T0254236

# Pro Open Source Mail

## Building an Enterprise Mail Solution

Curtis Smith

**Pro Open Source Mail: Building an Enterprise Mail Solution**

**Copyright © 2006 by Curtis Smith**

Softcover re-print of the Hardcover 1st edition 2006

All rights reserved. No part of this work may be reproduced or transmitted in any form or by any means, electronic or mechanical, including photocopying, recording, or by any information storage or retrieval system, without the prior written permission of the copyright owner and the publisher.

ISBN-13: 978-1-4302-1173-0

ISBN-13 : 978-1-4302-0234-9 (eBook)

Library of Congress Cataloging-in-Publication data is available upon request.

Trademarked names may appear in this book. Rather than use a trademark symbol with every occurrence of a trademarked name, we use the names only in an editorial fashion and to the benefit of the trademark owner, with no intention of infringement of the trademark.

Lead Editors: Jason Gilmore, Keir Thomas
Technical Reviewer: Jon Shoberg
Editorial Board: Steve Anglin, Ewan Buckingham, Gary Cornell, Jason Gilmore, Jonathan Gennick,
    Jonathan Hassell, James Huddleston, Chris Mills, Matthew Moodie, Dominic Shakeshaft, Jim Sumser,
    Keir Thomas, Matt Wade
Project Manager: Kylie Johnston
Copy Edit Manager: Nicole LeClerc
Copy Editors: Liz Welch, Heather Lang
Assistant Production Director: Kari Brooks-Copony
Production Editor: Kelly Gunther
Compositor: Lynn L'Heureux
Proofreader: Kim Burton
Indexer: Michael Brinkman
Artist: April Milne
Cover Designer: Kurt Krames
Manufacturing Director: Tom Debolski

For information on translations, please contact Apress directly at 2855 Telegraph Avenue, Suite 600, Berkeley, CA 94705. Phone 510-549-5930, fax 510-549-5939, e-mail info@apress.com, or visit http://www.apress.com.

*To my wife, whose encouragement and love I am eternally indebted to*

# Contents at a Glance

# PART 5 ▪▪▪ Filtering E-mail

# PART 6 ▪▪▪ Fighting E-mail Viruses and Worms

# PART 7 ▪▪▪ Fighting Spam

# PART 8 ▪▪▪ Managing Mailing Lists

# PART 9 ▪▪▪ Advanced Topics

# PART 10 ▪▪▪ Appendix

# Contents

# PART 1 ■■■ Preparing Your Infrastructure

# PART 2 ▪▪▪ sendmail

# PART 3 ▪▪▪ Remote Client Access to E-mail with POP3 and IMAP

# PART 4 ■ ■ ■ Webmail

# PART 5 ■ ■ ■ Filtering E-mail

# PART 6 ■ ■ ■ Fighting E-mail Viruses and Worms

# PART 7 ■ ■ ■ Fighting Spam

# PART 9 ■■■ Advanced Topics

# PART 10 ■■■ Appendix

# About the Author

**CURTIS SMITH** is a professional systems and network administrator residing in Westerville, Ohio. His experience includes designing, building, and maintaining open source e-mail and web solutions for an Internet service provider and the Max M. Fisher College of Business at The Ohio State University. Curtis earned his BA from Ohio State, majoring in philosophy.

Curtis is active in local community user and volunteer groups, both technical and nontechnical. He also enjoys photography, camping, canoeing, and hiking when not stuck indoors behind the keyboard.

# Acknowledgments

I'd like to thank Jason Gilmore for offering me this project. His enthusiasm for writing is infectious and a great motivation. It's inspiring to have an editor who is as much a geek as the author!

Many thanks are also due to my project manager, Kylie Johnston, and the rest of my Apress review and editorial team for their support and patience throughout this project.

Also a big thanks to all the developers behind the quality open source applications and tools presented in this book. Without their tireless efforts, we systems administrators would have a lot fewer quality options for providing the services we build and countless users come to depend on.

Finally, thank you to my wife, Kathleen, for her strength, patience, and encouragement, without which this would not have been a successful endeavor.

# Introduction

**S**omething as ubiquitous as e-mail can be taken for granted so easily. You may curse it, but as soon as "the server goes down," you can't stop from trying to check your e-mail twice as often until it is available again. Every Linux distribution comes with a mail server application. Perhaps you're already running a small e-mail system for your home network, personal domain, or a larger organization, but you want to take that service a notch or two or three higher.

In this book, I take my experience as a professional systems and network administrator and offer a design for a complete enterprise-quality e-mail system. I take away the difficulty of choosing which software to use for the project, and provide a blueprint of sorts you can follow to build an e-mail system any organization would be proud to use. Certainly I encourage you to take the skills and knowledge learned from this book and expand upon them. Possibilities are nearly limitless, and you should not feel constrained by any means.

The software featured in this book represents what I feel to be the best of breed of open source software. Administrators have come to depend on these components and entrust the successful delivery and filtering of countless e-mail messages through e-mail systems built with these components. I hope you get a sense of my enthusiasm for Linux and open source software, particularly the applications discussed in this book. Indeed, I hope you will come to find that there is little reason to pay big money for software to provide enterprise-quality e-mail service.

## Who This Book Is For

Certainly, this book is written in such a way that the novice to intermediate hobbyist or systems administrator will be able to walk away with a complete enterprise-quality mail solution. However, I also believe there are topics discussed that seasoned administrators will find useful.

If you currently do not have an e-mail system, or have only a basic one, this book will walk through everything necessary to build a complete e-mail system, from start to finish. If you already have a successful e-mail system in place, I think this book will still present fresh ideas that you could integrate into your existing solution, making it even better than before.

## How This Book Is Structured

This book is meant to ultimately be read from front to back in it entirety. Although many of the components featured in this book will operate independently of the others, much of the way I design the solution as a whole depends on each component being built and configured in a specific way, and each chapter builds on the previous chapters.

This book is divided into nine logical parts, organized into separate tasks. In Part 1, "Preparing Your Infrastructure," three chapters get you started with the basic building blocks common to an e-mail solution. In Chapter 1, I introduce the evolution of e-mail, the path e-mail travels from message draft to delivery, e-mail–borne threats, and webmail and mailing lists. In Chapter 2, I introduce Fedora Core, a free Linux distribution backed by Red Hat that will serve as the platform of choice in this book. We discuss physical server hardware needs and walk through the installation of Fedora Core together. In Chapter 3, we describe the steps necessary to bring your e-mail system online for the first time, including some introductory Linux system administration concepts and secure login with SSH.

In Part 2, "sendmail," four chapters focus on the installation, configuration, and customization of the sendmail program. In Chapter 4, I introduce SMTP, the underlying protocol of e-mail itself, and introduce and install the sendmail program, the venerable mail server of choice for countless e-mail system administrators before you. In Chapter 5, we start work on configuring and customizing your sendmail installation for your specific e-mail domain, including making sure your domain's DNS is properly configured. In Chapter 6, we complete the basic sendmail configuration by populating the sendmail database configuration files. In Chapter 7, we conclude the bulk of our sendmail discussion by finally testing your sendmail installation and configuration for successful e-mail delivery.

In Part 3, "Remote Client Access to E-mail with POP3 and IMAP," three chapters are dedicated to showing you how to offer remote access to e-mail through two proven protocols but with one application. In Chapter 8, I introduce the two prevalent protocols for offering remote access to e-mail, POP3 and IMAP. Without these, your e-mail system would be virtually useless—your users couldn't access their e-mail! In Chapter 9, I introduce one open source application that offers either POP3 or IMAP, or both at the same time: Dovecot. Designed for efficiency and security, Dovecot is a cinch to install and configure. In Chapter 10, I conclude the discussion on remote e-mail access by explaining how to secure POP3 and IMAP with SSL, the same technology popular for securing your online banking. I also discuss how SSL works, and how digital certificates fit into the picture.

In Part 4, "Webmail," two chapters are dedicated to web-based e-mail services. Providing webmail may be considered essential if any of your users are mobile. In Chapter 11, I introduce Apache and PHP, the web server and web server-side programming on top of which we will run our web-based e-mail application. In Chapter 12, I introduce SquirrelMail, the webmail application of choice that can offer much more than just web-based e-mail access.

In Part 5, "Filtering E-mail," two chapters introduce filtering basics. In Chapter 13, procmail is introduced to provide e-mail filtering and sorting. Along the way, we take a side trip into the world of regular expressions, useful for efficient and powerful pattern matching. In Chapter 14, I introduce MailScanner, the linchpin to our e-mail system design. MailScanner is the beginning of what differentiates this total solution from other basic mail servers. MailScanner will be the gatekeeper of your e-mail, and necessary if you continue with the rest of the book. I also walk you through the configuration of MailScanner to prepare for antivirus and antispam scanning discussed later in the book.

In Part 6, "Fighting E-mail Viruses and Worms," just one chapter is necessary to help you learn how to protect your users from e-mail–borne malware. In Chapter 15, I introduce the community-developed and -supported antivirus application ClamAV. I am confident ClamAV will protect your users as well as any commercial application, if not more so.

In Part 7, "Fighting Spam," I use three chapters to cover everything you need to know about fighting the scourge of the Internet: unsolicited bulk e-mail, a.k.a. spam. Chapter 16 includes my thoughts regarding general best practices, policy, and tactics for fighting e-mail spam. In Chapter 17, I introduce SpamAssassin, a highly sought-after application for identifying and filtering spam. In Chapter 18, we walk through the configuration and customization of SpamAssassin and finalize our MailScanner configuration to round off our discussion of fighting spam.

In Part 8, "Managing Mailing Lists," two chapters are dedicated to the installation, configuration, and management of mailing lists. In Chapter 19, I introduce Mailman, the GNU mailing list manager. We walk through the installation and configuration of Mailman. In Chapter 20, I complete our discussion of mailing lists with list administration and management, detailing the role of the list administrator, moderator, and member.

Finally, rounding off the book is Part 9, "Advanced Topics." In Chapter 21, I introduce optional, advanced technologies that aim at securing SMTP and e-mail, including SMTP AUTH and SMTP STARTTLS for authenticated and secure SMTP sessions and upcoming technologies meant to address e-mail forgery. Also in Chapter 21, I discuss two separate client-side technologies, S/MIME and OpenPGP, that are available to digitally sign and optionally encrypt e-mail messages.

# Prerequisites

In this book, I try to assume as little as possible. My aim is to make this information accessible to the novice and expert alike. Although I cover advanced concepts, I introduce the basic skills necessary to complete all of the tasks in this book.

However, there are a few technologies peripheral to Internet e-mail that I will either only mention or not cover at all. For example, I assume you have a basic understanding of general networking concepts, the OSI model layers, IP addressing, and DNS.

If you are new to the world of Linux system administration, you will find yourself interfacing with your system through a predominantly textual interface. You will need a secure shell (SSH) client application for remote access to your Linux e-mail system. Numerous SSH clients exist for various operating system platforms. If Microsoft Windows XP is your workstation operating system of choice, I recommend PuTTY (www.chiark.greenend.org.uk/~sgtatham/putty/). If Apple Mac OS X is your workstation operating system of choice, I recommend the command-line SSH client accessible from Terminal.app.

# Contacting the Author

I wholeheartedly encourage questions and comments of any kind at all. I've built a companion web site to this book at www.proopensourcemail.com where you can find links to all of the software featured in this book, a list of useful resources, and discussion forums. If you'd like to contact me directly, please feel free to e-mail me at curtis@proopensourcemail.com.

Additionally, the publishers of this book, Apress, host a forum for the book at http://forums.apress.com. There you can discuss this book or open source technologies in general and become part of the wider Apress community of readers.

# PART 1

∎∎∎

# Preparing Your Infrastructure

# CHAPTER 1

■ ■ ■

# An Introduction to E-mail

Today, electronic mail has become as ubiquitous as the telephone, television, or radio. Thanks to popular services like AOL, Hotmail, and the like, e-mail has become a vast communications medium accessible by anyone with a personal computer and Internet connection. But most people are completely unaware of the technology and infrastructure behind e-mail or what it takes to keep that infrastructure running smoothly.

What's worse is that running an Internet mail server isn't as simple as it once used to be. With the proliferation of e-mail viruses and worms, phishing scams, and e-mail spam—not to mention the fact that most users expect e-mail to always be available like their telephone or television service—running a mail server these days may seem like a daunting task. And what of the plethora of commercial products that claim to provide a particular service or protect a system and the end user from malicious e-mail content? How do you make sense of all this? This book aims to help you understand the fundamental mechanics of building and maintaining a complete enterprise e-mail system and how to provide the 24×7 availability and access many come to expect or take for granted.

This chapter will discuss some of the fundamental aspects of this ubiquitous technology by introducing key issues and topics, including the structure of an e-mail message and a day in the life of an e-mail message. I will also introduce e-mail–borne threats, web-based access to e-mail, and the basic notion of Internet e-mail mailing lists, each of which will get additional expanded treatment in Parts 4, 7, and 8, respectively, of this book. But first, let's take a look at the history and evolution of e-mail itself.

## The Evolution of E-mail

E-mail isn't a technology that was invented out of nowhere at any one point in history by any one person. Rather, modern Internet e-mail is more of an evolution of human communication. The first forms of e-mail were simply text files copied from person to person on the independent time-share behemoths of the 1960s at places like MIT and the University of California, Berkeley. When some of those independent computer systems were interconnected to create the US Defense Department's ARPANET in 1969, communication, let alone e-mail, wasn't even a formal part of the original design goals. However, over time it became clear that ARPANET was useful for more than sharing scientific resources.

■**Note**  Much of the following Internet and e-mail history comes from three primary resources. The first is the history thesis "The Evolution of ARPANET Email" by Ian R. Hardy (`www.ifla.org/documents/internet/hari1.txt`). The second is RFC 2235, which is titled "Hobbes' Internet Timeline" (`www.ietf.org/rfc/rfc2235.txt`). The third is Dave Crocker's "Email History" (`www.livinginternet.com/e/ei.htm`).

In addition to growing to 15 nodes, ARPANET laid out a foundation for e-mail as a medium for human communication across the network in late 1971. Ray Tomlinson sent the first e-mail message over the ARPANET network with a utility he wrote called SNDMSG. It was an unmemorable message he sent to himself, but the second e-mail message was to the whole ARPANET community describing the new form of communication and interaction.

Network e-mail quickly achieved success, becoming very popular among the ARPANET researchers. However, despite its popularity, initially e-mail was not considered a part of the "real" scientific research; researchers made constant use of e-mail, but kept it out of official publications and presentations. One reason was that e-mail was considered a natural use of computer networks. In a sense, e-mail had become a ubiquitous technology among the ARPANET community even as early as the 1970s!

Tomlinson's e-mail application SNDMSG laid the groundwork for a whole evolution of applications ported to different computer systems and networks. During the late 1970s and early 1980s, protocols like *Multipurpose Memo Distribution Facility (MMDF)* and *UNIX-to-UNIX Copy Protocol (UUCP)* were developed to relay e-mail over dial-up telephone lines to sites that could not establish a direct, permanent link to the larger computer networks like ARPANET. In fact, it is earlier work on similar technology that Eric Allman's famous sendmail program was based on! Now the Internet's most popular SMTP server application, sendmail will be the base of the open source Internet e-mail solution we will build together in this book.

Commercial adoption of electronic e-mail appears to have started around 1989 when an arrangement was made between the commercial e-mail provider MCI Mail and another research network called NSFNET to interconnect through the Corporation for National Research Initiatives (CNRI). Soon after, CompuServe connected to NSFNET through The Ohio State University, making its commercial e-mail service available to the Internet.

The emergence of different methods for delivering and receiving e-mail from network to network spurred efforts to standardize e-mail in 1976 and again in 1982. The popularity of Internet e-mail was due in part by its simplicity, but its standardization also played a big role in adoption. Next, we'll take a look at the simple standards that form the foundation of modern Internet e-mail.

■**Note**  One seemingly silly, yet quite interesting, development in Internet e-mail was the development of the use of the sideways smiley face, or emoticon. Generally attributed to Scott E. Fahlman, the use of :-) to indicate a joke or jovial mood was suggested in 1982, and the rest is history. Scott's account of the Internet lore behind the smiley can be found at `www.cs.cmu.edu/~sef/sefSmiley.htm`.

# The Structure of an E-mail Message

In 1982, a standard way for e-mail to be addressed and delivered over the Internet was defined. It built on some of the conventions adopted by Ray Tomlinson but updated the conventions to reflect the modern state of the Internet. Called *Simple Mail Transfer Protocol (SMTP)*, it is the underlying technology behind the transfer of e-mail from one Internet host to another. In the early days of the Internet, disparate e-mail systems required special gateway applications to transfer e-mail from one proprietary system to another. Don't sweat it; thankfully, that's no longer the case. In Chapter 4, I walk you through the complete process of installation and configuration of one of the oldest, most popular Internet SMTP servers: the sendmail program.

---

■**Note** SMTP is an Internet Engineering Task Force (IETF) standard defined by RFC 821 (www.ietf.org/rfc/rfc821.txt).

---

An Internet e-mail message must be in a specific format, and that basic format was originally defined by another standard also drafted in 1982. An Internet e-mail message is generally split into two parts: the message header and the message body.

## The Message Header

Every well-formed Internet e-mail message starts with a header. An e-mail message header is a continual, sequential series of lines. Each line must be nonempty and contains fields concatenated together. Some of the header fields are added by the Internet mail client application, and some of the header fields are added by each SMTP server that handles and processes the mail message. The following is an example of what an e-mail header might look like:

```
Received: from [192.168.69.100] ([192.168.69.100])
        by mail.example.com (8.13.4/8.13.4) with ESMTP id j8861oev004986
        for <curtis@example.com>; Thu, 8 Sep 2005 02:01:50 -0400
Message-ID: <431FD39E.3090001@example.com>
Date: Thu, 08 Sep 2005 02:01:02 -0400
From: Curtis Smith <curtis@example.com>
User-Agent: Mozilla Thunderbird 1.0.6-1.1.fc3 (X11/20050720)
X-Accept-Language: en-us, en
MIME-Version: 1.0
To: curtis@example.com
Subject: Example E-mail Header
Content-Type: text/plain; charset=ISO-8859-1; format=flowed
Content-Transfer-Encoding: 7bit
```

The fields added by each Internet mail server are useful for detailing what Internet hosts processed the e-mail message, when the message was processed, and so forth. The fields added by each Internet e-mail client application are useful for determining for whom the message is destined, and where, when, and from whom the message originated. The message header ends with an empty line, or by the end of the message itself; a body is not required. A line containing only spaces or tabs that appears to be empty is not empty and is still considered a part of the message header, albeit an ill-formed one not compliant with Internet standards.

Some message header fields are used for host-to-host delivery, while some fields are simply read by a mail client application meant for human consumption for informational purposes only (like the From field and To field). Although Internet standards suggest a certain order for some header fields, in practice fields can be in any order. In Chapter 7, we'll take a closer look at how to interpret e-mail headers in more detail. Learning how to read e-mail headers can help with troubleshooting delivery problems, especially when correlated with detailed log entries on your e-mail system.

---

**■Note**  RFC 822 is the original standard for detailing the Internet mail message header format, and is often called the *822 format*. RFC 1123 (www.ietf.org/rfc/rfc1123.txt) offered some corrections and clarifications to RFC822. Yet another IETF standard, RFC 2822 (www.ietf.org/rfc/rfc2822.txt), was meant to replace RFC 822 and RFC 1123. Considered to be less misleading than its predecessors in most cases, some find RFC 2822 more misleading in others. RFC 2822 is also often called *822bis*. It's important to recognize that not all Internet mail client applications perfectly adhere to RFC 822 to the letter; some clients ignore restrictions detailed in RFC 822.

---

Most header fields in an Internet e-mail message header are added by each mail server that handles that message. However, some information is added by the end user's e-mail client application. For example, the From field of an e-mail message header is usually automatically added by a client's e-mail application. What the application uses to fill out that line typically depends on how the application is configured, but it usually contains the end user's e-mail address. The e-mail application typically relies on the user to correctly configure the application with his proper address, properly spelled. If the address is incorrectly entered, it will show up in the From field incorrectly.

Neither an Internet e-mail application nor an Internet e-mail server can know if the From field address is correct, and each must trust what it's given. As such, it's very easy for a malicious mail virus or worm, or a knowledgeable end user, to forge some header lines like the From field with bogus information. We will discuss e-mail–borne threats that take advantage of this fact, how to identify such threats, and how to combat these threats to protect your end users, beginning in Chapter 14.

## The Message Body and Message Attachments

An Internet e-mail message body follows the message header, with an empty line demarking the two. The message body is typically human-readable plaintext; however, this is not required. Internet standards only discuss e-mail messages in ASCII text format. In fact, it's common for end users to attach files to an e-mail message, and these files are oftentimes binary data and not human readable. In addition to binary file attachments, it's also possible for Internet e-mail client applications to create message bodies in a format other than ASCII.

When a binary file is "attached" to an e-mail message, or the e-mail message is in another format other than ASCII, the text and binary file must be encoded and included as lines of ASCII text to the body of the mail message. One common method for such an encoding is uuencode. In addition, *Multipurpose Internet Mail Extensions (MIME)* was developed to structure and define an encoding and naming convention for sending non-ASCII e-mail message bodies.

---

■**Note** MIME is defined in a series of five IETF documents: RFC 2045 (www.ietf.org/rfc/rfc2045.txt), RFC 2046 (www.ietf.org/rfc/rfc2046.txt), RFC 2047 (www.ietf.org/rfc/rfc2047.txt), RFC 2048 (www.ietf.org/rfc/rfc2048.txt), and RFC 2049 (www.ietf.org/rfc/rfc2049.txt).

---

In short, MIME must be supported by both the sending and receiving Internet e-mail client applications; once a mail message body is encoded and formatted according to the MIME specifications, the message body or message attachment appears to the Internet e-mail server as a series of ASCII lines. Unless these lines are properly decoded by the receiving end, the lines will appear as gibberish. Nearly all modern e-mail client applications support MIME.

# A Day in the Life of an E-mail Message

Having discussed the underlying technology behind Internet e-mail, and the basic structure of an Internet e-mail message, let's track the path an Internet e-mail message takes from message draft to message delivery.

## The Mail User Agent (MUA)

First, the end user uses a *mail user agent (MUA)* to construct and compose an Internet e-mail message. MUA is just the technical term describing any e-mail client application, like Microsoft Outlook, Eudora, Mozilla Thunderbird, or Mutt. The MUA typically handles the proper mail header creation, and the end user uses the text editor built into the MUA to compose the message body. When the end user clicks the Send button, the mail message is handed off to her outgoing Internet e-mail server.

## The Mail Transfer Agent (MTA)

A user's outgoing mail server is called a *mail transfer agent (MTA)*. MTA is a technical term for an Internet electronic e-mail SMTP server. An Internet e-mail server can reside on the end user's Internet host, but it's more likely in practice to be a separate dedicated Internet server host maintained by somebody like yourself. The e-mail server will proceed to determine the recipient(s) of the e-mail message and whether or not they are local. If the recipient is not a local user hosted on that server, the server will initiate a network connection via SMTP to the destination Internet e-mail server. This server-to-server handoff will continue until the e-mail message hits the server that hosts the final recipient's mailbox.

I will walk you through the installation and configuration of the sendmail program, one of the Internet's most common and venerable e-mail server applications, in Chapter 4.

## The Mail Delivery Agent (MDA)

Once the final e-mail server receives the message, it is handed off to the *mail delivery agent (MDA)*. The MDA, also sometimes called the *local delivery agent (LDA)*, is the technical term for the mechanism that delivers the e-mail message to the recipient's mailbox. In some cases this mechanism is completely transparent. However, as we'll discover in Chapter 13, certain applications like procmail exist to process a message before it's delivered in order to scan or filter the message. This is quite useful for scanning, disinfecting, or tagging e-mail messages that might have malicious or unwanted content.

Once the e-mail message has been delivered to its final destination, the recipient can then collect the e-mail message in a number of ways. One of the most traditional ways to download e-mail off a server is through the *Post Office Protocol version 3 (POP3)*. A more robust remote e-mail access method can be provided by the *Internet Message Access Protocol (IMAP)*. Both remote e-mail services are the two most popular ways for someone to download mail off an e-mail server onto his personal computer. Both protocols are independent of each other, but they can be run simultaneously if you need to offer both to your users. I will introduce POP3 and IMAP later in Chapter 8, and I'll run through the installation and configuration of Dovecot, an open source POP3 and IMAP server, in Chapter 9. Figure 1-1 graphically depicts the complete life cycle of an e-mail message, from draft to delivery.

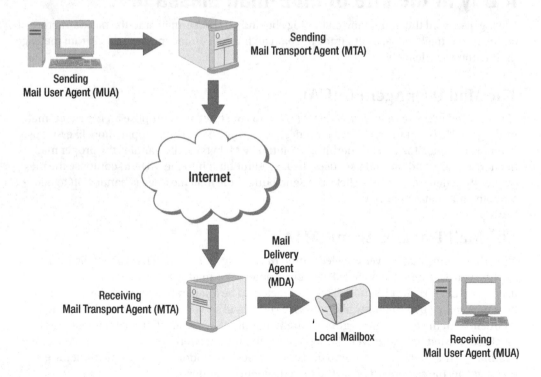

**Figure 1-1.** *A day in the life of an e-mail message*

# Internet E-mail Threats

In recent years, both server administrators and end users have had to deal with a huge proliferation of Internet e-mail–borne threats. These various threats range from the mildly
annoying to the devastating. Internet e-mail–borne threats can cause extreme excessive server
load, and they can carry executable programs that delete files on a user's computer or corrupt
a user's operating system beyond repair. e-mail–borne threats can require considerable effort
to mitigate. Three categories of threats are briefly introduced in the next section. But don't
worry; each is discussed in greater depth, with proposed methods for combating them, in subsequent chapters of this book. I'll point you in the right direction as we go along.

## Viruses and Worms

E-mail–borne viruses and worms rank among the most destructive threats found on the Internet. An *e-mail virus* is a piece of computer code attached to a mail message that attempts to
infect, or embed its code into, other files. An *e-mail worm* is a piece of computer code attached
to a mail message that makes copies of itself over and over, onto local computer drives, over the
network, or through mail; in other words, Internet e-mail worms simply exist to reproduce and
infect others with a copy of itself. Both viruses and worms infect a computer by exploiting some
vulnerability within the computer's operating system or a specific application.

New e-mail viruses and worms, or new variants of old ones, are found every day. Antivirus
vendors and researchers constantly intercept new threats and figure out how to protect
against them. Keeping track of new e-mail viruses and worms isn't something you should have
to constantly worry about. Let the free and open source product ClamAV filter your e-mail and
keep out the unwanted messages. Find comfort in the community support behind the product and product updates, and feel confident your users will be safe from e-mail viruses and
worms with up-to-the minute updates as new threats are discovered. Chapter 15 walks you
through the installation and configuration of ClamAV to help keep the threats from hitting
your users' mailboxes.

## Spam

Typically junk or unsolicited commercial Internet mail is called *spam*. Internet e-mail spam is
an ever-increasing problem for everybody. Current industry estimates put e-mail spam as conservatively as 45 percent, and as high as 90 percent, of all Internet e-mail received by individual
and corporate e-mail accounts. Some believe the use of Internet e-mail as a mass-marketing
tool has become an epidemic of sorts. Worse yet, it seems spam is a lucrative business for those
sending the spam (called *spammers*). When it's combined with enticing language and unbeliev-
able deals, people seem to regularly respond to spam.

Internet lore has it that the use of the word *spam* as a slang term to describe unsolicited
commercial e-mail comes from the Monty Python skit in which the SPAM meat was featured
(see http://en.wikipedia.org/wiki/Spam_(Monty_Python)). The skit takes place in a restaurant
in which two users are trying to order something without SPAM, despite the waitress only
offering breakfasts made with SPAM. In the skit, a group of Vikings often break out in a chorus
of "SPAM, lovely SPAM, wonderful SPAM." The Viking chorus gets louder and louder each
time, eventually drowning out all other conversations. Spam e-mail is seen in a similar light:
flooding people's e-mail accounts with unsolicited e-mail and making it difficult to sort
through to the legitimate e-mail.

No matter the humor behind the slang, spam e-mail is a nuisance, but it is something you can help your end users detect and combat. In Chapter 16, I will introduce a few basic methods for combating spam. Chapters 17 and 18 will detail the installation and configuration of SpamAssassin, the sophisticated antispam application that allows each of your users to detect spam with personalized rules based on the kinds of e-mail they receive.

---

**Note** The Hormel Foods Corporation owns the trademark "SPAM" and sells a product by the same name. It is acceptable to use the word *spam* to describe unsolicited e-mail, but it is not permissible to use the word *spam*, or a Hormel Foods SPAM product image, as a trademark (see `www.spam.com/ci/ci_in.htm`).

---

## Phishing

Lately, there have been widespread attempts by malicious hackers to trick consumers into giving sensitive information under false pretenses and using that information illegally for their own personal gain. These fraudulent attempts made through deceptive e-mail practices are called *phishing scams*. Phishing e-mail messages are purposely designed to look like messages from legitimate sources such as banks, eBay, and so forth. The mail messages might claim a need to update personal information, and provide an Internet link for the consumer to follow to do so. The link may look innocent or legitimate, but the site is usually not owned or controlled by the entity it claims to represent. Phishing scams exist solely to trick consumers into providing information to a third party. Unfortunately, these scams can lead to identity theft and loss of personal privacy.

---

**Note** The slang term *phishing* was coined to describe the way malicious hackers use e-mail to lure people into giving up private information in similar fashion to fishermen using bait to lure fish into biting their hook. Replacing *ph* for *f* is common among hackers, malicious or otherwise.

---

# Extending Basic E-mail Service

There are two components that I will explain in further detail later in this book. These components aren't necessarily required for a complete, fully working Internet e-mail server, but they do complement the services you install. These components enhance your users' experience, and provide easier, universal access to their e-mail and allow for collaboration and discussion of e-mail.

## Web-Based E-mail

One of the reasons Internet e-mail has become so ubiquitous is easy access to the Internet. What better way of offering access to e-mail than through the World Wide Web? E-mail's utility is drastically lessened if it cannot be accessed from anywhere with an Internet connection. Your users won't always have their own personal laptop with them when they're traveling, so they might have to check their e-mail from random remote kiosks or workstations. Offering a web-based solution for sending and receiving e-mail is a value-added service that can only make your users happier.

Web-based e-mail was made popular by the free e-mail accounts offered through online, web-only services like Hotmail or Yahoo! Mail. Some services have popped up, offering a web-based proxy service to check e-mail accounts without web access. However, in Chapter 12, I will start to describe a complete web-based e-mail solution, implementing the free and open source webmail suite SquirrelMail. With this solution, your users won't have to use one of those proxy accounts or forward their e-mail to one of the services offering web access in order to gain convenient access to their e-mail. Internet e-mail isn't just about individuals, though. Disseminating information, or carrying virtual conversations, is the job of e-mail mailing lists.

## Mailing Lists

Electronic mass communication with potentially thousands of recipients with one e-mail address? That's just what e-mailing lists are designed to do. Message board–like conversations virtually through e-mail? Yeah, e-mail mailing lists can do that, too. Create one e-mail address, address an e-mail message, and let your own mailing list software automatically deliver the message to thousands of recipients almost instantly. No need to address each recipient individually, and optionally protect the individual privacy of each list subscriber. Make your list a one-way announcement communication device, or allow your users to create public discussion groups on a topic of their choice. Either way, it's simple with the GNU Mailman mailing list software I will introduce in Chapter 20.

# Summary

Internet e-mail is steeped in deep history. Thankfully, it has evolved into a simple, standards-based technology. However, e-mail, and people's use of and reliance on it, continues to evolve as time goes on. We've taken a look at some of the basics behind a few of those standards and how the whole system ties together from message draft to final delivery. We will continue to drill down deeper into these concepts and produce an enterprise-grade e-mail system.

We've also seen that without proper controls and mechanisms in place, mitigation of Internet e-mail–borne threats can be an uphill battle for an Internet e-mail server administrator. New threats are created and occur daily and are explicitly designed to fool users. However, life can be greatly simplified with the right tools, and as we work together through each chapter of this book, I'm confident you will have the information and tools necessary to provide your users with a superior, enterprise-quality Internet e-mail solution.

■■■

# CHAPTER 2

# Building Your Server

In this chapter we'll build the base platform that will house the enterprise e-mail solution. This chapter will discuss determining your hardware needs and installing a Linux operating system. It shouldn't be a difficult process, but there may be a few things that are unfamiliar if you are new to Linux. The first thing to consider before starting any operating system or software installation is the server hardware.

## Sizing Your Needs

Determining your hardware needs may be one of the most important considerations, but it may also be the most difficult task you'll encounter throughout this project. Correctly sizing your server will mean the difference between handling whatever e-mail traffic is thrown at it and caving at the wrong time under especially heavy, peak load. Unfortunately, there is no magic formula for determining exactly how many processors, how much physical memory, and how much hard disk space is necessary to serve a thousand e-mails per hour. Perhaps the most important point to keep in mind is to always plan ahead and overshoot your estimate; once the system is put into production, demand can only increase with time. Luckily, the cost of hardware has fallen dramatically over the years. Linux operating systems can perform very well on so-called commodity hardware. As such, overestimating your hardware needs probably won't cost as much as upgrading the server should the need arise.

For the purposes of this book, I will assume that the final solution will be hosted on a single physical server. Network load balancing, high availability clustering, and complex service redundancy are outside the scope of this book. The server hardware you choose should reflect the size of your organization or user base. The hardware vendor of your choice can no doubt provide more advice. Always remember, it's never possible to have too much CPU power, physical memory, or hard disk space.

### Processor

The processing power necessary is quite difficult to estimate. For instance, having a *symmetric multiprocessing (SMP) system*, or a server that has more than one CPU, can only increase the efficiency of your e-mail solution. SMP systems come with CPUs in multiples of two. A dual-CPU system is sometimes referred to as a two-way processor system, while a quad-CPU system is referred to as a four-way processor system, and so forth. Having more than one CPU means more computing cycles can be completed simultaneously to increase performance. At a minimum, I would suggest a two-way processor system unless your needs are very minimal.

In this book I will assume the server platform will be based on the x86 architecture; whether it's an Intel-based or AMD-based processor system is of no consequence.

## Memory

Many components of the e-mail solution we build in this book take advantage of all the RAM they can get. For example, the antivirus component of the system will be considerably faster if the antivirus definitions can be loaded into memory for speed and efficiency. If your system does not have sufficient amounts of RAM to do this, then the antivirus software will have to constantly reread the definitions from the hard disk. Reducing reads and writes to the hard disk is always a good thing. At a minimum, 2GB of RAM is suggested.

## Disk Space

Hard disk space is very dependent on specific needs. For the operating system alone, I suggest reserving no less than 8GB of disk space. An exact breakdown of the system disk layout will be discussed later in this chapter during the installation process. This estimate is based on my experiences running Linux servers, and I must stress that this 8GB does not include room for user mailboxes. How much disk space will be necessary to host your users' mailboxes will depend on policy decisions. For instance, how much total storage are you willing to give per user? For some of the more advanced features of the e-mail solution we will build, all of your users' e-mail must remain on the server. Experience dictates that many people tend not to delete e-mail and save everything they receive. Over time, even if your number of users doesn't grow, their mailboxes will. Whatever number you come up with, factor in an additional 10 to 15 percent just for growth and room to play.

In my place of employment, we host e-mail for approximately 5,000 uses. Official policy is to allow a 25MB quota per user. Based on these numbers, you could assume we would need approximately 138GB of total disk space, assuming a bit of overhead and that everyone used their maximum quota. Before you say that can't possibly be a realistic assumption, stop and think how big some of your e-mail attachments can get. Does your organization use e-mail to pass around documents, presentations, and spreadsheets? After a year, we have reached approximately a quarter of this capacity.

In addition, you will need extra disk space for mail queues, quarantines, and temporary scratch space. The exact amount depends on policy and projected growth, but don't worry too much about these things. Later in the book when we discuss sendmail in Chapter 4 and filtering spam in Chapter 21, we will explain what queues and quarantines are.

If budget allows for it, hard disk drive redundancy should also be considered. A *redundant array of independent disks (RAID)* configuration requires more physical disk drives but provides data integrity and redundancy. Depending on the specific RAID implementation, redundancy can be as simple as a one-to-one direct mirroring and duplexing of a hard disk onto another (RAID level 1) or striping and duplication of data across three or more disk drives (RAID level 5). Each RAID level has varying levels of cost benefit and overhead, and some require trade-offs between reliability, recoverability, and performance. Table 2-1 briefly describes the popular RAID levels and a bit of information about each.

**Table 2-1.** *RAID Level Characteristics, Advantages, and Disadvantages*

| RAID Level | Characteristics | Minimum Number of Disks | Advantages | Disadvantages |
|---|---|---|---|---|
| 0 | Striped disk array, data broken in blocks, and blocks written to different disks | 2 | Little overhead, high performance | Not true RAID; no redundancy; loss of one disk results in data loss. |
| 1 | Mirroring and duplexing | 2 | Complete redundancy of data; transfer rate equal to a single disk | Least efficient and highest disk overhead. |
| 5 | Data blocks written to disk and parity generated, written in distributed manner, and checked on reads | 3 | Highest read rates; low ratio of parity disks to data disks | Disk failure has moderate impact on throughput and harder to rebuild. |
| 10 | Striped disk array, mirrored | 4 | Very high redundancy and high fault tolerance | Very high overhead and very expensive. |

In any case, if any one hard disk drive in the RAID configuration fails, the system will continue to operate with no data loss at all. Recovering from such a failure can be easier and reduce downtime. Otherwise, if you do not configure your hard disk drives into a RAID configuration, when a single drive system fails, the system must be taken offline and restored from a backup medium like magnetic tape. All major server-grade Linux distributions can support RAID either via hardware RAID controllers or through software emulation. A hardware RAID solution is more expensive, but it is transparent to the server operating system, whereas software RAID requires the operating system to emulate the features of a hardware RAID controller, which entails some processing overhead. Specifics on designing and implementing a RAID configuration are not covered further in this book, but nothing we do cover will depend on or exclude the possibility of such an implementation.

---

■**Tip** For more information, including more in-depth descriptions of the different RAID levels and how to implement software RAID in Linux, check out the Linux Software-RAID HOWTO by Jakob Østergaard and Emilio Bueso at www.tldp.org/HOWTO/Software-RAID-HOWTO.html.

---

# Introducing Fedora Core

The project described in this book uses Fedora Core 4, the open source Linux operating system developed by the Fedora Project (http://fedora.redhat.com). As of this writing, Fedora Core 4 was the current release by the Fedora Project. Fedora Core 4 is only used as the base solely for instruction and example. Everything we do or discuss in this book can be applied to, and implemented in its entirety on, another enterprise-grade open source Linux operating system. Where appropriate, I will point out anything that might be specific or unique to Fedora Core; otherwise, the operating system–specific material will be kept as general as possible.

---

**Note** By the time this book is published, Fedora Core 6 or later might be released. Just as the specific choice of Linux operating system distribution is irrelevant, so is the specific release of Fedora Core.

---

More often than not, a system administrator's choice of Linux operating system is a matter of personal taste, although I believe Fedora Core offers certain unique advantages. Many of the applications I introduce in this book are offered as prepackaged archives ready for installation. This saves time compared to having to build software from source and keeping your applications updated. Some of the other advantages include

- Backed by Red Hat, a large enterprise Linux operating system company

- Fantastic community support

- Easy installation

- Optimizations and performance enhancements

- Excellent selection of prepackaged software "out-of-the-box"

- Outstanding quality control/assurance

However, the aggressive release cycle and shorter-than-usual life of each Fedora Core release may be too much for your specific business.

## Obtaining Fedora Core

The latest release of Fedora Core can be obtained several ways. You also have the choice of getting the complete operating system in two formats: one DVD image or a set of four CD-ROM images. Both the DVD and CD-ROMs are bootable, if your system supports it.

The ISO images are available via the Web at http://download.fedora.redhat.com/pub/fedora/linux/core/4/i386/iso/. The ISO images are also available via anonymous FTP at ftp://download.fedora.redhat.com/pub/fedora/linux/core/4/i386/iso/.

Choose either the DVD ISO image or the set of four CD-ROM images, depending on the capabilities of your computer for creating such media. Keep in mind that some web browsers and FTP clients may not be able to properly download the DVD image because it is larger than 4GB, in which case you should refer to the application's documentation.

The official sites that distribute the ISO image files can experience very high traffic volume and may be slow. In that case, it is best to choose a mirror site that is closer to you. For a list of mirrors, visit http://fedora.redhat.com/download/mirrors.html.

### BitTorrent

Another alternative for downloading the necessary files is through BitTorrent. BitTorrent is a new, distributed way of publishing and distributing data across the Internet. BitTorrent does not depend on any one server to host the data centrally. Instead, a BitTorrent client can pull pieces of a file from other clients joined to the torrent. You can join the Fedora Project torrent at http://torrent.dulug.duke.edu/.

---

**Tip** For more information about BitTorrent in general, or for a list of BitTorrent clients, visit the official BitTorrent web site at www.bittorrent.com.

---

### Purchasing the CDs or DVDs

Yet another way to obtain the latest release of Fedora Core is by purchasing the media from CheapBytes (www.cheapbytes.com) or similar outfits around the world that perform the service of creating Linux CD/DVDs for a fee. CheapBytes offers the DVD and four-disc set of CD-ROMs for a small price covering the cost of media and shipping. This is especially useful for those with slow Internet connections or those without CD or DVD burners.

### Friends and Colleagues

Finally, your local Linux users group (LUG) can be an awesome general Linux and open source resource. You should find members willing to provide you with copies of various Linux operating systems in exchange for the cost of media. No matter how you obtain the media, you're finally ready to start the installation process.

---

**Tip** LUGs are a great way for you to meet others with similar interests. Your local LUG, if one exists, can also be an excellent technical resource. Search for a LUG near you at the Linux Users Group Worldwide project web site (http://lugww.counter.li.org/).

---

## Verifying the Download Integrity

Whenever downloading anything from the Internet, it is a good idea to verify the integrity of the download. Many distributors provide the md5sum of the original, known-good file, which can be used to compare to the md5sum of your downloaded file. If the two md5sums match, then it is reasonable to assume that you have successfully received the file in its entirety. For example, the following example demonstrates a successful verification of the integrity of the downloaded Fedora Core 4 DVD ISO using the Linux command md5sum:

```
[curtis@mail ~] md5sum FC4-i386-DVD.iso
```

---

```
c136e0bb691398e9d7b15d645f930628   FC4-i386-DVD.iso
```

---

and the following demonstrates a failed integrity verification attempt:

```
[curtis@mail ~] md5sum FC4-i386-DVD.iso
```

---

```
000ee00c6dd30039ccbf5004aa933300   FC4-i386-DVD.iso
```

---

> ■**Caution**  Verifying the md5sum of a file does not indicate the authenticity or origin of that file. Many file distributors will also cryptographically sign each file using *Pretty Good Privacy (PGP)* encryption. For a discussion of the GNU Project's implementation of PGP encryption, visit www.gnupg.org/.

# Installing Fedora Core

I won't get into the Fedora Core installation process in too much detail. I do, however, want to point out specific choices I made and recommend you follow them if you've never installed a Linux operating system. These choices are based on my experiences as a system administrator and form a solid base from which you should feel free to build on. Like sizing your physical server needs, specific installation details can be particular to your organization's needs or your particular administration style.

## Booting the Installation Media and Beginning the Installation

Maybe you've heard that installing Linux can be a horrible experience. I think the first thing you will find about the Fedora Core installation process is that it is definitely not a horrible experience. When you boot the installation DVD or CD-ROM discs, you will be greeted with a welcome splash screen, as shown in Figure 2-1. Typing nothing for several seconds will automatically start the default graphical installation process. Here starts the power and flexibility of a Linux operating system. You're immediately faced with the ability to choose between two installers or numerous custom boot options. The boot options are irrelevant for purposes of this discussion; however, the installer options are important:

- *Graphical installer*: The default graphical installer gives a very nice, intuitive interface from which to work and should be familiar to most. Throughout the process, help is offered on the left of the screen.

- *Text-mode installer*: The text-mode installer may be more comfortable to those of you who prefer an interface that does not require a mouse. The text-mode installer is also graphics-rich and only requires the most basic video card and monitor.

Both options offer the same features and installation options, just in different environments.

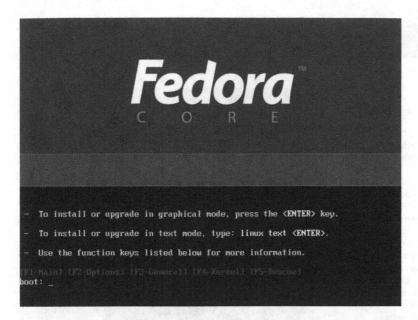

**Figure 2-1.** *When the Fedora Core 4 installation media boots, you're presented with choices immediately.*

## Altering the Installer Boot-Time Defaults

You can also pass special arguments, or instructions, that will alter the installer in various ways. For instance, for advanced administrators, you can pass the argument expert and certain advanced features will be enabled during the installation process that otherwise wouldn't be available. At the welcome boot splash screen, press the F2 key to retrieve a list of special boot options, press the F3 key for general boot and installation information, press the F4 key for help with passing kernel parameters, and press the F5 key for help with booting an existing installation into rescue mode. For most administrators, including myself under most circumstances, the default boot options and graphical installer will suffice.

Most of the installation is straightforward. You're first given the option to test your installation media. This process can take some time, but if you've never used the media, it can save you from wasting time when the install fails close to the end because the media was unreadable. When it's completed, the Fedora Core installer will continue. If you've booted into the default graphical mode, then your video card and monitor will be probed. The initial welcome screen will appear, shown in Figure 2-2, and you're ready to begin the bulk of the install process. Click the Next button and let's get started!

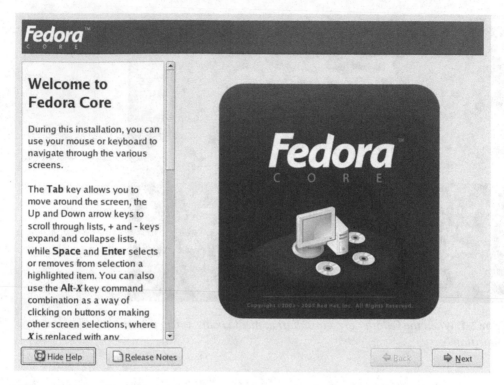

**Figure 2-2.** *The Fedora Core 4 graphical installer starts with a friendly welcome screen.*

## Selecting a Language and Making Keyboard Preferences

The next two steps are simply asking for your default language and basic keyboard preferences. You'll find that extensive work has been made to support a wide variety of languages. Select accordingly, and click Next. After selecting your language and keyboard preferences, you must choose the installation type from one of three predefined categories or create your own custom installation.

## Choosing an Installation Type

The Fedora Core installer gives you the choice of installing one of three predefined classes of Linux systems, or installing with your own custom settings (see Figure 2-3):

- *Personal Desktop*: Choosing this option will install a base system geared to the average user who needs to surf the Internet, check e-mail, and play games. For a server, this option is highly discouraged.

- *Workstation*: Choosing this option will install almost everything from the Personal Desktop, but also add more applications geared toward the power user or software developer. For a server, this option is highly discouraged.

- *Server*: Choosing this option will install a slightly stripped-down system but add several common Internet server applications. If you're looking for a quick-and-dirty introduction to Linux as a server platform, you might choose to use this installation option. Keep in mind that this is not guaranteed to install everything you will need for this project—it may also install extraneous applications that you'll never use.

- *Custom*: Choosing this option will allow you complete control over every aspect of how your Linux installation is done. This includes choice of installed applications and how your hard disks will be laid out and configured. This installation type requires a little more time as you will be presented with more options and the opportunity to fine-tune your installation to your specific needs.

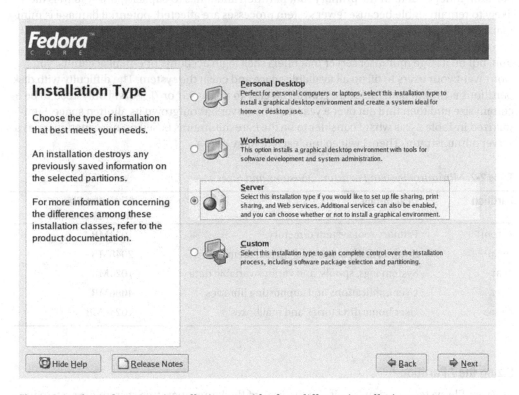

**Figure 2-3.** *The Fedora Core installation provides four different installation types.*

The fourth option, Custom, is what I recommend for the intermediate-to-expert system administrator. It gives you the ability to better fine-tune exactly what system components get installed and which do not. I personally do not prefer having extraneous server applications installed if I'm never going to use them, even if they never actually run as they were intended. Although I will assume you've chosen to use the Custom installation type throughout the rest of this chapter, it is not necessary. However, some of the subsequent steps might differ or not be presented at all if you select another installation type. The next major obstacle to overcome is how to partition the hard disk drives.

## Partitioning and Formatting the Hard Disk Drives

The Fedora Core installer will give you the option of allowing it to automatically partition and format the hard disk drives, or allow you to manually partition and format the hard disk drives. I would not recommend going with the automatic option as it chooses the most rudimentary configuration, designed to be generic and less complex. This is fine for a desktop workstation system, but not for an enterprise server.

In general, best practice is to segment key system directories into their own partitions. The reasoning is simple. If the primary root partition fills to capacity, the system can become highly erratic and possibly crash if left unattended. Some directories, like /var, where log files are stored for instance, can consume large amounts of disk. If /var is contained within its own partition independent of the primary root partition and it fills to capacity, the system is more likely to remain stable because fewer system processes are affected, potential damage is minimal, and the rest of the system is left to run as normal.

On a system that has few local user accounts, /home may not need to be a separate partition, but on a large multiuser server that offers shell login accounts or e-mail accounts, you won't want your users to fill up all available space and crash the system. The difficulty with disk partitions is how to plan for future growth. It's easy to think /var or /home will only need to be a certain size and then find out over a year that the server has outgrown its allotted space. Summarized in Table 2-2 is what I consider to be the bare minimums based on my experiences as a server administrator. Then, I will go into each in more depth.

**Table 2-2.** *Minimum System Partition Divisions and Sizes*

| Partition | Description | Minimum Size Recommendation |
| --- | --- | --- |
| / (root) | Primary root system directory | 1024MB |
| swap | Swap to disk partition for virtual memory | 2048MB |
| /var | System logs, spools, and various variable data | 1024MB |
| /usr | User applications and supporting libraries | 4096MB |
| /home | User home directories and mailboxes | 10240MB |

### Sizing the / Partition

The root file system, or simply /, is the top level of the Linux operating system file system hierarchy. The simplest of hard disk layouts would be to create one large / file system and install everything onto it. However, this is bad practice and can lead to system instability. The / partition will hold everything else not contained within the other partitions, including the Linux kernel, boot images, and systemwide configuration files. I recommend a minimum of 1024MB for the / partition.

### Sizing the Swap Partition

Every system has to have physical RAM to operate. The more memory a system has, the more efficient the system will run. However, under certain circumstances, whether it is too little

RAM or unusually high server load, RAM may become exhausted. This is where the swap partition comes in. Swap is used to extend the amount of fast physical memory with slower virtual memory on your hard disk drive.

Because reading and writing to the hard disk drives is much slower than reading and writing to RAM, a system should not use the swap partition on a regular basis. It is only meant for occasional, backup use. I recommend at least 2048MB dedicated to the swap partition on a server.

### Sizing the /var Partition

The /var partition will contain, among other things, system files that continually change. One example of such files is log files from the system itself and other applications. The /var partition is also where the e-mail server application will typically store temporary e-mail queues destined to be delivered remotely or locally. Because log files can suddenly grow very fast over a short period of time, I recommend no less than 1024MB for the /var partition.

### Sizing the /usr Partition

The /usr partition is where user-related documentation, applications, and application libraries are installed. Most applications will be installed on the /usr partition. However, once the system is built, /usr should not grow much at all. I recommend no less than 4096MB for the /usr partition.

### Sizing the /home Partition

The /home partition is the default location for user home directories. Every login user should have a home directory; it's where personal custom login environment and e-mail is stored. Creating a separate home directory under the /home partition promotes increased privacy and security. At the very least, the /home partition should be 10240MB for a system with only a small number of users.

### Choosing a File System

Once each partition is created, you must also choose which file system to format over each partition. I highly recommend choosing the ext3 file system, which is the default. The Linux ext3 file system is a journaling file system that offers additional data integrity features not found in the more traditional Linux ext2 or Microsoft's FAT32 file systems.

Although the ext2 file system has been around much longer, ext3 is little more than an extension to ext2. The ext3 file system is completely backward compatible with ext2. An ext3-formatted file system can also be treated as a traditional ext2 file system, albeit without any of the advanced journaling features. The journaling feature of ext3 keeps track of more information about the contents of the file system. If a system fails or loses power, there is considerably less chance of data loss if you chose the ext3 file system. Figure 2-4 shows a screenshot of this step completed using my partition recommendations.

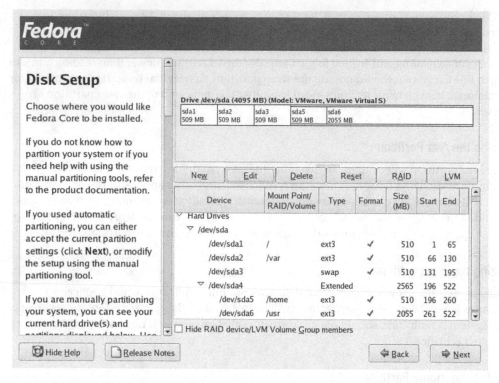

**Figure 2-4.** *How a sample partition layout might look*

Once you're satisfied with your hard disk drive partition layout and file system choices, let's continue with the rest of the installation.

## Configuring the Boot Loader

The boot loader is what tells your computer which operating system to boot and where it exists on your hard disk drives. Since we're building a server, there will be only one operating system installed, but the boot loader is still necessary. The Linux boot loader can also be used to boot a particular kernel version or pass special boot parameters to the kernel if your system needs any.

You're given two choices of boot loaders:

- The traditional Linux Loader (LILO) was the tried-and-true boot loader of choice for so many years. LILO is pretty basic in what it does, but it is notoriously difficult to configure and prone to error to misconfiguration. Further, whenever a new kernel is installed, LILO must be reconfigured and reinstalled, making it a bit more difficult to maintain.

- The newer alternative boot loader called the Grand Unified Bootloader (GRUB) has been developed by the GNU Project to provide a more feature-rich boot loader, addressing LILO's technical and management shortcomings. GRUB is easy to maintain, requiring only minimal configuration and no reinstallation when a new kernel is installed.

GRUB is now the boot loader of choice as it is a more feature-rich product. The default settings, shown in Figure 2-5, are more than adequate for the majority of installations under most conditions. In general, I feel GRUB is easier to maintain once installed. Changes here are more a matter of taste, but I usually accept the defaults and move on to configuring the network interfaces.

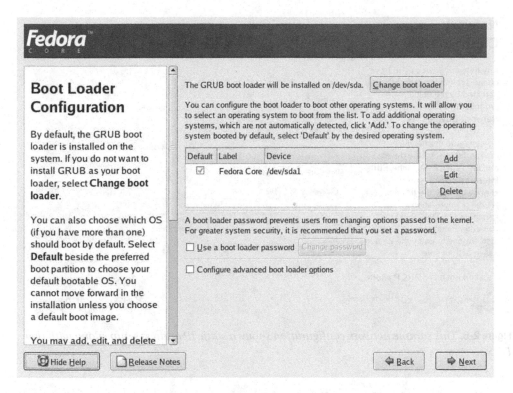

**Figure 2-5.** *Choosing GRUB with the suggested defaults is usually sufficient.*

## Configuring the Network

The Fedora Core installer will attempt to automatically detect if the system has any network interfaces. If any are found, they will show up in a list. Your primary network interface should be labeled *eth0*, which is short for Ethernet Interface 0.

The default configuration for eth0 is to automatically assign an IP address via *Dynamic Host Configuration Protocol (DHCP)*. DHCP is a way for your system to ask the network for a lease on an IP address. If a DHCP server is live on the network, it will respond back with a free IP address. DHCP is not usually appropriate for servers, and best practice is to statically assign an available IP address to the server. You can do so by selecting eth0 from the list of network interfaces, deselecting the Configure Using DHCP check box, and filling in the IP address and appropriate netmask.

This step is also where you define the server's network gateway if you statically assigned an IP address to a network interface and up to three separate DNS servers. DNS servers are absolutely vital to the Internet in general and your server in particular. If you do not specify any DNS servers, your server will not be able to properly resolve network names and IP addresses or receive and deliver e-mail properly. Figure 2-6 shows an example of this information properly filled out; be sure to fill in the appropriate information specific to your network.

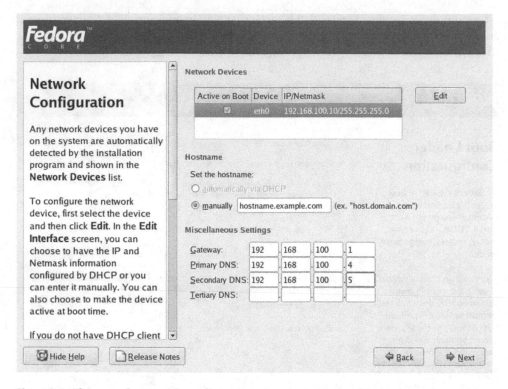

**Figure 2-6.** *This sample network configuration shows a static IP address setup, along with two DNS servers.*

## Configuring the Firewall and SELinux

Most Linux operating systems come with a built-in network firewall application. Fedora Core is no different. In this step you're given the opportunity to fine-tune the firewall settings a bit. You're also given the choice of disabling the firewall, but this is not at all recommended, even if your network border is protected by another independent firewall.

The default firewall settings are very restrictive and not appropriate to our e-mail server. So, go ahead and select the check boxes next to the following options to open holes in the firewall:

- Remote Login (SSH)

- Web Server (HTTP, HTTPS)

- Mail Server (SMTP)

This will still only be a base firewall configuration, and later we will have to tweak the firewall rules further to allow some of the other services through.

___

■**Note** The modern Linux firewall, called iptables, is provided by netfilter, a network packet filtering software framework. For more detailed information regarding advanced packet-filtering concepts, check out www.netfilter.org.

In addition to the network security the built-in host-based firewall provides, Fedora Core also incorporates a new, sophisticated set of security enhancements called *Security Enhanced Linux (SELinux)*. Originally developed by the US National Security Agency, SELinux adds granular security controls over various aspects of the system never before possible. However, maintaining SELinux can be a very complex thing to do. SELinux is well beyond the scope of this book, so I recommend disabling SELinux. If you do not do so, you may find one or more of the applications we install and configure later will not work.

---

**Tip** Disabling SELinux will not remove it altogether. It will simply operate in a warning state, alerting you to policy violations without blocking them. If you decide to dive into SELinux down the road, it is trivial to enable SELinux later. For more information, check out the Fedora Core SELinux FAQ at `http://fedora.redhat.com/docs/selinux-faq/`.

---

Figure 2-7 shows this step completed as suggested. After adding the exceptions to the network firewall and disabling SELinux, there are only four more steps to complete before you have a fully installed Linux system.

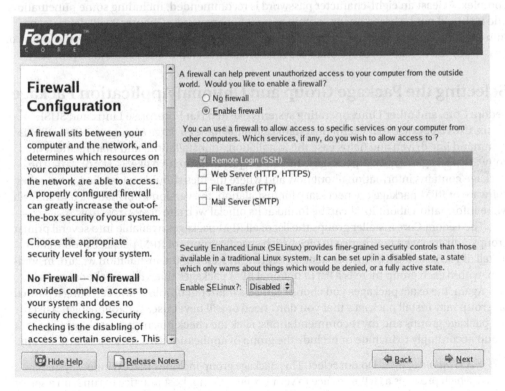

**Figure 2-7.** *Open a few holes in the firewall and disable SELinux.*

## Selecting Optional Additional Language Support

This step is optional, depending on your needs. If you need to support any additional languages, this step allows you to select the appropriate languages.

## Selecting a Time Zone

The time, date, and appropriate time zone of the server must always be properly set; otherwise services on the server may go out of synch, and e-mail messages delivered to, and received by, your mail server will be improperly time-stamped. Later, when you boot the system for the first time after installation, you will also be given the chance to set up the *Network Time Protocol (NTP)* for automatic time adjustment and synchronization. I highly recommend using NTP; once set up, it will keep your system time and date in synch from other Internet time servers down to the millisecond automatically.

## Setting the Root Password

The root account is the single most powerful and important account on any Linux system. The root account is analogous to the Administrator account on a Microsoft Windows system. This step prompts you for a password for root. This password should be unique and sufficiently complex. At least an eight-character password is recommended, including some punctuation, and it should not be based on, or contain any, dictionary words. Chapter 3 will delve deeper into the root account and how to manage your system. After you've typed and verified the root password, you're ready to move on to the final interactive step in the installation process.

## Selecting the Package Group and Optional Application Package

Fedora Core, and other Linux operating systems like Red Hat Enterprise Linux and SUSE Linux, uses a package management system called the *RPM Package Manager (RPM)*. RPM is command line driven and helps ease the installation, uninstallation, and management of software packages. An RPM package is more than just a file archive like a .tar or .zip. The package contains information about how and where the files should be installed, what other software or RPM package are necessary for installation, the version information, and so forth. More information about RPM can be found at its official web site at www.rpm.org.

The Fedora Core installer groups the list of all RPM packages available into several primary groups. You are given the chance to pick which specific groups of RPM packages you want to install, if you selected the Custom installation type in Step 4 of the installation wizard. In addition, within each group there is a list of optional RPM packages that you can choose from.

Again, the exact packages you choose can be a matter of opinion, and selecting a particular group may install packages that you don't need or will never use. The following is a list of the package groups and my recommendations; click the check box next to each package group accordingly to include or exclude the group of applications from the final installation.

- *X Window System*: Do not select. This package group includes the X Window System, which provides a GUI interface to your system. It is not best practice to run X on a server for security reasons. Also, by deselecting this option, your system will boot into text mode.

- *GNOME Desktop Environment*: Do not select. This package group will install the GNU desktop environment called GNOME and requires the X Window System.

- *Editors*: Highly recommended. This will install a couple extra text editors like GNU Emacs.

- *Graphical Internet*: Do not select. This package group includes the Mozilla web browser and graphical e-mail applications. Since we are not installing the X Window System, these packages should not be installed either.

- *Office/Productivity*: Do not select. This will install a graphical office suite called OpenOffice and requires the X Window System.

- *Sound and Video*: Do not select. This package group includes applications for listening to, and editing, music and video files. Since you are building a server, there's very little need for listening to music or watching videos.

- *Graphics*: Do not select. This package group includes the GNU Image Manipulation Program (GIMP), which allows for advanced graphics editing.

- *Web Server*: Required. This package group includes the Apache web server and supporting packages, which we will use later in Chapter 12.

- *Mail Server*: Required. This is the base of the whole project this book is dedicated to! By default, this package group will install sendmail, the SMTP server application that will send and deliver your e-mail.

- *Development Tools*: Required. This package group is necessary to build other applications, and various applications provided by this package group will be used throughout this book.

- *Administration Tools*: Optional. This package group includes various applications first developed by Red Hat and enhanced by the Fedora Project that aid the system administrator in day-to-day tasks like managing user accounts.

- *System Tools*: Optional. This package group is similar to the previous, but the applications are geared toward system configuration.

- *Printing Support*: Do not select. Since your system will be a server, not a personal desktop computer, there should be no cause to print.

Many of the package groups are simply not applicable or appropriate to a server. The administration and system tools are nice if you are not comfortable with editing configuration files with a text editor. They give you a graphical utility to make optional changes to many of the configurable applications installed.

Don't worry if you forget to select a package or an unnecessary package is installed. Once the installation is over and your new system is online, you can add and remove packages easily. Fedora Core offers the command line–driven utility called yum. In the next chapter you will learn how to use yum to update existing packages.

Once you've chosen which package groups to install, the installer will proceed with preparing the hard disk drives and then install each RPM package from the install media. If you've opted to install from the set of four CD-ROM discs, you will be prompted to switch discs where appropriate. Otherwise, sit back and monitor the progress. When everything has been installed, your CD-ROM or DVD disc will be ejected, and you can reboot your fresh Fedora Core installation (see Figure 2-8).

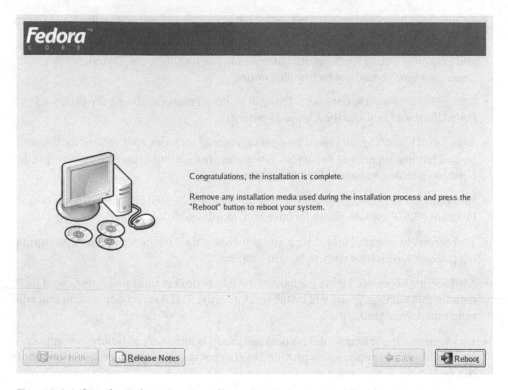

**Figure 2-8.** *When the Fedora Core installer is finished, your installation media will be ejected and your system will be rebooted.*

## Summary

One of the most difficult and vague topics of this chapter is determining your hardware needs. Due to the falling price of hardware, accounting for a little more growth than initially expected will actually save money in the long run. The trouble of upgrading a server you outgrew too fast can be a lot of work, especially if the server has been in production for some period of time. If you chose Fedora Core as your Linux operating system of choice, I hope you've found that the installation process isn't as intimidating as you might have thought. The graphical installer is quite intuitive. Don't worry too much if you think you might have missed a package group; I'll show you how to get everything if it wasn't installed during the initial system installation process.

By now your new system has probably started the reboot process. The next step is to get logged into your system for the first time and start preparing your system to be put into production. Chapter 3 will guide you through what to do once your server is booted for the first time after installation. This includes creating your own administrative user, learning the basics of system administration, and updating your system to keep it secure and bug-free.

# CHAPTER 3

■■■

# Bringing Your Server Online for the First Time

**N**ow that the new server is installed, you're probably anxious to move on and get your system live on the Internet. To get your system ready for a production environment, you need to do several things. During the installation you should have specified a static IP address and hostname for your new server. Once it's able to "talk" on the Internet like other Internet hosts, it's time to prepare your system to host your e-mail services. This chapter might seem longer than most, but it's chock-full of necessary information, especially if you are new to Linux in general, or Fedora Core specifically. I hope you stick with it; it will pay off in the end, and the rest of the book builds on the concepts discussed here.

## Postinstallation

There are a few things you need to do to get your system ready to start installing and configuring each of the components of your e-mail server. The two most important tasks are to create an administrator account for yourself and to make sure your server is updated, and remains so. But first, you'll need to log into the server for the first time.

### Logging In for the First Time

When your Linux server completes the boot process, you will be presented with a login prompt. What this looks like depends on the Linux operating system you chose and the hostname you specified at installation time, but in any case you will be prompted to enter a username. Assuming you're using Fedora, the prompt will look similar to that shown in Figure 3-1.

More than likely, the only login user account that exists on your system will be the root account, so go ahead and enter **root** for the username and press the Enter key. You'll next be prompted for a password. This was set during the installation process, so enter the password you chose and press Enter again. If you've entered the right password, you should find yourself logged into a text environment. This environment is called the *shell*.

```
Fedora Core release 4 (Stentz)
Kernel 2.6.11-1.1369_FC4 on an i686

apress login: _
```

**Figure 3-1.** *Example Fedora Core 4 login screen*

## Introducing the Shell

At the most basic level, the shell is little more than a command interpreter, providing an interface for interacting with the Linux operating system. Using this interface, you can easily
traverse the file system; modify, add, and delete files and directories on the file system; and
run and manage applications. It is also the environment from which we will do most of our
work throughout this book.

    The default shell in Fedora Core, and many other Linux operating systems, is GNU Bash.
Bash is a modern derivative of the sh shell, but has incorporated many features from the ksh
and csh shells. Bash offers features that enhance productivity, such as a sophisticated scripting environment, shell functions and command aliases, and an unlimited command history.
For more detailed information, check out the Bash Reference Manual at www.gnu.org/
software/bash/manual/bash.html.

---

■**Note** GNU stands for *GNU's Not UNIX* and is pronounced *guh-noo*. The GNU Project was originally started
in 1984 to develop a complete, free operating system upward compatible with the traditional UNIX operating
systems. The GNU Project also provides many software packages ranging from the Bash shell, a text editor,
games, and a graphical desktop environment. Some of the applications we will use later in this book are
hosted by the GNU Project. For more information about the GNU Project, the history and philosophy behind its
existence, and a directory of GNU software, visit the GNU Project web site at www.gnu.org.

---

    You interact with the shell by entering commands at a shell prompt. The shell prompt is
simply a bit of text at the beginning of every line where commands can be typed. For instance,
the default shell prompt for root in Fedora Core 4 looks like this:

```
[root@mail ~]#
```

This shell prompt includes the username of the account you're logged in as (root), the hostname of the system you're logged into (@mail), and the current working directory (~, which is short for the user's home directory, /root in this case). A prompt can look different from system to system, and is usually fully customizable. I prefer to add the current time in my prompt, while others may prefer as small a prompt as possible.

The most basic shell prompt will typically end with either a # or $; which one depends on which login user you are logged into the system with. Traditionally, the shell prompt for the root user is always denoted with a # and any other user's shell prompt is denoted with a $. Later in this chapter I'll offer a few short examples of how to customize your personal shell prompt.

### Learn to Respect root

The root account is the single most powerful account on a Linux server; it is also the most dangerous. root is the Linux superuser, analogous to the Administrator account on a Microsoft Windows server. I do not recommend that you log directly into a Linux server as the privileged root user to perform daily administrative tasks. Privilege separation is an important security and administrative concept in Linux server design and administration. Whenever possible, applications run without root privileges. Privilege separation maximizes users' personal privacy on a multiuser system, and minimizes security risks if application security vulnerability is exploited.

Given that, much of the system can only be manipulated by the superuser. So what do you do? The first thing you should do after the installation of your Linux server is create a system administrator user account for yourself. Then you'll set that account up to gain superuser root privileges only when necessary.

## Creating Your Administrative User Account

The reasoning behind creating a separate administrative user for you is twofold. First, it creates that privilege separation for security and privacy purposes. Second, as the primary system administrator, it allows you to maintain a custom interactive shell environment. As I've stressed before, many details are a subjective matter based on individual administrator taste and style. Some prefer the Bash shell; others may prefer the zsh shell. Some prefer a particular shell prompt and shell command aliases.

You can customize your virtual work environment on the server to fit your specific needs without modifying the root or anyone else's account. Most system operations depend on the root account to remain set up exactly as it is out of the box. For example, changing root's shell can have a negative impact on day-to-day operation of your system. First, let's create your administrative user account. Then I will give you a few quick pointers on customizing your new account.

### Introducing Users and Groups

Linux, by nature, is a multiuser environment. Users are simply individual accounts with which a person logs into a Linux system. An *account* is a virtual identity with which to gain access to the system and also partially determines what parts of the system the identity affords it. A *group* is a way to aggregate one or more users into the same class. In other words, a set of files on a Linux system might be owned by a handful of different users, and each user only has access to their files. Adding each user account to a single group, and giving that group access to the same files, can then also allow everyone access to share everyone else's files. Users and groups are used to compartmentalize a system; otherwise, the system would be monolithic and anyone sitting at the terminal would be able to access the entire system. Throughout this book, you will see examples of how this concept of users and group is used to manage the system and maintain privacy and security.

Users and groups are identified internally by a numeric *User ID (UID)* and *Group ID (GID)*, respectively. Usernames are mapped to their UID via the file /etc/passwd, and group names are mapped to their GID via the file /etc/group. The root user account is always UID 0, and the root group is always GID 0. Historically, usernames and group names were limited to eight characters each, and the maximum number of UIDs and GIDs was 65,536. However, technically speaking these limits no longer exist in the core of Linux operating systems, although many system administrators choose eight-character usernames out of tradition.

Not all users and groups are used for interactive login accounts. Some are used for applications running on a system. Those applications that run as a different user can be kept partitioned or restricted from the rest of the system. Having a number of specialized applications running as different unprivileged system users and groups minimizes potential security should a particular application be compromised. The user nobody is a perfect example of such a system user.

## Creating a New User

Let's create your first user account. To do so, use the useradd command. This account will be your personal administrative user for you to use for day-to-day administration. By default, Fedora Core will create a group by the same name as the username, make the GID identical to the UID, and make that group the initial login group. The command useradd takes several command-line arguments, but only the username is required. Most of the other arguments have systemwide defaults associated with them, and explicitly specifying an argument overwrites the default behaviors of the command. For example, the default user shell in Fedora Core is Bash, but by specifying the -s argument to useradd you can choose a different shell for a specific user.

Here's an example of adding a user with the useradd command; replace the sample username and real name with your own:

```
[root@mail ~]# useradd -c "Curtis Smith" -d /home/curtis -m -s /bin/bash curtis
```

The previous command will allow the system to determine the UID and GID of the new user and group automatically, but it specifies a comment (-c "Curtis Smith"), a home directory (-d /home/curtis) to create if one doesn't exist (-m), and the user's default shell (-s /bin/bash). Unless explicitly specified with the -u argument, the useradd command will automatically use the next available numeric UID and assign it to the username you create. Typically, the numeric range for nonsystem user account UIDs starts at 500.

---

**■Tip** Nearly every Linux command has an associated manual page, or man page, that describes its function, usage, and command-line arguments. Man pages can be a fantastic resource, and should be the first place you look for help. A man page can be invoked from the command line by typing man and the command itself. To read the man page for useradd, type man useradd at the command line. In addition, a particular command can have more than one section. If you see notation like "see the useradd(8) man page," this means see section 8 of the man page, which can be read by typing man 8 useradd. For more information about the man command itself, type man man at the command line.

---

You may find that you need to create a group for two or more users to share files, or you may decide that a user's primary login group should be named something different from their username. In that case, you would use the command groupadd.

## Creating a New Group

Like the useradd command, groupadd takes several optional command-line arguments, but the only required argument is the name of the group you wish to create. So, to create a new group with the name newgroup, simply type the following at the command line:

```
[root@mail ~]$ groupadd newgroup
```

Also like the useradd command, unless explicitly specified with the -g argument, groupadd will automatically use the next available numeric GID and assign it to the group name you create. Typically, the numeric range for nonsystem login group GIDs starts at 500. Creating special administrator groups is a great way to allow special read or write access to certain files or directories to a limited number of system administrators. One particular group is traditionally reserved for granting special privileges to select administrators. Further, that group can be used in conjunction with a powerful application to allow a nonprivileged administrative user to have the power of the root account.

## root Privileges without root

Earlier in this chapter I recommended never logging in directly as the root user for security reasons, but so far everything you've done has required root privileges. As I said before, most system operations require superuser power. Let's set up a way for you to use your newly created personal administrative account to be able to do the work of root.

### The Wheel Group

The reserved group I alluded to earlier is called *wheel*. Although you can use any arbitrary group name, many contemporary Linux operating systems like Fedora Core use the historical group name wheel for such occasions. As you'll learn a little later in this section, you can use the wheel group to simplify your life a bit and cut down on future administration. First, if you're not using Fedora Core, make sure the wheel group exists. Do so by typing grep wheel /etc/group at the command line. You should see some output like the following:

```
[root@mail ~]# grep wheel /etc/group
```

```
wheel:x:10:root
```

If nothing is output to the screen after executing this command, it probably means the wheel group does not exist. If so, create the wheel group with the following command:

```
[root@mail ~]# groupadd -g 10 wheel
```

Now add your newly created administrative account to the wheel group by typing

```
[root@mail ~]# usermod -G wheel curtis
```

Just as the command name implies, usermod is used to modify a user account. The command usermod is similar to the useradd in the command arguments it accepts and general usage. Check out its man page for detailed usage.

The wheel group has been historically used as an administrative group of sorts. For example, on some Berkeley Software Distribution (BSD) operating systems, only members of the wheel group had permission to use the command su, which allows nonprivileged users to log in as the root user if they know root's password. However, in the GNU system utilities, this specific functionality was removed from applications like su. However, it's a handy little group, still found on many Linux systems, to use as a general administrative group. Specifically, we'll use the wheel group in the configuration of another administrator tool called sudo.

### Introducing sudo

The program that allows an unprivileged user to run commands as root without logging in as root is called *sudo*. sudo stands for "superuser do," and will run any command as root, or as any other user, and log the command and command arguments in a secure system log file. The benefits of using sudo are threefold. First, there is an audit trail of administrator activity. Second, when sudo is used to run a command, the user is prompted for his password. This ensures that the person running the command is authorized to do so. Third, I believe it reminds users that they should consider carefully what they are running.

sudo must be configured to explicitly allow specific users to run some or all system commands. The sudo configuration gives granular access over who can use sudo, which commands they can run, and where on the system they may run those commands. For now, you'll need to give your new administrative user account unfettered access to the system. In fact, we're going to use the wheel group that we set up in the previous section to control the use of sudo. sudo configuration is controlled with the sudoers file and is located in /etc/sudoers by default. The recommended way to manipulate this file is with the command visudo.

visudo allows you to edit the sudoers file in a safe manner. It locks sudoers and keeps anyone else from making changes to that file at the same time. After you finish making your changes, it will also make sure there are no syntax or parse errors in the file before committing the changes. The visudo command uses the vi text editor by default. vi is a robust text editor, but if you've never used it before, it can seem a bit daunting. I assure you it's not as bad as it may seem at first, and after some practice vi will become second nature. Volumes can be written about vi, but I'll give the very basics to get you up and running.

■**Note** On most contemporary Linux operating systems, vi is actually Vim, or vi Improved. It has been written to work exactly like the old vi text editor traditionally found on UNIX operating systems. However, Vim offers many new features and functionality not available in the original version. More information can be found at the Vim project web site at www.vim.org.

### Crash Course in vi

The first thing you need to know about vi is that there are three modes: open mode, insert or replace mode, and last line mode. When you first open a file with vi, you are in open mode. This means that keystrokes are mostly meant for viewing and navigating the file. To navigate an opened file, you can use the arrow keys, or the h command to move left, j to move down, k to move up, and l to move right. This is illustrated in Table 3-1. Characters and words are deleted in open mode. Use x to remove one character under the cursor and X to remove one character before the cursor.

**Table 3-1.** *vi Movement Commands*

| Command | Movement | Alternate Command |
|---------|----------|-------------------|
| h | Left one character | Left arrow |
| j | Down one character | Down arrow |
| k | Up one character | Up arrow |
| l | Right one character | Right arrow |

To make changes to a file, there are a number of commands that will put you into insert or replace mode. Use a to begin inserting text after the cursor and i to begin inserting text under the cursor. When you have finished inserting or replacing text, press the Esc key to exit insert/replace mode and return to open mode to navigate the file. You must also press the Esc key before entering another insert/replace command; otherwise, the corresponding character represented by pressing the key itself will be inserted into the file. If you make a mistake, or an insert/replace command doesn't do what you had hoped, immediately press Esc and then u to undo the last set of changes. Table 3-2 lists more insert and replace commands.

**Table 3-2.** *vi Insert and Replace Commands*

| Command | Action |
|---------|--------|
| a | Enter insert mode one character after cursor position. |
| i | Enter insert mode at current cursor position. |
| A | Enter insert mode at the end of the current line. |
| I | Enter insert mode at beginning of the current line. |
| o | Enter insert mode below the current line. |
| O | Enter insert mode above the current line. |

When in open mode you have three ways to get into last line mode. Commands typed in last line mode literally appear on the last line of your screen in vi. The first two last line modes are entered by typing **/** or **?**. These keys will start searches for a target forward and backward in a file, respectively. For example, type **/** and press Enter to search forward from the location of the cursor for the string "the". Type **?** and press Enter to search backward for the string "the". If the search target is found, searching will stop and the cursor will be moved to the beginning of the target. Typing **/** or **?** and pressing Enter will continue the search for the same target, if it exists.

Typing **:** (colon) will put you into last line mode and allow you to use ex editor commands. The ex editor is a line editor historically found in the older UNIX operating systems. A line editor is not a full-screen application like vi; it edits files line by line. The ex commands you should familiarize yourself with are the ones that allow you to save changes to a file and quit vi. Type **:q** to quit a file if changes haven't been made, **:w** to save any changes, and **:wq** to save changes and quit vi. If you've made changes to a file but wish to quit without saving those changes, type **:q!**. Table 3-3 lists more ex commands. Now that you're a bit more familiar with vi, let's actually use those new skills to edit sudoers.

---

**Tip** For more practice with vi, I recommend the excellent vilearn interactive tutorial. It walks you through the major vi modes and commands while using vi itself. The tutorial immerses you into a vi session and breaks commands into intuitive categories. Each lesson builds on the previous. More information can be found at www.vilearn.org.

---

**Table 3-3.** *ex Commands for Use in vi*

| Command | Action |
|---|---|
| :w *filename* | Write changes to the new file called *filename*. If *filename* is not specified, changes are written to the current file. |
| :r *filename* | Read (and insert) the contents of the file *filename* at the current cursor location. |
| :q | Quit vi if no changes were made to the file. |
| :q! | Quit vi without saving any changes to the file. |
| :wq | Write changes to the file and quit vi. |

### Editing sudoers

Type **visudo** at the command line. The default configuration is very basic, but offers a few examples that are commented out. Any line that begins with a # is a comment and will be ignored by sudo when the sudoers file is parsed. About halfway down the screen, you should find two lines:

```
# User privilege specification
root    ALL=(ALL) ALL
```

This basically says that the user root has the right to run any command on any host as any user. This is the most basic, and least restrictive, configuration possible. This is also the configuration I recommend giving yourself as the server administrator. You could add an identical line, replacing root with your administrative user account name, but we'll use the wheel group instead. Other possibilities include restricting sudo privileges to a particular directory only, say your home directory, or limiting what particular system commands you can run with sudo. However, restricting your administrative user account would only limit what you can do on the system and negate the purpose of your account altogether.

So, first move the cursor to the beginning of the line and insert a # at the beginning of the line, effectively commenting out that configuration line. Now search for the following lines:

```
# Uncomment to allow people in group wheel to run all commands
#%wheel ALL=(ALL) ALL
```

Uncomment the second line by moving your cursor over the #and removing it. This says to allow anybody in the group wheel to run any command on any host as any user. From this point forward, instead of having to add a new line for every administrative user to the sudoers file, you simply have to add each new administrative user to the wheel group when you create their user account. Now that you've created your account, added yourself to the wheel group, and configured sudo so that you can administer your new server, all that's left is to set a password, log off the root account, and log in with your new account.

## Using Your Administrative User Account

A user cannot log into the system interactively without a password. No default password is applied when you create a new user. User passwords in modern Linux systems are stored in the file /etc/shadow. Nobody but root can read this file, for obvious security reasons. But in addition to restrictive file permissions, the actual clear-text passwords are not stored. Rather, when a password is generated, it is put through a one-way encryption algorithm so that, theoretically, the password can never be guessed from its encrypted version. However, the encrypted password is only as strong as the original; a weak, easily guessed password cannot be used, as we will see in the coming example.

To assign a password, or change an existing password, use the passwd command. When you run passwd as root, or as a regular user with sudo, you will not be prompted for the current password of the user you are trying to change the password of. When you run passwd for yourself, you will be prompted first for your current password before being allowed to change it. Here's an example of changing a password for a user as root:

```
[root@mail ~]# passwd curtis
```

```
Changing password for user curtis.
New UNIX password:
Retype new UNIX password:
passwd: all authentication tokens updated successfully.
```

The passwd command will attempt to do some checks to make sure the password is secure. For example, it will warn root when a password is too short or rudimentary. However, because root can do anything on a system, root will be allowed to set the password regardless of any warnings. See what happens when I try to change my password to foo:

```
[root@mail ~]# passwd curtis
```

```
Changing password for user curtis.
New UNIX password:
BAD PASSWORD: it's WAY too short
Retype new UNIX password:
passwd: all authentication tokens updated successfully.
```

But here's what happens when I try to do the same thing logged in as myself, an unprivileged user:

```
[curtis@mail ~]$ passwd
```

```
Changing password for user curtis.
Changing password for curtis
(current) UNIX password:
New UNIX password:
BAD PASSWORD: it's WAY too short
New UNIX password:
BAD PASSWORD: it's WAY too short
New UNIX password:
BAD PASSWORD: it's WAY too short
passwd: Authentication token manipulation error
```

No matter how hard I try, after three attempts, passwd quits with an error and my password is not changed.

Go ahead and change your password, but make sure it's equally complex as the password you chose for root. Now you can log off the root account by typing **logout** and log in with your new username and password pair. Now that you've set up your own personal administrative user account, set it up to gain superuser privileges when necessary, set the password, and logged in for the first time, let's go over a few basics to get you started on customizing your shell environment. But first, I need to introduce a few basic shell concepts.

## Introducing Shell Variables

First, *shell variables* are used to configure and customize your shell environment. In the Bash shell, a variable is denoted with a $ and is usually, but not necessarily, in all uppercase. Some common shell variables include $EDITOR, $HOME, and $PS1. The $EDITOR variable simply specifies your favorite default text editor and $HOME usually holds your home directory. The $PS1 shell variable is of particular interest if you want to customize your shell prompt.

To find out what a variable defines, use the shell built-in command echo:

```
[curtis@mail ~]$ echo $EDITOR
```

As you can see, the $EDITOR variable holds the value vi. For applications that look for the $EDITOR variable, vi will be your default text editor. Go ahead and see how the default Fedora Core $PS1 variable is defined:

```
[curtis@mail ~]$ echo $PS1
```

```
[\u@\h \W]\$
```

Note the \u, \h, and \W; these are special escape codes the shell recognizes and replaces with corresponding text when it displays the $PS1 variable. The \u stands for the username, the \h stands for the hostname, and the \W stands for the current working directory. Now let's change the $PS1 variable to customize the look of your shell prompt. To set a variable with a particular value in the Bash shell, use the command export, but do not specify the $ when assigning a value to a variable:

```
[curtis@mail ~]$ export PS1='[\t \u@\h \W]$ '
```

```
[01:28:19 curtis@mail ~]$
```

No, check your handiwork:

```
[01:28:19 curtis@mail ~]$ echo $PS1
```

```
[\t \u@\h \W]$
```

Notice how your shell prompt changes as soon as you press Enter? Note your prompt has the current time in it, and changes automatically whenever you type a new command the prompt refreshes. For a more complete discussion on customizing your shell prompt, check out the Bash Prompt HOWTO at www.tldp.org/HOWTO/Bash-Prompt-HOWTO/index.html.

So far, we've been running various commands without specify a full path to the command itself. When you type anything that the shell interprets as a command, it looks in each of the directories listed in the $PATH variable for that command. If that command isn't found in any of the directories, collectively called your *command path*, or *path* for short, the shell reports an error:

```
[01:35:33 curtis@mail ~]$ foobar
```

```
bash: foobar: command not found
```

To see what the default command path is for the root user, type echo $PATH as root:

```
[root@mail ~]# echo $PATH
```

```
/usr/kerberos/sbin:/usr/kerberos/bin:/usr/local/sbin:/usr/local/bin:/sbin: ➥
/bin:/usr/sbin:/usr/bin:/usr/X11R6/bin:/root/bin
```

Now compare your own command path of your regular, unprivileged user:

```
[curtis@mail ~]$ echo $PATH
```

```
/usr/kerberos/bin:/usr/local/bin:/bin:/usr/bin:/usr/X11R6/bin
```

To find out where, if at all, a command is found in your command path, use the command which:

```
[curtis@mail ~]$ which useradd
```

```
/usr/bin/which: no useradd in (/usr/kerberos/bin:/usr/local/bin:/bin: ➥
/usr/bin:/usr/X11R6/bin)
```

User accounts should typically not have access to various system utilities that administrators will need to use. A directory with sbin in its path is typically where administrative system binaries are found.

To see what variables are set within your shell environment, run the command env. Much of the output you might not understand just yet, but be aware that these variables are set to customize interaction with various aspects of the system.

## Introducing Shell Aliases

The second useful shell feature is *command aliases*. With command aliases, you can define an arbitrary alias to a particular command or lump of commands. For instance, the command ls will give a directory listing:

```
[curtis@mail ~]$ ls
```

```
some_directory   some_file   some_file_2
```

Well, the default ls output doesn't really give enough information; how are you supposed to tell the difference between a file and directory if the names aren't obvious? The -F argument will add a modifier after each file or directory to indicate just what it is:

```
[curtis@mail ~]$ ls -F
```

```
some_directory/   some_file   some_file_2
```

Note that directory names end with a / and regular files have nothing following their names. Suppose you want this to be default behavior but don't want to type the extra two characters every time. Not to worry! Create a command alias for ls:

```
[curtis@mail ~]$ alias ls='ls -F'
```

Then try a directory listing with ls again:

```
[curtis@mail ~]$ ls
```

```
some_directory/  some_file  some_file_2
```

From now on, every time you type **ls**, the shell will use your command alias and expand it to **ls –F**. If you decide you don't like this command alias, remove the alias like so:

```
[curtis@mail ~]$ unalias ls
[curtis@mail ~]$ ls
```

```
some_directory  some_file  some_file_2
```

### Making Your Shell Customizations Stick

If you were to log out after making these customized changes, they would be lost, and your shell environment would be reset to the system defaults. What good are these customizations if you have to make them every time you log in? Don't fret; shells have special files that allow you define your customizations, and have them configured every time you log in or invoke a new shell.

The Bash shell uses three primary initialization files, and each is located in your home directory. The first is .bash_profile. This file contains commands to be executed, or variables to be defined, during every new login shell. Basically, this file gets initialized every time you login or run a command. Your .bash_profile is the best place to define the $EDITOR and $HOME variables. To continue with the rest of this chapter, you should also define a different command path that includes the system utilities. Add the following line to your .bash_profile:

```
export PATH=$PATH:$HOME/bin:/sbin:/usr/sbin:/usr/local/sbin
```

The second file is .bashrc. This file contains individual command aliases, shell prompt customizations, and anything else that should be defined for interactive shell logins. This is where you would define your custom shell prompt with the $PS1 variable. This file is not executed when Bash isn't invoked interactively, say from a shell script.

Now that your personal environment is customized, it's time to finish preparing your system. The next administrative task is to update the RPM packages installed on your system. Managing security updates and bug fixes is simple with yum.

## Managing Software Packages with yum

Like other operating systems, Linux operating systems need updates to patch critical security vulnerabilities, fix bugs in software, and update features. If you chose Fedora Core as your server platform, you can use yum to manage system updates. yum is short for *Yellow dog Updater, Modified* and is more than an automatic updater. It can also be used to search for, install, and remove one or more RPM packages simultaneously.

RPM packages can be dependent on one or more other RPM packages, and manually resolving interdependencies between some packages can be difficult and frustrating. yum will do all the hard work, determining and resolving dependencies for you. The global configuration file for yum is /etc/yum.conf; for the most part, the default settings are sufficient. yum will only download RPM packages from yum repositories.

## Introducing yum Repositories

yum repositories are specially prepared sites that contain the RPM packages and the header files that list basic information about each RPM. yum will use the headers to compare to the headers of the packages installed on your system and determine whether newer packages need to be downloaded and upgraded. The headers are also used to resolve dependencies.

By default, yum is preconfigured to automatically choose repositories from a list of mirror sites on the Internet. Repositories are defined in separate files ending with .repo in their name in the directory /etc/yum.repos.d. Three repositories are enabled: the repository containing the base packages, the repository containing updates to the packages in the base, and the repository containing packages from the Fedora Extras project.

---

**Note** The Fedora Extras project is a community project, led by volunteers, that provides a repository of packages that is complementary to the base Fedora Core repository. You'll find more information, including a list of packages, at http://fedoraproject.org/wiki/Extras.

---

One particular option you should note in each of the yum repository configuration files is the line gpgcheck=1. This tells yum to check for, and verify the validity of, a GNU Privacy Guard signature on each package. I mentioned PGP and the GNU implementation of PGP briefly in a note in Chapter 2. GPG, as it's known as, is used by many to provide a way to ascertain the authenticity of a file. If the signature cannot be verified, then the package will not be installed. Essentially, this verifies that each package is legitimate and not a package that has been manipulated by a third party. All the RPM packages in an official Fedora Core or Fedora Extras repository are signed with their official GPG keys, respectively. These keys can be found in /usr/share/doc/fedora-release-4/ on Fedora Core 4 or online at http://fedora.redhat.com/about/security/. GPG keys can be imported globally into RPM itself. For example, to import the Fedora Project GPG public key so that package security can be verified, type **sudo rpm -- import /usr/share/doc/fedora-release-4/RPM-GPG-KEY-fedora** at a command prompt. Next, let's perform a systemwide update using yum.

## Updating Fedora Core with yum

To compare the RPM packages installed on your system to the packages in the repositories and upgrade to newer released packages, run the following command:

```
[curtis@mail ~]$ sudo yum update
```

This will look for an updated version of each package installed on your system, calculate dependencies, and report which packages need to be updated. If any packages need to be installed to satisfy dependencies, yum also will report those. If you want to continue, type **y** for yes, and yum will download each package and install it. If GPG checks are enabled in the repository configuration file, and you have not imported the public GPG key into RPM, yum prompts you to do so automatically.

When a package is updated, the older version of the package is usually replaced by the newer version. The one default exception to this is kernel updates. It is possible, and usually highly suggested, to install the new version of a kernel package alongside the older version. This allows you to restart the system, boot the new kernel, and make sure it is stable. Due to the ever-changing nature of the Linux kernel, sometimes a new kernel may be incompatible with particular hardware, or some other rare incompatibility exists between a software package and the new kernel. If the older kernel is left on the system, then it's a simple matter of restarting the system again and booting the older kernel. This provides a failsafe backup, one that would not exist if kernels were blindly upgraded, blowing away the older kernel. Although problems are few and far between, it's nice to have peace of mind that you can fall back to a known good kernel.

---

■**Caution** Sometimes, an RPM package will need to update a configuration file that's supplied by the package. If you have made changes to the original configuration file, there will be a conflict between the two files. Under most circumstances, RPM will back up the modified file and add an `.rpmsave` extension to the filename, then add the new file.

---

After the update process is complete, you typically do not need to restart the system. Usually, the only major package update that requires a full system reboot after upgrade is a newly installed kernel. Throughout the book there will be more examples of using yum to manage RPM packages, but for more immediate information check out the man page by typing **man yum** at the command line.

Running yum every day to see whether or not updates are available, downloading available updates, and then waiting for them to finish installing would be a real headache. This isn't the sort of thing you want to spend your time doing when there are other administration tasks to attend to. yum can be configured to run periodically on its own and automatically keep your system updated for you.

To enable the periodic updates, run the following:

```
[curtis@mail ~]$ sudo chkconfig --level 345 yum on
[curtis@mail ~]$ sudo service yum start
```

---

```
Enabling nightly yum update:                              [  OK  ]
```

---

This introduced two new commands: `chkconfig` and `service`. We'll make use of these commands more throughout the book, and each will be discussed in more depth later. But first I should briefly introduce init scripts and their role in the system.

## Introducing init, Runlevels, and init Scripts

Once the Linux kernel has been loaded by the boot loader and the boot process started, init, the process control initialization, is started. Think of init as the parent of all other processes. It does two primary things. First, init spawns one or more gettys, the console that you logged into at the beginning of this chapter. Second, init controls any other processes that are necessary to run the system. It is configured with a very simple configuration file, /etc/inittab. Under normal circumstances, you won't have to modify this file.

A Linux operating system has what are called *runlevels*. A runlevel is a specific set of applications that should start or stop when the system boots or switches from one runlevel to another. Table 3-4 lists the runlevels and their typical function.

**Table 3-4.** *Linux Runlevels*

| Runlevel | Function |
| --- | --- |
| 0 | Reserved; used to halt (power down) the system. |
| 1 | Reserved; used to take the system to single-user mode. |
| 6 | Reserved; used to reboot the system. |
| 2 | Used to switch to multiuser mode, with no networking. |
| 3 | Default; used to switch to multiuser mode, with full networking. |
| 4 | Rarely used; identical to runlevel 3. |
| 5 | Same as runlevel 3, but with graphical local interactive logins. *Not recommended for servers.* |
| 7–9 | Technically valid, but not used out of tradition to legacy UNIX systems. |

When init invokes a runlevel, init scripts are executed to start the subsequent applications appropriate to that runlevel. In Red Hat and Red Hat–based Linux operating systems like Fedora Core, init scripts are a bit more complex than some other variants. All Red Hat–style init scripts are found in /etc/rc.d. The init scripts that actually start an application are individually found in /etc/rc.d/init.d. Each runlevel has a corresponding directory as well. For example, runlevel 3, the runlevel a server should run in during normal operation, corresponds to the directory /etc/rc.d/rc3.d.

Inside this directory you will find a series of *symbolic links*, or symlinks for short. A symlink is simply a pointer to another real file or directory. If a symlink points to a nonexistent file or directory, then it is called a *dangling symlink*. In the case of init scripts, the symlink points to the actual application script in /etc/rc.d/init.d, but with either a K or S followed by a two-digit number. When init invokes runlevel 3, every script starting with a K is executed in the order of their corresponding number. Then all scripts starting with an S are executed in the order of their corresponding number.

This gives you, the system administrator, the ability to have init automatically start and stop certain applications when switching runlevels. In addition, by designating a specific number to the init script itself, you can make sure prerequisite applications are started before its dependent application starts. For example, in runlevel 3, networking must be started before any network applications like the mail server are started. Simply assigning the network init script a lower number than the sendmail init script will take care of this.

You're probably thinking the sounds complex. Perhaps you're worrying about having to maintain and manage all those symlinks? Well, remember the chkconfig command? It takes care of all the hard work for you:

```
[curtis@mail ~]$ chkconfig --list yum
```

| yum | 0:off | 1:off | 2:off | 3:on | 4:on | 5:on | 6:off |
|-----|-------|-------|-------|------|------|------|-------|

The chkconfig command tells you that the yum init script is turned off (starts with a K) in runlevels 0, 1, 2, and 6, and is turned on (starts with an S) in runlevels 3, 4, and 5. Of course, this is the case because we previously ran the command sudo chkconfig --level 345 yum on, which automatically created the appropriate symlinks in the appropriate directories.

The command service is simply an easy way of running the init script without having to type the whole path to the init script. For example, the command sudo service yum start is equivalent to sudo /etc/rc.d/init.d/yum start. To find out what arguments a particular init script takes, try the following:

```
[curtis@mail ~]$ sudo service yum
```

```
Usage: /etc/init.d/yum {start|stop|status|restart|reload|force-reload|condrestart}
```

Typically, most application init scripts will take the same arguments. You can especially count on start, stop, and restart.

So far, everything you've done has been done from the command line on the console, directly connected the system with a keyboard and monitor. With just a bit more configuration, your new Linux system comes fully equipped to be managed remotely over the Internet.

# Managing Your System Remotely

Chances are you're not going to have physical access to your server at all times. Besides, if you're anything like me, you'd prefer to work from the comfort of your office. Yet another powerful feature of a Linux operating system is the ability to manage nearly every aspect of the system remotely.

## Secure Remote Login with SSH

Secure remote login can be achieved with the traditional "r-servers": rsh, rlogin, and rsync, or through the Telnet protocol. However, each of these options is notoriously nonsecure, passing your username, password, and entire session in clear text. Obviously, you want to keep any user account secret, especially the root account and your administrative user account.

*Secure Shell (SSH)* is just what the name implies. SSH is a secure method for accessing the shell on a remote Internet host. SSH encrypts all traffic between your computer and the remote system, so you don't have to worry about sending your username and passwords over the Internet. When you log into your system via SSH, you get basically the same environment as if you had logged into the console directly. What's more, SSH also has a secure file transfer (SFTP) mode that can replace traditional FTP, which suffers from the same security risks as Telnet.

SSH should be installed by default on your Linux operating system. On Fedora Core, the SSH implementation of choice is OpenSSH (www.openssh.org). Your system should already be preconfigured to allow remote logins through SSH. If not, it's a simple matter of using yum to install OpenSSH and all of its dependencies with

```
[curtis@mail ~]$ sudo yum install openssh
```

If you specified to allow remote login via SSH through the firewall during the Fedora Core installation, you should be set to log off the console and connect with the SSH client of your choice. Otherwise, you may need to configure your server firewall to permit such traffic.

## Introducing netfilter/iptables

*netfilter* and *iptables* make up the framework that provides network address translation (NAT), firewalling, and general packet manipulation in the modern Linux kernel. Specifically, iptables is the term for the generic table structure in which rules can be defined. Each rule defines a match and an associated action for that match. For instance, a basic rule would match any IP traffic and arbitrarily block that traffic from passing on to the server.

This is how many Linux operating systems are set up. First, block all incoming Internet traffic, and then explicitly allow certain legitimate traffic. In the case of SSH, I recommend opening access to SSH on your server from anywhere on the Internet. On a Fedora Core server, that would mean adding the following to /etc/sysconfig/iptables, if it's not already there:

```
-A RH-Firewall-1-INPUT -m state --state NEW -m tcp -p tcp --dport 22 -j ACCEPT
```

Then restart iptables with the service command so the changes to the firewall take effect immediately:

```
[curtis@mail ~]$ sudo service iptables restart
```

```
Flushing firewall rules:                            [  OK  ]
Setting chains to policy ACCEPT: filter             [  OK  ]
Unloading iptables modules:                         [  OK  ]
Applying iptables firewall rules:                   [  OK  ]
```

This may seem like gibberish, but all it is saying is to allow any incoming connections destined for TCP port 22 from any Internet source. Much of the Internet traffic is over the *Transmission Control Protocol (TCP)* or *User Datagram Protocol (UDP)*. Every major application protocol like SSH is assigned a specific Internet port that it uses to communicate over the Internet. Since by default SSH uses TCP port 22 for incoming communications, your local SSH server is going to be expecting requests on that port. If the firewall is explicitly denying any communication to that port, the SSH server will never respond to the requests because the firewall is preventing the requests from reaching the SSH server.

Advanced networking and netfilter/iptables topics are well outside the scope of this book. For more information, visit the netfilter/iptables project web site at www.netfilter.org. Also, consider picking up a copy of James Turnbull's excellent book *Hardening Linux* (Apress, 2005). An in-depth discussion and tutorial on Linux packet filtering (firewalls) is also available from the Linux Packet Filtering HOWTO at www.netfilter.org/documentation/HOWTO/packet-filtering-HOWTO.html.

If you installed the System Administration package group during the Fedora Core installation, a GUI application called system-config-securitylevel will guide you through the configuration of the system firewall. If it did not get installed, you can install it now by entering the following command at the command line:

```
[curtis@mail ~]$ sudo yum install system-config-securitylevel
```

## Summary

In this chapter, we covered a lot of basic information, laying the groundwork necessary to start building your e-mail solution. You should have a basic understanding of the shell and command line. The commands we used to create your own administrative user account will come in handy later when you have to create the user accounts for your users. You'll also be able to work on your system in a more secure manner with sudo. Using the root account directly only when absolutely necessary will maintain the integrity of the system, and keep you more mindful of what you're doing on the system. Managing your system with yum will reduce your workload and make updating your system much easier. Now that your system is reachable from anywhere on the Internet, there is no more need for logging in directly over the console to perform day-to-day tasks—you can manage your system in a secure fashion from any remote Internet host.

Throughout the rest of this book, we will continue to develop the general skills you've developed in this chapter. In the next chapter, we delve right into the heart of an Internet e-mail server: the sendmail application.

# sendmail

# CHAPTER 4

■■■

# Introducing SMTP and sendmail

The linchpin in any Internet e-mail system is the MTA. As you may recall from Chapter 1, the MTA hands off mail from a client to a recipient. For years, countless server administrators have depended on the venerable sendmail program to deliver and receive their domain's e-mail. It has been the default MTA of many Linux operating systems, including Fedora Core, for years. This book covers the essentials of the sendmail program, though it just scratches the surface of the powerful features the program has to offer.

In this chapter, we will walk through the installation of the sendmail program. Whether you use your operating system vendor's prepackaged sendmail installation or install sendmail from the source distribution, this chapter will serve as a good introduction to the sendmail program in general. In Chapter 21, I will cover additional advanced security topics, some of which are specific to sendmail, that are not necessarily required but may offer additional value to your users. But first, I'd like to talk more about the primary Internet protocol that serves most Internet e-mail these days—the Simple Mail Transport Protocol, better known as SMTP.

## Introducing the Simple Mail Transfer Protocol (SMTP)

First, what does all this talk of protocols have to do with you? Simply put, a *protocol* is a (theoretically) well-defined method for two or more Internet hosts to communicate in a specific manner. Typically, proposed protocols go through an international standardization process in an effort to become widely approved by the global Internet community at large. Without these standardized protocols, electronic communication probably wouldn't have evolved past the early 1970s when every disparate network had its own unique form of electronic mail.

Throughout this book, I'll mention several protocols like SMTP, POP3, and IMAP. Each of these describes different ways for two Internet hosts to send and receive Internet e-mail messages. We will discuss the POP3 and IMAP protocols in more detail in Chapter 8. Before we try installing an SMTP server, let's take a quick look at the basics behind SMTP and how it affects you, the e-mail server administrator. E-mail server administrators should have at least a working knowledge of how each protocol functions, even if the dirty details on the Requests for Comments (RFC) might read like Greek. Understanding the basics will help you see how each piece of the puzzle fits together.

SMTP is the primary Internet protocol used to transfer Internet e-mail from one Internet host to another. SMTP is best thought of simply as a conversation conducted between the agent sending the message and the agent receiving the message on behalf of the recipient or recipients.

First, an e-mail client initiates the network connection with the appropriate e-mail server. The clients know how to connect to the appropriate server because of the *Domain Name Service* (DNS), another Internet protocol. This piece will be discussed in much more detail later in this chapter. Once the Internet connection to the server is initiated, the client will cordially begin the SMTP conversation by transmitting the HELO command. Optionally, a well-behaved client will identify its domain when it initiates the conversation, so that the server knows who the client is. After the conversation is initiated by the client, the server decides whether or not to continue the conversation. If it chooses to do so, it will send the client an SMTP reply code letting the client know it's ready and willing to continue.

If the client receives an affirmative response from the server, the client next indicates who is sending the e-mail with the MAIL command, which is typically the e-mail address of the original sender. Once again, the e-mail server will send an SMTP reply code back to the client indicating whether or not it's OK to proceed. If it's allowed to do so, the client can continue by sending the e-mail address of the recipient with the RCPT command. If there are multiple recipients, each recipient can be given with multiple RCPT commands. Once again, after each RCPT command, the server will send back an SMTP reply code indicating its acceptance or rejection of the recipient.

---

■**Caution** An Internet e-mail server that blindly accepts any e-mail recipient from any e-mail client is called an *open relay*. Spammers can exploit an open relay and use it as a springboard for their misdeeds. Chapter 21 goes into more detail on how to keep your server from being an open relay.

---

Next, the client will send the DATA command, indicating that the message body follows. The message text must end with the following five characters in this order: carriage return, line feed, period, another carriage return, and another line feed (\r\n.\r\n). After that five-character combination is received, the server will send yet another SMTP reply code indicating whether or not the message was accepted for delivery. After its message is accepted, the client can begin a new conversation with a new MAIL command, or it can finish the conversation with the QUIT command, after which the server will terminate the network connection between itself and the client.

An SMTP reply code is a three-digit number followed by a string of text describing the reply. Learning these few basic SMTP commands and the STMP reply codes can help you debug and troubleshoot e-mail delivery and routing problems in the future.

## An Example SMTP Conversation

It might surprise you that the simplest of SMTP clients are your favorite Telnet application and your keyboard! Watching a basic SMTP conversation in action is easy. You can use any Telnet client to connect to a publicly accessible mail server and issue SMTP commands. This effectively emulates what an SMTP client does, be it your e-mail client application or another mail server itself. Let's walk through an example SMTP session. If you want to try this yourself, substitute mail.example.com with the SMTP server address of your local Internet service provider and curtis@example.com with a valid e-mail address. In the examples, text in bold is sent by the client, so if you're following along, the bold text is what you type into the Telnet session.

**Note** The domain names `example.com`, `example.net`, and `example.org` have been set aside as reserved domains that are meant to be used for examples only and should never resolve to a real server. See RFC 2606 (`www.ietf.org/rfc/rfc2606.txt`) for more information.

On a Linux system, you can use the command-line application `telnet` to start a new session. To start a connection to a mail server, you must specify the well-known SMTP port number of 25; otherwise the Telnet application will default to port 23, the well-known default port for the `telnet` protocol. Let's take a look at how an SMTP conversation starts:

```
[curtis@mail ~]$ telnet mail.example.com 25
```

```
Trying 192.168.69.4...
Connected to mail.ods.org (192.168.69.4).
Escape character is '^]'.
```

You should get a response from the mail server that looks something like the following:

```
220 mail.example.com ESMTP Sendmail 8.13.4/8.13.4; Wed, 23 Nov 2005 ➡
16:59:29 -0500
```

Anything after the `ESMTP` can vary wildly from server to server and is informational only. Now try using the SMTP commands previously discussed to send a basic e-mail message to yourself that appears to come from yourself. The following example shows how to do just that:

```
MAIL FROM:<curtis@example.com>
```

```
250 2.1.0 <curtis@example.com>... Sender ok
```

```
RCPT TO:<curtis@example.com>
```

```
250 2.1.5 <curtis@example.com>... Recipient ok
```

```
DATA
```

```
354 Enter mail, end with "." on a line by itself
```

```
From: <curtis@example.com>
To: <curtis@example.com>
```

```
Subject: This was sent with Telnet!

Testing...1...2...3....

.
```

---

```
250 2.0.0 jANM68Yk020236 Message accepted for delivery
```

---

```
QUIT
```

---

```
221 2.0.0 mail.example.com closing connection
Connection closed by foreign host.
```

---

Open your e-mail client and check for new messages. You should see a new e-mail message waiting for you from yourself. Recall that you don't have to know every SMTP command, but a working knowledge of the basics helps you understand the process a little better and equips you with another tool to troubleshoot problems down the road. Table 4-1 lists common SMTP server reply codes for your reference. These will be handy to have readily available when your system is in production and you have to debug mail delivery problems for your users.

**Table 4-1.** *Common SMTP Reply Codes*

| Code | Description |
|------|-------------|
| 200 | Indicates a nonstandard success response (see RFC 876). |
| 211 | The following text is a system status or help reply. |
| 214 | The following text is a help message. |
| 220 | example.com SMTP service is ready; proceed. |
| 221 | example.com SMTP service is closing the transmission channel. |
| 250 | The requested mail action was OK and was completed. |
| 251 | The user is not local; the message will forward to *<forward-path>*. |
| 354 | Go ahead and start the mail message, and end it with <CRLF>.<CRLF>. |
| 421 | The example.com SMTP service is not available; the transmission channel is closing. |
| 450 | The requested mail action was not taken because the mailbox was unavailable. |
| 451 | The requested mail action was aborted because there was a local error in processing. |
| 452 | The requested mail action was not taken because there was insufficient system storage. |
| 500 | There was a syntax error; the command was unrecognized. |
| 501 | There was a syntax error in parameters or arguments. |
| 502 | The preceding command was not implemented. |

*continued*

| Code | Description |
|------|-------------|
| 503 | The preceding command was an invalid sequence of commands. |
| 504 | The preceding command parameter was not implemented. |
| 521 | example.com does not accept mail (See RFC 1846). |
| 550 | The requested mail action was not taken because the mailbox is unavailable. |
| 551 | The user is not local; please try the <*forward-path*>. |
| 552 | The requested mail action was aborted, because it exceeded the storage allocation. |
| 553 | The requested mail action was not taken because the mailbox name is not allowed. |
| 554 | The transaction failed. |

## The Role of an MTA

In the previous section, I used the terms "client" and "MTA" to describe SMTP as a sort of conversation to send and receive e-mail. Typically, the client is an MUA, as described in Chapter 1. For example, an MUA can be Microsoft Outlook, Mozilla Thunderbird, or Mutt, but in our example previously, Telnet and your keyboard serve as the MUA!

Also, in the previous section, I spoke of the MTA as an SMTP server accepting incoming connections from a client or MUA. However, an MTA can perform double duty—it can be both a server and a client. In which case, the previous discussion of SMTP as a conversation between a client and server can be taken a bit more broadly and can apply to two MTAs communicating. This would be the case after an MUA hands off an e-mail message to its MTA when the recipient is not hosted by the MTA. In this case, the MTA would have to look up the recipient's MTA and relay the message as a client to the recipient's server.

# Introducing the sendmail Program

The sendmail program is a freely available, open source MTA. sendmail's roots are in the days of ARPANET. Originally authored by Eric Allman at the University of California at Berkeley, the sendmail program was written to meet the need to bridge the various network mail protocols as ARPANET was expanding and evolving into what we know as the Internet today.

## A Brief History of sendmail

The first version of the sendmail program was shipped with Berkeley Software Distribution (BSD) 4.1c in 1983. In the years following its first public release, Allman went on a bit of development hiatus, but others continued to create variants of sendmail, adding features, fixing bugs, and making specific customizations. Some vendors also shipped their own customized versions of sendmail with their commercial variants of the UNIX operating system. Over time, this led to general confusion and compatibility and portability problems among the variants and offshoots.

Because he was bridging various networks' mail protocols in use at that time, Allman's initial approach to handling e-mail was a bit liberal. For example, UUCP mail didn't use headers, so sendmail was designed to accept these messages and add the appropriate SMTP headers to the message before sending it on. This behavior was necessary to make sure an e-mail message originating from one network would conform to the destination network's e-mail message and protocol formats. This is contrary to the more pragmatic, strict standards compliance of other contemporary MTAs. Rather than simply rejecting certain noncompliant addresses or expecting perfectly formed messages, sendmail will try to fix the message before delivering. This can be useful if you have to support myriad e-mail client applications that don't always do the right thing, but it also leaves open the possibility of letting spam through. Many of these concerns have been addressed, and security is in the forefront of sendmail development today. However, it isn't yet foolproof. Therefore, I will cover some of the things you can do to make sure spammers don't take advantage of your server, beginning in Chapter 16.

In 1992, Allman began work on adopting and consolidating some of the features and customizations introduced by other developers and vendors. The result was version 8 (V8), a new generation of the sendmail program. Since then, development has continued on a solid path of fixing bugs, patching security holes, maintaining standards compliance, and adding features. Major updates continued with the introduction of V8.8 in 1996 and V8.9 in 1999.

## Sendmail, Inc. and the Sendmail Consortium

In 1999, a new commercial company was incorporated to develop commercial support for the sendmail program—Sendmail, Inc. (www.sendmail.com). It also sponsors the Sendmail Consortium (www.sendmail.org), the group responsible for maintaining and developing the free, open source version of sendmail. The first offering from Sendmail, Inc. was sendmail V8.10 in 2000. Subsequent releases have culminated in V8.12.4 in early 2005.

Commercial and community support for sendmail remains strong even today. Over time, some have come to criticize sendmail as being overly complex, too slow, and difficult to maintain. However, even though popularity for sendmail may have begun to wane over the years, it remains the de facto standard for most UNIX and Linux operating systems. Recent surveys, including that of Credentia, a Seattle, Washington–based IT company, show that nearly 39 percent of all Internet e-mail servers still run sendmail; the next most popular MTA has only about 17 percent of the market share (See www.credentia.cc/research/surveys/smtp/200304/). Throughout this book, I hope to show that sendmail isn't quite the scary piece of software that some might claim and that it is still worthy of a place in your network. Although we may only scratch the surface of features and configurability, I'll present everything you need to know to maintain a secure, enterprise-quality e-mail system.

# Installing sendmail

Now it's time to install the sendmail program on your server, if it's not there already. As I've mentioned previously, chances are that sendmail is already installed and ready for you to customize and configure. If you've chosen to use Fedora Core as your server operating system, I will walk you through the sendmail packages and package management in the next section. If you have not chosen use Fedora Core specifically, but your Linux operating system does use the *RPM package manager* (RPM), the next section may still partially apply to your installation.

Finally, you might have decided to forgo any vendor package altogether, regardless your choice of Linux operating system, and roll your own sendmail installation from source code. Although I would not recommend this course of action for those new to Linux, or those not familiar with compiling source code from scratch, I will cover the basics of downloading and compiling sendmail from source code.

## The sendmail RPM Package

If you followed the Fedora Core installation in Chapter 2, then sendmail should have automatically been installed as an RPM package for you. To verify that this is, in fact, the case, use yum to find out:

```
[curtis@mail ~]$ yum list installed sendmail
```

```
Installed Packages
sendmail.i386                          8.13.4-2                    installed
```

This shows that sendmail version 8.13.4-2 is installed on your system. If you system does not have yum, use RPM itself to find out:

```
[curtis@mail ~]$ rpm -qv sendmail
```

```
sendmail-8.13.4-2
```

This command queries (-qv) the RPM database for any packages named sendmail. If any exists, it will list the package name and version. These methods are simply two different ways of getting the same information.

If you find that the sendmail RPM package is not installed, you can install it with yum:

```
[curtis@mail ~]$ sudo yum install sendmail
```

or you can download the latest RPM package from a download mirror with wget:

```
[curtis@mail ~]$ wget ➥
http://download.fedora.redhat.com/pub/fedora/linux/core/4/i386/os/Fedora/RPMS ➥
/sendmail-8.13.4-2.i386.rpm
```

```
--15:20:25-- http://download.fedora.redhat.com/pub/fedora/linux/core/4/i386/os ➥
/Fedora/RPMS/sendmail-8.13.4-2.i386.rpm
           => `sendmail-8.13.4-2.i386.rpm'
Resolving download.fedora.redhat.com... 209.132.176.221, 66.187.224.20, ➥
209.132.176.20, ...
Connecting to download.fedora.redhat.com[209.132.176.221]:80... connected.
HTTP request sent, awaiting response... 200 OK
Length: 611,890 [application/x-rpm]

100%[====================================>] 611,890       482.55K/s

15:20:27 (480.92 KB/s) - `sendmail-8.13.4-2.i386.rpm' saved [611,890/611,890]
```

and install the package with RPM:

```
[curtis@mail ~]$ sudo rpm -Uvh sendmail-8.13.4-2.i386.rpm
```

```
Preparing...                ######################################### [100%]
   1:sendmail               ######################################### [100%]
```

The preceding command uses the -U command-line argument to upgrade the sendmail RPM package if it's installed; otherwise, it installs a fresh copy. Then it prints out a hash mark progress indicator (-vh).

The Fedora Core package maintainers distribute sendmail in three different packages: sendmail, sendmail-cf, and sendmail-doc. The primary package, which the other two depend on, is the sendmail package, which we verified and installed in the preceding examples. For some stand-alone workstations or personal desktop systems, this one package could be sufficient for day-to-day operations. However, in Chapter 5, when we actually start customizing your sendmail configuration, you will also need the sendmail-cf package.

The sendmail-cf package includes all of the configuration and supporting files necessary to reconfigure sendmail to fit your custom needs. If you followed the installation instructions on Chapter 2, the sendmail-cf RPM package should have been automatically installed for you. If the package is not installed, the same steps apply as in the previous example, but using the sendmail-cf package name and version. If you have chosen not to use Fedora Core, you should check with your vendor to determine whether the configuration files are bundled separately.

The third sendmail RPM package is sendmail-doc. It is not installed by default, and it is entirely optional. If you'd like to have sendmail documentation handily installed on your local server, then I'd recommend installing the sendmail-doc RPM package to have around as a reference.

You now have a complete sendmail installation, ready to be configured and customized for your environment. You can skim the next section or skip it altogether, but I recommend at last checking out the section regarding RPM package management and dependencies. The rest of the chapter will be dedicated to installing sendmail from source.

## The sendmail Source Distribution

You should strongly consider using the vendor-supplied package available for your distribution unless you have very specific reasons for installing sendmail from source code, for example, if you require specific features not offered by the package provided with your system. Using your vendor-supplied packaged sendmail, if one exists, has several advantages. First, maintaining bug fixes and security patches in sendmail is a manual process with installations from source code, but utilizing a vendor's packaging system, like RPM in Fedora Core, allows you to rely on the vendor to supply regular updates to the sendmail packages as needed. If you followed my recommendation in Chapter 3 and enabled nightly updates with yum, the updates will be installed automatically without any intervention. Otherwise, you would have to download the latest source code and recompile and reinstall whenever an update was necessary. In addition, many vendors, like Red Hat and the Fedora community, maintain some advancements not always readily available from the raw source distribution, and they make sure the packages are specifically tested and tuned for the exact version of their Linux operating systems.

However, that is not to say that there aren't legitimate reasons for maintaining sendmail from source code on your own. You may require specific options or patches to the source code that are not available from a vendor. You may also desire to maintain a leading-edge installation, taking advantage of some new feature not yet available in the mainstream. Again, although these reasons are perfectly valid, I don't generally recommend taking this route.

Further, we will not cover any features or configuration that will not work with the standard RPM package distributed with the version of Fedora Core current at the time of this writing.

## An RPM Package Dependencies Warning

If you are using a Linux operating system like Fedora Core that offers sendmail RPM packages, you might consider removing those packages before installing sendmail from source code. However, be aware that there are bound to be other RPM packages installed on your system that depend on the sendmail package. If you use yum to remove all of the sendmail packages, it will calculate dependencies, if any exist, and suggest removing those packages also, shown in the following example using the yum command:

[curtis@mail ~]$ **sudo yum remove sendmail sendmail-cf sendmail-doc**

```
Setting up Remove Process
Resolving Dependencies
--> Populating transaction set with selected packages. Please wait.
---> Package sendmail-cf.i386 0:8.13.4-2 set to be erased
---> Package sendmail.i386 0:8.13.4-2 set to be erased
---> Package sendmail-doc.i386 0:8.13.4-2 set to be erased
--> Running transaction check
Setting up repositories
updates-released        100% |==========================| 951 B    00:00
extras                       100% |=========================| 1.1 kB    00:00
base                         100% |=========================| 1.1 kB    00:00
Reading repository metadata in from local files
--> Processing Dependency: /usr/sbin/sendmail for package: redhat-lsb
--> Processing Dependency: smtpdaemon for package: mdadm
--> Processing Dependency: smtpdaemon for package: fetchmail
--> Processing Dependency: smtpdaemon for package: mutt
--> Restarting Dependency Resolution with new changes.
--> Populating transaction set with selected packages. Please wait.
---> Package redhat-lsb.i386 0:1.3-10 set to be erased
---> Package fetchmail.i386 0:6.2.5-7.fc4.1 set to be erased
---> Package mdadm.i386 0:1.11.0-4.fc4 set to be erased
---> Package mutt.i386 5:1.4.2.1-2 set to be erased
--> Running transaction check

Dependencies Resolved

=============================================================================
Package              Arch      Version       Repository      Size
=============================================================================
Removing:
 sendmail            i386      8.13.4-2      installed       1.3 M
 sendmail-cf         i386      8.13.4-2      installed       939 k
 sendmail-doc        i386      8.13.4-2      installed       1.7 M
```

```
Removing for dependencies:
    fetchmail           i386        6.2.5-7.fc4.1       installed       1.4 M
    mdadm               i386        1.11.0-4.fc4        installed       1.3 M
    mutt                i386        5:1.4.2.1-2         installed       2.9 M
    redhat-ls           i386        1.3-10              installed       17 k

Transaction Summary
==============================================================================
Install     0 Package(s)
Update      0 Package(s)
Remove      7 Package(s)
Total download size: 0
Is this ok [y/N]:
```

Removing these packages will probably not be a wise choice, so answer "no." Now try using RPM instead:

```
[curtis@mail ~]$ sudo rpm -ev sendmail sendmail-cf sendmail-doc
```

```
error: Failed dependencies:
        /usr/sbin/sendmail is needed by (installed) redhat-lsb-1.3-10.i386
        smtpdaemon is needed by (installed) mdadm-1.11.0-4.fc4.i386
        smtpdaemon is needed by (installed) mutt-1.4.2.1-2.i386
        smtpdaemon is needed by (installed) fetchmail-6.2.5-7.fc4.1.i386
```

RPM will simply report a dependency error and exit. If you're sure you want to remove the sendmail packages, ignoring any dependency failure, and leave the dependent packages installed, tell RPM to ignore dependencies.

**Caution** Ignoring RPM package dependencies can be extremely detrimental to the proper working of your Fedora Core installation. Please do so *only* if you're sure of what you're doing and what the repercussions are. This may or may not come back to haunt you later if you're not careful.

Ignoring dependencies is not generally recommended, but because we know what we're removing and that we'll actually be replacing the packages with the same thing from source code, we can ignore the warnings and dependencies with the --nodeps argument to RPM:

```
[curtis@mail ~]$ sudo rpm -ev --nodeps sendmail sendmail-cf sendmail-doc
```

## Downloading and Verifying the sendmail Source Distribution

Now that the vendor sendmail packages have been removed from your system, the next step is to download the latest source code distribution. Find a local mirror located near to you from www.sendmail.org/mirrors.html, and use wget to download the latest version of the sendmail program source code, shown in the following example. At the time of this writing, the latest version is 8.13.4, and it is found at www.sendmail.org/8.13.4.html.

```
[curtis@mail ~]$ wget ➥
ftp://ftp.sendmail.org/pub/sendmail/sendmail.8.13.4.tar.gz
```

From the sendmail web site, we are given the MD5 signatures of the source tarballs, so use the md5sum command to verify the integrity of your download:

```
[curtis@mail ~]$ md5sum sendmail.8.13.4.tar.gz
```

```
61e336750b48b01abaa69b4d7c9473b5  sendmail.8.13.4.tar.gz
```

If the signature calculated by md5sum matches the signature published on the Sendmail Consortium web site, then you have a good download. Otherwise, delete the file, and retry from another mirror.

## Compiling the sendmail Source Distribution

The downloaded file is what's commonly called a *tarball*, because it's a tar archive (.tar) that has been compressed with gzip (.gz). Sometimes a tarball file name ends in .tgz, which is just a short form of .tar.gz. A tarball is loosely analogous to a ZIP file, except a tarball is archived and compressed by two different programs (tar and gzip respectively), while a ZIP file is archived and compressed using the same program.

Next you must uncompress and rip apart the tarball. This can be done with one command if you are on a modern Linux operating system and have GNU tar available (output trimmed for brevity):

```
[curtis@mail ~]$ tar -xzvf sendmail.8.13.4.tar.gz
```

```
sendmail-8.13.4/
sendmail-8.13.4/Makefile
sendmail-8.13.4/Build
sendmail-8.13.4/CACerts
sendmail-8.13.4/FAQ
sendmail-8.13.4/INSTALL
sendmail-8.13.4/KNOWNBUGS
sendmail-8.13.4/LICENSE
sendmail-8.13.4/PGPKEYS
sendmail-8.13.4/README
sendmail-8.13.4/RELEASE_NOTES
```

The previous command is unbundling the tarball file (-xvf) and using gunzip to uncompress the file compressed with the gzip compression utility (-z).

Building sendmail consists of several steps. The following steps are necessary to get sendmail to build on a Fedora Core server as described in Chapter 2.

The first step is to move inside the source directory for the sendmail program and run the build script (screen output trimmed for brevity):

```
[curtis@mail ~]$ cd sendmail-8.13.4/sendmail/
[curtis@mail sendmail]$ sh Build
```

```
Configuration: pfx=, os=Linux, rel=2.6.12-1.1398_FC4, rbase=2, ➥
rroot=2.6.12-1, arch=i686, sfx=variant=optimized
Using M4=/usr/bin/m4
Creating /home/curtis/sendmail-8.13.4/obj.Linux.2.6.12-1.1398_FC4.i686/ ➥
sendmail using /home/curtis/sendmail-8.13.4/devtools/OS/Linux
Making dependencies in /home/curtis/sendmail-8.13.4/ ➥
obj.Linux.2.6.12-1.1398_FC4.i686/sendmail
rm -f sm_os.h
ln -f -s ../../include/sm/os/sm_os_linux.h sm_os.h
cc -M -I. -I../../include  -DNEWDB    main.c alias.c arpadate.c bf.c ➥
collect.c conf. control.c convtime.c daemon.c deliver.c domain.c ➥
envelope.c err.c headers.c macro.c map.c mci.c milter.c mime.c ➥
parseaddr.c queue.c ratectrl.c readcf.c recipient.c sasl.c save-mail.c ➥
sfsasl.c shmticklib.c sm_resolve.c srvrsmtp.c stab.c stats.c sysexits.c ➥
timers.c tls.c trace.c udb.c usersmtp.c util.c version.c
```

Next, change to the cf/cf/ directory, copy the generic Linux .mc file, and build a new sendmail configuration file, thusly:

```
[curtis@mail sendmail]$ cd ../cf/cf
[curtis@mail cf]$ cp generic-linux.mc sendmail.mc
[curtis@mail cf]$ sh Build sendmail.cf
```

```
Using M4=/usr/bin/m4
rm -f sendmail.cf
/usr/bin/m4 ../m4/cf.m4 sendmail.mc > sendmail.cf || ➥
( rm -f sendmail.cf && exit 1 )
echo "### sendmail.mc ###" >>sendmail.cf
sed -e 's/^/# /' sendmail.mc >>sendmail.cf
chmod 444 sendmail.cf
```

Now install the sendmail configuration files to /etc/mail/:

```
[curtis@mail cf]$ sudo sh Build install-cf
```

```
Using M4=/usr/bin/
../../devtools/bin/install.sh -c -o root -g bin -m 0444 ➥
sendmail.cf /etc/mail/sendmail.cf
```

```
../../devtools/bin/install.sh -c -o root -g bin -m 0444 ➥
submit.cf /etc/mail/submit.cf
```

As a security precaution, as discussed in Chapter 3, part of sendmail is run as a separate, unprivileged user and group. If the smmsp user and group do not already exist, create them:

```
[curtis@mail cf]$ groupadd -g 51 smmsp
[curtis@mail cf]$ useradd -g smmsp -d /var/spool/mqueue ➥
-m -s /sbin/nologin smmsp
```

Now install the sendmail binary:

```
[curtis@mail sendmail]$ sudo mkdir -p /usr/man/man8
[curtis@mail sendmail]$ sudo mkdir -p /usr/man/man5
[curtis@mail sendmail]$ sudo mkdir -p /usr/man/man1
[curtis@mail sendmail]$ sudo sh Build install
```

```
Configuration: pfx=, os=Linux, rel=2.6.12-1.1398_FC4, ➥
rbase=2, rroot=2.6.12-1, arch=i686, sfx=, variant=optimized
Making in /home/curtis/sendmail-8.13.4/ ➥
obj.Linux.2.6.12-1.1398_FC4.i686/sendmailif [ ! -d ➥
/etc/mail ]; then mkdir -p /etc/mail; else :; fi
install -c -o bin -g bin -m 444 helpfile /etc/mail/helpfile
if [ ! -d /etc/mail ]; then mkdir -p /etc/mail; else :; fi
install -c -o root -g bin -m 0600 statistics /etc/mail/statistics
install -c -o root -g smmsp -m 2555 sendmail /usr/sbin
for i in /usr/bin/newaliases /usr/bin/mailq ➥
/usr/bin/hoststat /usr/bin/purgestat; do \
        rm -f $i; \
        ln -s /usr/sbin/sendmail $i; \
done
install -c -o bin -g bin -m 444 sendmail.0 /usr/man/man8/sendmail.8
install -c -o bin -g bin -m 444 aliases.0 /usr/man/man5/aliases.5
install -c -o bin -g bin -m 444 mailq.0 /usr/man/man1/mailq.1
install -c -o bin -g bin -m 444 newaliases.0 /usr/man/man1/newaliases.1
```

Then install the various supporting sendmail utilities by moving into the utilities' individual directories and running sudo sh Build install. For example, to build and install editmap, use the following command (screen output trimmed for brevity):

```
[curtis@mail sendmail]$ cd ../editmap
[curtis@mail editmap]$ sudo sh Build install
```

Each utility, and its purpose, is listed in Table 4-2. I recommend installing all of the utilities, as all are useful, and most will be used in subsequent chapters.

**Table 4-2.** *sendmail Utilities*

| Utility/Directory Name | Utility Purpose |
| --- | --- |
| editmap | Edit and view configuration maps created with the makemap utility. |
| mailstats | Display the current mail statistics saved by sendmail. |
| makemap | Create the keyed map configuration files discussed in Chapter 6. |
| praliases | Display the current system aliases discussed in Chapter 6. |
| smrsh (sendmail restricted shell) | Use for security as discussed in Chapter 13. |

Finally, various Fedora Core applications may require a special set of symbolic links in /etc/alternatives. A symbolic link, or symlink for short, is a kind of *shortcut*, a file pointing another file. If you are running Fedora Core, and if you removed the sendmail RPM package and installed sendmail from source, you will need to create or change the set of symlinks:

```
[curtis@mail sendmail]$ cd /etc/alternatives
[curtis@mail alternatives]$ sudo ln -s /usr/sbin/sendmail mta
[curtis@mail alternatives]$ sudo ln -s /usr/sbin/mailq mta-mailq
[curtis@mail alternatives]$ sudo ln -s /usr/sbin/newaliases mta-newaliases
[curtis@mail alternatives]$ sudo ln -s /usr/sbin/rmail mta-rmail
[curtis@mail alternatives]$ sudo ln -s /usr/sbin/sendmail mta-sendmail
```

Congratulations! You now have a newly installed sendmail application hand built from source code. Building sendmail from source code isn't for the faint of heart, but it can be a rewarding experience for those who attempt it. Now that sendmail is installed, Chapter 5 will start you down the path of configuring sendmail to meet your particular needs.

# Summary

In this chapter, we first discussed SMTP. As you saw, it's little more than a well-defined, friendly conversation between a client and server. Learning a few necessary SMTP commands and SMTP server reply codes will definitely help you debug your e-mail system, should the need arise. You also saw that an MTA doesn't have to be just a server, passively accepting SMTP connections from users' e-mail clients; an MTA also acts as a client when relaying messages to a recipient's own MTA. Finally, I've presented two ways of installing the sendmail program, depending on your chosen server operating system or personal preference.

sendmail has a long, rich history and has been the dominant MTA for years. Even today, many Linux operating system vendors still ship with sendmail as their default MTA. Relying on the vendor-supplied sendmail packages can help keep your installation up to date and secure along with the rest of your system. However, I've shown it's also possible to install sendmail from source code, if you choose to do so. Whether you stick with the Fedora Core sendmail RPM packages or chose to build sendmail from source code, you are ready to move on to the configuration and testing of your new MTA!

# CHAPTER 5

■ ■ ■

# Configuring sendmail and DNS

**M**any regard configuring sendmail as a daunting task, which seems true if you stare at the long list of raw, supported features and consider the sheer number of configuration options. However, the average administrator simply won't need the majority of those features, and much of the configuration need not be changed. For instance, you can configure sendmail to work with UUCP mail gateways. However, since UUCP is no longer used, you can disregard these options. When you start looking at sendmail from this point of view, it isn't as daunting as you might think at first.

In this chapter, I will cover the basic configuration necessary to bring your MTA listening live on the network for the first time. I will also introduce the primary sendmail configuration files and a few DNS concepts that are necessary for others to route mail to your e-mail server once it is online. Without the proper DNS configuration, e-mail will never make it to your Internet domain.

## Introducing the sendmail Configuration Files

The primary configuration files for sendmail are found in the directory /etc/mail/, unless you explicitly changed the configuration directory when you installed sendmail from source code. A sample directory listing from our default Fedora Core installation ought to look something like this:

```
[curtis@mail ~]$ cd /etc/mail/
[curtis@mail mail]$ ls -l
```

```
total 188
-rw-r--r--  1 root root   331 May  6 08:35 access
-rw-r-----  1 root root 12288 Aug  8 20:28 access.db
-rw-r--r--  1 root root     0 May  6 08:35 domaintable
-rw-r-----  1 root root 12288 Aug  8 20:28 domaintable.db
-rw-r--r--  1 root root  5588 May  6 08:35 helpfile
-rw-r--r--  1 root root    64 May  6 08:35 local-host-names
-rw-r--r--  1 root root     0 May  6 08:35 mailertable
-rw-r-----  1 root root 12288 Aug  8 20:28 mailertable.db
-rw-r--r--  1 root root  1035 May  6 08:35 Makefile
-rw-r--r--  1 root root 58079 Aug  8 20:28 sendmail.cf
-rw-r--r--  1 root root  7069 May  6 08:35 sendmail.mc
```

```
drwxr-xr-x  2 root root  4096 Aug  8 10:06 spamassassin
-r--r--r--  1 root root 41348 May  6 08:35 submit.cf
-rw-r--r--  1 root root   952 May  6 08:35 submit.mc
-rw-r--r--  1 root root   127 May  6 08:35 trusted-users
-rw-r--r--  1 root root     0 May  6 08:35 virtusertable
-rw-r-----  1 root root 12288 Aug  8 20:28 virtusertable.db
```

In Fedora Core, the sendmail RPM package installs these files, and the sendmail program is preconfigured to listen for and accept mail from the local computer only. This means that sendmail is running and will deliver e-mail locally, but it will not listen on any public network interfaces or receive e-mail from other network nodes. The main configuration files for sendmail are sendmail.cf and submit.cf; we will discuss these two files and their corresponding files, sendmail.mc and submit.mc, in depth later in this chapter. All of the other sendmail files in /etc/mail/ are configuration files included by sendmail.cf meant to manipulate other various sendmail features, which are discussed in further detail in Chapter 6. For now, ignore the directory spamassassin altogether, if it exists; SpamAssassin and the role of /etc/mail/spamassassin/ are topics in Chapter 18.

Later in this chapter, when we configure sendmail, you will see that the main sendmail.cf configuration file actually depends on a number of other sendmail configuration files, which contain features and operating system–specific configuration directives necessary for sendmail to run correctly on your system. Luckily, even though they are explicitly necessary for reconfiguring sendmail, it is unlikely that you will have to touch any of them at all.

## A Word About sendmail Security

The sendmail program has to run as the privileged root user for several reasons. One primary reason is that only applications run by the root user may bind to an address and port for sending and receiving connections over the network. Also, root privileges are needed for read/write permissions to all of the queue directories; on a multiuser system, you wouldn't want to make all users' mail queues readable by unprivileged users. The inability of sendmail to run as anything other than the root user has been a major criticism of sendmail over the years, because of the potential security risks of running solely as the privileged root user.

### sendmail.cf vs. submit.cf

Beginning with version 8.12 of sendmail, this issue has been addressed. Unfortunately, there is no way around the necessity to run sendmail as the root user to open a network address and port, but the queue problem has been addressed. The solution involves splitting sendmail into two separate processes. One is used for receiving e-mail only, and the other is for e-mail delivery. The sendmail process used for receiving e-mail still runs as the root user and has its own queue (/var/spool/queue/) that it, and only it, has access to read from and write to. The second sendmail process runs using a nonprivileged user (typically smmsp) and owns another, separate queue (/var/spool/clientmqueue/) that it can read from and write to, and that other nonprivileged users can execute in a secure manner through a command-line application. The former receives mail from other e-mail systems over the network and uses the normal sendmail.cf configuration file, and the latter is for local mail submission and delivery and uses the submit.cf configuration file.

On any system that makes use of this split configuration, like Fedora Core, two different sendmail processes can be seen working in the two modes of operation with a combination of the ps and grep commands:

```
[curtis@mail ~]$ ps auxw | grep sendmail
```

```
root     13390  0.0  0.6   7952  3176 ?           Ss   11:26   0:00 ➥
sendmail: accepting connections
smmsp    13396  0.0  0.5   6968  2668 ?           Ss   11:26   0:00 ➥
sendmail: Queue runner@01:00:00 for /var/spool/clientmqueue
```

Note the first column (in bold) of the output of the command ps, which shows the input from the user running the corresponding process.

This security matter is of relevance to you only if you decide to allow interactive login accounts for your users, from which, they may send e-mail to and receive e-mail from traditional UNIX command-line mail clients like mail, Mutt, or Pine; this is not as common anymore, since most people check their e-mail remotely from their desktop computers. The default behavior is to treat local mail essentially like incoming mail from the public network, passing messages to the local delivery sendmail application. If you install the Fedora Core sendmail-doc RPM package, you can read more about this in the file /usr/share/doc/sendmail/SECURITY; otherwise, it's available online at www.sendmail.org or in the source distribution. Unless you have special requirements, you should not have to change /etc/mail/submit.cf at all. However, you will need to make changes to sendmail.cf, so let's take a look at sendmail's default configuration and learn how to customize sendmail for your specific needs.

## The Default Fedora Core sendmail.cf

Again for security reasons, some Linux operating systems like Fedora Core specifically configure sendmail, so that it will only accept incoming connections from the local computer through the loopback network interface. The IP address for the loopback interface is 127.0.0.1 and is commonly referred to by the generic hostname localhost. The reasoning behind this is the general acknowledgment by vendors that not everybody who installs a Linux operating system intends to offer public Internet e-mail services, as is the case for most desktops. Yet the ability to send and receive e-mail, even just locally, is necessary to many of the components on a Linux system. Reducing the number of applications accepting incoming connections over the public network limits the avenues miscreants can take advantage of to break into an improperly configured or secured server application that the user neglects or simply isn't aware of.

---

**Note** The loopback network interface is a virtual interface, emulating a physical network card via software, without any real hardware connected to it. The reason for having such a network interface is to allow a system to privately contact its own local network applications, like sendmail, instead of over the public network.

---

However, in your case, you need sendmail to accept incoming network connections over the public network. (Otherwise, you probably wouldn't be reading this book!) Changing this default configuration behavior, and much more, is covered in the following section of this chapter.

# Configuring sendmail

If you installed Fedora Core, I must reemphasize the need for the separate prerequisite sendmail-cf RPM package. If that package is not installed, you will not be able to successfully reconfigure sendmail; refer to Chapter 4 for more details. If you installed sendmail from source code, all the necessary support files should be in place as part of the installation process. For the rest of this chapter, I will assume you are working from a Fedora Core system, using the vendor-supplied sendmail packages. Although the configuration file names should be identical between the two installation methods, the actual locations may vary, and you will need to refer to the documentation that came with the source code you downloaded for exact installation directories.

Throughout this chapter, I've said that the default sendmail configuration file is sendmail.cf. However, as you might have noted when we looked at the directory listing of /etc/mail/, for every file ending with a .cf file extension, a file with the same name ending with the .mc file extension also exists. When configuring sendmail, you never edit the .cf file directly. Indeed, if you just browse sendmail.cf, I think you'll quickly see why! To simplify the configuration process, we edit the .mc files and use those simpler files to produce the final, more complex sendmail.cf. This is done with the macro processor called GNU m4.

## Introducing the m4 Macro Processor

Generally speaking, a *macro* is simply a representation, or abbreviation, of a set of commands or strings of text. Macros are used in popular word processors all the time. Executing one macro command can initiate several keystrokes or commands, easing repetitive tasks.

The m4 macro processor is an application that does just as the name implies—it processes macros. To be more precise, m4 copies its input, expands macros as it reads the input, and then presents the results as its output. The original is untouched and a new file with the macros expanded is generated. If the input is modified, and m4 is run again, the output is expanded accordingly.

m4 is *stream-based*, meaning is has no notion of lines; it simply sees its input as a continuous line of characters. Because of this, you will see the special m4 keyword dnl throughout the .mc files. It stands for "delete through newline." m4 ignores the characters following dnl up to, and including, the newline character, effectively removing the string of characters from the output. This can be used to remove redundant empty lines and make the resulting output more readable. It can also be used to insert comments in the input that won't show up in the output. I think a simple example can illustrate this point fairly well.

Type the following text into a temporary text file called something like test.m4 (a great chance to practice those vi skills!); the file should begin and end with empty lines:

```
See? dnl

dnl
dnl Ignore everything after a "dnl"
dnl

m4 dnl foo dnl
isn't so bad!
```

Now, from the command line in the same directory as the file you just created, use the command m4 to process the input text by typing the following:

```
[curtis@mail ~]$ m4 test.m4
```

See?

m4 isn't so bad!

It almost seems like magic!

But the real power is in macros. Recall that a macro is simply a short, meaningful representation for a set of elaborate, complex strings of characters or commands. For instance, if you find that you are typing /usr/share/sendmail-cf/ a lot, why not define a macro to replace every occurrence of the string cf with the longer string /usr/share/sendmail-cf/? There are some built-in macros that m4 automatically recognizes and processes, but you can create your own macros with the m4 directive define. For example, define(`foo',`bar') creates the macro named foo with the value bar. Every instance of foo in the input will be replaced by bar in the output. Let's edit test.m4 and change it accordingly (changes are noted in bold):

```
See? dnl

dnl
dnl Ignore everything after a "dnl"
dnl
define(`bad', `hard')
m4 dnl foo dnl
isn't so bad!
```

Note that the syntax of the define directive is a backtick (`), a text string, and a single quote (') enclosed in parenthesis.

Process the new input text with m4, and compare the output to the previous example:

```
[curtis@mail ~]$ m4 test.m4
```

See?

m4 isn't so hard!

Even though sendmail.cf is the primary sendmail configuration file, you don't edit it directly. Instead, edit sendmail.mc, and use the m4 macro processor to generate a new sendmail.cf. Let's look at how to do that next.

## Editing sendmail.mc

The first thing I suggest, before making any major changes to any configuration file at all, is to back up the original. So, let's back up sendmail.mc:

```
[curtis@mail ~]$ cd /etc/mail/
[curtis@mail mail]$ sudo cp sendmail.mc sendmail.mc.orig
[curtis@mail mail]$ ls -l sendmail.mc sendmail.mc.orig
```

```
-rw-r--r-- 1 root root 7069 May  6 08:35 sendmail.mc
-rw-r--r-- 1 root root 7069 Aug 17 20:07 sendmail.mc.orig
```

Now it's time to start editing sendmail.mc. Open the sendmail macro configuration file in your text editor of choice with sudo. (Aren't you glad you practiced hard with vi?) The first thing you should notice is that this file is heavily commented, so if you ever have to make changes to an existing option not covered in this book, basic information is at your fingertips. I won't go through the entire file line by line. Rather, we'll walk through the few options that are relevant to the goals of this book and to getting sendmail ready to accept SMTP connections from the public network.

The six basic macros and groups of macros follow:

- VERSIONID: Macro to insert optional versioning information into sendmail.cf

- OSTYPE: Macro to define the operating system sendmail is running on

- FEATURE: Macro to turn on special built-in features, like procmail delivery

- *Local macro definitions*: Macros defined to customize features

- DAEMON_OPTIONS: Macro to define options fed to the sendmail daemon, such as the network port to listen on

- MAILER: Macro used to define the protocols or program used to receive and deliver e-mail

In general, these rules, or groups of rules, should appear in sendmail.mc in the order listed, the exception being any local macro definitions that affect a particular FEATURE definition. In that case, the local macro definition should appear before the FEATURE definition that it modifies.

### Defining the VERSIONID Macro

This macro is actually optional, but I highly recommend using it. It simply inserts simple versioning information into sendmail.cf. It can be used to keep track of different revisions to sendmail.mc. You can use a revision control system, like CVS or Subversion. Neither of these are covered in this book, but more information can be found in Garrett Rooney's excellent book *Practical Subversion* (Apress, 2004). If you use a revision control system, version tags can be entered here. Otherwise, you can just change this by hand and rebuild sendmail.cf each time you make a change. Defining VERSIONID is useful, so you can tell whether sendmail.cf was successfully rebuilt after making your changes by comparing the version strings before and after. If multiple administrators will be making changes to the sendmail configuration files, this also might be a useful way to track who made changes last. The default set by the Fedora Core team is:

```
VERSIONID(`setup for Red Hat Linux')dnl
```

Using some combination of the date in ISO 8601 format and the administrator's initials might be a useful way of tracking changes and times of changes, so let's change the default setting to something a bit more informative for future reference. I suggest something like the following:

```
VERSIONID(`Config last revised 2005-08-17 cjs')dnl
```

At any rate, the VERSIONID can be set to whatever you prefer, or left out completely; it has no bearing on the operation or customization of sendmail itself. This information is not given out publicly, so it is only meaningful to you to track your configuration changes. However, the next macro to be defined is not optional and is crucial to the operation of sendmail.

## Defining the OSTYPE Macro

The OSTYPE macro defines the operating system environment in which you are configuring sendmail. Defining the operating system is necessary so that sendmail knows how to set certain macro values, like the path to the aliases file, the location of the mail queues, or how sendmail should interact with the operating system. Sendmail supports a vast list of UNIX and UNIX-like BSD and Linux operating systems, each with various idiosyncrasies that need to be taken into account.

If this macro is not defined, sendmail.mc will not compile or generate a sendmail.cf configuration file at all. The sendmail source comes with many operating system environments already configured and available to be included in your local sendmail configuration. The complete list of available operating system environments can be found in the ostype directory of the sendmail source or in /usr/share/sendmail-cf/ostype/ on a Fedora Core system with the sendmail-cf RPM package installed.

It is absolutely necessary to define this macro before any MAILER macro definitions (which we will discuss a bit later in this chapter) and to define only one OSTYPE in your configuration. The default set by the Fedora Core development team is:

```
OSTYPE(`linux')dnl
```

and should remain defined as such, since you are, presumably, configuring sendmail for a Linux operating system environment.

The next several definitions you'll come across in the default Fedora Core sendmail.mc are various options, features, and local macro definitions used to customize your sendmail configuration.

## Looking at sendmail Features, Local Macro Definitions, and Options

The next few macros define various options that affect how sendmail handles mail. The Fedora Core sendmail.mc sets some standard settings, and we will not make any changes to those. Some of the options are for advanced functionality that does not need to be altered under most circumstances. Several options are commented out and define how SMTP AUTH is configured; we will ignore these options until Chapter 21.

Various special features can be turned on with the FEATURE macro. For example, the following line in the default Fedora Core sendmail.mc file:

```
FEATURE(`smrsh',`/usr/sbin/smrsh')dnl
```

defines a special security feature for mail delivery, which we will specifically cover in more depth in Chapter 13.

Following FEATURE definitions are local macro definitions. Again these are simply ways of changing the default behavior of sendmail. If a local macro influences a feature, it should generally occur before the FEATURE definition itself. One local macro definition in the default Fedora Core sendmail.mc that we need to change is the following line:

```
DAEMON_OPTIONS(`Port=smtp,Addr=127.0.0.1, Name=MTA')dnl
```

This configuration line tells sendmail to only listen on the localhost loopback IP interface (127.0.0.1) on port smtp (a setting we discussed earlier in this chapter). Port smtp is a reference to a services string as defined in the file /etc/services. So, in this case, smtp is looked up in /etc/services and replaced with 25 when sendmail starts; port 25 is the well-known, standard port for communication over SMTP.

---

**Note** The file /etc/services is a text file that maps standard service names to port numbers. The service names and appropriate ports were historically defined by RFC 1700 (www.ietf.org/rfc/rfc1700.txt), but RFC 1700 has since been replaced by the Internet Assigned Numbers Authority (IANA) web database found at www.iana.org/assignments/port-numbers. For most well-known ports like SMTP, these assignments did not change, so it's not necessary to update /etc/services.

---

Because the whole intent of our work here is to run an Internet e-mail server, we want sendmail to listen for incoming connections from the public network. So, go ahead and comment out the previous line by adding dnl to the beginning of it. It should look something like the following line when you're done:

```
dnl DAEMON_OPTIONS(`Port=smtp,Addr=127.0.0.1, Name=MTA')dnl
```

Now insert a new line directly below the option you just commented out, and add the following line:

```
dnl #
dnl # Make sendmail listen on our public Internet IP address.
DAEMON_OPTIONS(`Port=smtp,Addr=192.168.69.4, Name=MTA-Public')dnl
dnl #
```

Replace the IP Address 192.168.69.4 with the public IP address of your server. Save your changes to sendmail.mc without exiting your text editor. Now let's explore the final primary class of sendmail configuration macros.

## Defining MAILER Macros for E-mail Delivery

The MAILER macros should be the very last set of macro definitions. Different mailers are defined to tell sendmail what protocols to use to send and receive e-mail. For example, the local mailer is used to deliver e-mail sent to users hosted on the local server and is always automatically included. As we discussed early in this chapter, the standard protocol for the exchange of Internet e-mail is SMTP, so you should also define the SMTP mailer. Other mailers, like the UUCP mailer, exist for historical purposes but are very rarely used anymore.

For the purposes of this book, we only need the local and SMTP mailers, which are defined by the following:

```
MAILER(smtp)dnl
MAILER(procmail)dnl
```

These happen to be the defaults in the Fedora Core sendmail.mc and should be left as such.

Our first attempt at customizing sendmail is complete. The next thing to do is save your changes, if you haven't done so already, exit your text editor, and compile the sendmail.cf with the m4 macro processor.

# Compiling sendmail.mc

Now it's time to compile your customized sendmail macro configuration file. It's necessary to recreate a new sendmail.cf every time you make changes to sendmail.mc. And remember, doing so on a Fedora Core system requires the sendmail-cf RPM package to be installed. First, make a backup of your current sendmail.cf, in case you need to fall back on a configuration that you know is good should some problem arise. I usually name backup files with the date and my initials, so it's clear when the file was backed up and by whom. Go ahead and back up sendmail.cf now, just to be safe:

```
[curtis@mail ~]$ cd /etc/mail/
[curtis@mail mail]$ sudo cp sendmail.cf sendmail.cf.20050817.cjs
[curtis@mail mail]$ ls -l sendmail.cf*
```

```
-rw-r--r--  1 root root 58079 Aug  8 20:28 sendmail.cf
-rw-r--r--  1 root root 58079 Aug 17 14:34 sendmail.cf.20050817.cjs
```

■**Caution** When rebuilding a new sendmail.cf from a modified sendmail.mc, the existing sendmail.cf is overwritten, so I strongly advise you to make backups of important files before proceeding.

Next, to actually rebuild sendmail.cf on a Fedora Core system using the sendmail and sendmail-cf RPM package installation, use the GNU make command to perform the rebuild process in one easy step:

```
[curtis@mail mail]$ sudo make -C /etc/mail
```

```
make: Entering directory `/etc/mail'
make: Leaving directory `/etc/mail'
```

The two lines of output from make are normal. If you don't get any errors, you successfully rebuilt a new sendmail.cf based on your customizations of sendmail.mc!

## Manually Starting and Stopping sendmail

Now, let's start the newly configured sendmail daemon. This can be achieved with the init script, typically /etc/init.d/sendmail or /etc/rc.d/init.d/sendmail, depending on which flavor of Linux operating system you've chosen. For example, to start sendmail with the init script, you might try the following command:

[curtis@mail mail]$ **sudo /etc/init.d/sendmail start**

or to stop sendmail, use this command:

[curtis@mail mail]$ **sudo /etc/init.d/sendmail stop**

On Fedora Core, you can use the shortcut command called service, which makes it a little easier to use the init scripts without having to guess or type the whole path to the init script:

[curtis@mail mail]$ **sudo service sendmail start**

```
Starting sendmail:                                    [  OK  ]
Starting sm-client:                                   [  OK  ]
```

or to stop sendmail, you can use the following command:

[curtis@mail mail]$ **sudo service sendmail stop**

```
Shutting down sendmail:                               [  OK  ]
Shutting down sm-client:                              [  OK  ]
```

When you start sendmail, you should see log entries like the following ones indicating successful process start-up in /var/log/maillog:

```
Aug 26 22:43:14 mail sendmail[32624]: starting daemon (8.13.4): ➥
SMTP+queueing@01:00:00
Aug 26 22:43:14 mail sm-msp-queue[32630]: starting daemon (8.13.4): ➥
queueing@01:00:00
```

The first line is the sendmail program listening and accepting incoming connections over the public network, and the second line indicates the local client security sendmail program.

## Starting sendmail Automatically

On a Fedora Core system using sendmail installed from the RPM package, you can use the command chkconfig to configure an application to automatically start up and shut down. By default, sendmail comes preconfigured to always start up when your system boots. You can see this by passing the --list argument to chkconfig:

```
[curtis@mail ~]$ sudo chkconfig --list sendmail
```

```
sendmail        0:off   1:off   2:on    3:on    4:on    5:on    6:off
```

As you can see, sendmail is already configured to automatically start in the appropriate run levels. For a more complete introduction to Linux run levels and Fedora Core init scripts, refer to Chapter 3.

Now that sendmail is started, make sure your system firewall has been configured to pass network traffic to sendmail.

## Opening Your Firewall to sendmail

We've already discussed the Linux firewall and opened a hole for the SSH server. We've got to do the same thing for the sendmail server, too. SMTP typically listens on the well-known port TCP 25. On a Fedora Core system, add a line like the following one to /etc/sysconfig/iptables:

```
-A RH-Firewall-1-INPUT -m state --state NEW -m tcp -p tcp --dport 25 -j ACCEPT
```

Don't forget to restart the firewall after you've made your changes! Now, you're all set. Since you've successfully reconfigured your sendmail installation and have it running and ready to send and receive e-mail, there's one more thing to configure, so other MTAs can find your server to deliver e-mail for your domain—the DNS.

# Configuring DNS for Successful E-mail Delivery

Other Internet e-mail servers have to know how to deliver e-mail destined for your Internet domain to your e-mail server. Everyone is at least familiar with the Internet DNS, even if they don't know it. DNS is the Internet protocol used to translate domain names that are easily recallable for humans, like www.apress.com, to their computer-routable IP addresses.

The most common DNS server application is the Internet Systems Consortium's Berkeley Internet Name Domain (BIND) application (www.isc.org/index.pl?/sw/bind/). It's possible to run your own BIND server, though the details of doing so are well outside the scope of this book. If you're unfamiliar with BIND and would like to learn more, consider picking up Ron Aitchison's excellent book *Pro DNS and BIND* (Apress, 2005).

The first thing to do is make sure your server itself is configured with a resolvable Internet domain name. This domain name must be assigned to an IP address that is controlled by you or your ISP. This is the same IP address you assigned your server during the installation process, but now you've got to publish a name for that IP address. The domain name that is mapped to an IP address is called a DNS A record and looks like this for a BIND configuration:

```
mail.example.com    IN    A    192.168.2.4
```

When a DNS lookup is done on the domain name of your server, it should resolve to the IP address of your server. This is called a *reverse lookup*. It is controlled by the DNS PTR record, and looks like this for a BIND configuration:

```
192.168.2.4    IN    PTR    mail.example.com
```

Well, the same system is used for routing e-mail from a client's MTA to another domain's MTA. Specifically, the DNS mail exchange (MX) record type is used to define one or more mail destinations for any given Internet domain. When an e-mail client or MTA looks up the mail destination for a domain, the authoritative DNS server for that domain returns an ordered list.

## Introducing the DNS MX Record

MX, short for *mail exchange*, is no more than an Internet host that either forwards e-mail for a domain to a final destination or is the final destination itself. A domain can have more than one MX record if you have more than one mail exchange for your domain, but for the purposes of this book, we'll assume that you have only one mail exchange for simplicity's sake. An example MX record follows:

```
example.com.    IN  MX  10    mail.example.com.
```

The first field is the domain for which this MX record is defined; the second field defines the class to be Internet; the third field indicates this is an MX record; the fourth field defines the preference; and the last field defines the name of the mail exchange. The mail exchange should be defined by the appropriate BIND A record, mapping the name to a valid IP address. Strictly speaking, a DNS MX record should not point to a CNAME, or alias, record, but pointing to a CNAME is common, so most MTAs will accept it.

## Testing Your DNS Configuration

To test to make sure your DNS configuration is correct, whether your DNS is hosted by you or your ISP, on most Linux systems, including a Fedora Core system, you find the command host. The host command can be used to make various DNS queries from the command line.

To make sure that the hostname of your e-mail system resolves to the correct IP address, run the following command from the command line:

```
[curtis@mail ~]$ host mail.example.com
```

```
mail.example.com has address 192.168.2.4
```

To make sure that the reverse lookup on your IP address resolves to the correct hostname, run the following command from the command line:

```
[curtis@mail ~]$ host 192.168.2.4
```

```
4.2.168.192.in-addr.arpa domain name pointer mail.example.com.
```

And finally, to check that your MX record for your e-mail domain is set up correctly, run the following command from the command line:

```
[curtis@mail ~]$ host -t mx example.com
```

```
example.com mail is handled by 10 mail.example.com.
```

# Summary

In this chapter, you took a whirlwind tour of the sendmail configuration files. I showed you how sendmail has addressed some local security problems by running a separate sendmail application specially configured for local e-mail submission only. Typically configured with individual configuration files, sendmail.cf and submit.cf, running sendmail as two separation applications helps achieve the privilege separation discussed in Chapter 3. Next, I introduced the GNU m4 macro processor and showed how you could use it to simplify sendmail configuration. By editing the sendmail.mc macro configuration file and running one command, we were able to generate a brand new sendmail.cf customized for your specific installation. Without proper DNS MX records, nobody would know where to deliver e-mail destined for your domain. Although a complete discussion of DNS is outside the scope of this book, I gave an example of an MX record for the BIND application, a DNS server almost as venerable as the sendmail program. In Chapter 6, we will continue to build on the foundation we've built so far to further fine-tune and customize sendmail to meet your specific needs.

# CHAPTER 6

■ ■ ■

# Populating Your sendmail Databases

Now that we have a basic sendmail configuration in place, let's take a look at a few other files that modify how some of the features that we turned on operate. These files are split into two main kinds of configuration files: flat text files that contain one value per line and flat text files that contain a key and value pair per line and get placed into special database files. We'll cover the first flavor of configuration file first, and then conclude the chapter with the second.

## Looking at the Simple Files

By "simple files," I merely mean these files require no processing after editing. As I alluded to previously, these files take one value per line. Indeed, these files can be empty, depending on your particular needs.

### Defining Local Host Names

Typically, any given Internet host is known by one name. For example, suppose your e-mail server is called `mail`, and the domain is `example.com`. However, sometimes it's possible to have aliases for an Internet host. For example, maybe you want to present your mail server as `mailexchange.example.com` instead of its real host name `mail`.

In that case, add any host aliases that you have set up in DNS for your server to the file `/etc/mail/local-host-names`. Any line that starts with a number sign (#) is a comment and is ignored by sendmail. Each line should contain at most one alias. You should also add your Internet e-mail domain, `example.com` in our previous example, to `local-host-names`. An example of what this file might look like follows:

```
# local-host-names - include all aliases for your machine here.
example.com
mail.example.com
mailexchange.example.com
```

Every time sendmail is started, this file will be reread, so make sure to restart sendmail after making any modifications to `local-host-names`.

This file will only be read if sendmail is configured to do so. To enable this optional feature, the following m4 FEATURE macro should be defined in `/etc/mail/sendmail.mc`, if it's not already:

```
FEATURE(use_cw_file)dnl
```

Defining this FEATURE macro in sendmail.mc forces sendmail to look for the file named local-host-names in the directory /etc/mail/. To override the location of local-host-names, use the following m4 macro definition in sendmail.mc:

```
define(`confCW_FILE', `/path/to/local-host-names')dnl
```

replacing /path/to/local-host-names with the desired directory and file name. The default configuration in the Fedora Core sendmail.mc is to define the FEATURE macro but leave local-host-names in its standard location in /etc/mail/.

## Defining Trusted Users

When a local user sends e-mail from the local e-mail server with a command-line mail application like mail, Mutt, or Pine, sendmail uses that user's local account to automatically create the message envelope source address . However, it is possible to override this by running the sendmail program with the -f argument, effectively allowing anyone to forge the message envelope source address with anything they like. Allowing this feature enables anybody with an interactive login account on your e-mail system to mask the true sender address of an e-mail, something better left to sendmail.

The root superuser is the only user that has the privilege to address an e-mail as another user other than himself without any warnings. Under most circumstances, this configuration is desirable to ensure that no one can send fraudulent e-mails. If an unprivileged user sends a message using the -f argument, forging the message envelope sender, sendmail will generate a log message in /var/log/maillog:

```
Dec 21 22:46:15 mail sendmail[24908]: jBM3kFtq024908: Authentication-Warning: ➡
mail.example.com: curtis set sender to curtis@foo.example.com using -f
```

and an informational message header will be added to the message:

```
X-Authentication-Warning: mail.example.com: curtis set sender to ➡
curtis@foo.example.com using -f
```

However, you may find that a particular application, running as a different, unprivileged user account, might have cause to manipulate the message envelope source address to send e-mail on behalf of other users with their e-mail addresses. To make a user *trusted* and allow that user to override the message envelope source address, simply add each username to a line by itself in the file /etc/mail/trusted-users. Just like in local-host-names, any line that begins with a number sign (#) is a comment and ignored by sendmail. Each line should contain at most one username. An example of what this file might look like follows:

```
# trusted-users - users that can send mail as others without a warning
# apache, mailman, majordomo, uucp, are good candidates
apache
curtis
```

The preceding example will add the users apache and curtis, in addition to root, to the list of trusted users. Every time sendmail is started, this file will be reread, so make sure to restart sendmail after making any modifications to trusted-users.

This file will only be read if sendmail is configured to do so. To enable this optional feature, the following m4 FEATURE macro should be defined in /etc/mail/sendmail.mc, if it's not already:

```
FEATURE(use_ct_file)dnl
```

Defining this FEATURE macro in sendmail.mc forces sendmail to look for the file named trusted-users in the directory /etc/mail/. To override the location of trusted-users, use the following m4 macro definition in sendmail.mc:

```
define(`confCT_FILE', `/path/to/trusted-users')dnl
```

replacing /path/to/trusted-users with the desired directory and file name. The default configuration in the Fedora Core sendmail.mc is to define this FEATURE macro but leave trusted-users in its standard location in /etc/mail/.

# Taking On the More Complex Files

The next five configuration files I'd like to cover are also flat text files, but they are a bit more complex. Like the previous two configuration files, the next five configure the following specific sendmail features:

- *The* mailertable *feature*: Used to override the routing of mail to domains that are not local
- *The* domaintable *feature*: Used to map one or more domains to your local e-mail domain
- *The* virtusertable *feature*: Used to alias one or more domains to a local e-mail address or e-mail domain
- *The* access *database*: Used to restrict mail from specific e-mail domains
- *The user* aliases *database*: Used to create e-mail aliases for one or more e-mail users

Each of these files contains key-value pairs separated with a colon, one pair per line. Like the local-host-names and trusted-users files, any line that begins with a number sign (#) is considered a comment and is ignored. What also makes these configuration files unique is that the flat text files that you directly edit are not used directly by the sendmail program at all. Some of these configuration files can contain thousands of records, so in order to parse the files more efficiently, database maps are created from the flat text files. Then sendmail can perform keyed map lookups on the database maps themselves, a much more efficient way of getting at the information. To create the appropriate database map from the flat text file, the m4 macro processor isn't used, as it is when generating sendmail.cf. Instead, the makemap utility is used.

## Introducing the makemap Utility

The makemap utility comes with the sendmail source code or vendor RPM package distribution. It simply reads input from standard input and generates the database map file. makemap can generate three different database formats, but the default is the hash format, and it's the most common. The Fedora Core sendmail distribution uses the hash format for its database maps, and unless you explicitly configure it otherwise, your sendmail installation probably also uses this database format.

Recall that database maps are generally created from a text file that contains lines with key-value pairs. Usually, the key and value are separated by some sequence of nonempty whitespace characters, like one or more tabs.

I cover the more common database maps in this chapter. Each is generated from a text file with the makemap utility, except the last, the aliases file. The aliases file is a bit different, and we will discuss it specifically later in this chapter. As I introduce each feature and its use, I will show you how to use makemap to build the appropriate database map that sendmail uses.

---

**Note** The key and value are also oftentimes referred to as the *left-hand side* (LHS) and *right-hand side* (RHS), respectively, in other sendmail documentation and literature.

---

## Introducing the mailertable Feature

This database map may not be used under most circumstances, but I feel it prudent to at least mention it since it's usually a defined feature by default. We won't use this feature for the purposes of this book, but you may find it useful should you find yourself building further on the concepts discussed and creating a more-advanced installation.

Essentially, the mailertable feature allows you to override the routing of mail for any domain not listed in the local-host-names configuration file. Keys in this database map are domains, either partial domains or *fully qualified domain names (FQDN)*. An example FQDN is mail.example.com, and a partial domain is .example.com. Note the period (.) preceding the partial domain; otherwise, it would be considered an FQDN.

Suppose your e-mail domain is example.com, and the server that accepts mail from example.com is the MX for example.com. If you decide to host your e-mail mailing lists (discussed in detail in Chapter 19) with the domain lists.example.com on a physical server other than the e-mail server for example.com, then you, your ISP, or the entity that handles your DNS for example.com adds a separate DNS MX record for lists.example.com pointing to the alternate server.

Perhaps you need antivirus scanning on the mailing list server, but you do not want to maintain two antivirus installations. Well, instead of having the DNS MX record point to another server for your mailing list domain, point it to the same server that handles the mail for example.com. Then have that server pass off the e-mail destined for lists.example.com to the alternate mailing list server. To achieve this, simply add an entry in the mailertable configuration file to route e-mail destined for lists.example.com directly to the alternate server. Now you have one server that accepts all e-mail for every domain, scans the e-mail once, and sends the mail to another server for final delivery.

The default mailertable flat text file is /etc/mail/mailtertable, and the default database map is /etc/mail/mailertable.db. Keys, or the LHS, are FQDNs or partial domains preceded by a dot. In mailertable, values, or the RHS, must be defined in a specific format—two values separated by a colon. The first half of the value is the name of the internal mailer that should be used, and the second half tells where to send the matching messages.

## Choosing a Mailer for a mailertable Value

The mailer you choose to use in a `mailertable` value is what tells sendmail how to forward, or reject, messages with recipients that match the FQDN or partial domain in the key. The two most useful mailers that you will probably ever find are the `local` and `smtp` mailers.

The `local` mailer will forward the message to the local user that you define in the second half of the `mailertable` value. For example, to send all e-mail sent to the domain `foo.bar.example.com` to the local user `curtis`, add the following line to the `mailertable` database:

```
foo.bar.example.com local:curtis
```

In this example, `foo.bar.example.com` is the key, and `local:curtis` is the value.

The `smtp` mailer will forward the message to another MTA using SMTP. This forwarding process is useful in the initial example in this chapter—use one server as a domain mail exchange and forward mail for a mailing list domain to another mailing list server. To do so, add a line like the following one to the `mailertable` database:

```
lists.example.com    smtp:listserver.example.com
```

where the key, `lists.example.com`, is the domain to forward, and the value, `smtp:listserver.example.com`, says to forward all mail destined for the key to the MTA, `listserver.example.com`, using the `smtp` mailer.

I alluded previously to the possibility of rejecting messages sent to a domain. This can be achieved by using the `error` mailer. Say, for example, your organization decides, after receiving e-mail with the `example.com` domain for some time, to stop using this domain altogether. Of course, if you remove the DNS MX record altogether, mail won't get routed to your domain anymore, but perhaps you'd like to receive mail for some time, reject the messages, and send a specific error message alerting the sending MTA that the e-mail domain is out of service. To reject all e-mail destined for the domain `example.com`, add a line like the following one to the `mailertable` database:

```
example.com    error:This domain is no longer in use effective 2004-01-01
```

Once mail is received for the exact FQDN `example.com`, sendmail will reject the message and send an SMTP reply code with the error message "This domain is no longer in use effective 2004-01-01."

To catch any e-mail that contains the partial domain `example.com`, like `bar.example.com` or `foo.bar.example.com`, modify the previous example by preceding the key with a dot to make it a partial domain:

```
.example.com    error:This domain is no longer in use effective 2004-01-01
```

Finally, it's possible to send a specific SMTP reply code in addition to the error message with a line like the following:

```
example.com    error:D.S.N:This domain is no longer in use effective 2004-01-01
```

where `D.S.N` is a valid SMTP reply code as defined in RFC 1893 (`www.ietf.org/rfc/rfc1893.txt`). Anything defined in the `mailertable` database will not show up in or make changes to an e-mail message's headers.

Make your changes to `/etc/mail/mailertable`, and run the following command to generate a new `mailertable` database map:

```
[curtis@mail ~]$ cd /etc/mail
[curtis@mail mail]$ sudo makemap hash mailertable.db < mailertable
```

Don't forget to restart sendmail after making changes to and rebuilding the mailertable database.

The mailertable feature is turned on by defining the following FEATURE macro in sendmail.mc:

```
FEATURE(`mailertable',`hash -o /etc/mail/mailertable.db')dnl
```

Defining this FEATURE macro in sendmail.mc forces sendmail to look for the file named mailertable.db in the directory /etc/mail/. The flat text file /etc/mail/mailertable is never used by sendmail and is only used to generate the hash database map. The default configuration in the Fedora Core sendmail.mc is to define the mailertable FEATURE macro.

## Introducing the domaintable Feature

The domaintable database is used simply to map one FQDN to another FQDN. The excellent example scenario given in the sendmail documentation (/usr/share/sendmail-cf/README on your Fedora Core system or www.sendmail.org/m4/README.txt on the Web) shows one use of this feature. If a particular company decides to change names and transition from an old e-mail domain to a new one, they could add a line like the following one to the domaintable database:

```
old-corp.example.com    new-corp.example.com
```

The key in the domaintable feature is the domain to map, and the value is the new domain to map the key to. Incoming e-mail messages that match a key in the domaintable will have their message headers modified to match the appropriate value accordingly.

Make your changes to /etc/mail/domaintable, and run the following command to generate a new domaintable database map:

```
[curtis@mail ~]$ cd /etc/mail
[curtis@mail mail]$ sudo makemap hash domaintable.db < domaintable
```

Don't forget to restart sendmail after making changes to and rebuilding the domaintable database.

The domaintable feature is turned on by defining the following FEATURE macro in sendmail.mc:

```
FEATURE(`domaintable',`hash -o /etc/mail/domaintable.db')dnl
```

Defining this FEATURE macro in sendmail.mc forces sendmail to look for the file named domaintable.db in the directory /etc/mail/. The flat text file /etc/mail/domaintable is never used by sendmail and is only used to generate the hash database map. The default configuration in the Fedora Core sendmail.mc is to define the domaintable FEATURE macro.

## Introducing the virtusertable Feature

The virtual user feature is a quite powerful one. This feature, among other things, effectively allows you to set up fake e-mail addresses that map to real user accounts. Or, you can deliver wildcard matches for anything sent to a domain to one or more real accounts.

The key in the virtusertable database map is a specific e-mail address or some form of wildcard match on one or more e-mail addresses for a given domain. The value is the real e-mail account that should receive the e-mail matched on the key. Let me explain with a few examples.

Suppose your organization's primary e-mail domain is some-corp.example.com, and I, as an employee at your organization, have the real e-mail account curtis@some-corp.example.com. Perhaps I am the vice president of sales for a division of your organization, and I need to receive sales requests for a second e-mail domain called division.some-corp.example.com. Instead of setting up a second e-mail server for the division.some-corp.example.com and creating another real account for me, all you have to do is add the appropriate MX record for division.some-corp.example.com to your DNS, add division.some-corpexample.com to local-host-names, and add the following line to the virtusertable database:

sales@division.some-corp.example.com    curtis@some-corp.example.com

Next, regenerate the virtusertable database map by running the following command:

```
[curtis@spider ~]$ cd /etc/mail
[curtis@spider mail]$ sudo makemap hash virtusertable.db < virtusertable
```

and don't forget to restart sendmail after making changes to and rebuilding the virtusertable database.

Now all e-mail sent to sales@division.some-corp.example.com will be delivered to the real e-mail account curtis@some-corp.example.com without needing a second mail server!

This concept can be taken a step further. Suppose I need to receive any e-mail sent to the division.some-corp.example.com e-mail domain. No problem; simply change the previous example as follows:

@division.some-corp.example.com    curtis@some-corp.example.com

and regenerate the virtusertable database map. Now any e-mail sent to any address for the domain division.some-corp.example.com will be forwarded to the real e-mail account curtis@some-corp.example.com.

Now suppose that your corporation's division has grown and more employees in your organization are taking some of the e-mail load off of my shoulders. In that case, configure a one-to-one map of virtual e-mail addresses on a virtual e-mail domain to a real address on a real e-mail domain, by changing the previous example as follows:

@division.some-corp.example.com    %1@some-corp.example.com

and regenerate the virtusertable database map. Now e-mail sent to sales@some-corp.example.com will be sent to sales@some-corp.example.com; e-mail sent to curtis@divsion.some-corp.example.com will be sent to curtis@some-corp.example.com, and so forth.

The possibilities are endless, and I encourage you to explore them in more detail if you feel so inclined. Although this book generally assumes a single e-mail domain, nothing precludes the possibility of adapting to support multiple virtual e-mail domains and virtual users.

The virtusertable feature is turned on by defining the following FEATURE macro in sendmail.mc:

```
FEATURE(`virtusertable',`hash -o /etc/mail/virtusertable.db')dnl
```

Defining this FEATURE macro in sendmail.mc forces sendmail to look for the file named virtusertable.db in the directory /etc/mail/. The flat text file /etc/mail/virtusertable is never used by sendmail and is only used to generate the hash database map. The default configuration in the Fedora Core sendmail.mc is to define the virtusertable FEATURE macro.

## Limiting Access to Your Mail Server with the access Database

By turning on the access database feature, you have the ability to control access to your MTA. This means it would be possible to explicitly allow or disallow whole Internet domains or networks to send e-mail to your e-mail system. You can also choose to explicitly allow or disallow specific remote e-mail accounts to send e-mail to your e-mail system. More-specific information regarding how to effectively use the access database feature can be found in the antispam discussion later in Chapter 16. For now, I just want to introduce this feature, since it is usually defined by default, and its database map is generated differently than the other database maps.

This feature is turned on by defining the following FEATURE macro in sendmail.mc:

```
FEATURE(`access_db',`hash -T<TMPF> -o /etc/mail/access.db')dnl
```

The first thing you should notice is that this has an extra option defined. The -T<TMPF> is not a typo and is required when rebuilding the access database map; simply replace <TMPF> with a temporary filename. Therefore, to regenerate the access database map, run the following command:

```
[curtis@spider ~]$ cd /etc/mail
[curtis@spider mail]$ sudo makemap hash –Taccess.tmp access.db < access
```

which simply writes to a temporary file called access.tmp during the process of generating access.db. Don't forget to restart sendmail after making changes to and rebuilding the access database.

Defining this FEATURE macro in sendmail.mc forces sendmail to look for the file named access.db in the directory /etc/mail/. The flat text file /etc/mail/access is never used by sendmail and is only used to generate the hash database map. The default configuration in the Fedora Core sendmail.mc is to define the access FEATURE macro.

## Introducing the E-mail aliases Feature

The last database map I'm going to cover is the aliases database. The aliases database allows you to offer e-mail aliases to your users. The aliases database is distinct from the other databases in a few respects. First, it's defined in the OSTYPE m4 macro configuration file, not the primary sendmail.mc m4 macro configuration file, so the location of the aliases database can vary from operating system to operating system. Second, the key-value pairs are separated by a colon, not a sequence of nonempty whitespace characters. Third, the default location of the aliases text file and aliases.db database map are found in /etc/, not /etc/mail/, on a Fedora Core system and are defined in the OSTYPE m4 macro configuration file you included in sendmail.mc. Finally, you don't use makemap at all to generate the database map.

To illustrate how the aliases database is useful, let's continue with the previous example from the virtusertable feature. Suppose, in addition to my primary e-mail address curtis@some-corp.example.com, I'd like to also receive e-mail sent to the address

VicePresidentCurtis@some-corp.example.com in my mailbox. You'd simply add the following line to /etc/aliases:

```
VicePresidentCurtis:    curtis
```

and then recreate the aliases databases map with the newaliases command:

```
[curtis@spider ~]$ sudo newaliases
```

---

```
/etc/aliases: 77 aliases, longest 10 bytes, 790 bytes total
```

---

Now the alias is created. Aliases apply only to real users hosted on the local e-mail server itself. Fake, or virtual, users and aliases should be added to the virtusertable database instead.

---

■**Tip** Remember to always rerun newaliases every time /etc/aliases has been modified! sendmail need not be restarted for newly added aliases to take affect after newaliases has been run.

---

An e-mail alias can be applied to multiple users. For example, to send sales e-mails to me and an associate named Jon, add the following line to /etc/aliases:

```
sales@some-corp.com:    curtis, jon
```

and rerun newaliases. In addition, it's possible to send e-mail aliases to a program; you'll see examples of that in Chapter 19 when we discuss e-mail mailing lists.

If you take a look at the /etc/aliases file that comes with the default sendmail installation, you'll notice a number of already-defined user aliases. If you investigate further, you find that each entry corresponds with a local system user account for various applications and servers on your system. These aren't real users, but the system doesn't know that and may try to send e-mail to those users. So, best practice dictates aliasing any mail for a system account to the root account.

Of course, that means the root account is receiving e-mail. How are you supposed to get to that if you're never supposed to log in directly as the root user? Simple—alias the root user's e-mail to your account by modifying the following lines:

```
# Person who should get root's mail
#root:          marc
```

to read like these:

```
# Person who should get root's mail
root:           curtis
```

replacing curtis with your local account and running newaliases. Now, all e-mail sent to root is aliased to you, and you can keep track of your system better. This illustrates the fact that aliases can be chained—userA is an alias for userB is an alias for userC, which is a real user account.

That wraps up the primary sendmail database map and configuration files. We're finally ready to start testing your customized system in the next chapter! I'm confident all this hard work will pay off, and you'll be pleased with what we've accomplished in the end.

## Summary

This chapter hasn't provided an exhaustive list of features and feature configuration files by any means. Remember, sendmail is a powerful application with an extensive list of features. In this chapter, we did cover the essentials, most of which will suffice even for the largest of Internet e-mail systems under normal circumstances. First, you saw the two basic kinds of database files: flat text files with single values and database maps with key-value pairs (also called LHS and RHS). Along the way, you've seen how to support multiple e-mail domains, custom mail routing, virtual users, and e-mail aliasing. You're now ready to begin sending and receiving e-mail and to test your custom sendmail configuration.

■■■

# CHAPTER 7

# Testing Your sendmail Installation

**N**ow that we've covered the basic sendmail configuration options, and then some, it's finally time to start sending some e-mail! All this preparation means nothing if your server can't deliver e-mail, so in this chapter we'll cover how to track and debug e-mail message delivery. Then I will survey a couple of alternative open source client e-mail applications that can be configured to work with your e-mail system. But first, let's make sure sendmail was started and is listening for new incoming connections of the network.

## Looking for the sendmail Processes

First, let's take a look on your e-mail server to make sure the appropriate processes are started. Using the Linux command ps can show you a snapshot of the current processes on your system. Typing **ps** alone on the command line will show the list of your user processes only—not quite useful if you are interested in seeing all system processes, as we are now. So, adding the command arguments aux to the ps command will show all processes, their state and system resources usage, and the user it is running as.

If you tried ps aux, you might have noticed that the output was limited to the width of your SSH terminal window, cutting off text from view. Well, add the argument w to your ps command, and the output will wrap, showing the whole line. Go ahead and try it on your e-mail server, and look for two lines that look something like the following. In this example, the screen output is truncated for brevity and the processes themselves are highlighted in bold:

```
[curtis@mail ~]$ ps auxw
```

```
root       7173  0.0  0.3   7944  2048 ?          Ss   15:47   0:00 ➥
sendmail: accepting connections
smmsp      7179  0.0  0.3   6960  1648 ?          Ss   15:47   0:00 ➥
sendmail: Queue runner@01:00:00 for /var/spool/clientmqueue
```

If you don't see two sendmail processes, then sendmail might not have been started at all, or could not start due to some configuration error. Review Chapter 5 to see how to start and stop the sendmail program. If sendmail still does not start up, then the next thing to do is check the system log files for more information.

# Checking Log Files

Traditional UNIX-based operating systems, like Linux in general and Fedora Core in particular, has a *system logger*. Called syslog for short, it's a central, systemwide mechanism by which
useful information can be collected from various applications running on your system. syslog
writes this information to various flat text log files. Now, the exact information that is logged,
and to which log files it's written, as well as where those log files exist, can vary widely from
various traditional UNIX and contemporary Linux operating systems. However, the general
format for syslog files is always the same: the date and time the message is logged, the hostname or IP address of the server on which the message was logged, the application process
and process ID that generated the message, and the message itself.

There will be several log files you will come to rely on in countless situations. On Fedora Core,
and many other contemporary Linux operating systems, system logs of all kinds can be found
under the directory /var/log/. Specifically, two log files are important to familiarize yourself with.

## The messages Log File

For general system-related information and critical errors, review /var/log/messages. Usually
the first place to look if you are having trouble, the messages log can contain various bits of
information from many applications. To view the messages log, use the less pager command:

```
[curtis@mail ~]$ sudo less /var/log/messages
```

The less command is basically a file viewer, showing a page at a time. less generally uses
the same commands as the Vim text editor: arrow keys to move up and down, and :q to quit.
Alternatively, if you want to view just the last few lines—useful if you want to see the end of a
large file but don't want to scroll so much—try the tail command:

```
[curtis@mail ~]$ sudo tail /var/log/messages
```

Go ahead and take a look at the messages log and see if sendmail reported any errors. Otherwise, the next place to check for sendmail errors is the maillog file.

## The maillog File

The most important log file with respect to an Internet e-mail server is the maillog file. Found
in /var/log/maillog, this is where sendmail sends all of its information, logging SMTP sessions
in great detail. Go ahead and open it up with less:

```
[curtis@mail ~]$ sudo less /var/log/maillog
```

If sendmail started successfully, you should see two log messages in maillog like the
following:

```
Dec 30 15:50:56 mail sendmail[22904]: starting daemon ➡
(8.13.4): SMTP+queueing@01:00:00
Dec 30 15:50:56 mail sm-msp-queue[22910]: starting daemon ➡
(8.13.4): queueing@01:00:00
```

which indicates that the two sendmail processes have successfully started.

If you don't see these two lines in `maillog`, then you look to see if you can find any error messages that might indicate the failure in startup. Otherwise, work through Chapters 5 and 6 again to make sure you didn't skip anything and look for typos in your sendmail configuration files.

I will cover `maillog` in more detail later in this chapter when I discuss debugging and tracking mail delivery. If it looks as if sendmail was started successfully, then let's make sure sendmail and your system are configured properly to accept incoming connections over the network.

## Testing sendmail with Telnet

The sendmail application may have started, but you don't know whether it has been properly configured to accept network connections over the server's public network interface. Remember that Fedora Core comes configured to specifically disallow this, only accepting network connections over the private loopback network interface. The simplest way to test an SMTP session over the network is with the `telnet` command.

First, from your e-mail server itself, try connecting to sendmail over the private loopback network interface `localhost` on port 25. To suspend the Telnet session, press Ctrl+] and then type **quit** at the `telnet>` prompt. An example of a successful network connection follows, with user input highlighted in bold:

```
[curtis@mail ~]$ telnet localhost 25
```

```
Trying 127.0.0.1...
Connected to localhost.localdomain (127.0.0.1).
Escape character is '^]'.
220 mail.example.com ESMTP Sendmail 8.13.4/8.13.4; ➥
Fri, 30 Dec 2005 16:07:55 -0500
^]
telnet> quit
Connection closed.
```

If you receive the SMTP reply 220 and a server banner, then you can be sure that sendmail is receiving connections over the private loopback network interface.

Now try the same thing from another computer on the same public network as your e-mail server. If you are trying from another Linux system, you can use the same `telnet` command, but connect to the hostname or IP address of your mail server instead of the `localhost` address. If you are testing from a Microsoft Windows system, click the Start button, then click Run. Type **telnet mail.example.com 25**, and click the OK button. A window like that in Figure 7-1 should pop up with your e-mail server's SMTP reply code 220 and server banner. Simply close the Telnet window to kill the session.

If you cannot connect from another system over the public network, then check to make sure your sendmail configuration is properly modified to allow such connections and that your e-mail system's firewall is configured to pass network traffic over the public network interface through port TCP 25; both modifications are outlined in Chapter 5.

Otherwise, if your sendmail responds to both Telnet tests, then you are ready to try passing your first e-mail traffic using an e-mail client application.

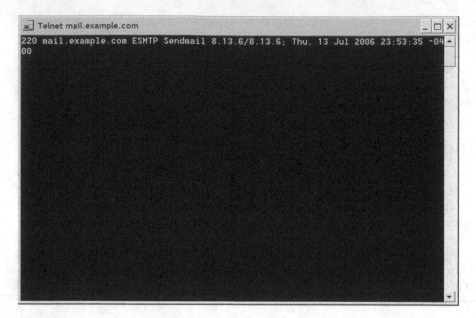

**Figure 7-1.** *Testing sendmail from a Windows Telnet client*

# Generating Your First E-mail Traffic

There are two different ways to send messages to your e-mail system. The first is from the command line on the e-mail system itself using any number of popular text-only, command line–oriented e-mail clients. This used to be the only way to send e-mail in the early days, and the applications I'll introduce are variants of the originals found on the older legacy UNIX systems years ago.

The second type of e-mail client I'll introduce are more contemporary graphical applications; these tend to be more familiar and your users are more likely to send mail this way. Some of the e-mail clients I will introduce are cross-platform, too, so they can run on Linux, Windows, or Mac OS, making it easier to support one mail client that works identically regardless of what operating system your users use.

Remember, the technical term for a client e-mail application, regardless if it's text-only or graphical, is *mail user agent (MUA)*. For simplicity's sake, I'll use the term MUA throughout this chapter.

## Sending with a Local E-mail Client

Any number of command-line e-mail applications exist for the Linux operating system. One of the original UNIX command-line e-mail applications is mailx. mailx is a simple but fully functional MUA that operates in two basic modes: send mode and read mode. On contemporary Linux operating systems, mailx has been replaced with an enhanced version found in /bin/mail.

## Introducing mailx

mailx, sometimes called "binmail" named for its typical full command path /bin/mail, is almost guaranteed to be installed on nearly every Linux operating system you might encounter because it is such an essential part of any Linux system. On Fedora Core, mailx is supplied by the mailx RPM package, which is a core installation requirement and is installed by default.

First, let's use mailx in send mode to send an e-mail to yourself. From the command line on your mail server, type the following:

```
[curtis@mail ~]$ echo "Hello world." | mail -s "First e-mail" ➥
curtis@example.com
```

replacing my e-mail address with your own.

---

**Tip** If you're new to the command line, this command might look alien to you, but it's really a simple example of redirecting the output of one command to the input of another. For a more in-depth discussion of the command line and shell scripting, check out *From Bash to Z Shell: Conquering the Command Line*, by Oliver Kiddle, Jerry Peek, and Peter Stephenson (Apress, 2004).

---

After several seconds, your shell will tell you have new mail waiting. On the e-mail system itself, press Enter a couple of times, and you should get a new mail alert like this:

---

```
[curtis@mail ~]$
You have mail in /var/spool/mail/curtis
[curtis@mail ~]$
```

---

So, let's check your mail with the mailx program in read mode:

```
[curtis@mail ~]$ mail
```

---

```
Mail version 8.1 6/6/93.  Type ? for help.
"/var/spool/mail/curtis": 1 message 1 unread
>U  1 curtis@example.com        Thu Sep  8 00:44  17/593   "First e-mail"
&
```

---

The ampersand is the traditional mailx prompt. As you can see, when invoking mailx with no command-line arguments, it will open your mailbox in read mode. It looks like we've got one unread message, as indicated by the capital U next to the message index number. mailx will also give a quick look at the message sender, the date received, and the subject. If other messages existed, those too would be listed here. Type **1** to read the first message:

```
Mail version 8.1 6/6/93.  Type ? for help.
"/var/spool/mail/curtis": 1 message 1 unread
>U  1 curtis@example.com         Thu Sep  8 00:44  17/593    "First e-mail"
& 1
Message 1:
From curtis@example.com  Thu Sep  8 00:44:20 2005
Date: Thu, 8 Sep 2005 00:44:20 -0400
From: Curtis Smith <curtis@example.com>
To: curtis@example.com
Subject: First e-mail

Hello world.

&
```

For now, let's leave the message for reviewing in more depth later, and simply quit mailx by typing **q** at the mailx & prompt:

```
Mail version 8.1 6/6/93.  Type ? for help.
"/var/spool/mail/curtis": 1 message 1 unread
>U  1 curtis@example.com         Thu Sep  8 00:44  17/593    "First e-mail"
& 1
Message 1:
From curtis@example.com  Thu Sep  8 00:44:20 2005
Date: Thu, 8 Sep 2005 00:44:20 -0400
From: Curtis Smith <curtis@example.com>
To: curtis@example.com
Subject: First e-mail

Hello world.

& q
Saved 1 message in mbox
```

For more information on mailx usage, in send or read mode, check out the man page by typing **man mail** on the command line, or typing **?** in read mode. mailx is especially useful as the occasional quick-and-dirty MUA or from shell scripts, but few users typically choose to use mailx for day-to-day interaction with their e-mail. The Mutt application is, however, the tool of choice for many.

### Introducing Mutt

Mutt is an interactive, heavily featured, fully customizable mail user agent. Based on the original elm e-mail client application, Mutt was written from scratch and has become a sort of hybrid of several other popular text-only mail user agents. Mutt is available as a Fedora Core RPM package, named (yep, you guessed it) mutt. If you selected the Internet RPM package group during the Fedora Core installation, then the mutt RPM package is installed; otherwise you can install it by using the yum command or by downloading and installing the RPM package by hand.

Unfortunately, I can't possibly do Mutt justice in just a few paragraphs and therefore intend only to introduce it here. I encourage you to check it out, and read more about Mutt from its home on the Internet at www.mutt.org.

# Sending with a Remote E-mail Client

Up to this point, the mail user agents I've introduced are run locally from the command line of your e-mail server. It's not clear whether you'll actually give your users complete interactive login accounts on your e-mail server, but the command-line tools are useful for system and e-mail administration. At any rate, who wants to try to support more complex text-only applications to users accustomed to graphical interfaces in more modern computing environments?

So, let's take a look at a relative newcomer to the world of client e-mail applications that holds a lot of promise.

### Introducing Mozilla Thunderbird

You might recognize Mozilla as the name of a popular alternative Internet browser, but it is also the name of the nonprofit corporation that provides legal, financial, and organizational support to the Mozilla open source software projects. One of the Mozilla Foundation's (www.mozilla.org) latest products is the elegant client e-mail application Thunderbird (www.mozilla.com/thunderbird/). Thunderbird is a free, open source, and multiplatform MUA with countless advanced options (like built-in email security and privacy; more on that later in Chapter 21) and a simple, easy-to-learn graphical interface. Thunderbird is available for free download for Windows, Mac OS X, and Linux operating systems.

You should not install or run Mozilla Thunderbird from your mail server itself. Instead, install it on your personal workstation of choice. Prepackaged binaries for all three supported platforms can be downloaded from the Thunderbird web site, or if you choose to run a Fedora Core workstation, a Thunderbird Fedora RPM package can be installed with yum. Once you install it for the first time, you will be walked through the new account setup wizard.

#### Configuring Mozilla Thunderbird for the First Time

Let's walk through the setup wizard of Thunderbird version 1.5 on a Windows XP workstation. The first step is to select the type of account to create and set up. As you can see, in addition to supporting e-mail, Thunderbird can also perform as a *Really Simple Syndication (RSS)* aggregator or Usenet newsgroup reader (shown in Figure 7-2). However, these features are beyond the scope of this book, and we want to create a new e-mail account. First, select E-mail Account, and then click Next.

**Figure 7-2.** *Step 1 of the Thunderbird new account setup wizard allows you to create a new e-mail, RSS, or newsgroup account.*

Next, fill out your name and e-mail address in the text boxes accordingly, and click Next. The following step will prompt for the incoming mail server type and hostname; for now, leave POP selected and enter the hostname of your e-mail server in the Incoming Server box. Also enter the hostname of your e-mail server in the Outgoing Server box, as shown in Figure 7-3, and click Next when you are finished.

**Figure 7-3.** *Step 3 of the Thunderbird new account setup wizard allows you to add POP or IMAP incoming server and SMTP outgoing server names.*

The fourth step in the wizard prompts for the incoming username. This is the username you use to log into your e-mail server. Click Next to continue after you have entered your username. The next screen prompts for an account name with which to identify the account you are configuring. Enter something short and descriptive if you do not like the default, and click Next.

Finally, you are given a chance to review the account setup details you entered in the wizard, shown in Figure 7-4. Although we configured an incoming mail server, we have not installed a remote e-mail retrieval application on the e-mail system yet, so deselect Download Messages Now. If everything looks OK, then finish the account wizard by clicking Finish.

**Figure 7-4.** *The final step of the Thunderbird new account setup wizard gives you a chance to check the settings before committing to them.*

---

■**Note** Again, remember not to worry if you immediately receive an error that complains Thunderbird cannot contact your POP server and cannot download new e-mail. Whether you use Thunderbird, Microsoft Outlook, or any other e-mail client at this point to check mail, they will fail. We have not installed a POP or IMAP server as yet; we are only using Thunderbird to test SMTP at this point, and we'll cover remote e-mail retrieval later in Chapter 8.

---

Now you should be presented with the main Mozilla Thunderbird application window with a welcome message, as shown in Figure 7-5. Let's go ahead and compose a new e-mail message to test SMTP with Thunderbird.

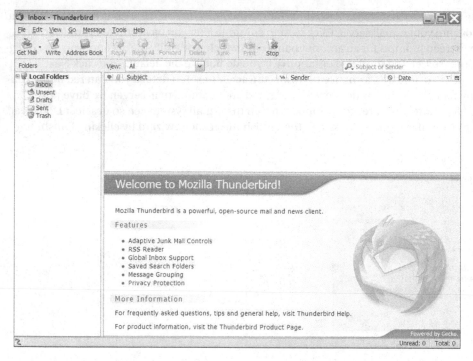

**Figure 7-5.** *The main Mozilla Thunderbird application window*

### Composing and Sending an E-mail Message with Mozilla Thunderbird

Now you should be ready to compose a new e-mail message by clicking the Write button on the top toolbar of the Mozilla Thunderbird main application window. Address the e-mail to yourself with the subject "Test from Thunderbird" and some body text, as shown in Figure 7-6. Click the Send button; Thunderbird should initiate an SMTP connection to your e-mail system, and sendmail should accept and deliver your test e-mail message.

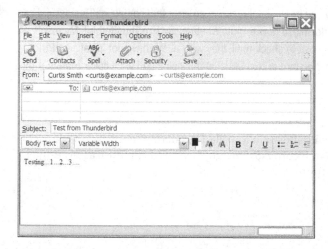

**Figure 7-6.** *Compose a new e-mail message to yourself to test SMTP on your e-mail system.*

For now, you'll have to check for that new message with mailx or Mutt from the command line on your e-mail server because we haven't configured POP or IMAP on the server yet:

```
[curtis@mail ~]$ mail
```

```
Mail version 8.1 6/6/93.  Type ? for help.
"/var/spool/mail/curtis": 1 message 1 new
>N  1 curtis@example.com        Thu Sep  8 02:01  18/631   "Test from Thunderbird"
& 1
Message 1:
From curtis@example.com  Thu Sep  8 02:01:50 2005
Date: Thu, 08 Sep 2005 02:01:02 -0400
From: Curtis Smith <curtis@example.com>
User-Agent: Mozilla Thunderbird 1.0.6-1.1.fc3 (X11/20050720)
X-Accept-Language: en-us, en
MIME-Version: 1.0
To: curtis@example.com
Subject: Test from Thunderbird
Content-Type: text/plain; charset=ISO-8859-1; format=flowed
Content-Transfer-Encoding: 7bit

Testing...1...2...3...

& q
Saved 1 message in mbox
```

**■Note** Remember, whether you decided to send a test message from Mozilla Thunderbird, Outlook, Eudora, or any other MUA, you will not be able to check for new e-mail at this time. In Chapter 8 I begin introducing remote e-mail protocols and explain how to configure Thunderbird to check mail remotely using those profiles. At this point you are only equipped to send, not receive, mail with a remote graphical e-mail client application.

Congratulations; you've effectively tested mail delivery from an external mail client to your new e-mail system! The rest of this chapter will be dedicated to debugging e-mail delivery should a message turn up missing or is not delivered properly for some reason. Even if your test messages from the server's command line and Thunderbird were delivered successfully, I highly encourage you to continue reading the rest of this chapter as it will be useful knowledge to have later.

# Tracking and Debugging E-mail Delivery

To be honest, one of my least-liked responsibilities as an e-mail administrator is tracking e-mail messages and debugging e-mail delivery. However, one of my favorite reasons for running a Linux-based e-mail system with open source software is the amount of information and the hundreds of powerful programs and utilities available to make this responsibility much easier.

## Checking maillog

Earlier in this chapter, I introduced syslog in general, and the messages and mail logs in particular. We've seen how logs are useful for tracking system processes and applications. Now I'd like to show how maillog is of particular use for tracking and debugging e-mail delivery.

Summaries of every SMTP session your MTA handles, both incoming and outgoing transactions, are also logged in maillog. If you open /var/log/maillog with less and scroll toward the bottom of maillog, you might see some log entries that look familiar. You should find blocks of log entries that indicate the beginning of the SMTP session and the final delivery of the two test e-mail messages we sent earlier in this chapter. For example, here's the block of messages generated when I sent the first e-mail from mailx on the command line on my example server:

```
Sep  8 00:44:20 mail sendmail[4347]: j884iKHj004347: from=curtis, size=54, class=0, ➡
nrcpts=1, msgid=<200509080444.j884iKHj004347@mail.example.com>, ➡
relay=curtis@localhost
Sep  8 00:44:20 mail sendmail[4348]: j884iKmC004348: ➡
from=<curtis@mail.example.com>, size=331, class=0, nrcpts=1, ➡
msgid=<200509080444.j884iKHj004347@mail.example.com>, proto=ESMTP, ➡
daemon=MTA, relay=localhost.localdomain [127.0.0.1]
Sep  8 00:44:20 mail sendmail[4347]: j884iKHj004347: to=curtis@example.com, ➡
ctladdr=curtis (500/500), delay=00:00:00, xdelay=00:00:00, mailer=relay, pri=30054, ➡
relay=[127.0.0.1] [127.0.0.1], dsn=2.0.0, stat=Sent (j884iKmC004348 Message accepted ➡
for delivery)
Sep  8 00:44:20 mail sendmail[4349]: j884iKmC004348: to=<curtis@example.com>, ➡
ctladdr=<curtis@mail.example.com> (500/500), delay=00:00:00, xdelay=00:00:00, ➡
mailer=local, pri=30545, dsn=2.0.0, stat=Sent
```

Every log message comes in the following general format:

*date host* sendmail[*pid*]: *qid*: *foo*=value, ...

All messages start with the date, hostname, or IP address of the server reporting the log message, the process name (sendmail, in this case) and the system *process ID (PID)*, and the sendmail *queue ID (QID)*. Following that are one or more *foo*=value messages, separated by commas, where *foo*=value is one of numerous syslog equates. The syslog equates are the meat of the log message, giving you the information you need to track or debug e-mail delivery. Table 7-1 lists the most common *foo*=value syslog equates that get logged when a message delivery succeeds, fails, or is deferred.

**Table 7-1.** foo=value *syslog Equates in maillog Entries*

| foo= syslog Equate | Description |
| --- | --- |
| class= | The numeric value of the Precedence mail header if one exists, otherwise 0. |
| ctladdr= | The local controlling user, set when a message is delivered through a local program. The value is in the form of <user@domain> (UID/GID). |
| daemon= | This logs the name of the daemon that handled the e-mail message. The value is defined by the Name= option in the DAEMON_OPTIONS m4 macro in sendmail.mc. |
| delay= | The total time it took to deliver the e-mail message. This is in the format DD+HH:MM:SS. |
| dsn= | The numeric SMTP reply code, as dictated in RFC 1893. |
| from= | The e-mail address of the enveloper sender for an e-mail message. |
| mailer= | The name of the mailer that delivered the e-mail message. |
| msgid= | The unique identifier applied to all e-mail messages sent, also found in the Message-ID header. Message IDs are a requirement of RFC 2822. |
| nrcpts= | The number of recipients an e-mail message is sent to. This number is reported after all address aliases are looked up, so the number might not match the number of addresses in the envelope recipients. |
| proto= | The protocol used when the e-mail message was originally received. |
| relay= | Lists the hostname, IP address, or e-mail address of who sent or accepted the e-mail message. |
| size= | The total size, in bytes, of the e-mail message body sent during after the DATA SMTP command. |
| stat= | A textual log of the delivery status of the e-mail message. |
| to= | The e-mail address or program the e-mail message was delivered to. |
| xdelay= | The time it took to complete the current transaction, like the time to transmit or defer. Should not be confused with delay=, which is total time from receipt to delivery. This is in the format HH:MM:SS. |

Information overload! But I assure you that when the time comes to troubleshoot your boss's e-mail delivery, you will find that amount of information is worth more than gold. You'll also find that much of that information can be matched up with e-mail headers for a specific message to aid in further investigations.

## Reading E-mail Headers

Reading e-mail headers can almost be as daunting as wading through the thousands of lines in a large maillog. However, as with anything new, with time and practice comes experience. As we discussed in Chapter 1, every e-mail message is made up of message headers and a message body. Whereas a user is most concerned with the contents of the message body, the message headers are more interesting from an Internet e-mail administrator's point of view.

An e-mail message's headers log the life of that message and the path it took to get from an MUA, to a remote MTA, to your MTA, and ultimately to your user's MUA. If you remember my description of SMTP as a well-defined conversation, then parsing e-mail message headers

will seem much easier. First, let's take a look at the message headers from the first example
e-mail earlier in this chapter and the relevant example log entries found in maillog:

```
From curtis@example.com  Thu Sep  8 00:44:20 2005
Return-Path: <curtis@example.com>
Received: from mail.example.com (localhost.localdomain [127.0.0.1])
        by mail.example.com (8.13.4/8.13.4) with ESMTP id j884iKmC004348
        for <curtis@example.com>; Thu, 8 Sep 2005 00:44:20 -0400
Received: (from curtis@localhost)
        by mail.example.com (8.13.4/8.13.4/Submit) id j884iKHj004347
        for curtis@example.com; Thu, 8 Sep 2005 00:44:20 -0400
Date: Thu, 8 Sep 2005 00:44:20 -0400
From: Curtis Smith <curtis@example.com>
Message-Id: <200509080444.j884iKHj004347@mail.example.com>
To: curtis@example.com
Subject: First e-mail
Status: RO
```

When tracking the path an e-mail message has taken to get from one MTA to another,
look for the SMTP Received headers. The Received headers are in ascending order, so the last
Received header was the first to be added. Think of each Received header as a hop in the path
the message took from submission to delivery.

Each Received header also reflects that SMTP conversation between a client and server.
The first Received header

```
Received: (from curtis@localhost)
        by mail.example.com (8.13.4/8.13.4/Submit) id j884iKHj004347
        for curtis@example.com; Thu, 8 Sep 2005 00:44:20 -0400
```

reflects the submission by an MUA (mailx, in this case, but you can't tell from the header) to an
MTA (mail.example.com). The transaction ID, final recipient, and date and time received are
also there.

Then the next Received header

```
Received: from mail.example.com (localhost.localdomain [127.0.0.1])
        by mail.example.com (8.13.4/8.13.4) with ESMTP id j884iKmC004348
        for <curtis@example.com>; Thu, 8 Sep 2005 00:44:20 -0400
```

reflects the submission MTA mail.example.com, acting as an SMTP client now, submitting the
message to the queuing MTA on mail.example.com. The transaction ID, final recipient, and
date and time received are also there.

You now see that the transaction IDs and dates match to the block of log messages sendmail sent to /var/log/maillog pointed out in the previous section. See how nicely it all ties
together? Different parts of the SMTP conversation match with the Received headers of an
e-mail message. For instance, the HELO command at the beginning of an SMTP session is used
in the Received header. Also, various information found in an e-mail message header is logged
in maillog, like the unique message identifier. In all that confusing mess of seemingly cryptic
messages exists useful information that can be used to track a message and debug potential
delivery problems.

# Summary

In this chapter, we covered some potentially confusing topics. I strongly suggest going back through your own e-mail message headers and log files to see if you can correlate each together to get an idea of what it's like to track specific SMTP sessions. Don't get bogged down in the sheer amount of information you have to wade through; efficiency comes with repetition and practice. After tracking a few messages, you're sure to get the hang of it all. You'll be amazed at the large amounts of useful information you can find in the various log files, as you'll see as we press on further into this book.

# PART 3

# Remote Client Access to E-mail with POP3 and IMAP

# CHAPTER 8

■ ■ ■

# Introducing POP3 and IMAP

This chapter is the first in a series of chapters dedicated to showing you how to provide remote access to e-mail. After all, what good is e-mail if you can't reach it from wherever you or your users might find themselves with an Internet connection? Further, if you have dial-up users, they might still want access to their e-mail on their computer when they are offline—something that's not possible if you only offer webmail. In this chapter, I introduce the Post Office Protocol, version 3 (POP3) and the Internet Mail Access Protocol (IMAP). POP3 has been the remote mail protocol of choice for years and is supported by nearly every e-mail client out there. IMAP is a slightly newer remote mail protocol that offers many more options and flexibility to users and is gaining more support as storage becomes cheaper and broadband Internet access becomes more commonplace.

Both protocols are perfectly legitimate ways of offering remote access to e-mail. In this chapter, I cover each protocol in general terms and show the pros and cons of each to help you choose which fits your environment best. You might even wish to offer both at the same time—in Chapter 9 I will introduce Dovecot, a terrific open source server application that supports both protocols, if you so choose.

## Introducing the Post Office Protocol (Version 3)

The *Post Office Protocol* is a simple remote e-mail Internet protocol. These days, many users simply refer to POP, but more than likely they really mean POP3, or the third version of the protocol. POP3 is defined by RFC 1939 (www.ietf.org/rfc/rfc1939.txt).

POP3 is a fairly simple protocol, offering largely only the essential features. The typical POP3 session consists of a user authentication, listing new e-mail messages since the last time checked, and downloads either the headers only or the headers and message body of each new e-mail message. One key feature POP3 lacks is that it is only meant to list new messages and download them to an MUA. This is at its heart of simplistic design, but also limits its usefulness for some power users constantly on the go, switching from desktop to laptop and back again. Let's take a look at some of the advantages and disadvantages, as I see them from personal and professional experience.

### Choosing to Offer POP3

One of the best reasons I can give in favor of offering POP3 to your user base as an option is its widespread support among a large variety of mail user agents. If any given MUA is going to support any remote e-mail protocol at all, it's probably going to support POP3. This has been especially true of many of the personal data assistants (PDAs) and powerful cell phones, although less so lately. You also need to decide whether you will support older, legacy e-mail client applications, many of which may only support POP3.

Also in its favor, POP3 is a relatively easy protocol to support and debug because of its simplistic design and feature set. Later, I'll show you how to "speak" POP3 by connecting to a POP3 server with Telnet and issuing POP3 commands, much in the same way we did with SMTP in Chapter 4. Regardless, in my opinion, POP3 should only be offered if a commonplace, legacy remote e-mail access protocol is necessary to meet the best interests of your user base.

## Choosing Not to Offer POP3

One of the best reasons I can give for not offering POP3 is its lack of robustness. As I mentioned earlier, POP3 is only meant for simple e-mail retrieval. Mail can only be stored in the Inbox on the server, although mail can be manually sorted and stored into mail folders in their MUA on their local computer. POP3 does not support multiple remote mail folders.

Although the option to leave mail on the server exists in most MUAs, it is not a good way of managing e-mail if you have to check your e-mail from multiple locations. If your users need to access and download e-mail from only one location, and they are comfortable with storing their e-mail on that computer, then POP3 is sufficient. However, as soon as a user starts down the slippery slope of leaving mail on the server and tries to use multiple POP3 applications on different computers, mail is bound to be missed or lost. That's why I suggest offering IMAP for your users and consider leaving out POP3 if possible.

# Introducing the Internet Mail Access Protocol

The *Internet Mail Access Protocol (IMAP)* is a very feature-rich remote e-mail Internet protocol. Traditionally, IMAP is not as well supported and commonplace as POP3, but that is quickly becoming not the case. Most popular e-mail clients will fully support IMAP. At the moment, however, mobile devices like PDAs and cell phones may be less likely to fully support IMAP, although this is quickly changing as the adoption of IMAP becomes more widespread on the desktop and users begin to demand access to the mail they stored in remote mail folders. The latest version of IMAP, version 4, revision 1, is defined by RFC 3501 (www.ietf.org/rfc/rfc3501.txt).

The protocol was originally conceived in 1986 at Stanford University, but the University of Washington now hosts much of the continuing development and advocacy of IMAP. After waning support in the past by the industry, IMAP is quickly becoming a necessity for the mobile user.

---

■**Tip** A great general resource for IMAP can be found at www.imap.org, a site hosted by the University of Washington.

---

## Choosing to Offer IMAP

To put it simply, IMAP was built to provide universal e-mail access from more than one computer or device to your e-mail. In this day and age of always-on, instant access, and a heavy reliance by most users on their e-mail, the ability to read both new and saved e-mail from a central server can be crucial. Specifically designed to do just that, IMAP supports three modes of e-mail access as described in RFC 1733 (www.ietf.org/rfc/rfc1733.txt):

*Offline mode*: Relatively speaking, this is the simplest of the three modes. The client opens a connection to the server, e-mail is retrieved by the client from the server, typically mail is deleted off the server after retrieval, and the client closes the connection to the server. Actions are on demand, with the server acting as a temporary storage for e-mail. This is the way POP3 generally works.

*Online mode*: The client opens a connection to the server, maintaining a constant connection throughout the whole session, as e-mail is retrieved, manipulated, and permanently stored on the server itself, not the client. IMAP is developed to implement this mode in an efficient manor, taking up as little bandwidth as possible.

*Disconnected mode*: Best of the offline and online modes, disconnected mode is a hybrid of sorts. The client opens a connection to the server, any number of e-mail headers or entire messages are retrieved and copied to the client but also left on the server, and the client disconnects. Messages can be manipulated offline on the client, and then at any time later the client can connect to the server and synchronize the changes with the server. This is the true power of IMAP; synchronization is maintained by keeping unique message identifiers, but the server is always authoritative. Messages are cached locally in the client, but still stored on the server for future retrieval or manipulation. This mode is especially useful for PDAs and smart cell phones with limited network connectivity.

A summary of strengths and weaknesses of each mode, taken directly from RFC 1733, can be found in Table 8-1.

**Table 8-1.** *Strengths and Weaknesses of the Three Modes of Remote E-mail Access*

| Feature | Offline | Online | Disconnected |
|---|---|---|---|
| Can use multiple clients | No | Yes | Yes |
| Minimum use of server connect time | Yes | No | Yes |
| Minimum use of server resources | Yes | No | No |
| Minimum use of client disk resources | No | Yes | No |
| Multiple remote mailboxes | No | Yes | Yes |
| Fast startup | No | Yes | No |
| Mail processing when not online | Yes | No | Yes |

Further, IMAP fully supports multiple remote e-mail folders. This empowers users to store their e-mail in an organized fashion not unlike directories on a computer. Since the messages are physically stored on the server until permanently deleted, there is little danger of losing e-mail, yet storing cached copies locally allows for instant, offline access to e-mail. And it's possible to do all this with two or more IMAP clients concurrently!

Finally, the most compelling reason for implementing IMAP is that some of the other applications I will cover in this book do require IMAP. Most notably, if you plan on offering web-based access to e-mail, we will take a look at SquirrelMail in Chapter 12.

## Choosing Not to Offer IMAP

One possible problem to overcome if you decide to offer IMAP is disk space. Although user mailboxes can grow if mail is always left on the server with POP3, IMAP is specifically designed to store all e-mail on the remote server and inherently encourages archival through the sorting and storage of mail in remote folders. If your users are anything like the ones I've dealt with, they will keep every e-mail they receive over the years. This can add up to a significant amount of disk usage over time if your customer base is large. However, the trend has been for the price of storage to drop fairly significantly over the years.

Another possible downside to IMAP is the additional bandwidth an online mode session can include. This is especially a concern for those who pay for their Internet connection by the minute or by the number of bytes transferred (like cell phones). However, any intelligent IMAP client should support the disconnected mode of e-mail access, and give the option to only download headers or partial messages initially to conserver bandwidth, and then download entire message bodies at the request of the user. The features you offer to your users by implementing IMAP are fairly significant, and can enable a level of mobility and flexibility not possible with POP3.

# Surveying Popular E-mail Clients

These days, there are countless e-mail client applications. It would be impossible to list them all here, but I did want to list several of the most popular for the Microsoft Windows XP and Windows Mobile, Palm OS, Mac OS X, and Linux operating systems. Tables 8-2 through 8-6 also list whether each application supports POP3 or IMAP at the time of this writing. Some, but not all, are free or open source applications, and are noted as such. I hope this quick survey will help you determine what the majority of your customers might be using and help you decide which protocol to support.

**Table 8-2.** *Microsoft Windows XP E-mail Client Applications*

| Application Name | Web Site | POP3 Support | IMAP Support | Free | Open Source |
|---|---|---|---|---|---|
| Microsoft Outlook | http://office.microsoft.com/ | Yes | Yes | No | No |
| Mozilla Thunderbird | www.mozilla.com/thunderbird/ | Yes | Yes | Yes | Yes |
| Qualcomm Eudora | www.eudora.com/email/ | Yes | Yes | Yes | No |

**Table 8-3.** *Microsoft Windows Mobile E-mail Client Application*

| Application Name | Web Site | POP3 Support | IMA Support | Free | Open Source |
|---|---|---|---|---|---|
| Built-in Messaging Client | www.microsoft.com/ windowsmobile/ | Yes | Yes | No | No |

**Table 8-4.** *Mac OS X E-mail Applications*

| Application Name | Web Site | POP3 Support | IMA Support | Free | Open Source |
|---|---|---|---|---|---|
| Apple Mail | www.apple.com/macosx/features/mail/ | Yes | Yes | No | No |
| Microsoft Entourage | www.microsoft.com/mac/products/entourage2004/entourage2004.aspx | Yes | Yes | No | No |
| Mozilla Thunderbird | www.mozilla.com/thunderbird/ | Yes | Yes | Yes | Yes |

**Table 8-5.** *Palm OS 5.0 E-mail Application*

| Application Name | Web Site | POP3 Support | IMA Support | Free | Open Source |
|---|---|---|---|---|---|
| VersaMail | www.palm.com/us/support/accessories/versamail/ | Yes | Yes | No | No |

**Table 8-6.** *Linux E-mail Applications*

| Application Name | Web Site | POP3 Support | IMA Support | Free | Open Source |
|---|---|---|---|---|---|
| Novell Evolution | www.novell.com/products/desktop/features/evolution.html | Yes | Yes | Yes | Yes |
| KMail | http://kmail.kde.org/ | Yes | Yes | Yes | Yes |
| Sylpheed | http://sylpheed.good-day.net/ | Yes | Yes | Yes | Yes |

# Summary

In this short chapter, I introduced the two most popular remote e-mail access Internet protocols in wide use today. POP3 is the old, venerable workhorse so many mail administrators have relied on for years. Enjoying support by nearly every e-mail client around, it is sure to meet the basic needs of the majority of your users. However, POP3 is showing its age, so to speak. POP3's simplistic, small feature set is its own worse enemy.

IMAP has been designed specifically with mobility in mind. With IMAP, users can access their e-mail easily from multiple computers using different e-mail clients without worrying about losing e-mail. Also, some of the other components, like webmail, explicitly require IMAP. However, not everything is without its hurdles. If disk space consumption is a concern, IMAP might not fit your environment. You'll find that one open source application can offer both at the same time—in Chapter 9, I will introduce Dovecot, the secure POP3 and IMAP server.

CHAPTER 9

∎∎∎

# Introducing and Installing Dovecot

In this chapter, I introduce Dovecot, an open source application that can provide both POP3 and IMAP services, which might make the decision to offer one or the other, or both concurrently, a bit easier. It's definitely nice from the standpoint of only having to administer one application instead of two—especially true when that one product is specifically written with security in the forefront of its development process, as you'll see is the case with Dovecot.

## Introducing the Secure POP3 and IMAP Server

Dovecot (www.dovecot.org) is an open source, lightweight yet robust, and secure POP3 and IMAP server application. The Dovecot development team's primary goal is to create and maintain a product designed with security as the main concern. Although many assume this means a slower, more resource-hungry application, Dovecot has proven to be quite efficient, both in terms of speed and resource use.

Dovecot is also unique in its compatibility with other legacy POP3 and IMAP server implementations, its support of both mbox and maildir mailbox formats, and its support of not only traditional IMAP and POP3 services, but also IMAP Secure (IMAPS) and POP3 Secure (POP3S). The latter two secure options are discussed in depth in Chapter 10. Few applications can make all of these claims, much less pull them off so well in an enterprise-quality mail server environment.

## Installing Dovecot

Dovecot is available as a Fedora Core RPM package, or you can download and install from the source distribution found on www.dovecot.org. The Dovecot RPM was included in our default Fedora Core installation as outlined in Chapter 2. This and subsequent chapters will assume you're using the Fedora Core RPM package, but the general topics discussed in this chapter and specific configuration in this and subsequent chapters should still apply to an instance of Dovecot installed from source. From which of the two you choose to install and maintain Dovecot is a matter of personal preference, but as always I prefer the RPM package for easy maintenance whenever possible.

## The Dovecot RPM Package

To determine whether Dovecot was installed on your Fedora Core system, you can use the following command to query the RPM database:

```
[curtis@mail ~]$ rpm -qv dovecot
```

```
dovecot-0.99.14-4.fc4
```

This command shows the version of Dovecot and the revision of the RPM, if it is installed. Of course, your version may vary. Otherwise, if the package is missing, the previous command won't output anything and you can install Dovecot with yum:

```
[curtis@mail ~]$ sudo yum install dovecot
```

This command will search for, and install if found, the latest version of Dovecot available from the yum RPM package repositories you have configured on your e-mail system. In addition, any required prerequisite RPM packages will also be downloaded and installed if they aren't already.

If you decide RPM packages are not an option, then follow along the next section if you'd rather install Dovecot from the source distribution.

## The Dovecot Source Distribution

To install from source, download the latest stable source distribution from www.dovecot.org. At the time of this writing, this was version 1.0.beta1; however, it might be different by the time you read this.

**Note** Do not be alarmed by the version label alpha or beta. Sometimes software developers will use these version labels to indicate the maturity of their code. However, sometimes software developers will also use these same labels to indicate that a particular release is nearing a new major release, perhaps indicating new features or major changes from the previous major release. Also, some developers are very conservative with how they indicate progress through version strings, while others are not; trust the applicable web site to find what the developers feel is the stable release, and download that. Dovecot is a very mature, stable application, although sometimes its version number might appear to claim otherwise.

Throughout this book, I've suggested using wget to download the latest stable source distribution; Dovecot is no different. Copy the URL to the source distribution from the download link on the Dovecot web site, but be sure you download the latest stable source distribution:

```
[curtis@mail ~]$ wget http://www.dovecot.org/releases/dovecot-1.0.beta1.tar.gz
```

Next, unpack, build, compile, and install the source distribution (screen output is not shown for the sake of brevity):

```
[curtis@mail ~]$ tar xzvf dovecot-1.0.alpha3.tar.gz
[curtis@mail ~]$ cd dovecot-1.0.alpha3/
```

```
[curtis@mail ~]$ ./configure
[curtis@mail ~]$ make
[curtis@mail ~]$ sudo make install
```

Whatever your choice of installation method might be, you're now ready to configure Dovecot. I think you'll find this an extremely easy thing to do—another reason Dovecot is a favorite among the many POP3 and IMAP server applications these days.

# Configuring Dovecot

Configuring Dovecot is an extremely simple process. There is only one configuration file, and it is very well documented. All aspects of Dovecot, including both of the POP3 and IMAP features, are controlled through its configuration file, dovecot.conf. Typically found in /etc/, both in the Fedora Core RPM package and source distribution, dovecot.conf may be in a different location depending on modifications you made at compile and installation time. Let's take a look at the main options and customize Dovecot for our specific needs. I won't go through the configuration file line by line, but you should skim the rest of dovecot.conf to familiarize yourself with it.

## Customizing dovecot.conf

The Dovecot configuration file consists of a series of application option keywords, followed by the equal sign (=) and the option's modifier. For example, the typical configuration line might look something like this:

```
keyWord = optionModifier
```

As with most configuration files, a number sign (#) is a comment and is ignored by Dovecot itself. First, let's make a backup copy of the default configuration file:

```
[curtis@mail ~]$ cd /etc/
[curtis@mail etc]$ sudo cp dovecot.conf dovecot.conf.orig
```

Go ahead and open dovecot.conf with your favorite text editor (you'll need superuser privileges to modify dovecot.conf, so don't forget sudo!). The first items of interest are the following lines:

```
# Protocols we want to be serving:
#   imap imaps pop3 pop3s
protocols = imap imaps pop3 pop3s
```

The protocols option keyword tells Dovecot which remote e-mail protocols to serve. As can be seen from the preceding comment, Dovecot supports the following keywords representing specific protocols:

- imap: The Internet Mail Access Protocol, discussed in Chapter 8
- imaps: IMAP through a secure, encrypted tunnel, discussed in detail in Chapter 10
- pop3: The Post Office Protocol, version 3, discussed in Chapter 8
- pop3s: POP3 through a secure, encrypted tunnel, discussed in detail in Chapter 10

For now, let's only enable the nonsecure versions of both POP3 and IMAP; I'd like to cover secure remote e-mail access in much more detail in the next chapter, as it's such an important topic. Also, I'm going to assume the system we're building will need to support both POP3 and IMAP simultaneously. This is partially for illustrative and instructional purposes, but also because, with Dovecot, it's trivial to support both protocols with little to no overhead in terms of system resources or administration. Which protocol you choose is a matter of particular needs and policy, which should be decided on a case-by-case basis in order to meet your specific users' needs.

So, let's go ahead and modify the protocols option to enable only imap and pop3 for now. Comment out the protocols option with # and add a new protocols option like so:

```
#protocols = imap imaps pop3 pop3s
protocols = imap pop3
```

This will tell Dovecot to only support the traditional, nonsecure IMAP and POP3 remote e-mail Internet protocols.

Next, scroll down to the following lines:

```
imap_listen = [::]
pop3_listen = [::]
```

These lines tell Dovecot what IP address and port to listen for IMAP and POP3 connections. The default is to allow Dovecot to decide this for you automatically. Unless your system is multihomed (see the corresponding Note), or you have a special need to offer IMAP and POP3 on a different port other than the traditional ones, you should leave these options as they are.

---

**Note** A multihomed system is one that has more than one Internet IP address assigned to it. In addition, many contemporary server applications like Dovecot support what's known as IPv6, the next generation of the current Internet addressing protocol called IPv4. Both of these concepts are out of the scope of this book, but are covered in *Pro DNS and BIND*, by Ron Aitchison (Apress, 2005).

---

Next, scroll down to the following lines:

```
imaps_listen = [::]
pop3s_listen = [::]
```

These lines tell Dovecot what IP address and port to listen on for IMAPS and POP3S connections. Again, the default is to let Dovecot decide this for you automatically. Let's comment out these two lines since we're not configuring secure connections at the moment.

In the same vein, we're going to completely disable secure communication support altogether. Locate this line:

```
#ssl_disable = no
```

and then change it to

```
ssl_disable = yes
```

Note this is backward from how we've been disabling features by simply commenting them out.

In addition, we will skip the next few options, including `ssl_cert_file`, `ssl_key_file`, `ssl_parameters_file`, and `ssl_parameters_regenerate` as they only apply to our discussion in Chapter 10. Leaving them there without commenting them out is fine; they will be ignored since we just disabled SSL and TLS support.

The next option we need to consider is

```
#disable_plaintext_auth = yes
```

You'll notice this option is already commented out; that is to say, plaintext authentication is *not* disabled. Uncommenting this option will disable all plaintext login and authentication methods if a connection is not secured or encrypted. Although this might seem like a good security precaution, doing so will break some traditional e-mail clients as it requires special functionality not typically found or configured by default. Further, supporting and configuring non-plaintext authentication with nonsecure protocols is not within the scope of this book.

If security is of particular concern, as it should be, then you ought to consider disallowing nonsecure POP3 and IMAP altogether and implementing only POP3S and/or IMAPS, as illustrated in Chapter 10. If you find you must support legacy clients, then you'll have little choice but to leave this option commented out.

The rest of `dovecot.conf` is security-related, privilege separation, and miscellaneous authentication options. Since security is at the forefront of Dovecot's design, the default configuration represents best-practice suggestions for an optimally secure installation and configuration. Changing these options is outside the scope of this book and should only be done with advanced knowledge of Dovecot and solid experience with Linux systems in general. For more in-depth discussion of options not discussed here, read the last section of this chapter for suggestions on where to go from here if the default installation doesn't fit your organization's needs.

## Opening Your System Firewall

Before you can connect to Dovecot through POP3 or IMAP, you must modify your system's network firewall to allow corresponding traffic to pass through. Remember, our system firewall should be configured to deny all incoming network traffic and then explicitly allow specific network traffic through.

The Internet Assigned Numbers Authority (IANA) has assigned the Post Office Protocol, version 3, to TCP port 110 and the Internet Mail Access Protocol to TCP 143. Although it's technically possible to run any service on any port you wish, adhering to the port assignments given by IANA will make life simpler as they are the generally recognized default ports for these services.

To open TCP 110 for POP3 permanently on a Fedora Core system, add the following line to /etc/sysconfig/iptables:

```
-A RH-Firewall-1-INPUT -m state --state NEW -m tcp -p tcp --dport 110 -j ACCEPT
```

and to open TCP 143 for IMAP permanently on a Fedora Core system, add the following line to /etc/sysconfig/iptables:

```
-A RH-Firewall-1-INPUT -m state --state NEW -m tcp -p tcp --dport 143 -j ACCEPT
```

For reference, or more details about iptables, check back in Chapter 3.

Don't forget to restart iptables to commit the changes. On Fedora Core, you can use the `service` command to do so:

```
[curtis@mail ~]$ sudo service iptables restart
```

```
Flushing firewall rules:                             [  OK  ]
Setting chains to policy ACCEPT: filter              [  OK  ]
Unloading iptables modules:                          [  OK  ]
Applying iptables firewall rules:                    [  OK  ]
```

Next you'll learn how to start and stop Dovecot, as well as configure it to both start up and shut down automatically. This is the final step before testing POP3 and IMAP on your new e-mail system.

## Manually Start and Stop Dovecot

To start Dovecot installed on a Fedora Core system from the RPM package for the first time, use the `service` command to start Dovecot with its init script:

```
[curtis@mail ~]$ sudo service dovecot start
```

```
Starting Dovecot Imap:                               [  OK  ]
```

If Dovecot didn't start successfully (the `service` command reports a failure), then check the system and mail logs (typically `/var/log/messages` and `/var/log/maillog`, respectively) to see if Dovecot reported any errors. Dovecot is usually pretty verbose in reporting the specific problem that kept it from starting; it's probably just a simple typo, so check the section about configuring Dovecot earlier in this chapter. Also, if you configured a specific IP address or alternate port for Dovecot to listen on, then make sure the IP address is configured properly on your system, and make sure no other applications are listening on the same address/port combination.

If you wish to shut down Dovecot manually, you can use the `service` command to do so:

```
[curtis@mail ~]$ sudo service dovecot stop
```

```
Stopping Dovecot Imap:                               [  OK  ]
```

Otherwise, you can configure Dovecot to automatically start up and shut down when appropriate, which I will show you next.

# Starting Dovecot Automatically

On a Fedora Core system using Dovecot installed from the RPM package, you can use the command `chkconfig` to configure an application to automatically start up and shut down. By default, Dovecot comes preconfigured not to start up at all. You can see this by passing the `--list` argument to `chkconfig`:

`[curtis@mail ~]$ sudo chkconfig --list dovecot`

```
dovecot          0:off   1:off   2:off   3:off   4:off   5:off   6:off
```

As you can see, Dovecot is disabled for all runlevels. To configure Dovecot to start up when your system comes online, use the `chkconfig` command again:

`[curtis@mail ~]$ sudo chkconfig --level 2345 dovecot on`

Check your handiwork and compare the output of the following to your earlier output:

`[curtis@mail ~]$ sudo chkconfig --list dovecot`

```
dovecot          0:off   1:off   2:on    3:on    4:on    5:on    6:off
```

For a more complete introduction to Linux runlevels and Fedora Core init scripts, refer to Chapter 3. Now that Dovecot is turned on and listening for POP3 and IMAP connections, let's test it out!

# Testing Remote E-mail Access

In Chapter 7, we started setting up the cross-platform Thunderbird e-mail client. Let's fill in the POP3 and IMAP settings to test your new Dovecot installation.

## Configuring Mozilla Thunderbird for POP3

Fire up Thunderbird and select Tools ➤ Account Settings, which brings up the Account Settings window shown in Figure 9-1. Click the plus sign next to the account we set up in Chapter 7 to expand it (if it's not already). Under your test account, click Server Settings. If the server type reads "POP Mail Server," then enter the fully qualified domain name of your POP3 server, mail.example.com for example, in the Server Name box. Also fill in your account username in the User Name box.

For the purposes of testing, go ahead and check the option Leave Messages on Server; we want to be able to check for messages with IMAP later. Click OK to save the changes you just made and the Account Settings window should disappear.

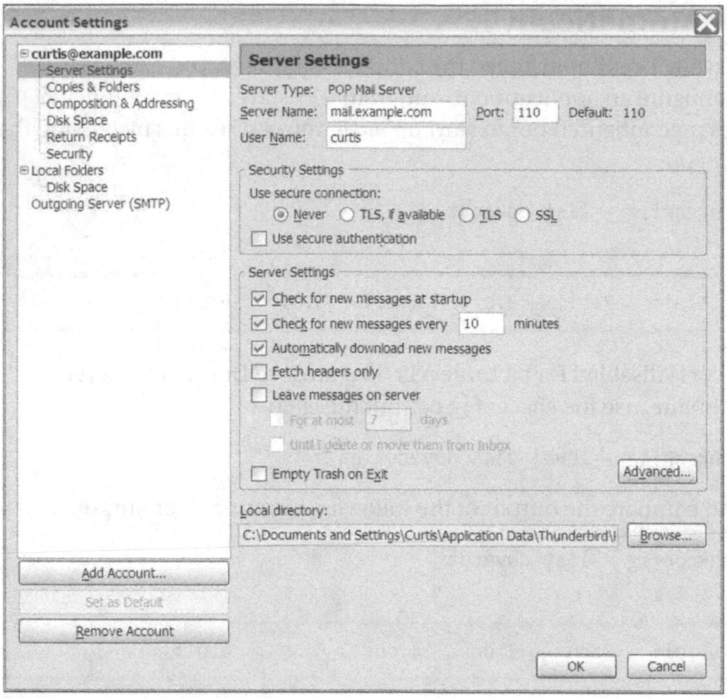

**Figure 9-1.** *The Account Settings dialog box allows you to change an existing e-mail account already configured in Thunderbird.*

Finally, click the Get Mail button on the toolbar to force Thunderbird to check for new e-mail. If your Dovecot installation was properly configured to accept POP3 connections, you should be prompted to enter your password. Do so and click OK. If you authenticate success-fully, you should see the test e-mail message we sent way back in Chapter 7 waiting for you in your Inbox!

### Configuring Mozilla Thunderbird for IMAP

Next let's reconfigure Thunderbird for IMAP. Again select Edit ➤ Account Settings. We need to create a new account that's configured to use IMAP as the incoming mail server, so click the Add Account button. This will run the same new account wizard we walked through in Chap-ter 7. You can follow the same instructions detailed in that chapter to create a new account, but configure the account to use IMAP instead of POP3. Use the same fully qualified domain name and username as with your POP3 settings.

Now when you click Get Mail on the Thunderbird toolbar you will be prompted for your password again, this time to check your mail through the IMAP connection you just set up. Thunderbird will present your new account on the left side of the window, and the very same message that we sent in Chapter 7 and that showed up in POP3 will be there in your IMAP mailbox (see Figure 9-2)!

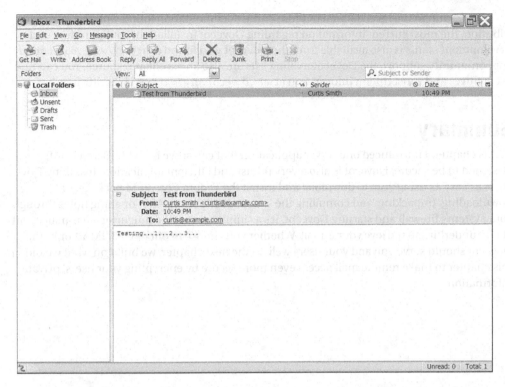

**Figure 9-2.** *Thunderbird will download POP3 messages to your Inbox under Local Folders, while IMAP server accounts will appear as a separate account.*

# Further Dovecot Resources

Dovecot is an extremely well-documented software package. Documentation can be found locally on your Fedora Core system in /usr/share/doc/dovecot-[version]/, where [version] represents the base version string of the RPM package installed. For example, at the time of this writing, the RPM package installed was dovecot-0.99.14-4.fc4, so documentation can be found in /usr/share/doc/dovecot-0.99.14/; to check the version of Dovecot, run the following command:

```
[curtis@mail ~]$ rpm -qv dovecot
```

```
dovecot-0.99.14-4.fc4
```

Of particular interest are the files design.txt and securecoding.txt, which detail the design guidelines and secure coding practices by which the Dovecot development team has created Dovecot.

In addition to the local documentation, or the documentation found with the source distribution, the most current information regarding Dovecot installation, configuration, and development status is also available from the Dovecot wiki found at `http://wiki.dovecot.org`. For community support, the Dovecot mailing lists are also an excellent resource. You can find list archives and subscription information at `www.dovecot.org/mailinglists.html`.

## Summary

In this chapter, I introduced one server application that can serve both POP3 and IMAP. Designed to be secure, Dovecot is also a very robust and efficient application. Installing Dovecot is as easy as using yum to download and install the Fedora Core RPM package, or downloading, unpacking, and compiling the source distribution. After opening holes through your system's firewall and starting Dovecot, it's a simple matter of configuring an e-mail client like Thunderbird to retrieve your e-mail. Whether you choose to offer POP3, IMAP, or both, Dovecot should serve you and your users well. In the next chapter, we build on what we did in this chapter to make remote mail access even more secure by encrypting your users' private information.

# CHAPTER 10

■ ■ ■

# Securing Remote Client Access with SSL

In the previous chapter, I introduced Dovecot and showed how it can be configured to offer both POP3 and IMAP simultaneously with minimal configuration or overhead. I mentioned a bit about securing the traditional remote e-mail access protocols, but glossed over the specifics and recommended ignoring or disabling those features for a later time. I promised to cover those features, and in this chapter I will make good on that promise.

My reason for keeping security for a later chapter is not because I don't feel it's an important issue. Quite the contrary; I feel secure remote e-mail access is so important it warrants its very own chapter. This chapter will build on the previous ones and will cover securing both POP3 and IMAP. I will also examine general topics that will apply to subsequent chapters when discussing secure web access.

## Introducing Secure Network Communication

The Internet developed out of a desire to share information. Today we find that the World Wide Web is full of public information of all kinds imaginable. In the past, the precursors to the Internet as we know it today were pockets of a few trusted nodes networked together. Today, millions of seemingly anonymous computer nodes connect to the modern Internet from all over the world.

However, so many businesses and individuals use the Internet to share information but expect it to stay private among them. After all, the Web is used for online banking and other financial transactions, not just for sharing the latest research papers. Furthermore, there's an expectation that one's e-mail is personal and ought to be kept private.

But where there's private information, there's somebody who wants to get at it. Authentication methods were developed to give access to certain resources, like e-mail or banking records, to the appropriate person while keeping out other persons not privy to those same resources. The most common mechanism for someone to prove who they are to a computer is through a private username and password only that person ought to know. This is nothing new; after all, a username and password are required to log into your Linux system. This sort of basic general mechanism for proving one's identity digitally has been around since the first multiuser computers were in use.

However, most authentication schemes are designed to send a username and password in clear text over a network connection. This has the unfortunate side effect of opening up the likely possibility that someone can, and will, capture your network traffic and freely read your username and password. Now the one thing you relied on to prove who you are isn't individual to you and only you. A miscreant who has captured your username and password has the ability to access private and personal resources previously available to you alone.

Most Internet protocols did not take this level of security into mind. Although most protocols have some sort of authentication mechanism built in, unfortunately such mechanisms are not sufficient anymore. Luckily, a way to take existing network protocols and wrap them in an electronic security blanket of sorts was developed to combat those who eavesdrop on your Internet communications.

## The Secure Sockets Layer Protocol

Developed in 1996 by Netscape Communications Corporation, the most popular method for securing Internet communication is called *Secure Sockets Layer (SSL)*. Almost anyone who has done secure banking or made any purchases online should be familiar with SSL. You know that SSL has been used when you see the yellow padlock in the status bar of Internet Explorer or when the address bar turns golden in Firefox. SSL is approved by all of the major credit card agencies and banks for ensuring safe and secure communication between the user and server.

SSL was specifically designed to work with any well-known existing Internet protocol, like POP3 or IMAP, without changing the way those protocols work. SSL was to be modular, extendable, and forward- and backward-compatible with new and previous versions of any communications protocol. This means SSL occurs at a different level, or layer, than most Internet protocols.

For example, as we saw in Chapter 9, we require users to authenticate with a username and password when initiating a connection via POP3 or IMAP before downloading any e-mail. This authentication is done completely in the clear and is available for anyone to see with a protocol analyzer. With a system using SSL to secure POP3 or IMAP, the connection between the client and server is encrypted *first*, before any part of the POP3 or IMAP session is initiated. Then, once a secure channel is created, all POP3 or IMAP protocol communication is sent through that encrypted channel. Anyone with a protocol analyzer can see the secure channel, but it will appear to be little more than garbage—useless bits of data unless you are a part of that secure channel! This can be illustrated very easily by example.

## A Quick and Dirty Introduction to Sniffing Network Traffic with tcpdump

Using the venerable network traffic sniffer tcpdump (www.tcpdump.org), we can see how open your sensitive information can really be when not encrypted in a secure channel. Network traffic and packet analysis in general, and tcpdump in particular, is well out of the scope of this book. Suffice it to say, the ability to sniff, or watch, what is being sent and received between two Internet hosts can be a powerful tool for troubleshooting any number of advanced network problems. This example is only meant as an introduction to tcpdump and to emphasize the risk one faces when Internet communication is not secure.

In this example, I will start tcpdump listening on the e-mail system itself. Then I will start Thunderbird and log in with POP3 and IMAP, authenticating with my username and password in clear text. The command-line arguments to tcpdump are simply limiting what traffic it logs to the public network interface and IP address of the server itself:

```
[curtis@spider ~]$ sudo tcpdump -i eth0 -w dumpfile dst host 192.168.69.4
```

After running Thunderbird, authenticating via POP3 and IMAP, kill tcpdump by pressing Ctrl+C. Then use tcpdump to print the raw data it logged to the file dumpfile in a human-readable format:

```
[curtis@spider ~]$ sudo tcpdump -xn -r dumpfile
```

This will print any network traffic that was logged with the time-stamp, source IP address and Internet port, destination IP address and Internet port, and the contents of the network packet. The left half is the representation of the packet in hex, and the right is the ASCII representation. If you look through the output of dumpfile, you should come across something like the following (I've highlighted the interesting bit in bold):

```
00:10:06.939934 IP 192.168.69.106.55242 > 192.168.69.4.pop3: P 12:25(13) ➥
ack 120 win 1460 <nop,nop,timestamp 8295041 1303809643>
    0x0000: 4500 0041 c042 4000 4006 6eb5 c0a8 456a  E..A.B@.@.n...Ej
    0x0010: c0a8 4504 d7ca 006e dd29 b3ec b849 d418  ..E....n.)...I..
    0x0020: 8018 05b4 de6f 0000 0101 080a 007e 9281  .....o.......~..
    0x0030: 4db6 8e6b 5553 4552 2063 7572 7469 730d  M..kUSER.curtis.
    0x0040: 0a                                        .
```

Now look at this next packet (again, the particularly interesting bit is highlighted in bold):

```
00:10:06.965660 IP 192.168.69.106.55242 > 192.168.69.4.pop3: P 25:42(17) ➥
ack 125 win 1460 <nop,nop,timestamp 8295066 1303811550>
    0x0000: 4500 0045 c046 4000 4006 6ead c0a8 456a  E..E.F@.@.n...Ej
    0x0010: c0a8 4504 d7ca 006e dd29 b3f9 b849 d41d  ..E....n.)...I..
    0x0020: 8018 05b4 30be 0000 0101 080a 007e 929a  ....0.......~..
    0x0030: 4db6 95de 5041 5353 206c 3333 742e 6861  M...PASS.l33t.ha
    0x0040: 7830 720d 0a                             x0r..
```

In the first packet, you can see (in plaintext) the POP3 command USER and my username (curtis). Then, in the second packet you can see the POP3 PASS command and my password (l33t.hax0r)! Although much of this might look like gibberish, once you develop a feel for how to read tcpdump output, it becomes painfully obvious that Internet communication is not very private after all.

---

**Tip** For more information on how to use tcpdump, read the `tcpdump(8)` man page. It goes into great detail, including examples. A quick search on the Web should also yield plenty of packet sniffing and tcpdump tutorials if you want to learn more.

---

SSL is used so much these days and is such a big part of so many online experiences that it's hard to believe it's not even really an Internet standard like other popular protocols such as POP3 and IMAP. Originally developed by one forward-thinking corporation for the specific task of creating a way to secure web traffic, SSL has become a standard of sorts through its popular industry use and acceptance. However, to ensure compatibility and adherence to best practices, an enhanced, standards-track draft has been developed under the IETF's RFC process.

## The Transport Layer Security Protocol

Originally introduced in 1999, version 1.0 of *Transport Layer Security (TLS)* is a formal IETF Internet standards-track protocol defined by RFC 2246 (`www.ietf.org/rfc/rfc2246.txt`). TLS was designed to be a formal standard driven, and formally accepted, by the general Internet community. It was designed both to enhance and be backward-compatible with the SSL version 3.0 specification.

Although the SSL version 3.0 specification and TLS version 1.0 RFC are very similar, and TLS maintains a compatibility of sorts with SSL, there are a few main differences in their design and operation. When securing a nonsecure protocol like POP3 or IMAP with SSL, you cannot serve both nonsecure and secure communication over the same Internet port. A POP3 server typically listens on port 110 for regular POP3 connections and on port 995 for secure POP3-over-SSL connections. If you secure a protocol with SSL, it's all or nothing.

In 1997, the IETF recommended modifying existing application protocols like POP3 and IMAP in such a way to upgrade a session that begins nonsecured, guiding it through a secured tunnel. This effectively allows both nonsecure and secure sessions of the application protocol to be served on the same well-known port, eliminating the need to listen on two different ports for each. This enables a POP3 or IMAP client to connect to its primary well-known port without a secure connection. The client can then optionally initiate a secure session without disconnecting and reconnecting on a different port. This offers seamless support for both types of connections through one server application on one well-known Internet port—something that's not possible with traditional SSL. TLS is designed specifically to allow for such a situation.

The process of starting a secured session is shown in Figure 10-1. A client always initiates a secure communication channel, negotiates the type of secure communication, and authenticates the server through a digital certificate. This is called the *handshake*.

Then, the client and server switch to the encryption cipher agreed on during the handshake and use the server certificate and public key to create the secured channel. We'll discuss server certificates, public, and private keys shortly.

Once the secured channel is created, all subsequent application communication is continued, in an encrypted channel, using the original protocol (such as POP3 or IMAP). More detailed information about the exact process involved in creating the secure channel is beyond the scope of this book, but this is a good start from a conceptual level.

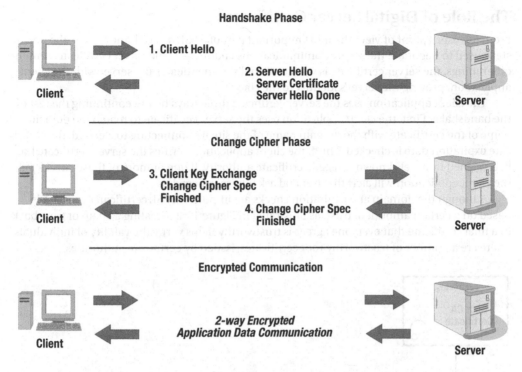

**Figure 10-1.** *Overview of an encrypted application session from start to finish*

---

**■Tip** Although most contemporary client and server applications support either SSL or TLS, or both, others might not. By using an application called Stunnel (www.stunnel.org), a universal SSL wrapper, it's possible to secure some protocols that do not support SSL/TLS natively.

---

Both mechanisms, SSL and TLS, work under the same basic principles. Although not an official IETF Internet standard, SSL works so well, and has been so widely adopted and utilized, that it has essentially achieved standards-like status due to its ubiquity. It has the benefit of working without changes to, or explicit support by, existing applications. TLS, although compatible with SSL version 3.0, is a standards-track protocol developed and approved by the Internet community and has been designed to enhance SSL without the administration overhead, but at the minor price of having to extend already deeply entrenched Internet application protocols.

SSL has become almost a generic term for any kind of secure, private communication between a client and server. This is mostly due to the fact that SSL is still the protocol of choice for secure web communication, despite the development of the TLS protocol standard. Although I might conflate the two throughout this book when speaking in general terms, it is important to distinguish between the two where technically appropriate.

## The Role of Digital Server Certificates

From the user's point of view, the most important part of a SSL or TLS handshake—the first steps used to negotiate the secure communications channel—is the server certificate. Among other things, the server certificate is what essentially authenticates the server with the client application, proving the server's identity to the client.

The client application uses the server certificate three ways before continuing the rest of the handshake. First, the client application uses the server certificate to match the domain name of the certificate with the domain name of the site it's connecting to. Second, the certificate expiration date is checked. Third, the client application verifies the server certificate has been signed by a well-known, trusted certificate authority. If one or more of these checks fail, the client application will alert the user and ask how to proceed.

Although the domain and expiration checks are important, SSL certificates are largely based on a certain amount of trust, as illustrated in Figure 10-2. Creating a chain of trust back to a final certificate that everyone agrees is trustworthy helps verify the validity of individuals. There are a number of trustworthy root certificates, issued by certificate authorities.

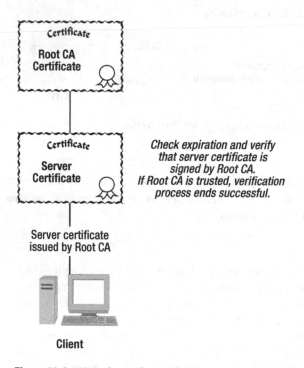

**Figure 10-2.** *Digital certificate chain to a trusted certificate authority root certificate*

## The Role of Certificate Authorities

A *certificate authority (CA)* is the basis for maintaining the chain of trust back to a server certificate. Any well-known authority is responsible for making sure that only legitimate sources register a server certificate for each domain. The most trustworthy CAs require a rigorous process for identifying those legitimate parties who ought to be assigned a certificate for a domain. For example, a registrar may require potential registrants to provide their organization's *Data Universal Numbering System (DUNS)* number or some such unique identifier incorporated with an elaborate process for verifying the registrant through faxes and online verification. Other registrars utilize a combination of an automated phone and e-mail verification system using an e-mail address that only the domain administrator could possibly have access to. This provides a mechanism for making sure not just anyone off the street can obtain a server certificate for ebay.com or paypal.com, and only those entities that have control of those domains have the authority to request a server certificate for those domains.

Once the requesters' identity and legitimacy has been verified by the vendor selling certificates, the requester creates a *certificate signing request (CSR)*. This is essentially an unsigned, unverified server certificate with the proper identifying information for the server. This CSR is sent to the CA, at which time it is signed by the certificate authority's root certificate, indicating the CA trusts the CSR and has validated it to be legitimate. Now the CSR becomes a valid, signed server certificate, and a client application can link the signed CSR to a valid, well-known, and trusted root CA certificate.

Most operating systems and some applications like the Mozilla Firefox Internet browser store a set of well-known root CA certificates in which they trust. For example, Microsoft Windows XP contains a certificate store where the most well-known root CA certificates are held for testing server certificate chains. Mac OS X has a similar mechanism called the Keychain. If a server certificate chain is rooted in one of the root CA certificates stored and bundled on your computer, it is considered trusted and valid since the root CA certificate is considered trusted and valid. Sometimes it's possible for a server certificate to have a longer chain, called *intermediate root certificates*. But as long as that chain of two or more certificates ultimately ends with a valid root CA certificate, you can be reasonably sure that the server certificate can be trusted. Table 10-1 lists some of the current popular root certificate authorities.

**Table 10-1.** *Popular Certificate Authorities*

| Certificate Authority | Web Site |
| --- | --- |
| VeriSign | www.verisign.com |
| Thawte | www.thawte.com |
| GeoTrust | www.geotrust.com |
| CAcert | www.cacert.org |

## Self-Signed Certificates

A *self-signed*, or *snake oil*, certificate is a certificate that has been signed by itself, creating no chain of trust back to any valid certificate authorities. Typically, snake oil certificates are only used for testing SSL or TLS servers before purchasing a regular server certificate. They can also be used permanently if the server is only accessed by a very small number of clients, but this is not recommended because it lacks any of the trust measures valid server certificates have for users to validate.

A self-signed certificate's chain consists of one node: itself. In other words, it is both the server certificate and the root CA, providing a circular chain that does not lead to a valid root CA certificate. In most cases, snake oil certificates are usually easy to identify, and your users should not accept a snake oil certificate as a trusted source without being absolutely sure of the source of the certificate. For example, if your business cannot afford a valid CA-signed certificate, your server's snake oil certificate can be stored and trusted as a valid root CA certificate. However, with the numerous cheaper alternative CAs available, this would not be considered a best practice.

### Introducing the Community-Driven Certificate Authority, CAcert

A relative newcomer to the arena of certificate authorities is CAcert (www.cacert.org). CAcert is a community-driven certificate authority whose goal is educate the general public about certificates and provide SSL certificates for free. It's the spirit of the free and open source community applied to a certificate authority.

CAcert has something for the occasional enthusiast, providing simple, free client certificates that can be used to sign or encrypt e-mail. CAcert also offers resources for the corporate systems administrator, providing server certificates appropriate for e-mail and web servers.

At the heart of CAcert is its Assurance Program, based on the *web of trust* concept. Essentially, this allows registered users to collect assurance points that can be applied toward additional member benefits and features. Those with enough Assurance Points may perform as Assurers, personally identifying and vouching for a person's identity. The Assurance Program creates a network of people who have been identified either directly or indirectly through a web of trust. When your identity has been verified and you collect enough Assurance Points, some benefits include the ability to apply for certificates with a longer expiration date and the ability to personalize e-mail certificates with your name.

At the time of this writing, the CAcert root certificate is not immediately recognized as a known, trusted root certificate by most Internet browsers or e-mail clients. However, it is possible to accept the root certificate, storing it in your operating system's or browser's certificate store.

Joining CAcert is free. If you're interested in this new concept, and want to help further the global acceptance of CAcert, visit www.cacert.org and look for an Assurer near you to get started in becoming a part of the CAcert web of trust.

## Obtaining and Installing Valid Server Certificates

Deciding whether to purchase a valid CA-signed certificate is up to you and your organization's specific needs. While I typically use self-signed certificates regularly for personal systems, I would never consider running a production, enterprise-quality services without a CA-signed certificate.

These days you have the option to purchase a globally accepted and widely recognized server certificate from a number of vendors. Some will be more recognized than others, but as long as you choose an industry-recognized and reputable vendor, the certificate will be worth the money compared to the peace of mind you're giving your users.

## Generating a CSR

To generate a certificate signing request (CSR) on a Fedora Core system, or virtually any other Linux operating system distribution, to send to the CA of your choice for validation and signing, use the openssl command. This will also create the server private key used to sign the certificate request. When you run this, fill in what I show in bold here with the information of your organization. The most important part of this process is the *Common Name (CN)*; this must match the fully qualified domain name (FQDN) exactly as your users will type it into their mail client for secure POP3 or IMAP:

```
[curtis@spider ~]$ sudo openssl req -new -nodes -keyout server.key ➥
-out server.csr
```

```
Generating a 1024 bit RSA private key
..............................................++++++
.....++++++
writing new private key to 'server.key'
-----
You are about to be asked to enter information that will be incorporated
into your certificate request.
What you are about to enter is what is called a Distinguished Name or a DN.
There are quite a few fields but you can leave some blank
For some fields there will be a default value,
If you enter '.', the field will be left blank.
-----
Country Name (2 letter code) [GB]:US
State or Province Name (full name) [Berkshire]:Ohio
Locality Name (eg, city) [Newbury]:Columbus
Organization Name (eg, company) [My Company Ltd]:Example Enterprise
Organizational Unit Name (eg, section) []:Information Technology
Common Name (eg, your name or your server's hostname) []:mail.example.com
Email Address []:postmaster@example.com

Please enter the following 'extra' attributes
to be sent with your certificate request
A challenge password []:
An optional company name []:
```

Submit the file server.csr to the CA of your choice and wait for the signed certificate to arrive. Hang on to the certificate private key server.key; we will use it and the signed server certificate you receive from the CA later when configuring Dovecot for secure POP3 and IMAP.

# Configuring Dovecot for Secure Remote Client Access

Now it's time to return to the Dovecot configuration file introduced in Chapter 9 and enable the security features to enable POP3 and IMAP over SSL and TLS. Because the security and privacy risks of allowing user authentication over a nonsecure connection are so high, I highly recommend enabling these security options for your own system. Offering POP3 and IMAP over SSL/TLS adds little to no overhead, both in terms of administration and in system resources. The only real downside to doing so is the maintenance of the server certificate itself. Server certificates typically have a two-year expiration date, so you will have a recurring biannual task of renewing your certificates. However, most CA vendors provide online tools, including reminder and certificate management services, to help you.

## Editing dovecot.conf

Before making any changes to the Dovecot configuration we created in Chapter 9, let's make a backup first:

```
[curtis@spider ~]$ cd /etc/
[curtis@spider etc]$ sudo cp dovecot.conf dovecot.conf.nossl
```

Now open dovecot.conf in your favorite text editor. First, tell Dovecot to enable POP3, IMAP, POP3S (POP3 over SSL/TLS), and IMAPS (IMAP over SSL/TLS) by modifying the protocols option to enable all four:

```
# Protocols we want to be serving:
# imap imaps pop3 pop3s
protocols = imap imaps pop3 pop3s
```

Next, uncomment the imaps_listen and pop3s_listen options and edit them to look just like the imap_listen and pop3_listen options. Following the example from Chapter 9, they should look something like this:

```
# IP or host address where to listen in for SSL connections. Defaults
# to above non-SSL equivalents if not specified.
imaps_listen = [::]
pop3s_listen = [::]
```

Now reenable SSL/TLS support by setting

```
# Disable SSL/TLS support.
ssl_disable = no
```

The next two options, ssl_cert_file and ssl_key_file, need to point to the location of your public server certificate and the private key used to created the server certificate. These options can be set to different defaults depending on how you installed Dovecot. If you installed Dovecot with the Fedora Core RPM package, then these options should be set to

```
ssl_cert_file = /etc/pki/dovecot/dovecot.pem
ssl_key_file = /etc/pki/dovecot/private/dovecot.pem
```

If you installed Dovecot from the source distribution, these options should be set to

```
ssl_cert_file = /etc/ssl/certs/dovecot.pem
ssl_key_file = /etc/ssl/private/dovecot.pem
```

In either case, a generic snake oil server certificate was created when Dovecot was installed. For the purpose of testing secure POP3 and IMAP, these snake oil certificates are sufficient, but they should not be used in production. Later in this chapter we will discuss how to obtain and install a valid server certificate.

That's all there is to configuring Dovecot for secure POP3 and IMAP. Next, you will need to open up the well-known ports to allow incoming connections.

## Punching Holes through Your System's Firewall

IANA has assigned secure POP3 to TCP port 995 and secure IMAP to TCP 993. Although it's technically possible to run any service on any port you wish, adhering to the port assignments given by IANA will make life simpler as they are the generally recognized default ports for these services and the ports most e-mail clients will use by default.

To open TCP 995 for secure POP3 permanently on a Fedora Core system, add the following line to /etc/sysconfig/iptables, or a line similar to your iptables configuration file:

```
-A RH-Firewall-1-INPUT -m state --state NEW -m tcp -p tcp --dport 995 -j ACCEPT
```

and to open TCP 993 for secure IMAP permanently on a Fedora Core system, add the following line to /etc/sysconfig/iptables, or a line similar to your iptables configuration file:

```
-A RH-Firewall-1-INPUT -m state --state NEW -m tcp -p tcp --dport 993 -j ACCEPT
```

Commit your firewall changes and restart Dovecot with the service command as was demonstrated in the last chapter, and you're ready to test secure remote e-mail access.

# Testing Secure POP3 and IMAP

Now it's time to put your configuration to the test. Let's modify the POP3 and IMAP accounts we created. Reconfiguring each mail account profile in Thunderbird is as easy as checking the Use Secure Connection (SSL) option under the Server Settings for each account. This will change the default port for each account automatically. Save your changes, and click the Get Mail button.

When you connect, you may find that Thunderbird will present you with a window notifying you that it cannot verify the validity of the server certificate if you used an unverifiable certificate like a snake oil certificate (Figure 10-3).

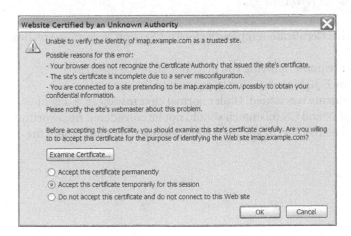

**Figure 10-3.** *Server certificate validation failure*

You are given the option to examine the certificate, decline to accept the certificate, accept the certificate temporary, or always accept the certificate for subsequent sessions. Go ahead and view the certificate just to get familiar with how certificates look (Figure 10-4). You're able to see who the certificate was issued to, including the CN, and who the certificate was issued by. Because the issuer is not known or trusted, the chain failed. You can also see identifying information unique to this certificate, namely the SHA1 and MD5 fingerprints. A fingerprint is just like a human fingerprint—an attribute, digital in this case, of the item that uniquely identifies it.

**Figure 10-4.** *Viewing a snake oil server certificate*

For now, let's click Accept This Certificate Temporarily for This Session to continue testing your connection.

You'll receive a second error window notifying you of a domain name mismatch (Figure 10-5). This means that the FQDN you're using to connect to the server does not match the CN for which the certificate was issued. Under normal circumstances, a digital server certificate that has an FQDN and CN mismatch should not be considered trustworthy, particularly if it's an especially sensitive site. Again, for testing purposes, let's just ignore the error and continue.

**Figure 10-5.** *Server certificate domain name mismatch failure*

After that, you should be prompted for your username and password. If all goes well, you've successfully authenticated and received your e-mail over a secure, encrypted channel. If you're curious, you could rerun tcpdump when you try those last few steps again; all you'll see is unintelligible gibberish.

These errors are extremely educational as they imitate the failure of two out of the three server certificate tests and illustrate how important the need for a real CA-signed certificate is. Although it is technically possible to continue using a snake oil or self-signed digital server certificate, doing so is extremely ill advised. Your users deserve the reassurance a valid certificate chain provides that their session is private. So, let's go ahead and look at replacing the temporary snake oil certificate with a real one.

# Installing Your Signed Digital Certificate

Rename and move the private key file server.key created earlier when you generated the CSR to the private key directory defined by the option ssl_key_file in dovecot.conf, overwriting the snake oil private key that comes bundled with Dovecot:

```
[curtis@spider ~]$ sudo mv server.key /etc/pki/dovecot/private/dovecot.pem
```

Once you've received your signed server certificate from the CA of your choice, rename and move the new signed certificate to the certificate directory defined by the option ssl_cert_file in dovecot.conf, overwriting the snake oil certificate:

```
[curtis@spider ~]$ sudo mv server.crt /etc/pki/dovecot/dovecot.pem
```

Some certificate authority vendors require an intermediate certificate bundle to be installed in order for the complete certificate chain to validate properly. An intermediate certificate or certificates can be a series of certificates that are needed to help a client follow the certificate chain all the way back to the root certificate. This is fine as long as each certificate validates to the next in the chain. Without the intermediate certificate, some server certificates will have a gap in the certificate chain. Figure 10-6 illustrates this situation, showing one additional intermediate certificate necessary to complete a certificate chain.

If this is the case with your vendor, simply obtain the bundled certificate file and copy the file into the same directory as your server certificate. Add the following line to dovecot.conf:

```
ssl_ca_file=/etc/pki/dovecot/ca-bundle.crt
```

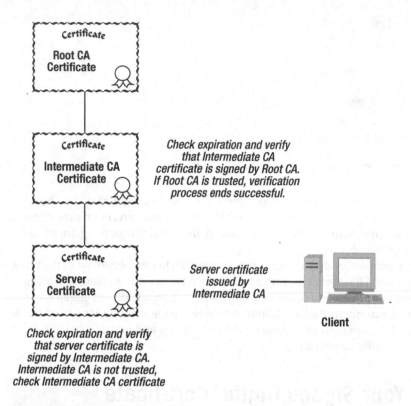

**Figure 10-6.** *Sometimes intermediate certificates are necessary to complete a certificate chain.*

Don't forget to restart Dovecot with the `service` command to put your changes into effect. The next time you connect to your secure services on your e-mail system with Thunderbird, you should not get any errors as your certificate fully validates!

## Summary

In this chapter, we covered a lot of general information about the two protocols used to secure various Internet communications: Secure Sockets Layer and Transport Layer Security. These concepts will apply to subsequent chapters as we use them again to secure other services on your e-mail system. We also finished our Dovecot configuration, adding the SSL and TLS options back into `dovecot.conf`. Lastly, I outlined the basics of generating a CSR and installing your certificate private key and signed certificate. If your CA of choice requires an intermediate certificate bundle to complete the chain to the root CA certificate, Dovecot can support that with no problem.

In Chapter 11, we're going to switch gears a little: we cover the Internet's most popular web server and start the process of installing and configuring web-based access for ubiquitous access to e-mail.

# PART 4

###

# Webmail

■ ■ ■

# Introducing and Installing Apache and PHP

**N**ow you have secure, remote access to e-mail on your system. That's great, but have you ever wondered why those free web-based e-mail accounts are so darn popular? If you think those accounts are only popular with poor saps who can't afford anything else, think again. Past personal experience shows that a staggering number of users forward the e-mail accounts that my organization provides them to their web-based e-mail accounts!

They don't forward their mail because those services are any better than ours. They primarily do it because we didn't offer, and many need or want universal access to their e-mail with any browser, from any computer, anywhere in the world. With web-based e-mail, you don't have to set up any e-mail clients, choose between POP3 and IMAP, or worry about whether or not your POP3 or IMAP session is secure. With a good web-based e-mail system, all you have to do is fire up your favorite browser and go.

In this chapter, we lay the foundation for offering a web-based e-mail service. The first step is building a web server, so this chapter shows you how to install and configure the open source Apache HTTP server. We also install and learn to use the PHP scripting language. Both Apache and PHP can provide the framework to build web-based e-mail access for your users. Then, in Chapter 12, we will build on this framework to complete your web-based e-mail service with the open source package SquirrelMail.

## Introducing the Apache HTTP Server

Apache is the most popular and widely used web server in the world. Development of the Apache server started in mid-1994 as a small, coordinated effort to update the then most-popular web server at the National Center for Supercomputing Applications (NCSA), at the University of Illinois at Urbana-Champaign. Eight core contributors formed the original Apache Group, and their efforts culminated in a public release in April 1995. After issuing several updates and completely overhauling and redesigning the code and documentation, not to mention renaming the server, Apache 1.0 was released in December 1995. A mere year after the Apache Group began their efforts, the Apache server surpassed NCSA's server as the most popular web server in the world. According to Netcraft web surveys, this is a distinction Apache has maintained every year since then (archived Netcraft web surveys can be found at http://news.netcraft.com/archives/web_server_survey.html).

The Apache Group further organized its efforts by forming the Apache Foundation (www.apache.org) in 1999. A nonprofit organization originally formed to provide formal organizational, financial, and legal support for the Apache web server project, the Apache Foundation has grown to include numerous other open source projects, including Spam-Assassin, the open source antispam product I introduce in Chapter 17.

## A Quick Word About the Hypertext Transfer Protocol

The *Hypertext Transfer Protocol (HTTP)* is the core of the World Wide Web. Although not specifically a mail-related protocol, it is the transport protocol used to present web-based e-mail to the user. The Apache web server is specifically designed to serve HTTP requests.

You're more familiar with HTTP than you might think. Look at a web address in your web browser. Chances are the address of the web page you're viewing has http:// prepended to it—this tells your browser to use HTTP to access the resource you're requesting.

If you do any online banking, you might notice that http:// in the address is replaced by https://, which simply denotes the address is accessed by HTTP wrapped in a SSL session. This secured HTTP session is based on the very same principles explained in Chapter 10. HTTPS, as HTTP over SSL is usually called, is simply a way to secure a web session with SSL. This chapter covers both HTTP and HTTPS to maximize your users' privacy and security.

---

**Note** The current HTTP revision, version 1.1, is defined in RFC2616 (www.ietf.org/rfc/rfc2616.txt).

---

## Surveying Methods for Serving Web Content

Originally designed simply to serve static textual information for research, the Web has evolved into a dynamic, multimedia medium. The Web is made up of linked media called *hypertext*, or text that contains embedded links to other texts. The primary means of linking texts and creating web pages is through the *Hypertext Markup Language (HTML)*.

Hypertext documents created and written in HTML are static. HTML was originally just a way to apply basic formatting, like centered and bold text, and to create links to text. Every time a static HTML web page is accessed, it appears exactly the same; it never changes unless the document is edited by somebody, and the updated text is downloaded. Hypertext documents created with HTML can also be dynamically changed programmatically through various client-side and server-side scripting languages. Let's take a quick look at some of the ways this is possible.

As the Web expanded in size and popularity, webmasters began to push the envelope, making HTML documents do new, wild things. The Web has become a multimedia experience with graphics, pictures, and animation. The need to present dynamic content has arisen, changing content on demand based on user interaction. Two basic ways of presenting dynamic content were developed: client-side and server-side scripting.

**■Note** HTML is a standard specification developed by the World Wide Web Consortium. More information about HTML, including extensions and updates to the original specification, can be found at www.w3c.org/MarkUp.

The best-known client-side mechanism is JavaScript, a scripting language that is processed by the client's system. In the past, JavaScript was slow, and webmasters couldn't guarantee complete compatibility among all web browsers. In addition, access to databases or other remote server resources was not possible with client-side scripting. Therefore, server-side scripting mechanisms have been developed. These are scripting languages that are processed on demand by the web server, putting most of the processing burden on the server and creating a mechanism compatible with clients of all kinds.

**■Note** A resurgence in the use of JavaScript can be found in AJAX. This is a new technique for developing dynamic and interactive Web content using a myriad of client- and server-side scripting languages, markup languages, and style sheets. For more information about AJAX development, check out Ryan Asleson's *Foundations of AJAX* (Apress, 2005).

Today, the most popular server-side language is the PHP hypertext preprocessor, PHP for short (www.php.net). It is a free, open source, multiplatform scripting language that is processed by the HTTP server when accessed by a client. PHP can be embedded inside an HTML document and used to create on-demand, dynamic content that is generated on the fly when it's accessed and presented as a static HTML document to the client. Think of it as an HTML document that has been personalized specifically for that client. PHP is at the core of SquirrelMail, our chosen web-based e-mail application (see Chapter 12).

**■Note** Although it's possible to run a PHP script from the command line like a shell script, PHP was truly meant to interact through an HTTP server like Apache, specifically designed to create and generate dynamic content.

# Installing Apache and PHP

Apache and PHP form the foundation on which SquirrelMail will be built. If you do not own or control your own web server, or do not wish to maintain your own web server, you could host SquirrelMail on the managed or hosted web service of your choice, provided they offer PHP that meets the specifications outlined later in this section. If so, you can skim or skip this section on the installation of Apache and PHP.

If you are using a Fedora Core system as outlined in Chapter 2, both Apache and PHP are available as RPM packages and are probably already installed. Otherwise, you can choose to install the RPM packages, or you can build them from their source distributions. In this chapter and subsequent chapters, I assume you're using the Fedora Core RPM package, but the general topics and the specific configuration discussed in these chapters should still apply to instances of Apache and PHP installed from source code. Whether you choose to install and maintain Apache and PHP as an RPM package or from the source code is a matter of personal preference, but as always, I prefer the RPM package whenever possible for easy maintenance.

## The Apache and PHP RPM Packages

The Apache RPM package name is not what you might expect. To determine whether Apache is installed on your Fedora Core system, you can use the following command to query the RPM database to see if the Apache httpd RPM package is already installed:

```
[curtis@mail ~]$ rpm -qv httpd
```

```
httpd-2.0.54-10.2
```

This command shows the version of Apache and the revision of the RPM package, if it is installed. Of course, your version may vary. If you get an error message indicating the package httpd is not installed, go ahead and install the Apache RPM and its dependencies with yum:

```
[curtis@mail ~]$ sudo yum install httpd
```

This command will search for and install, if found, the latest version of the Apache HTTP server available from the yum RPM package repositories you have configured on your system. In addition, any required prerequisite RPM packages are also downloaded and installed, if they aren't already.

The same process applies to PHP; first check if the PHP package is installed:

```
[curtis@mail ~]$ rpm -qv php
```

```
php-5.0.4-10.4
```

If you get an error or lack of output, install PHP and its dependencies with yum:

```
[curtis@mail ~]$ sudo yum install php
```

If you decide RPM packages are not an option, follow along the next section if you'd rather install the Apache HTTP server and PHP from their source distributions.

## The Apache and PHP Source Distributions

Installing Apache and PHP from their respective source distributions is as simple as anything else we've compiled and built so far. Again, Fedora Core offers everything you need in easy-to-manage and frequently updated RPM packages, but you might want the control and customization that building from source offers—the choice is yours.

Download the latest stable source distribution of the Apache web server from a mirror that's geographically close to you at http://httpd.apache.org/download.cgi. At the time of this writing, the latest stable version was 2.0.55. Always use the latest version recommended by the Apache developers to make sure you are not installing buggy, insecure, or out-of-date software.

As always, it's a good idea to check the MD5 signature to make sure that you got the entire file:

```
[curtis@mail ~]$ md5sum httpd-2.0.55.tar.gz
```

```
b45f16a9878e709497820565d42b00b9 httpd-2.0.55.tar.gz
```

Compare the MD5 signature with the signature given on the download pages; if they differ, you could have a corrupt or incomplete download.

Let's build Apache first. To begin, unpack the source distribution:

```
[curtis@mail ~]$ tar xzvf httpd-2.0.55.tar.gz
```

We're going to configure the Apache source with a few command-line arguments to manipulate the way it is built. The first option is --enable-so. It enables *dynamic shared objects* to allow us to add PHP as a loadable module after we've installed Apache. The second option is --enable-rewrite, and it turns on the rewrite module bundled with the Apache web server source code. The rewrite module is extremely useful and is necessary for the proper installation of SquirrelMail later. Lastly, just as we used SSL and TLS to secure POP3 and IMAP, we want to do the same thing for webmail, so we use the option --enable-ssl to build the Apache SSL module.

**Tip** I'm only suggesting two modules that I considered to be essential to every Apache installation. However, many more modules are available for all sorts of specific tasks. These are not essential to a working web server, but they do enhance Apache. For a list and description of standard modules bundled with the Apache web server source, visit http://httpd.apache.org/docs/2.0/mod/.

Putting those options together configures the Apache source code and prepares it to be compiled:

```
[curtis@mail ~]$ cd httpd-2.0.55/
[curtis@mail httpd-2.0.55]$ ./configure --enable-so ➥
--enable-rewrite --enable-ssl
```

Then compile and install the Apache web server source code:

```
[curtis@mail httpd-2.0.55]$ make
[curtis@mail httpd-2.0.55]$ sudo make install
```

Next, download the latest version of PHP source from www.php.net. At the time of this writing, the latest stable version was 5.05. Always use the latest recommended by the PHP developers to make sure you are not installing buggy, insecure, or out-of-date software.

As always, it's a good idea to check the MD5 signature to make sure you got the entire file:

```
[curtis@mail ~]$ md5sum php-5.0.5.tar.gz
```

```
ae36a2aa35cfaa58bdc5b9a525e6f451 php-5.0.5.tar.gz
```

Compare the MD5 signature with the signature given on the download pages; if they differ, then you could have a corrupt or incomplete download.

Next, unpack the source tarball:

```
[curtis@mail ~]$ tar xzvf php-5.0.5.tar.gz
```

Only the following configure option is necessary for our purposes; it tells PHP where to find the Apache apxs command. The Apache extension tool apxs is used to build and install new modules into an existing Apache installation:

```
[curtis@mail ~]$ cd ../php-5.0.5/
[curtis@mail php-5.0.5]$ ./configure --with-apxs2=/usr/local/apache2/bin/apxs
```

Next compile and install the PHP source:

```
[curtis@mail php-5.0.5]$ make
[curtis@mail php-5.0.5]$ sudo make install
```

Finally, copy the recommended PHP configuration file found in the PHP source distribution tarball to a systemwide location:

```
[curtis@mail php-5.0.5]$ sudo cp php.ini-recommended /usr/local/lib/php.ini
```

Whatever your choice of installation method, you're now ready to configure Apache and PHP. I think you'll find this an extremely easy thing to do—both Apache and PHP can get a working web server up and running with little effort.

# Configuring Apache and PHP

Now that you've got Apache and PHP installed, let's configure them. In this chapter, I will cover the essentials for creating a secure, working framework suitable for SquirrelMail. Advanced Apache configuration is beyond the scope of this book.

---

**Tip** The Apache HTTP server has become the most popular web server for good reason; its power and flexibility are unmatched by any and rivaled by none. For a detailed discussion on further Apache configuration, check out the most recent edition of *Pro Apache* by Peter Wainwright (Apress, 2004).

---

Apache is controlled by a series of runtime configuration directives found primarily in one configuration file, typically httpd.conf. The location will depend on whether you install from RPM or source code. If you build from source code, Apache is installed in /usr/local/ apache2/ by default. You should find httpd.conf in /usr/local/apache2/conf/. The source distribution splits configuration into two configuration files: `httpd.conf` and `ssl.conf`. As the file names imply, SSL-specific configuration directives go into `ssl.conf`; everything else goes in `httpd.conf`. The Fedora Core `httpd` RPM package places `httpd.conf` in `/etc/httpd/conf/`. The Fedora Core RPM installation splits the configuration into several logical files found in `/etc/httpd/conf.d/`. Splitting the files simply helps organize Apache configuration directives, but `httpd.conf` is always the primary configuration file called by Apache directly. All other configuration files are included by `httpd.conf` when read and parsed by Apache.

Go ahead and open `httpd.conf` in a text editor. The first configuration directive that should be changed is `ServerAdmin`; replace the default with a valid e-mail address, usually as follows:

```
ServerAdmin webmaster@example.com
```

`webmaster` has long been the de facto standard alias for the person or persons in charge of a web server and its content. Apache will use the `ServerAdmin` directive and the next directive, `ServerName`, to identify itself to the public.

You should find the `ServerName` directive a few lines further along. Remove the comment symbol from this directive and replace the default with the FQDN your organization chooses to use to identify this web server. For example, a good choice might be the FQDN of the server itself:

```
ServerName mail.example.com
```

You can optionally use a trailing colon and number to force Apache to serve on a specific port. If left out, Apache will default to the well-known TCP port 80. So, the previous configuration directive and the following one are equivalent:

```
ServerName mail.example.com:80
```

Do not add `http://` to the `ServerName` directive; that's only used for web browsers when fetching a web page. Also, do not forget to make sure the FQDN you choose is properly configured in your domain's DNS configuration.

You might be wondering if you're stuck with the same FQDN as your server itself or if you can serve up different server names from the same web server. Rest assured—this is quite possible with the Apache HTTP server. Once we complete the basic Apache configuration, I will introduce ways of doing so.

Next, note the default location for the `DocumentRoot` directive. This defines where Apache serves web files from. The Fedora Core RPM installation sets this as follows:

```
DocumentRoot /var/www/html/
```

The default for the source distribution is

```
DocumentRoot /usr/local/apache2/htdocs/
```

Without the `DocumentRoot` directive set, Apache will not know where to look for files when they are requested by an HTTP client. The `DocumentRoot` directive should be set to a valid directory path on your system. If an HTTP client requests the following URL:

```
http://mail.example.com/index.html
```

Apache would look for the file `index.html` in the following directory:

```
/var/www/html/index.html
```

or in

```
/usr/local/apache2/htdocs/index.html
```

depending on the DocumentRoot setting.

The last crucial step to basic Apache configuration is to configure the PHP module properly. To make the module available, the following lines must be added to your Apache configuration, if they are not there already. These Apache directives can go in httpd.conf or in a separate file like /etc/httpd/conf.d/php.conf, similar to the default Fedora Core configuration. If you installed the Fedora Core httpd RPM, then you can skip this part.

```
LoadModule php5_module modules/libphp5.so
AddHandler php5-script .php
AddType text/html .php
DirectoryIndex index.php index.html index.htm
```

The first directive, LoadModule, does just as its name implies. It effectively tells Apache to turn on the PHP module and make PHP available for preprocessing web pages containing PHP code. The next directive, AddHandler, tells Apache to use the PHP interpreter to preprocess any file ending with the file extension .php. The third directive, AddType, simply tells Apache that any file ending with the .php file extension is of the MIME type text/html (refer to Chapter 1 for more on MIME).

Finally, the DirectoryIndex directive tells Apache to treat a file named index.php, index.html, or index.htm as a directory index instead of listing the contents of the directory. This means if an HTTP client requests a URL with a directory name and a trailing /, then Apache will look for and serve, if found, index.php, index.html, and index.htm in that order. If none of the files listed in the DirectoryIndex directive are found, then Apache will try to list the contents of the directory.

## Opening Your System Firewall for HTTP Traffic

Before you can connect to your web server using HTTP, you must modify your system's network firewall to allow for corresponding traffic to pass through. Remember, your system firewall should be configured to deny all incoming network traffic and then explicitly allow specific network traffic through.

IANA has assigned HTTP to TCP port 80. Although it's technically possible to run any service on any port you wish, adhering to the port assignments given by IANA makes life simpler, as they are the generally recognized default ports for these services. Therefore, modern web browsers assume port 80 when you type a URL starting with http:// into the location or address bar.

To open TCP 80 for HTTP permanently on a Fedora Core system, add the following line to /etc/sysconfig/iptables:

```
-A RH-Firewall-1-INPUT -m state --state NEW -m tcp -p tcp --dport 80 -j ACCEPT
```

For reference, or more details about iptables, look back at Chapter 3. Don't forget to restart iptables to commit the changes. On Fedora Core, you can use the service command to do so:

```
[curtis@mail ~]$ sudo service iptables restart
```

```
Flushing firewall rules:                    [ OK ]
Setting chains to policy ACCEPT: filter     [ OK ]
Unloading iptables modules:                 [ OK ]
Applying iptables firewall rules:           [ OK ]
```

Next you'll learn how to start and stop Apache, as well as configure it to start up and shut down automatically. This is the final step before testing the HTTP server on your new e-mail system.

## Starting and Stopping Apache Manually

If Apache has been installed on a Fedora Core system from the RPM package, use the `service` command to start Apache for the first time with its init script (remember the init script matches the RPM package name):

```
[curtis@mail ~]$ sudo service httpd start
```

```
Starting httpd:                             [ OK ]
```

The source distribution comes with a control script called `apachectl` that can also be used to start and stop Apache; use it similarly to a traditional init script:

```
[curtis@mail ~]$ sudo /usr/local/apache2/bin/apachectl start
```

Of course, replace the path to `apachectl` with the installation root if it's different.

If Apache didn't start successfully (if the `service` or `apachectl` command reported failure), then check the Apache logs to see if the Apache daemon reported any errors. Typically, Apache logs are, at a minimum, separated into to two main files: `access_log` and `error_log`. These files can be found in `/var/log/httpd/` on a Fedora Core system or in `/usr/local/apache2/logs/` on a default source code installation.

Apache is usually pretty verbose in reporting the specific problem that keeps it from starting; it's probably just a simple typo, so check the previous section about configuring Apache earlier in this chapter. Also, if you specified a specific IP address or alternate port for Apache to listen on, make sure the IP address is actually configured properly on your system, and make sure no other applications are listening on the same address/port combination.

If you do not find anything useful in `error_log`, you could have a syntax error in one of your Apache configuration files. Apache can test your configuration files for such errors, using the following Fedora Core init script:

```
[curtis@mail ~]$ sudo service httpd configtest
```

```
Syntax error on line 249 of /etc/httpd/conf/httpd.conf:
Invalid command 'SeverName', perhaps mis-spelled or defined by a ➥
module not included in the server configuration
```

Similarly, you can use apachectl:

```
[curtis@mail ~]$ sudo /usr/local/apache2/bin/apachectl configtest
```

```
Syntax error on line 291 of /usr/local/apache2/conf/httpd.conf:
Invalid command 'SeverName', perhaps mis-spelled or defined by a ➡
module not included in the server configuration
```

In both cases, a typo seems to exist in httpd.conf. After fixing the typo, rerun the configuration test (the output of the initiscript and apachectl are identical):

```
[curtis@mail ~]$ sudo service httpd configtest
```

```
Syntax OK
```

Your Apache configuration should be free of any syntax errors. If Apache continues to fail to start, check the Apache logs again.

If you wish to shut down Apache manually, you can use the service command to do so:

```
[curtis@mail ~]$ sudo service httpd stop
```

```
Stopping httpd:                         [ OK ]
```

or you can use apachectl to do the same thing:

```
[curtis@mail ~]$ sudo /usr/local/apache2/bin/apachectl stop
```

Otherwise, you can configure Apache to automatically start up and shut down when appropriate, which I will show you next.

## Starting Apache Automatically

On a Fedora Core system using the Apache HTTP server installed from the RPM package, you can use the command chkconfig to configure an application to automatically start up and shut down. By default, Apache is preconfigured not to start up at all. You can see this by passing the --list argument to chkconfig:

```
[curtis@mail ~]$ sudo chkconfig --list httpd
```

```
httpd    0:off  1:off  2:off  3:off  4:off  5:off  6:off
```

As you can see, Apache is disabled for all runlevels. To configure Apache to start up when your system comes online, use the chkconfig command again:

```
[curtis@mail ~]$ sudo chkconfig --level 345 httpd on
```

To check your handiwork, compare the following output to the output from your previous check:

```
[curtis@mail ~]$ sudo chkconfig --list httpd
```

```
httpd    0:off  1:off  2:off  3:on  4:on  5:on  6:off
```

For a more complete introduction to Linux runlevels and Fedora Core init scripts, refer to Chapter 3. Now that Apache is turned on and listening for HTTP connections, let's test it!

## Testing Your Apache Installation

Open your favorite web browser and enter, into the location or address box, the domain you previously configured Apache to respond to with the ServerName directive. You should be presented with a generic Welcome test page similar to the one shown in Figure 11-1.

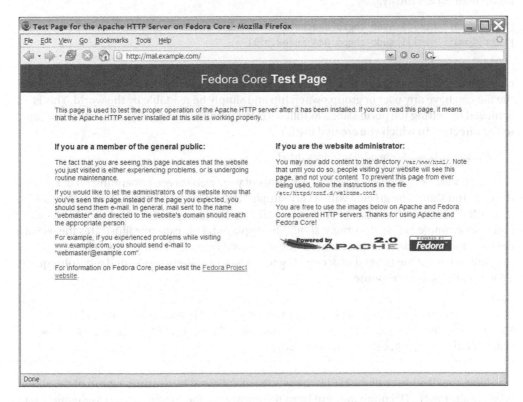

**Figure 11-1.** *The default Welcome test page greets you after a successful Apache installation.*

---

**Tip** The Mozilla project team, the fine people who developed Thunderbird, also offers a free, multiplatform, open source web browser called Firefox. It is feature-rich and extendable through add-ons called *extensions*. Downloads for several operating systems can be found at www.mozilla.org/products/firefox.

Now try creating a test HTML file in the root of your web directory as defined by the DocumentRoot directive. Call it index.html, or something similar, and use the following basic HTML code:

```
<html>
<head><title>Hello World!</title></head>

<body>
 <h1>Hello World!</h1>
</body>

</html>
```

For a file to be publicly accessible and served by Apache, the file permissions must allow the Apache web server to access the file. This can be achieved a couple of different ways. One way is to change the file group ownership to the group that Apache is running as and set group read access thusly:

```
[curtis@mail html]$ sudo chgrp apache index.html
[curtis@mail html]$ sudo chmod 644 index.html
```

However, if you do not own or host your own Apache web server, you may not be able to change file group ownership without having administrative access to the system. Therefore, the file can have any user or group ownership and simply be readable by the world. This is achieved by setting file permissions as follows (assuming you have read and write permissions to the directory in which you created the file):

```
[curtis@mail html]$ chmod 644 index.html
```

Now point your web browser to the address of your web server, appending /index.html to the end. You should be greeted with a very simple "Hello World!" message. Also note that if you leave off "index.html" and just visit the same URL as previously, the content should change, and your example HTML document should be displayed. This example illustrates the use of a default directory index file that is automatically served when a directory is accessed.

Take a look at the tail end of access_log to see your browser request and any subsequent Apache HTTP server response:

```
192.168.0.106 - - [08/May/2006:20:01:30 -0400] "GET /index.html HTTP/1.1" ➥
200 97 "-" "Mozilla/5.0 (X11; U; Linux i686; en-US; rv:1.7.12) Gecko/20060211 ➥
Fedora/1.0.7-1.3.fc3.legacy Firefox/1.0.7"
```

First, the IP address of the HTTP client is listed, followed by the time-stamp of the action. Next comes the HTTP command sent from the browser to the server, in this case requesting the file /index.html using HTTP version 1.1. Next, Apache logs the HTTP status code, 200 in this case, indicating that the request was received and successfully fulfilled.

The rest of the HTTP server response is the client operating system and browser identification information, as reported by the web browser itself. You'll find that this information is very useful for debugging problems and tracking usage statistics based on IP address, operating system, and browser.

# Testing Your PHP Installation

Before we can move on, we need to make sure that PHP is working properly and that Apache has been properly configured to load the PHP preprocessor accordingly. PHP has a function called phpinfo(), which creates a tabular list of configuration settings. This PHP function is a good test of your PHP installation and configuration, and it provides useful information regarding your installation.

In your server document root, defined by the Apache DocumentRoot directive, modify the index.html file created earlier, adding the following code snippet highlighted in bold:

```
<html>
<head><title>Hello World!</title></head>

<body>
 <h1>Hello World!</h1>
 <?php
  phpinfo();
 ?>
</body>

</html>
```

Now point your browser to the address of your web server, appending /index.html to the end of the address. You probably notice that no change has occurred. Hopefully, your first thought was to check access_log to see if the request came through OK (it probably did) and error_log for any errors indicating why you didn't get the expect results. Chances are, nothing is in error_log, either. If you use your web browser to view the page source, you see that the web page contains exactly what you entered into the file index.html, but the browser apparently ignored the PHP code you entered.

You might recall that PHP is a server-side scripting language, so the browser was right to ignore the code. You might also recall that we have to tell Apache which files to preprocess with the PHP module, and files ending with .html are not in the list. However, files with the .php extension are configured to be preprocessed by the PHP module. Therefore, rename index.html to helloworld.php with the mv command:

```
[curtis@mail html]$ sudo mv index.html helloworld.php
```

and point your browser to the new file, appending /helloworld.php to your server name. Success! Figure 11-2 shows an example of the output resulting from this exercise.

When your browser requests the file helloworld.php, Apache sees that it ends with the .php file extension, so the PHP module is used to preprocess the file before sending the results and content to the browser. If the PHP interpreter comes across the <?php starting tag, it knows to start looking for PHP code. In our example, its parses phpinfo(); as a valid function, evaluates the function, and adds the extra text we see to the HTML file on the fly. When the PHP interpreter reaches the closing tag (?>), processing stops until another opening tag is found, if one exists at all. We didn't include any of that content manually in helloworld.php, yet if you view the page source now, it appears there magically! The browser only knows that it received an HTML document to parse and display. However, before that ever happened, the web server processed it first, adding content dynamically.

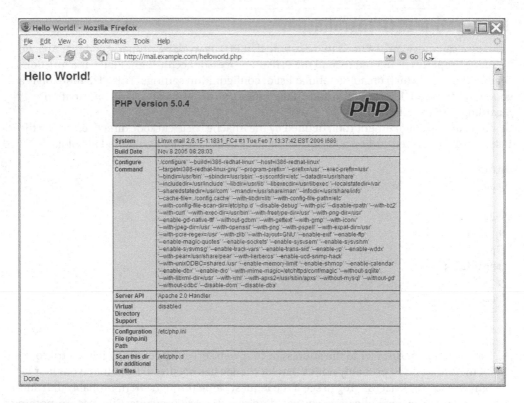

**Figure 11-2.** *You can use the function phpinfo() to test your PHP installation.*

---

■**Caution** The PHP `phpinfo()` function reveals information about your e-mail system and PHP installation and configuration. Although this information is useful for testing and debugging PHP, you might want to disable this function by adding `disable_functions = "phpinfo"` to `php.ini`.

---

Even though you've successfully installed, configured, and tested Apache and PHP, we still need to consider two more things: virtual hosts and secure HTTP sessions. Although what you have now might be sufficient to install and run SquirrelMail, you would be ill-advised to do so. Just as we secured POP3 and IMAP communication, best practices dictate that you also serve webmail over a secure channel. Before we configure Apache to secure HTTP sessions, let's take a look at virtual hosts.

# Introducing Apache Virtual Hosts

Virtual hosts are simply a way to run more than one web site from the same Apache server. Perhaps the FQDN for your e-mail system, by which users send and receive e-mail, is `mail.example.com`, but you'd rather have your users access webmail with the FQDN of `webmail.example.com`. Or perhaps you want a website that resolves to `mail.example.com` to be a simple web site listing your corporate e-mail services and make `webmail.example.com` resolve directly to webmail itself. Perhaps you'd even like to run your corporate web site `www.example.com` on the same server as webmail. All three scenarios are simple with virtual hosts.

There are two different kinds of virtual hosts. The first requires a separate IP address for each web site hosted on a server with Apache. The second allows you to run multiple web sites with the same IP address on a server with Apache. I'll introduce both types of virtual hosts and show you how virtual hosts apply to webmail.

## Configuring Apache Name-Based Virtual Hosts

The ability to support name-based virtual hosts is a powerful feature, and these hosts are the least complex of the two types, particularly for web hosting companies that provide hundreds or thousands of web sites or small businesses with limited numbers of precious (sometimes expensive) static IP addresses. With name-based virtual hosts, we can configure many individual web sites with FQDNs that resolve to the same static IP address but have entirely different content.

Previously in this book, I assumed our example e-mail system has a static IP address of `192.168.1.4`, which is configured in DNS to resolve to the FQDN `mail.example.com`. Earlier in this chapter, our example Apache configuration includes setting `ServerName` to `mail.example.com`. Say, for the sake of illustration, that we want `mail.example.com` to present different content from the web site `webmail.example.com`, which is also configured in DNS to resolve to `192.168.1.4`. We begin by turning on name-based virtual hosts in `httpd.conf`. First, search for the `NameVirtualHost` directive in `httpd.conf`; most likely, it is commented out as follows:

```
# Use name-based virtual hosting.
#
#NameVirtualHost *:80
```

Remove the comment symbol (#) from the last line of the previous example, or add the following directive to `httpd.conf`:

```
NameVirtualHost *:80
```

This directive will enable name-based virtual hosts for TCP port 80 on all configured IP addresses on your system. Enabling this directive is important; if you do not, you will not be able to configure more than one virtual host. Specifying port 80 is also important, as the port number will conflict when we configure SSL later if you do not.

To define a new virtual host, you use the `<VirtualHost>` directive. The `<VirtualHost>` directive might seem a bit different from other directives we've dealt with thus far, because it is enclosed in the opening and closing angle brackets (`<` and `>`). The `<VirtualHost>` directive begins a new group of directives that apply to a specific virtual host. The group of directives starting with a new `<VirtualHost>` is closed by the `</VirtualHost>` directive.

A virtual host can contain nearly any other Apache directive that would otherwise go into `httpd.conf`. However, virtual hosts inherit configuration settings from `httpd.conf` globally, so explicitly setting duplicate directives is not necessary. A name-based virtual host configuration for `mail.example.com` would, at a minimum, look something like the following one:

```
<VirtualHost *:80>
  DocumentRoot /var/www/html
  ServerName mail.example.com
</VirtualHost>
```

Replace /var/www/html with the directory that was assigned to the DocumentRoot directive, previously configured in this chapter. Now add the virtual host for webmail.example.com:

```
<VirtualHost *:80>
  DocumentRoot /var/www/html/webmail
  ServerName webmail.example.com
</VirtualHost>
```

Again, replace /var/www/html/webmail with the location where you'd like to create the new webmail.example.com document root directory. Note that, in this example, the two document roots overlap, which means content served as http://mail.example.com/webmail/ would be identical to http://webmail.example.com/. However, virtual hosts' document roots can be exclusive.

After making the changes to httpd.conf, save your changes, and run the configtest argument to the httpd init script or to apachectl to make sure you made no typos or syntax errors:

```
[curtis@mail ~]$ sudo service httpd configtest
```

```
Syntax OK
```

Create the new document root for the webmail.example.com virtual host, create an index.html with some distinguishing text for testing this new virtual host, and restart Apache with the httpd init script of apachectl:

```
[curtis@mail webmail]$ sudo service httpd restart
```

Now when you point your browser to http://mail.example.com/, you should still get the same old default test page, but when you visit http://webmail.example.com/, you should be presented with the content you added to index.html in /var/www/html/webmail/!

## A Quick Word About IP-Based Virtual Hosts

As mentioned previously, IP-based virtual hosts require a separate IP address for each web site, possibly requiring your system to be multihomed with multiple network adapters or virtual network interfaces. Under most circumstances, name-based virtual hosts are sufficient. However, the usefulness and necessity of IP-based virtual hosts might seem obvious when you consider securing HTTP connections with SSL.

# Securing HTTP with SSL

As we know from our discussion in Chapter 10, digital certificates are linked to a particular domain name. Although some certificates can have alternative domain names from the primary subjects that they are valid for, most certificates only apply to one specific host or domain name. When a web connection is secured using SSL, a web browser—the HTTP client—initiates the secure communication channel with the HTTP server, Apache in our case. Part of that negotiation is the certificate validation, the same process your e-mail uses to validate and negotiate a secure connection with your secure POP3 or IMAP server.

As we know, one of the tests for validation is that the domain in the URL requested by the HTTP client matches the subject of the digital certificate that was given by the HTTP server. If the two match, they must also resolve to the same IP address. If there is any inconsistency between the domains and the DNS resolution, the browser will warn you, indicating perhaps the communication channel is not properly secured with the intended HTTP server.

If you want to secure two web sites with SSL, you need two digital certificates (one for each web site) and you need to configure Apache virtual hosts for each secure web site on port 443, the traditional HTTPS port. However, if your system has only one IP address and you use name-based virtual hosts, the validation of one or both of the digital certificates will fail, depending on what the IP of the server resolves to. To prevent this failure, you must configure SSL virtual hosts as IP-based virtual hosts; each web site must have a unique IP address that resolves to the same domain used to access the web site and to create the digital certificate.

If you only want to secure one web site on your Apache web server, you won't have any conflict, but you still must configure at least the default SSL virtual host, including the special configuration necessary for the Apache SSL module.

## Introducing and Installing the Apache SSL Module

To secure web sites with SSL, you must have the Apache SSL module installed properly. If you installed the Fedora Core httpd RPM package, you simply need to make sure the Fedora Core mod_ssl RPM package is also installed:

```
[curtis@mail ~]$ rpm -qv mod_ssl
```

```
mod_ssl-2.0.54-10.3
```

This command shows the version of the Apache SSL module and the revision of the RPM package, if it is installed. Of course, your version may vary. If you get an error message indicating the package httpd is not installed, go ahead and install the mod_ssl RPM with the yum command:

```
[curtis@mail ~]$ sudo yum install mod_ssl
```

This command will search for and install, if found, the latest version of the Apache SSL module available from the yum RPM package repositories you have configured on your system. In addition, any required prerequisite RPM packages will also be downloaded and installed if they aren't already.

If you install Apache from source code, you must make sure you build the Apache source code with the configure script option --enable-ssl, as described previously in this chapter. That's it. Now you need to generate a digital certificate CSR and obtain a signed digital certificate.

Deciding whether or not to purchase a valid CA-signed certificate is up to you and depends your organization's specific needs. While I typically use self-signed certificates for personal systems, I would never consider running production, enterprise-quality services without a CA-signed certificate.

These days, you have the option to purchase a globally accepted and widely recognized server certificate from a number of vendors. Some are more recognized than others, but as long as you choose a reputable, industry-recognized vendor, the certificate is worth the money when compared to the piece of mind you give your users.

## Generating a CSR

To generate a CSR on a Fedora Core system, or virtually any other Linux operating system distribution, send the request to the CA of your choice for validation and signing using the openssl command. This also creates the server private key used to sign the certificate request. When you run this request, fill in the following bold code with the information for your organization. The most important part of this process is the Common Name, or CN for short; this must match the FQDN exactly as your users will type it into their web browser.

```
[curtis@mail ~]$ sudo openssl req -new -nodes ➥
-keyout server.key -out server.csr
```

```
Generating a 1024 bit RSA private key
.............................................++++++.....++++++
writing new private key to 'server.key'
-----
You are about to be asked to enter information that will be incorporated
into your certificate request.
What you are about to enter is what is called a Distinguished Name or a DN.
There are quite a few fields but you can leave some blank
For some fields there will be a default value,
If you enter '.', the field will be left blank.
-----
Country Name (2 letter code) [GB]:US
State or Province Name (full name) [Berkshire]:Ohio
Locality Name (eg, city) [Newbury]:Columbus
Organization Name (eg, company) [My Company Ltd]:Example Enterprise
Organizational Unit Name (eg, section) []:Information Technology
Common Name (eg, your name or your server's hostname) []:webmail.example.com
Email Address []:webmaster@example.com
```

```
Please enter the following 'extra' attributes
to be sent with your certificate request
A challenge password []:
An optional company name []:
```

Submit the server.csr file to the CA of your choice, and wait for the signed certificate to arrive. Hang on to the certificate private key server.key; we will use it and the signed server certificate you receive from the CA later, when configuring your SSL virtual host.

## Configuring the Default SSL Virtual Host

The SSL virtual host and SSL module configuration can go into httpd.conf or a separate file like /etc/httpd/conf.d/ssl.conf on a Fedora Core RPM installation. In any case, Apache comes with a default example configuration that constitutes the bare minimum for securing a web site with SSL. First, you must make sure that the SSL module is enabled as follows:

```
LoadModule ssl_module modules/mod_ssl.so
```

and add a Listen directive to open and listen for incoming connections on TCP port 443, the well-known port for HTTPS:

```
Listen 443
```

Now create the virtual host for the SSL web site. First, I'll give you the necessary configuration and afterward explain it in more detail:

```
<VirtualHost _default_:443>
  DocumentRoot /var/www/html/webmail
  ServerName webmail.example.com

  SSLEngine on

  SSLCertificateFile /etc/pki/tls/certs/server.crt
  SSLCertificateKeyFile /etc/pki/tls/private/server.key
  #SSLCertificateChainFile /etc/pki/tls/certs/server-chain.crt
  #SSLCACertificateFile /etc/pki/tls/certs/ca-bundle.crt
</VirtualHost>
```

By now, the first three lines should be familiar and self-explanatory. Make sure to change the DocumentRoot and ServerName directives as needed, but they should match the corresponding virtual host on port 80 that's not secured with SSL.

Next, the SSLEngine directive simply enables SSL for this virtual host; without it, you would just have another normal web site on port 443. The next four directives are important, as they configure your digital certificates for this SSL virtual host. First, the SSLCertificateFile should point to the path to the valid, signed server digital certificate you obtained through a CA or elsewhere. Second, the SSLCertificateKeyFile should point to the server digital certificate's private key generated when you created the CSR. The next two directives are optional and are only necessary if the certificate authority that signed your certificate requires intermediate certificates to chain to its root; these are obtained from the CA that signed your certificate, if they are necessary.

Don't forget to copy your server signed certificate, private key, and any necessary CA-certificate bundles to their appropriate locations as configured. Save your changes, test your configuration for syntax errors, and restart Apache for your changes to take affect. Before you can test your SSL virtual host configuration, you need to open HTTPS traffic through your system firewall.

## Opening Your System Firewall for HTTPS Traffic

Before you can connect to your web server using HTTPS, you must modify your system's network firewall to allow corresponding traffic to pass through. Remember, your system firewall should be configured to deny all incoming network traffic and then explicitly allow specific network traffic through.

IANA has assigned HTTPS to TCP port 443. Although it's technically possible to run any service on any port you wish, adhering to the port assignments given by IANA makes life simpler, as they are the generally recognized default ports for these services. Therefore, modern web browsers assume port 443 when you type a URL beginning with https:// into the location or address bar.

To open TCP 443 for HTTP permanently on a Fedora Core system, add the following line to /etc/sysconfig/iptables:

```
-A RH-Firewall-1-INPUT -m state --state NEW -m tcp -p tcp --dport 443 -j ACCEPT
```

For reference, or more details about iptables, review Chapter 3. Don't forget to restart iptables to commit the changes. On Fedora Core, you can use the service command to do so:

```
[curtis@mail ~]$ sudo service iptables restart
```

```
Flushing firewall rules:                    [ OK ]
Setting chains to policy ACCEPT: filter     [ OK ]
Unloading iptables modules:                 [ OK ]
Applying iptables firewall rules:           [ OK ]
```

Congratulations, you now have a complete Apache HTTP server implementation with virtual hosts and secure HTTP communication with SSL! When your users visit your web site and prepend https:// to the domain in their browser location or address bar, they can rest assured that communication between their browser and your server is secure and encrypted. Figure 11-3 shows an example session secured with SSL, as evidenced by the lock icon in the Firefox browser window status bar.

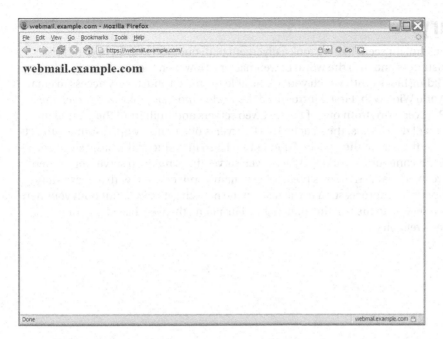

**Figure 11-3.** *Your users will be more comfortable when they see their sessions are secure, as indicated by the browser's padlock icon.*

# Further Apache and PHP Resources

Both Apache and PHP are extremely well-documented software packages. Documentation can be found locally on your Fedora Core system in /usr/share/doc/httpd-[version]/ and /usr/share/doc/php-[version]/, where [version] is replaced by the base version string of the RPM package installed. For example, at the time of this writing, the RPM package installed was httpd-2.0.54-10.3, so documentation can be found in /usr/share/doc/ httpd-2.0.54-10.3/. To check the version of Apache, run the following command:

[curtis@mail ~]$ **rpm -qv httpd**

```
httpd-2.0.54-10.3
```

In addition to the local documentation or the documentation found with the source distribution, the complete Apache manual, including extensive documentation on Apache configuration directives, can also be found on your system via the URL http://webmail. example.com/manual/ by replacing webmail.example.com with the FQDN of your web server.

If you're interested in PHP development, the PHP manual is available online at http://www. php.net/manual/. In addition, if you need help with a particular function, phpinfo() for example, simply add the function name to the end of php.net like so: www.php.net/phpinfo. Another worthy read for more-intensive treatment of PHP development is *Beginning PHP and MySQL 5: From Novice to Professional* by W. Jason Gilmore (Apress, 2006).

## Summary

In this chapter, it might seem like we took a divergent path out of the world of enterprise e-mail administrators and into the world of webmasters. However, the topics in this chapter are simply building blocks with which you will be able to create robust, easy access to email through the World Wide Web. First, I introduced the world's most popular web server, the Apache HTTP server. Born from one of the first web servers and built from the ground up by a small group of developers, the Apache HTTP server is one of many open source projects developed under the care of the Apache Foundation. I also introduced the basic steps necessary to install and configure a working Apache web server that's ready to serve web content. Finally, I showed you that PHP makes presenting dynamic web content with a heavy-duty server-side hypertext preprocessor a trivial task. In the next chapter, we'll put both your new e-mail and web servers to the test, introducing and installing the web-based e-mail application SquirrelMail.

# CHAPTER 12

∎∎∎

# Introducing and Installing SquirrelMail

**A**s an e-mail administrator, never underestimate how much your users rely on their e-mail. Certainly, industry-leading uptime and service availability are expected, as is the demand for ubiquitous access to e-mail.

If you have mobile users, you might find that they forward their e-mail to other accounts with webmail if your service doesn't offer web-based access. Sure, POP3 and IMAP are the de facto standards for remote e-mail access, but they both require a client application. Users who are constantly on the go might find themselves at Internet kiosks or on computers they don't control. In addition, many network administrators block outgoing SMTP traffic to any SMTP server other than their own; some even go as far as blocking POP3 and IMAP access to foreign servers. With blocks like these, even if your users find themselves with Internet access and their own e-mail clients on laptops, they may find they still cannot send or receive e-mail.

Webmail can mean nearly universal access to e-mail; every Internet-connected computer has a web browser. With a web-based e-mail application, your users can use a web browser to send, receive, and organize their e-mail from any network that allows normal Web traffic anywhere in the world. In this chapter, I'll introduce the open source package SquirrelMail, which has long been one of the most popular webmail packages.

## Introducing SquirrelMail—Webmail for Nuts!

SquirrelMail (www.squirrelmail.org) is a standards-based webmail package written in PHP. Despite its funny name and tagline, "Webmail for Nuts," SquirrelMail is one serious and professional software package. SquirrelMail attempts to provide the same basic functionality as other e-mail client applications while maintaining compatibility with all major web browsers. SquirrelMail supports the following basic features found in modern e-mail client applications:

- MIME support for proper e-mail attachment handling and multipart e-mail messages.

- Personal address book support, allowing easy message addressing and basic contact management.

- Complete IMAP e-mail folder access and manipulation, fully providing the abilities to add and remove remote e-mail folders and to organize e-mail into folders. Folders accessed with any regular IMAP e-mail client application are also accessible through SquirrelMail.

- Customization through user preferences and options, allowing your users to change the basic look and feel, default language, and other aspects of the SquirrelMail interface.

- Extendibility through plugins. Numerous plugins add a plethora of feature sets, including calendar, task, and note management. Later in this chapter, I will introduce a set of useful plugins that I suggest installing.

# Installing SquirrelMail

Like the other applications in this book, you have at least two options for installing the SquirrelMail webmail package, and both are introduced in this section. SquirrelMail is available as a Fedora Core RPM package, or you can download and install it from the source distribution found at www.squirrelmail.org. Although not included in the default Fedora Core installation outlined in Chapter 2, installing the SquirrelMail RPM is simple. This chapter and subsequent chapters assume you're using the Fedora Core RPM package, but the general topics and specific configuration discussed in these chapters should still apply to an instance of SquirrelMail installed from source code. Which of the two options you use to install and maintain Squirrel-Mail is a matter of personal preference, but as always, I prefer the RPM package for easy maintenance whenever possible.

## The SquirrelMail RPM Package

The SquirrelMail RPM package is one of the few packages not included in the standard Fedora Core installation discussed in Chapter 2. To verify that SquirrelMail is not installed, use the following command:

```
[curtis@mail ~]$ rpm -qv squirrelmail
```

```
package squirrelmail is not installed
```

This command shows the version of SquirrelMail and the revision of the RPM package if it is installed; in this case, it is not installed. However, SquirrelMail is available from the standard Fedora Core distribution as an optional software package. We know the RPM package is but a simple yum command away:

```
[curtis@mail ~]$ sudo yum install squirrelmail
```

This command searches for and installs, if found, the latest version of SquirrelMail available from the yum RPM package repositories configured on your e-mail system. In addition, any required prerequisite RPM packages are downloaded and installed, if they aren't already. Refer to Chapter 3 for information about yum and yum repositories.

The SquirrelMail RPM does a lot of work for you beyond the obvious installation of the SquirrelMail source files. The Fedora Core SquirrelMail RPM package installs the base Squirrel-Mail package in /usr/share/squirrelmail/. You might wonder how this is accessible to your users, since it is not within your configured Apache document root. Well, the RPM package also creates the Apache configuration file /etc/httpd/conf.d/squirrelmail.conf that contains the following Apache directive:

```
Alias /webmail /usr/share/squirrelmail
```

The Alias directive simply means that when you request the URL http://mail.example.com/ webmail/, Apache will not look for the physical directory webmail under its document root; instead, it knows to serve content from the directory /usr/share/squirrelmail/. Depending on what you choose for the web site address for your web server, you might want to change or override this Apache Alias directive.

For example, in Chapter 11, the example Apache installation includes virtual host directives for two web addresses: http://webmail.example.com and https://webmail.example.com. Using the default Alias directive installed by the SquirrelMail RPM, you can access the SquirrelMail package through either http://webmail.example/webmail/ or https://webmail. example.com/webmail/. Two different ways of accessing the same thing may seem redundant. Perhaps there's an expectation by you and your users that when they access webmail. example.com, the webmail login is immediately presented. To do this, you can override the default Alias directive by adding an Alias directive of your own to *both* of the webmail. example.com virtual hosts, which may be found in /etc/httpd/conf/httpd.conf and /etc/httpd/conf.d/ssl.conf (see Chapter 11). Add the following Apache directive between the appropriate <VirtualHost> and </VirtualHost> directives in your Apache configuration:

```
Alias / /usr/share/squirrelmail/
```

Now when you test your SquirrelMail installation later in this chapter, it will be accessible as the root of your webmail virtual host server name.

In addition to the source files that constitute the SquirrelMail web application itself, there is also a temporary attachment upload directory. This directory on the web server acts as a temporary storage location for files that are uploaded from a client's computer and sent as attachments to an e-mail message. Once the message and message attachments are sent through the SMTP server, the local, intermediate copy of the file is removed from the upload directory. The cron script /etc/cron.daily/squirrelmail.cron cleans up this directory daily, removing anything abandoned for more than ten days. The directory /var/spool/squirrelmail/attach/ is the default location created for this purpose.

A location to store user preferences and data is also created in /var/lib/squirrelmail/prefs/. This directory also contains default user preferences, which all users inherit if they do not customize their environments.

If you decide RPM packages are not an option, follow the instructions in the next section to install SquirrelMail from the source distribution.

## The SquirrelMail Source Distribution

Installing SquirrelMail from the source distribution is a very simple and straightforward process. To install from source code, download the latest stable source distribution from www.squirrelmail.org. At the time of this writing, this was version 1.4.6. Always use the latest version recommended by the SquirrelMail developers to make sure you are not installing buggy, insecure, or out-of-date software.

As always, it's a good idea to check the MD5 signature to make sure you have the entire file:

```
[curtis@mail ~]$ md5sum squirrelmail-1.4.6.tar.gz
```

```
da9e22416fca21ed0636458641187cdb squirrelmail-1.4.6.tar.gz
```

Make sure to compare the MD5 signature with the signature given on the download pages; if they differ, you could have a corrupt or incomplete download.

To begin the SquirrelMail installation, unpack the source distribution:

```
[curtis@mail ~]$ tar zxvf squirrelmail-1.4.6.tar.gz
```

SquirrelMail is written in PHP, and PHP code does not need to be compiled into system binaries like other applications we've installed so far. However, SquirrelMail and the Squirrel-Mail environment must be set up properly.

## Copying the SquirrelMail Source Files

First, you must decide where to install the SquirrelMail source files. These are the files accessed and served by the Apache web server and constitute the SquirrelMail package itself. The most logical place would be somewhere inside the document root of your Apache server as defined by the DocumentRoot directive in your Apache configuration.

For instance, presume the document root of your Apache installation is /usr/local/apache2/htdocs/, the default for the source distribution of the Apache HTTP server. Creating a physical directory /usr/local/apache2/htdocs/webmail/ and copying the SquirrelMail source files into that directory makes your SquirrelMail installation Web accessible through the URL http://mail.example.com/webmail/, assuming the FQDN of your web server is mail.example.com.

Of course, if you use the example Apache configuration in Chapter 11, this also makes SquirrelMail accessible through the URL http://webmail.example.com, because the examples in Chapter 11 create a name-based virtual host for webmail.example.com and configure the document root to be inside the document root of the default website mail.example.com.

Now that you've decided where to install SquirrelMail, let's get to work. First, create the web directory of your choice, if it doesn't already exist, and make sure it has the appropriate permissions to make it Web accessible:

```
[curtis@mail ~]$ sudo mkdir /usr/local/apache2/htdocs/webmail/
[curtis@mail ~]$ sudo chmod 755 /usr/local/apache2/htdocs/webmail/
```

Next, move the SquirrelMail source files from the source tarball to the new web directory:

```
[curtis@mail ~]$ cd squirrelmail-1.4.6
[curtis@mail squirrelmail-1.4.6]$ sudo mv class/ config/ functions/ ➥
help/ images/ include/ index.php locale/ plugins/ src/ themes/ ➥
/usr/local/apache2/htdocs/webmail/
```

Make sure the SquirrelMail source files and directories are set to the appropriate permissions:

```
[curtis@mail squirrelmail-1.4.6]$ cd /usr/local/apache2/htdocs/webmail
[curtis@mail webmail]$ find . -type d | xargs sudo chmod 755
```

This last command finds all directories, starting in the current working directory, denoted by the period (.), and assigns that list as the argument to the command sudo chmod 755 with the xargs command. See the find(1) and xargs(1) man pages for other uses of those common commands. Repeat the previous step, but use the find command to search for all files:

```
[curtis@mail webmail]$ find . -type f | xargs sudo chmod 644
```

Next, you must choose and create a location for uploading e-mail attachments.

## Creating the SquirrelMail Attachment Upload Directory

A temporary attachment upload directory must be created. This directory on the web server acts as a temporary storage location for files that are uploaded from a client's computer and sent as attachments to e-mail messages. Once the messages and message attachments are sent through the SMTP server, the local intermediate copy of the file is removed from the upload directory.

The temporary attachment directory must be writeable by the web server itself and must be fairly sizable. Otherwise, the web server won't be able to save the file, and your users won't have enough space to send attachments. This directory can be in any arbitrary location, for example, /var/spool/squirrelmail/attach/.

Now create the temporary attachment upload directory:

```
[curtis@mail ~]$ mkdir -p /var/spool/squirrelmail/attach/
```

and make sure it is secured, so no users can snoop and see other users' possibly private e-mail, but system administrators and the Apache web server still have read and write access:

```
[curtis@mail ~]$ chown apache:wheel /var/spool/squirrelmail/attach/
[curtis@mail ~]$ chmod 770 /var/spool/squirrelmail/attach/
```

This command assumes that your Apache server is running as the apache user and that you are using the wheel group for system administrators.

## Creating the SquirrelMail User Preferences Location

Lastly, you'll need to specify a location to store user preferences and data. The user preferences directory is self-explanatory, but what might not be immediately obvious is that the directory must also be writable by the Apache web server and secured from other users. Remember, SquirrelMail is served and run by the same user as your Apache instance (the apache user, by default), not by individual users themselves. This directory, too, can be in any arbitrary location, for example, /var/lib/squirrelmail/prefs/.

Create the user preferences directory:

```
[curtis@mail ~]$ mkdir -p /var/lib/squirrelmail/prefs/
```

and make sure it is secured, so no users can snoop and see other users' possibly private e-mail, but system administrators and the Apache web server still have read and write access:

```
[curtis@mail ~]$ chown apache:wheel /var/lib/squirrelmail/prefs/
[curtis@mail ~]$ chmod 770 /var/lib/squirrelmail/prefs/
```

This command assumes that your Apache server is running as the apache user and that you are using the wheel group for system administrators.

Finally, copy the user preferences index document and the global default preferences from the source distribution to the user preferences directory:

```
[curtis@mail squirrelmail-1.4.5]$ sudo mv data/* /var/lib/squirrelmail/prefs/
[curtis@mail squirrelmail-1.4.5]$ sudo chown apache:wheel ➥
/var/lib/squirrelmail/prefs/*
[curtis@mail squirrelmail-1.4.5]$ sudo chmod 440 /var/lib/squirrelmail/prefs/*
```

Whatever your choice of installation method, you're now ready to configure SquirrelMail. I think you'll find this an extremely easy thing to do—just a few more steps to get a working webmail system up and running.

# Configuring SquirrelMail

Whether you install SquirrelMail from the Fedora Core RPM or from the source distribution, SquirrelMail configuration is identical. Although the SquirrelMail package itself is written in the PHP scripting language, you do need to use the Perl programming language to configure SquirrelMail. Don't fret—Perl is almost certainly installed on your chosen Linux system.

The script conf.pl is used to customize your local SquirrelMail installation. The script is a menu-driven utility that edits the actual configuration files for you. It is found in the configuration subdirectory of the SquirrelMail web directory, usually /usr/share/squirrelmail/config/conf.pl, if you install by RPM, or /usr/local/apache2/htdocs/webmail/config/conf.pl, if you install from source distribution following my example installation in this chapter. Let's run through some of the important configuration options:

```
[curtis@mail ~]$ /usr/share/squirrelmail/config/
[curtis@mail config]$ sudo ./conf.pl
```

```
SquirrelMail Configuration : Read: config.php (1.4.0)
---------------------------------------------------------
Main Menu --
1. Organization Preferences
2. Server Settings
3. Folder Defaults
4. General Options
5. Themes
6. Address Books
7. Message of the Day (MOTD)
8. Plugins
9. Database
10. Languages

D. Set pre-defined settings for specific IMAP servers
```

```
C  Turn color off
S  Save data
Q  Quit

Command >>
```

First, type **1**, and press Enter to change Organization Preferences. Change each entry where appropriate to match your organization's specific information. Type **r**, and press Enter to return to the main menu when finished.

Next, type **2**, and press Enter to change Server Settings. You are presented with the following menu with several configurable options:

```
SquirrelMail Configuration : Read: config_default.php (1.4.0)
---------------------------------------------------------
Server Settings

General
-------
1. Domain          : example.com
2. Invert Time     : false
3. Sendmail or SMTP    : SMTP

A. Update IMAP Settings  : localhost:143 (other)
B. Update SMTP Settings  : localhost:25

R  Return to Main Menu
C  Turn color on
S  Save data
Q  Quit

Command >>
```

Modify the domain to match your organization's primary e-mail domain (*not* the FQDN of your mail or web servers), example.com for example.

Next, modify the sendmail or SMTP option by typing **3**, and pressing Enter. SquirrelMail must be able to send e-mail, and it can do that either by invoking the system sendmail command directly or using SMTP. Although invoking sendmail directly might be slightly more efficient, that option is not necessarily the most secure. In addition, outgoing mail won't be processed through your customized filters (set up in Chapters 14 and 18). Finally, using SMTP allows for the ability to run SquirrelMail on a web server that is not the same physical system as your mail server itself, separating services into a redundant infrastructure if desired. I recommend typing **2** and pressing Enter to configure SquirrelMail to use SMTP.

Type **a**, and press Enter to update IMAP Settings. SquirrelMail depends on IMAP, whether the IMAP server is local or remote. For the sake of simplicity, let's assume you are running SquirrelMail on the same server that's running IMAP, so keep option 4 set to localhost. If you're connecting the IMAP server on the local host, you do not need to add the overhead of SSL and TLS, as connecting to your e-mail system through the loopback network interface localhost is secure. However, if your webmail server is a different system than your mail server, enter the FQDN of the IMAP server. In this case, it behooves you to connect over a secure, encrypted channel with SSL or TLS.

Change option 8 to set the server software option to other, as we are not running any of the listed IMAP servers. Don't worry; there is no danger in this. Integrating SquirrelMail with some IMAP servers requires SquirrelMail to invoke particular workarounds or features specific to the IMAP server. In this case, none are necessary with Dovecot. Type **r**, and press Enter to once again return to the main menu.

Once back to the main menu, type **4**, and press Enter to change General Options. You are presented with the following menu with several configurable options:

```
SquirrelMail Configuration : Read: config_default.php (1.4.0)
---------------------------------------------------------
General Options
1. Data Directory        : ../data/
2. Attachment Directory  : $data_dir
3. Directory Hash Level  : 0
4. Default Left Size      : 150
5. Usernames in Lowercase : false
6. Allow use of priority  : true
7. Hide SM attributions   : false
8. Allow use of receipts  : true
9. Allow editing of identity : true
   Allow editing of name    : true
   Remove username from header : false
10. Allow server thread sort  : false
11. Allow server-side sorting  : false
12. Allow server charset search : true
13. Enable UID support       : true
14. PHP session name        : SQMSESSID

R  Return to Main Menu
C  Turn color on
S  Save data
Q  Quit

Command >>
```

The two important options to change here are options 1 and 2: the Data Directory (user preferences) and the temporary attachment upload directory, respectively. Set these to their respective directory paths, which were created by the RPM package or manually if you installed SquirrelMail from the source distribution. Return to the main menu one last time by typing **r** and pressing Enter.

I've outlined the few settings that need to be changed at a minimum; you might want to read more about the other options and decide whether you'd like to change them from their defaults. Tweaking these setting may be necessary under special circumstances, but the defaults suffice for most typical installations.

Once you're finished making changes, type **s**, and press Enter to save your changes. Type **q**, and press Enter to quit the configuration utility. Congratulations—you're finished configuring SquirrelMail! Let's test your new SquirrelMail webmail installation.

# Testing Your SquirrelMail Installation

After you run the configuration utility, it suggests testing your installation. But first, make sure you've restarted Apache so that changes to its configuration take affect:

`[curtis@mail config]$` **`sudo service httpd restart`**

```
Stopping httpd:                      [ OK ]
Starting httpd:                      [ OK ]
```

Now try pointing your favorite Internet web browser to the URL https://webmail.example.com/src/configtest.php, replacing webmail.example.com with the FQDN of your web server. Please keep in mind from here on out that the exact URL may change based on your choices that deviate from the example installation outlined throughout this book. At the very least, your server name will be different. If you did not decide to alias SquirrelMail to the root of your website virtual host, as I suggested earlier in this chapter, the path to configtest.php might also be different (/webmail/src/configtest.php, for example). Figure 12-1 shows example output from the SquirrelMail configuration test.

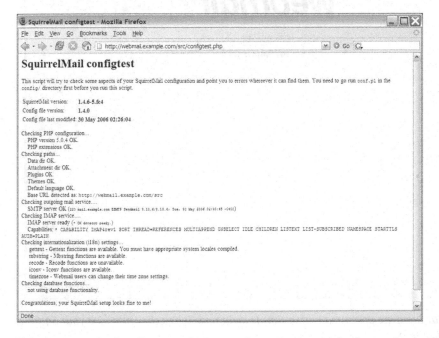

**Figure 12-1.** *SquirrelMail can perform a configuration test to check your SquirrelMail configuration for errors.*

Check the contents of this page to make sure no errors or problems were reported. At this point, you can confirm that the proper SMTP and IMAP server settings were applied. If the bottom of the webpage reads "Congratulations, your SquirrelMail setup looks fine to me!" you've successfully installed and configured SquirrelMail, and you're ready to log in for the first time. You can log in by pointing your web browser to https://webmail.example.com or clicking the "Login now" link at the bottom of the configuration test page.

Either method should bring up the SquirrelMail login page, shown in Figure 12-2, customized with your corporate name as configured previously. Log in with the same username and password you use to log in to your e-mail system interactively. You now have a fully functional e-mail client accessible through any modern web browser from anywhere in the world.

---

■**Caution** Surely the importance of creating and configuring a proper SSL Apache virtual host (see Chapter 11) is obvious by this point. You would be ill-advised to support authentication into your webmail system through insecure means instead of through a secure HTTP session.

---

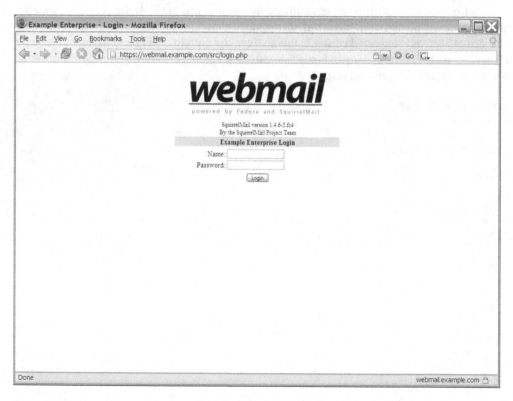

**Figure 12-2.** *Your users are presented with a simple login page when they first visit your Squirrel-Mail webmail system.*

One you've successfully logged into SquirrelMail, you will see your Inbox (see Figure 12-3). If you still have any of the previous test messages sent to test your e-mail system, they should be there. I think you will find the user interface as intuitive as any other full-featured desktop e-mail application.

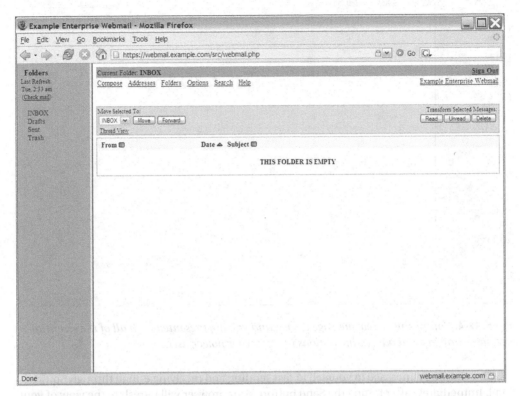

**Figure 12-3.** *Just like any desktop e-mail application, the first thing you will see after logging in to SquirrelMail is your Inbox.*

Composing a new e-mail message is easy. Simply click on the Compose link at the top of the page to open the e-mail composition window, shown in Figure 12-4. You'll find that all the standard features are there, including the ability to carbon copy or blind carbon copy, add a personal e-mail signature, set a message priority level, and request a return receipt when a message is successfully delivered and read. In addition, you can add any number of attachments to a message by browsing for a file and clicking the Add button individually for each attachment. When you're finished, click the Send button to send the message immediately, or click the Save Draft button to save the message for later.

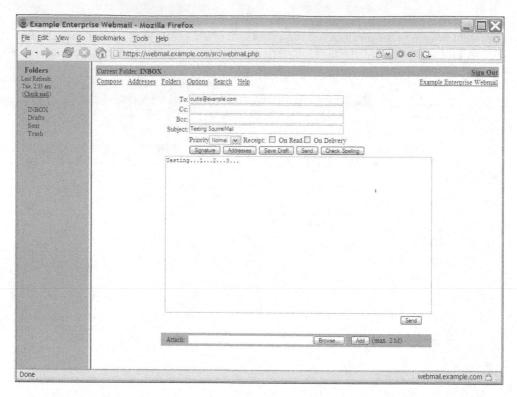

**Figure 12-4.** *Composing a new message is easy, and you are presented with all of the essential message drafting and addressing options necessary for power users.*

Try sending a message to yourself to test sending and receiving e-mail through Squirrel-Mail. Immediately after hitting the Send button, your browser will refresh to the view of your Inbox again. If your test message isn't there already, simply click the Inbox link in the folder index list on the left side of the screen to check for new mail. Click on the subject of any new message you've received to view the message contents, download any attachments, reply to or forward the message, move the message to another e-mail folder, or delete the message. An example message viewed with SquirrelMail is shown in Figure 12-5.

Once you've tested SquirrelMail by successfully sending and receiving e-mail through SquirrelMail and your e-mail system, explore the interface further. I've only scratched the surface of the basic features you'd expect from an e-mail application. In the next section, I discuss some of the more advanced and unique features of SquirrelMail itself, which enhance your users' experience.

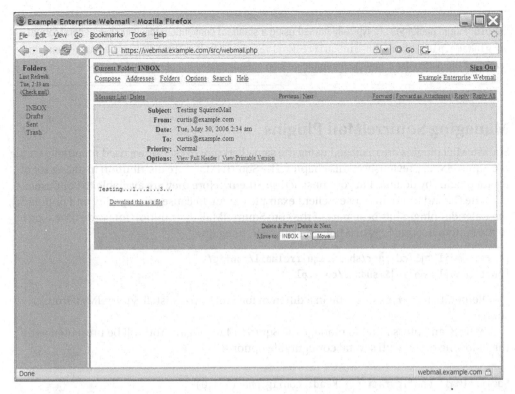

**Figure 12-5.** *Reading e-mail is just as easy as composing new messages. You can easily reply to, forward, or delete messages, or move them to another e-mail folder.*

# Advanced SquirrelMail Features

SquirrelMail aims to be a complete web-based e-mail solution and, in many ways, can be a wholly adequate replacement for the average e-mail client. Therefore, aside from the normal e-mail functions, SquirrelMail has several other advanced features available. For example, a full-featured address book is available in the base installation. You might be surprised to find other features available through SquirrelMail that you expect to find in any of the modern desktop e-mail applications, for example, complete support for remote IMAP preferences and folder manipulation, custom display preferences, and the ability to view full e-mail headers. One of the most powerful features of SquirrelMail is the inherent ability to extend the basic feature set of SquirrelMail with additional feature plugins.

## Introducing SquirrelMail Plugins

SquirrelMail supports a plugin system that allows developers to create add-ons to enhance various aspects of the SquirrelMail webmail package. *Plugins* are additional packages that allow you to enhance and customize your SquirrelMail installation. Many plugins have been developed by other SquirrelMail users like you, who found the need for a particular feature and shared their work with the rest of the SquirrelMail community. You can find an official list of community-supported plugins on the SquirrelMail website www.squirrelmail.org.

**■Note** Plugin packages are typically named using a standard convention, following the general format pluginName.pluginVersion-minSquirrelMailVersion.tar.gz. This tells you the plugin name, the version of the plugin itself, and the minimum version of SquirrelMail the plugin requires.

## Managing SquirrelMail Plugins

SquirrelMail plugins are managed using the same Perl conf.pl script we used to initially configure SquirrelMail previously in this chapter. The SquirrelMail core distribution installs a set of useful plugins by default, but you must activate them before they are available to your users.

The Calendar plugin is an excellent example plugin. Because of its quality and popularity, the Calendar plugin has been part of the core SquirrelMail distribution for some time. Log in to the system hosting SquirrelMail, and run conf.pl again:

```
[curtis@mail ~]$ cd /usr/share/squirrelmail/config/
[curtis@mail config]$ sudo ./conf.pl
```

Remember, conf.pl might be in a different location if you install SquirrelMail from source.

Type **8**, and press Enter to manage the SquirrelMail plugins. You will be presented with the following menu with several configurable options:

```
SquirrelMail Configuration : Read: config.php (1.4.0)
---------------------------------------------------------
Plugins
 Installed Plugins
  1. delete_move_next
  2. squirrelspell
  3. newmail

 Available Plugins:
  4. fortune
  5. abook_take
  6. info
  7. mail_fetch
  8. bug_report
  9. calendar
  10. message_details
  11. spamcop
  12. administrator
  13. listcommands
  14. translate
  15. sent_subfolders
  16. filters
```

```
R  Return to Main Menu
C  Turn color off
S  Save data
Q  Quit

Command >>
```

This output is from the Fedora Core RPM installation of SquirrelMail. As you can see, 16 plugins are available with the SquirrelMail core, three of which are already installed by default.

To activate a new plugin from the list of available plugins, simply select the plugin from the menu. For example, to activate the Calendar plugin, select **9**, and press Enter. You should find that the screen refreshes, and Calendar is now an installed plugin:

```
SquirrelMail Configuration : Read: config.php (1.4.0)
---------------------------------------------------------
Plugins
 Installed Plugins
  1. delete_move_next
  2. squirrelspell
  3. newmail
  4. calendar

 Available Plugins:
  5. fortune
  6. abook_take
  7. info
  8. mail_fetch
  9. bug_report
  10. message_details
  11. spamcop
  12. administrator
  13. listcommands
  14. translate
  15. sent_subfolders
  16. filters

R  Return to Main Menu
C  Turn color off
S  Save data
Q  Quit

Command >>
```

Type **s**, and press Enter to save your changes. Type **q**, and press Enter to quit conf.pl. If you're still logged into SquirrelMail, log out and log in again. A link for your own personal calendar should be available in the top navigation links (right after Help)! Click on the Calendar link to be presented with the current month view, shown in Figure 12-6.

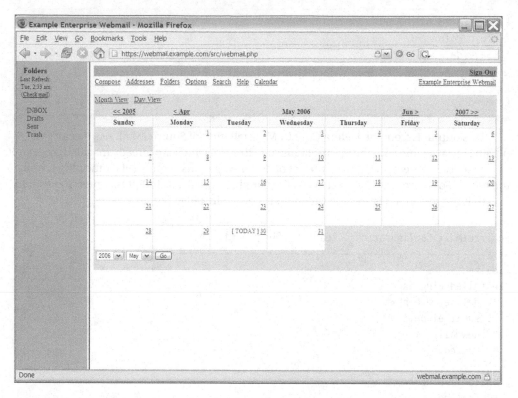

**Figure 12-6.** *Activating the SquirrelMail Calendar plugin provides your users with a web-based personal calendar application inside SquirrelMail.*

Perhaps you need a plugin that's not already available in your SquirrelMail installation but is available for download. No sweat—using a downloadable plugin is nearly as easy as using an installed one, requiring just one extra step. Let's say, for example, you'd like to provide a mechanism for your users to change their passwords themselves. A Change Password plugin is available that offers this functionality.

First, download the latest version of the Change Password plugin from www.squirrel-mail.org, which is change_passwd-4.0-1.2.8.tar.gz at the time of this writing. Next, move or copy the plugin tarball to the plugins directory of your SquirrelMail installation, which is /usr/share/squirrelmail/plugins/, if you installed the Fedora Core RPM, or /var/www/html/webmail/plugins/, if you installed from source following the examples in this book:

```
[curtis@mail ~]$ sudo mv change_passwd-4.0-1.2.8.tar.gz ➥
/usr/share/squirrelmail/plugins/
```

In addition to the Change Password (change_passwd) plugin itself, using this particular plugin also requires version 1.3 of the Compatibility (compatibility) plugin, downloadable from the same location as change_passwd. Move or copy the Compatibility plugin to the SquirrelMail plugins directory:

```
[curtis@mail ~]$ sudo mv compatibility-1.3.tar.gz /usr/share/squirrelmail/plugins/
```

and unpack the two plugin tarballs inside the plugins directory:

```
[curtis@mail ~]$ cd /usr/share/squirrelmail/plugins/
[curtis@mail plugins]$ sudo tar zxvf change_passwd-4.0-1.2.8.tar.gz
[curtis@mail plugins]$ sudo tar zxvf compatibility-1.3.tar.gz
```

I'm sure you can guess that the final step is to run conf.pl to activate the installed plugins the same way we did to activate the Calendar plugin. You're right, but before doing so, you should always check each new plugin to see if there are any individual prerequisite steps. Check for a README or INSTALL file in each individual plugin directory for any additional steps necessary. For example, the Change Password plugin does require a bit of modification and customization for your individual system before it can be activated.

First, according to the change_passwd plugin's INSTALL file, you must copy the sample plugin configuration file and modify it to match your specific system:

```
[curtis@mail ~]$ cd /usr/share/squirrelmail/plugins/change_passwd/
[curtis@mail change_passwd]$ sudo mv config.php.sample config.php
[curtis@mail change_passwd]$ sudo vi config.php
```

Simply look over the few available plugin configuration options. The configuration file config.php is a PHP script, so the syntax follows that of the PHP programming language. For example, any line starting with // is a comment and is ignored by the PHP preprocessor. For most Linux systems, the defaults are sufficient. However, you might want to note the following option:

```
// Set this to the minimum length of passwords you want
// to enforce. Set to zero to disable this check
//
$minimumPasswordLength = 8;
```

and change this option to reflect the password requirements for your organization. In addition, using the following two options is good practice:

```
// Set this to 1 if you want the user to have to enter
// their new password twice. Set to zero otherwise,
// but why would you do that?
//
$confirmNewPass = 1;
```

```
// Set this to 1 to require the user to enter their current
// password in order to change it (FreeBSD ('pw' utility)
// users typically set this to zero; others can (and should!)
// leave this as is.
//
$confirmOldPass = 1;
```

The last thing you need to do to configure the Change Password plugin is to make sure the permissions and ownership on the chpasswd command are set correctly. This binary will actually change the password for the user and is called by the SquirrelMail change_passwd plugin. Set this utility to be owned by the user running your web server, typically the apache user:

```
[curtis@mail change_passwd]$ sudo chown root:apache chpasswd
```

and assign sufficiently secure file permissions:

```
[curtis@mail change_passwd]$ sudo chmod 4750 chpasswd
[curtis@mail change_passwd]$ ls -l chpasswd
```

```
-rwsr-x--- 1 root apache 17917 Apr 25 2004 chpasswd
```

That's it for the change_passwd plugin. Now check the README and INSTALL files in the Compatibility plugin directory. You should find that the Compatibility plugin does not require anything special, so you're finished with the installation and preconfiguration of these plugins. Once you're finished, run conf.pl to activate the Change Password plugin the same way we activated the Calendar plugin. The Compatibility plugin doesn't add any features itself, only additional functionality that other plugins like change_passwd use, so it does not need to be activated like the Calendar or Change Password plugins.

The next time you log in to your SquirrelMail installation, select the Options link from the top navigation. You should find a new Change Password option, which, when clicked, offers the ability to change your password. Figure 12-7 shows what users will see when they successfully change their passwords using the SquirrelMail Change Password plugin.

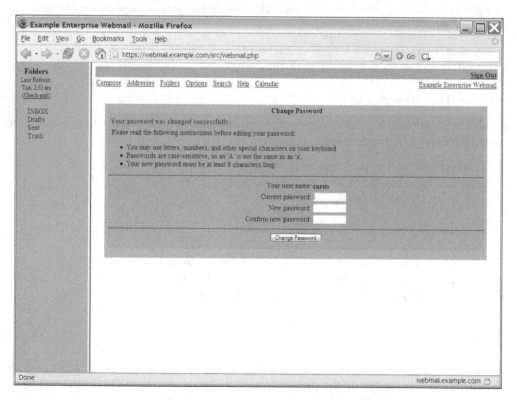

**Figure 12-7.** *Users can easily change their passwords with a SquirrelMail plugin.*

Another interesting feature of SquirrelMail is the ability to change the SquirrelMail interface itself. Let's take a look how easy it is to customize the look and feel of SquirrelMail.

## Customizing the SquirrelMail Interface

Various aspects of the look and feel of SquirrelMail are customizable without having to make direct changes to the SquirrelMail source files. When you initially run conf.pl, you edit various organization details, including the name of your company. It should be obvious where this is used, since the title and headings of the SquirrelMail web pages are now branded with your organization's name.

In addition, you can replace the SquirrelMail webmail logo on the login page of your SquirrelMail installation with your company's or organization's own logo, which is a unique way of customizing and branding the very first page every user accesses. Drop your replacement logo into the images directory of SquirrelMail: /usr/share/squirrelmail/images/, if you installed the Fedora Core RPM, or /var/www/html/webmail/images/, if you installed from source code following the examples in this book. Next, rerun conf.pl, type 1, and press Enter to edit the organization preferences.

Type 2, and press Enter to enter the path to your logo file. Enter the relative path to the logo file itself. For instance, if you copied the file companyLogo.png to the images directory, type .../images/companyLogo.png, and press Enter. If your logo is a different size than the SquirrelMail logo (308 pixels wide by 111 pixels high), type 3, and press Enter to supply the new dimensions, in pixels, of your logo. Type s, and press Enter to save your changes. Type q, and press Enter to quit conf.pl.

In addition to these global branding options, users themselves can customize many aspects of the SquirrelMail interface individually. In fact, these customizations are saved from session to session, no matter where or when users access SquirrelMail. To access various preferences, click on the Options link in the top navigation list. For example, the following short list includes just a few of the attributes that are customizable by users under Display Options:

- *Themes*: You can choose a color theme that changes the various background and text colors within the SquirrelMail interface.

- *Language*: SquirrelMail has been localized to many languages.

- *Custom Style Sheet*: Those who need larger fonts and those who simply prefer a serif font over a sans-serif font can use the custom style sheet.

- *Element Placement*: Various aspects of the placement of elements within the interface itself are customizable as well.

This list just barely scratches the surface of customizable display elements, and perhaps the most compelling feature is the ability to set the theme. SquirrelMail offers a mechanism for creating and choosing color themes for the SquirrelMail interface, so you can create a custom theme for your site.

## Introducing SquirrelMail Themes

The SquirrelMail interface is fully customizable by you, the administrator, and by each individual user. This customization is possible through a simple pluggable theme system that allows you to customize the colors of the SquirrelMail interface. Numerous themes come with the standard SquirrelMail core distribution, or you can develop your own theme customized to your organization or personal preferences.

Creating a theme is simple. A theme consists of a PHP array called $color with 16 elements. Each element contains the hexadecimal representation of a color. For example, $color[0] defines the background color for the top title bar page header. If set to the value #FFFFFF, the color of that particular element would be white. Table 12-1 lists each element and its description.

**Table 12-1.** *The 16 SquirrelMail Theme Color Elements*

| Element | Background or Foreground | Description |
| --- | --- | --- |
| 0 | Background | The background color of the page header title bar. |
| 1 | Foreground | The border around error messages, typically red. |
| 2 | Foreground | The text color of error messages, typically red. |
| 3 | Background | The background color of the left folder list pane. |
| 4 | Background | The common background color. |
| 5 | Background | The background color of the message index text (e.g., From, Date, Subject). |
| 6 | Foreground | The color of the common text in the left folder list pane. |
| 7 | Foreground | The color of links in the right pane. |
| 8 | Foreground | The color of common text, typically black. |
| 9 | Background | A darker shade of element 0. |
| 10 | Background | A darker shade of element 9. |
| 11 | Foreground | The text color of special folders (e.g., Inbox, Trash, Sent). |
| 12 | Background | The second background color for the message list, used to alternate between this element and element 4. |
| 13 | Foreground | The color of single-quoted text (i.e., > text) when viewing a message. The default is #800000. |
| 14 | Foreground | The color of text that has more than one quote (i.e., >> text) when viewing a message, the default is #FF0000. |
| 15 | Foreground | The text color of folders in the left frame that are not selectable. The default is the value of element 6. |

Create a new file called something like myTheme_theme.php inside the SquirrelMail themes directory, typically /usr/share/squirrelmail/themes/, if you installed the Fedora Core RPM, or /var/www/html/webmail/themes/, if you installed from the SquirrelMail source distribution as illustrated in this book. The format of the file is very simple. A sample template for a SquirrelMail theme follows; simply replace #xxxxxx with a valid hex color code:

```php
<?php

/*
 My Custom SquirrelMail Theme
```

```
   Author: Your Name

   Optional description
   */

global $color;
$color[0]  = '#xxxxxx';
$color[1]  = '#xxxxxx';
$color[2]  = '#xxxxxx';
$color[3]  = '#xxxxxx';
$color[4]  = '#xxxxxx';
$color[5]  = '#xxxxxx';
$color[6]  = '#xxxxxx';
$color[7]  = '#xxxxxx';
$color[8]  = '#xxxxxx';
$color[9]  = '#xxxxxx';
$color[10] = '#xxxxxx';
$color[11] = '#xxxxxx';
$color[12] = '#xxxxxx';
$color[13] = '#xxxxxx';
$color[14] = '#xxxxxx';
$color[15] = '#xxxxxx';

?>
```

Because a PHP array is zero-indexed, the sixteenth element of the $color array is element 15 ($color[15]).

Once you've created your theme and copied it into the SquirrelMail themes directory, you must activate the theme to make it available, much the same way you do for SquirrelMail plugins. Simply run conf.pl, type **5**, and press Enter to modify the SquirrelMail sitewide theme configuration:

```
SquirrelMail Configuration : Read: config.php (1.4.0)
---------------------------------------------------------
Themes
1. Change Themes
    Default                      Plain Blue
    Sand Storm                   Deep Ocean
    Slashdot                     Purple
    Forest                       Ice
    Sea Spray                    Blue Steel
    Dark Grey                    High Contrast
    Black Bean Burrito           Servery
    Maize                        BluesNews
    Deep Ocean 2                 Blue Grey
    Dompie                       Methodical
    Greenhouse Effect (Changes)  In The Pink (Changes)
```

```
     Kind of Blue (Changes)           Monostochastic (Changes)
     Shades of Grey (Changes)         Spice of Life (Changes)
     Spice of Life - Lite (Changes)   Spice of Life - Dark (Changes)
     Holiday - Christmas              Darkness (Changes)
     Random (Changes every login)     Midnight
     Alien Glow                       Dark Green
     Penguin
  2. CSS File :

  R  Return to Main Menu
  C  Turn color off
  S  Save data
  Q  Quit


Command >>
```

As you can see, a number of themes have been installed and are already available for use.
Type 1, and press Enter to modify the list of themes. Typing ? and pressing Enter gives you the
list of commands you can use to modify the list of themes:

```
Define the themes that you wish to use. If you have added a theme of your own,
just follow the instructions (?) about how to add them. You can also change
the default theme.
[theme] command (?=help) > ?
.---------------------------.
| t     (detect themes)     |
| +     (add theme)         |
| - N   (remove theme)      |
| m N   (mark default)      |
| l     (list themes)       |
| d     (done)              |
`---------------------------'
[theme] command (?=help) >
```

To add your new theme, type +, and press Enter. Enter a descriptive name for the theme;
the name should be obvious to you and your users and a company-specific SquirrelMail
theme. Next, press Enter. Enter the relative path to the theme file. For instance, if you created
the previous sample theme, type . . ./themes/myTheme_theme.php, and press Enter.

Once you're done modifying the theme list, type d, and press Enter. Your new theme
should show up in the list of available themes. Type s, and press Enter to save your changes.
Type q, and press Enter to quit conf.pl.

Now, when you log in to SquirrelMail again, you can change your theme preference by
selecting Options from the main navigation links at the top of the page and clicking Display
Preferences. The first drop-down box is the Theme selector. Select the theme you prefer, and
click the Submit button. From now on, the colors of the SquirrelMail interface should match
those of your chosen theme, and your choice sticks whether you log out or access SquirrelMail
from another computer or browser!

# Further SquirrelMail Resources

SquirrelMail is an extremely well-documented software package. Documentation can be found locally on your Fedora Core system in /usr/share/doc/squirrelmail-[version]/ where [version] is replaced by the base version string of the RPM package installed. For example, at the time of this writing, the RPM package installed is squirrelmail-1.4.6-5.fc4, so documentation can be found in /usr/share/doc/squirrelmail-1.4.6-5.fc4/. To check the version of SquirrelMail, run the following command:

```
[curtis@mail ~]$ rpm -qv squirrelmail
```

```
squirrelmail-1.4.6-5.fc4
```

In addition to the local documentation, or the documentation found with the source distribution, the most current information regarding SquirrelMail installation, configuration, and development status is also available from the SquirrelMail wiki found at www.squirrelmail.org/wiki/SquirrelMail. For community support, the SquirrelMail mailing lists are also an excellent resource. You can find list archives and subscription information at www.squirrelmail.org/wiki/MailingLists.

Finally, if you or any of your users need help with the SquirrelMail interface itself, nearly every page or view has contextual help available. Simply click the Help link at the top of any SquirrelMail page, and you are presented with the appropriate information describing the page.

# Summary

Like all of the other open source applications featured in this book so far, SquirrelMail enjoys a generous and resourceful user and developer community that only makes this great application better! Providing feature-rich, robust SquirrelMail to your users is a must. In this chapter, I walked you through the installation and configuration of the SquirrelMail webmail package. I also introduced the advanced SquirrelMail features of plugins and themes. SquirrelMail plugins, although not necessary, enhance the services you can offer through your webmail installation. Likewise, the ability to brand and customize the SquirrelMail interface is very desirable for any company or organization.

In the next chapter, we're going to switch gears and focus on e-mail filtering, laying the groundwork for dealing with e-mail virus protection and spam management. This work is a bit more advanced, but it is necessary for any successful e-mail system. The better you can protect your users from e-mail–borne viruses and unsolicited bulk e-mail, the happier they are to use the complete e-mail system you're building.

# PART 5

# Filtering E-mail

PART 3

Practice Exam II

# CHAPTER 13

■ ■ ■

# Introducing E-mail Filtering with procmail

**O**ne of the most powerful features you can offer to your users is e-mail filtering. Using e-mail filtering, your users can organize or sort their e-mail before they ever start reading their mail. E-mail filtering also allows users to manipulate their incoming e-mail in nearly unlimited fashion before it is finally delivered to their mailboxes. But e-mail filtering can be used even without your users knowing. For example, you can configure sendmail to deliver to a filtering program instead of delivering right to a mailbox file. Or you can filter mail through antivirus or antispam applications and catch unwanted or dangerous messages before they reach your users' mailboxes. This chapter offers some general information that will make it obvious why filtering would be a highly useful thing for an administrator to do. I will first introduce basic filtering concepts, but most of this chapter will be devoted to filtering e-mail with procmail, the autonomous mail processor.

## Introducing Filtering Basics

E-mail filtering is simply a way to perform some arbitrary action on e-mail based on search criteria. This can be as simple as intercepting all e-mail from your mother and moving it to a subfolder under your Inbox. After all, someone as special as Mom deserves special treatment of every piece of electronic correspondence! An e-mail filter could also be as powerful as sending each matching e-mail message to another program for further processing. Or perhaps your ex has been sending along harassing e-mail and you've decided to ignore it rather than let it bring you down. No problem; simply send those e-mails to the Linux black hole: /dev/null. Or maybe you want to trigger a particular event when a particular e-mail message arrives, such as creating a custom auto-responder that notifies the sender that you received the e-mail. All of these things are possible with e-mail filtering; using the concepts and programs discussed in this chapter spells the demise of the days of thousands of e-mail messages cluttering your Inbox.

But where does the e-mail filtering occur? There are two logical places for e-mail filtering to occur: the client side, by an e-mail client application on users' desktops or laptops, or on the server side, by a filtering program.

Client-side and server-side filtering shares many of the same advantages as client-side and server-side web scripting, respectively. On the one hand, all e-mail filtering can occur on your users' computer by their e-mail client application. One advantage to this is that there is no overhead on the e-mail server. No additional applications or software are required on the e-mail system itself for client-side filtering. Many contemporary e-mail client applications offer client-side filtering of various sorts. For example, Mozilla Thunderbird can sort incoming e-mail based on any arbitrary search criteria. However, some of your users might find this inconvenient if they use multiple computers to check their e-mail; having to maintain the same complex set of filters in multiple locations is decidedly annoying, not to mention error prone.

On the other hand, e-mail can be filtered on the server side, possibly without your users ever knowing. Or you can allow your customers the ability to configure their own special filters. In this chapter, we'll take a look at how we can use server-side e-mail filtering to combat spam. The server-side filtering program will perform as the mail delivery agent (MDA) in lieu of allowing sendmail to simply deliver to the system mail spool. Refer to Figure 13-1 for a graphical representation of how the MDA fits into the flow of e-mail just before mail is delivered to users' mailbox.

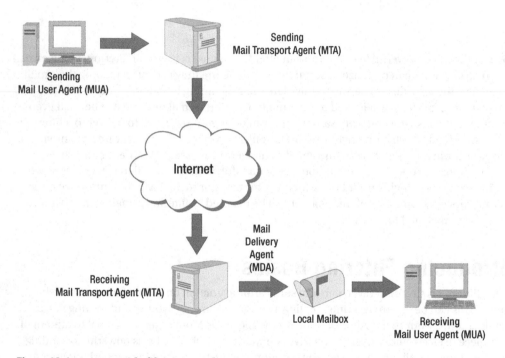

**Figure 13-1.** *A server-side filtering application can act as the MDA, sitting in between the MTA and your users' mailbox, filtering and delivering mail.*

In my mind, the reasons for implementing server-side filtering are twofold. First, server-side filtering would include taking the burden of filter management and computing resources from your users' e-mail applications and computers. Second, server-side filtering provides flexible e-mail delivery options that you, the e-mail administrator, can use to help manage mail flow, thus protecting your users from malicious or unsolicited content.

Both client-side and server-side filtering can be used on the same e-mail system. You might decide to filter viruses and spam only, but deliver all other mail directly to your users' Inbox. This allows your users the flexibility of filtering other e-mail as they sit fit. If you decide to filter e-mail further, or offer server-side filtering to your users, you could choose to use procmail, a powerful server-side e-mail filtering program.

# Introducing and Configuring procmail

procmail (www.procmail.org) is the venerable e-mail filtering program of choice for many e-mail administrators around the globe. procmail can sort your e-mail based on patterns, processing your e-mail before it's delivered to your Inbox, or trigger another application when any or all of your e-mail is delivered. If you subscribe to more than a few medium- to high-volume mailing lists, you'll appreciate the ability to perform any one of these actions to keep your mail organized and easier to read.

---

**Caution** Although it's possible to use procmail to forward e-mail to other e-mail accounts, it is important to remember procmail is not an MTA. procmail's real strength lies in filtering e-mail and writing to mailbox files on the local system; let sendmail forward your e-mail (I show you how later in this chapter).

---

When a message is fed to procmail, or when procmail is called to process an entire mailbox full of messages, the program must be configured so that it knows what to do with the messages. procmail simply reacts to a message when one or more search criteria match any part of the message. You control procmail with runtime configuration files; let's take a closer look.

---

**Note** Remember, if you choose to filter and sort e-mail into multiple e-mail folders, it will be necessary to use an IMAP client application since POP3 does not support server-side folder capabilities.

---

## The procmail Runtime Configuration File

If procmail is invoked without any command-line arguments, then it will first interpret the systemwide *runtime configuration file* (or rcfile, for short) /etc/procmailrc if it exists. This is where an e-mail administrator can put a global configuration set that affects all users that run procmail. This can be highly useful; you can force spam checking globally, or configure sendmail to use procmail as a mailer, for instance. Next, procmail will look for the local rcfile .procmailrc in the home directory of the user invoking procmail. Here is where individual users using procmail can specify personal filtering rules. If none of the default rcfiles are found, one or more of the rcfiles are empty, or each rule found in an rcfile is processed successfully without being redirected to another e-mail folder or account, then procmail will simply deliver the e-mail message to the default system location.

A procmail runtime configuration file is made up of environment variables and blocks of directives or rules typically called *recipes* and are covered in detail later in this chapter. Environment variables are meant to change the default behavior of procmail and to make sure procmail runs in a safe environment. There are a few special environment variables that every .procmailrc rcfile ought to have, so let's take a look at these before tackling procmail recipes.

## procmail rcfile Environment Variables

procmail runtime configuration file environment variables can be defined in one or more places. To customize procmail globally for all users, place systemwide environment variables in /etc/procmailrc. Anything else user-specific should be relegated to .procmailrc in the users' home directory. However, an environment variable in a user's .procmailrc will override the same variable if it's set in /etc/procmailrc.

One of the most common uses for procmail is sorting e-mail into different e-mail folders. So, the first thing you should do is point procmail to the root directory where your e-mail folders are stored. This can vary, based on what MTA and IMAP server you're running. For instance, our sample Dovecot installation outlined in this book uses the mbox mailbox format, storing all mailbox files in $HOME/mail/, so the procmail MAILDIR environment variable should be defined as follows:

MAILDIR=$HOME/mail

The HOME variable is set by the Linux system itself and would expand to the home directory of the user running procmail. For example, when I log in with the username curtis, $HOME/mail would expand to /home/curtis/mail. The MAILDIR variable is necessary to set a working directory for all mailboxes, from within which all other e-mail mailbox files are created by procmail by default.

Next, you should define a procmail working directory. This is where various procmail-related items are placed, including log files and other runtime configuration files discussed a bit later in this section. The PMDIR environment variable specifies this and is typically defined in the following manner:

PMDIR=$HOME/.procmail

But this can be any arbitrary directory within a user's home directory. Don't forget to create the directory if it does not already exist.

It's possible to have procmail log its actions in various levels of verbosity for informational or debugging purposes. You'll find this approach useful if you need to determine why procmail isn't acting as you expected or you simply want to keep an eye on what procmail is doing. First, define the procmail log file with the LOGFILE environment variable:

LOGFILE=$PMDIR/procmail.log

Note the use of the PMDIR variable, which presupposes the PMDIR variable was set earlier in /etc/procmailrc or .procmailrc.

The amount of information procmail logs can change with a couple of environment variables. By default, procmail will log some basic information about each processed message to the log file, including the From and Subject headers, the final delivery destination, and the size of the message in bytes:

```
From curtis@example.com Sat Jun 3 20:13:12 2006
 Subject: Testing
 Folder: Testing                              786
```

To override this default behavior and thus suppress the logging of this information, set the LOGABSTRACT environment variable as shown here:

LOGABSTRACT=no

To derive much more verbose information out of procmail for debugging purposes, set the VERBOSE environment variable:

VERBOSE=yes

Sample verbose logging, in addition to the standard LOGABSTRACT enabled, looks like this:

```
procmail: Match on "^Subject:.*test"
procmail: Locking "Testing.lock"
procmail: Assigning "LASTFOLDER=Testing"
procmail: Opening "Testing"
procmail: Acquiring kernel-lock
procmail: Unlocking "Testing.lock"
procmail: Notified comsat: "curtis@0:/home/curtis/mail/Testing"
From curtis@example.com Sat Jun 3 20:13:12 2006
 Subject: Testing
 Folder: Testing                              786
```

However, I recommend leaving this set only when you're debugging procmail since it can result in information overload and create a quite large file over time, thus wasting disk space. Otherwise, you will need to periodically rotate the procmail log file and remove old log entries when they are no longer needed.

If you find that .procmailrc becomes too large and complex, it's possible to modularize your runtime configuration by moving like recipes to different files. For example, all Linux-related mailing list recipes, designed to sort your Linux-related mailing list subscriptions to various e-mail folders, could be moved into another rcfile called linux_lists.rc. A home directory could get cluttered with all those rcfiles laying around, so why not move them into the procmail working directory defined by the PMDIR variable and then include them in .procmailrc? Use the INCLUDERC environment variable to tell procmail to read configuration information from another file:

INCLUDERC=$PMDIR/linux_lists.rc

Add additional INCLUDERC variables to include as many rcfiles as you'd like, depending on how you'd like to organize your procmail runtime configuration files.

In this section, I covered the most commonly modified procmail environment variables. Table 13-1 lists the majority of the procmail environment variables, some mentioned earlier in this section. However, keep in mind that most of these are taken from each user's shell environment, or have perfectly acceptable defaults that do not, under most circumstances, need to be changed or modified.

**Table 13-1.** *procmail Environment Variables*

| Variable Name | Default Value | Description |
| --- | --- | --- |
| DEFAULT | $ORGMAIL | The default mailbox file to write mail to if one is not explicitly given. This does not need to be set, as it defaults to the system default mailbox. |
| DELIVERED | *None* | If set to yes, procmail will report to the MTA that the message has been successfully delivered. If the message is not delivered for some reason, the message will be lost. |
| EXITCODE | 0 | This sets the exit code when procmail finishes a task. |
| INCLUDERC | *None* | This defines an additional rcfile to process; multiple INCLUDERC variables may be defined that point to additional rcfiles. |
| LOCKEXT | .lock | This defines what is appended to a name of the local lockfile, if one is set in a procmail recipe. |
| LOCKFILE | *None* | This defines the filename of a global lockfile. If this file exists, procmail will wait until the lockfile is removed before proceeding, creating the lockfile itself when continuing. Using a global lockfile is not a good idea; I recommend you use individual local lockfiles on a per-recipe basis instead. |
| LOCKSLEEP | 8 | This sets the time, in seconds, procmail will wait before retrying an operation when a lockfile exists. |
| LOCKTIMEOUT | 1024 | This sets the time, in seconds, that procmail considers a lockfile to be stale or left over. If set to 0, procmail will never override a lockfile, potentially creating an indefinite operation hang-up. Otherwise, if a lockfile has not been created or modified within the value of this variable, procmail will force its operation. |
| LOG | *None* | This defines text to add to the end of $LOGFILE. |
| LOGFILE | *None* | This defines a file to log error or debugging information to. If set to none, then errors are mailed to the original sender of the message that triggered an error. |
| LOGABSTRACT | *None* | Additional information regarding the message, including the From and Subject headers, the destination mailbox, and the size of the message in bytes is logged to the $LOGFILE if it is set. If set to no, no abstract will be logged. If set to all, additional information for successful deliveries will be logged. |
| LOGNAME | $USER | Typically set by the system, this defines the user's username, as identified by the command id -un. |
| MAILDIR | $HOME | This defines the location of mailbox files. All paths to mailbox files are relative to $MAILDIR. |
| NORESRETRY | 4 | This defines the number of times procmail will retry an operation if system resources, like disk space, are unavailable or full. If this is set to a negative number, then procmail will retry indefinitely. procmail will wait for the time set by $SUSPEND between retries. |

| Variable Name | Default Value | Description |
| --- | --- | --- |
| ORGMAIL | /var/mail/$LOGNAME | This defines the user's system mailbox file, and is used for the value of $DEFAULT, by default. On a Fedora Core system, this does not need to be changed. |
| SUSPEND | 16 | This sets the time, in seconds, which procmail will wait between retrying an operation. |
| VERBOSE | *None* | If set to yes or on, then additional debugging information is logged. This will generate a lot of information, so use this only when testing procmail. |

The action procmail performs on your e-mail is controlled with blocks of instructions called recipes. An rcfile can have any number of either environment variables or recipes mixed inside the same or multiple rcfiles. Without recipes, procmail would be useless, as they define patterns for searching messages that procmail processes and the subsequent action to perform on matching messages. I discuss procmail recipes in depth next.

## Introducing procmail Recipes

A procmail *recipe* consists of a well-defined block of text telling procmail how to start, what to search for, and how to handle matching e-mail messages. Or perhaps more simply, if the conditions defined in the recipe are met, then the corresponding actions are performed. As we'll see later, an action might consist of any event, such as delivering to an arbitrary mailbox file, executing another program, or forwarding the message to another e-mail account. Let's dissect a procmail recipe and learn how they are built and executed.

In its simplest form, a recipe is a single pattern that procmail uses to search the header of an e-mail message. procmail starts from the top of the first rcfile, through each recipe, until it finds a matching recipe, or falls off the end of every rcfile without a match. The first recipe that matches a message determines the action procmail performs on the message. If no recipes match, then the message is delivered normally, typically to the system default mailbox. A procmail recipe is either a delivering recipe or a nondelivering recipe.

A delivering recipe is one that results in any or all parts of an e-mail message being successfully delivered to a mailbox, forwarded to another e-mail account, or handed off to another application on the system. Once the action of a matching delivering recipe is completed, procmail will stop processing the rcfile and exit with a successful status code.

A nondelivering recipe is one that results in the output of a program to be passed back to procmail or a recipe that begins a nested recipe block. procmail will continue to process the message when a nondelivering recipe matches. Nondelivering recipes are typically used to collect message statistics or to keep track of message IDs to trap duplicate e-mail messages; an example of such a recipe can be found later in this chapter.

The basic structure of a recipe looks something like the following (taken direct from the procmailrc(5) man page):

```
:0 [flags] [ : [locallockfile] ]
<zero or more conditions (one per line)>
<exactly one action line>
```

A procmail recipe always starts with :0, a colon followed by a zero. This alerts the program that the next line will contain a conditional statement to perform its match on the e-mail message. Anything following the :0 on the first line is optional, but this space can be used to define special flags and a specific local lockfile, if one is necessary. These are options that, under most circumstances, are not typically defined, but we discuss them later in this chapter. In general, blank or empty lines should not be added in between the three lines of a recipe block.

The majority of procmail recipes only need to start with :0:, which indicates the start of a new recipe that requires no flags and that utilizes the default system file-locking mechanism and lockfile name based on the delivery destination. However, sometimes you will need to modify how procmail executes a recipe by defining special flags or an explicit local lockfile.

## procmail Recipe Flags

procmail recipe flags, among other things, can alter how procmail interprets the recipe condition, what part of the message to search against, or under which circumstances to execute the recipe. You can specify more than one flag at a time. Remember, the default behavior is to search the message headers only, and is probably what most people use procmail for. Later in this chapter, I will introduce examples of recipes that do more than this, using some of the available procmail recipe flags. Table 13-2 lists the procmail flags and a brief description of each.

**Table 13-2.** *procmail Recipe Flags*

| Flag | Description |
| --- | --- |
| H | Uses the built-in egrep interpreter to search the message *header*. The procmail internal egrep is compatible with the system egrep(1) extended regular expressions. This is the default behavior. |
| B | Uses the built-in egrep interpreter to search the message body. The procmail internal egrep is compatible with the system egrep(1) extended regular expressions. This flag can be used in conjunction with the H flag to search the entire e-mail message. |
| D | Makes pattern matching *case-sensitive*. The default behavior of the built-in egrep interpreter is to perform *case-insensitive* searches. |
| A | This flag allows chained actions, and specifies the recipe will only be executed if the preceding recipe was matched on the same message. The preceding recipe cannot have the A or a flag specified. |
| a | This is the same as the A flag, but this recipe will not be executed unless the preceding recipe finished successfully. |
| E | This flag allows else-if type conditional recipes, and specifies the recipe will only be executed if the preceding recipe was not executed. If this recipe is executed, and the next recipe also has the E flag, the next recipe will not be executed. |
| e | This flag specifies the recipe will only be executed if the preceding recipe was executed but the action failed. |
| h | Feeds the contents of the message header to the destination of the action of the recipe, typically a mailbox file, another application, or another e-mail account. This is the default behavior. |
| b | Feeds the contents of the message body to the destination of the action of the recipe, typically a mailbox file, another application, or another e-mail account. This is the default behavior. |

| Flag | Description |
|------|-------------|
| f | Considers the pipe in the action of the recipe to be another filter, not a final destination. Typically this recipe flag would indicate a nondelivering recipe, and can be used to pipe messages through another application for further tagging or manipulation and return messages to procmail for further processing. |
| c | This specifies that a carbon copy of the message ought to be generated after the recipe is executed. procmail will continue processing the rcfile on the copied message. This will effectively allow a copy of a message that matches a delivering recipe to be further processed by procmail after the delivering recipe with the c flag is executed. |
| w | Specifies that procmail should wait for the filter or application to exit with a successful status code before continuing. If the action does not complete, then the message will not be filtered, effectively ignoring the recipe. By default, procmail will ignore the exit code of the action destination, assuming the message was filtered successfully. |
| W | This is the same as the w flag, but will not output an error message if the action was unsuccessful. |
| i | Specifies that procmail should ignore any write errors if the execution of the action does not complete unexpectedly and continues as it normally would despite the error. |
| r | Specifies that the procmail should execute the recipe in raw mode. By default, procmail will make sure that an e-mail message ends with an empty line, but this option will suppress this behavior. |

## procmail Lockfiles

Lockfiles are necessary so that two or more programs, or, more specifically, two or more instances of procmail, do not try to manipulate the same mailbox file at the same time. Under most circumstances, it makes sense to allow procmail to use the Linux kernel file-locking mechanism, allowing it to create its own lockfile accordingly, and to not define a specific local lockfile, as per the default behavior.

For example, when two nearly concurrently running procmail processes match two different messages to a recipe that delivers mail to the same mailbox file, the first process to start delivery will create a lockfile for the destination mailbox file. When the second procmail process attempts to deliver to the same mailbox file, it tries to create the very same lockfile on the very same mailbox file. However, if the first process has not completed its delivery, the mailbox is still locked, and the second procmail process must wait for it to complete.

Specifying a local lockfile for a delivering recipe is essentially redundant given that procmail already creates a lockfile based on the mailbox name by default. If the Mailbox file name is MailFromMom, then procmail will look for, or create, a lockfile named MailFromMom.lock while executing a recipe that delivers to this mailbox. It's possible to override the default lockfile naming conventions with the LOCKEXT procmail environment variables, changing the default filename prefix from .lock to something else.

Specifying a local lockfile is handy, however, when writing and executing nondelivering recipes. For instance, if you are filtering all mail through a separate application via a procmail recipe, you need to wait for every message to be sent to, and return from, the filter. Because the action is not delivering to a specific file, you must specify a local lockfile that every procmail process that executes this recipe will look for or create. An example of such a need for a local lockfile can be found later in this chapter.

Specifying a global lockfile with the procmail environment variable LOCKFILE is not a good idea, as this means that every time procmail is invoked, each process will have to wait for its predecessor to finish, regardless of whether they are manipulating the same file or performing the same operation. Because e-mail messages don't always get delivered one at a time slowly, but rather several or more a second during high load, mail filtering, and subsequently final delivery, would be significantly delayed.

## procmail Recipe Conditions

A condition starts with a * and any given recipe can have zero or more conditions, each defined on a separate line. If a recipe has one condition, then each e-mail message is tested against the condition. If two or more conditions exist, all conditions must match before procmail will execute the action. If a recipe does not have any conditions, then the result of the recipe will always be true, and the action will be performed—which is useful if you'd like to include one final catchall recipe that filters any messages that did not match any other recipes, for example.

Everything after the * is a condition, aside from the leading and trailing whitespace, and is used by procmail's pattern-matching mechanism. By default, the message header is searched for a match to the condition, but we've seen earlier in Table 13-2 that this behavior can be changed through the use of special flags. This matching mechanism is an internal *regular expression* engine that operates almost identically to the system command egrep. Before we can offer any significant procmail examples, some preliminary discussion must be devoted to regular expression syntax, which procmail relies on for pattern matching. If you are already familiar with regular expressions, or simply want to get to the example procmail recipes, skip this next section, or come back later if necessary.

### Crash Course in Regular Expressions

Many users consider regular expressions to be very confusing at first blush. For instance, let's look at the following regular expression, whose purpose I will keep a mystery until later in this chapter:

```
^[_a-z0-9-]+(\.[_a-z0-9-]+)*@[a-z0-9-]+(\.[a-z0-9-]+)*$
```

This example looks like little more than a bunch of garbage, doesn't it? By the end of this section, its purpose should be much clearer and you should be able to identify its use yourself.

The definition of a *regular expression* (*regex* for short) from the egrep(1) man page is so good, I'd rather quote it than make up a new one:

> *A regular expression is a pattern that describes a set of strings. Regular expressions are constructed analogously to arithmetic expressions, by using various operators to combine smaller expressions.*

Regular expressions come in different flavors: basic regular expressions, Portable Operating System Interface (POSIX) regular expressions, extended regular expressions, Perl-compatible regular expressions, and so forth. Each uses slightly different syntax, but they all do the same basic thing. Getting into the intricacies of the differences of different regex flavors is beyond the scope of this section, but I will introduce extended regular expressions, as these are what procmail uses.

Regular expressions are best taught by example, and I will use the command egrep to help illustrate their usage. The egrep command, actually the same command as grep -E, specifies that the command grep should interpret the search patterns as extended regular expressions rather than basic regular expressions. GNU grep is a pattern search program that can be run from the command line of your Linux system, and it has been around for years in various UNIX operating systems. You will find GNU grep (www.gnu.org/software/grep/) in most modern Linux distributions, including Fedora Core.

■ **Tip** If you need to develop or test regular expressions, check out the handy application Kodos, a regular expression debugger (http://kodos.sourceforge.net/).

For the following examples, first create a text file called test.txt with these contents:

```
This is a test.
smith.999@example.com
Test this is.
```

A regular expression can be as simple as a literal string. For example, to search for any occurrence of the word "test" in test.txt, try the following:

```
[curtis@mail ~]$ egrep test test.txt
```

```
This is a test string.
```

By default, egrep will print to the screen any line that matches the search pattern. To simply get a count of how many lines match, then supply the -c argument to egrep:

```
[curtis@mail ~]$ egrep -c test test.txt
```

```
1
```

or you can tell egrep to just print the portion of the string or line that matches the pattern with the -o argument:

```
[curtis@mail ~]$ egrep -o test test.txt
```

```
test
```

Wait a minute; the word "test" occurs twice in our example text file. Why did egrep only find one match? Well, that's because basic regular expression patterns are case-sensitive. We can use the -i argument and tell egrep to make its search case insensitive:

```
[curtis@mail ~]$ egrep -c -i test test.txt
```

2

But that's just cheating, and it doesn't help when we have to write regular expressions for procmail conditions. If you want to look for any line that contains either "Test" or "test", try this:

```
[curtis@mail ~]$ egrep -c '(test)|(Test)' test.txt
```

2

This regex introduces a couple of new important concepts. First, the opening and closing parentheses have special meaning in the context of extended regular expressions. They group together anything between them into one single element. We'll see why this is important in a second.

Second, | (the pipe character, found on the same key as the backslash on your keyboard) is the or operator in regular expressions. This means matching the subexpression either to the right or to the left of the pipe is sufficient for the regex to match. This is why we group the words "test" and "Test" with parentheses; we want to find any occurrence of either of the words.

Third, the following characters have special meaning to the shell, different from their regex meanings:

```
| & ; ( ) < > $ ` ' " \
```

So they must be quoted with ' (the single quote character), hiding the special meaning of these characters from the shell and passing them as the literal characters.

If you want to use a regex special character, then you must *escape* the character. Escaping a special character simply means taking away its special meaning as a regular expression metacharacter. If you escape the parentheses and pipe inside the single quotes, it would hide the special meaning from those characters from both the shell and the regular expression and match the (, ), and | characters literally. Table 13-3 describes these two grouping regular expressions.

---

**Note** When using regular expressions in procmail recipes, you do not need to quote your patterns or escape special characters as you do when supplying them to the shell from the command line. procmail passes each regular expression in a condition to its internal egrep literally. Escaping the parentheses and pipe character in a procmail recipe would match those characters literally, taking away their special meaning as regular expression metacharacters.

---

**Table 13-3.** *Regular Expression Grouping Patterns*

| Regex Metacharacter(s) | Function |
|---|---|
| (....) | Group one or more items into one single element, which can be used with other grouping, anchor, or repetition modifiers. |
| \| | Or operator; match the subexpression either to the right or the left of the pipe. |

The previous example can be simplified into a smaller regex:

```
[curtis@mail ~]$ egrep -c '[t|T]est' test.txt
```

---

2

---

which introduces yet another new regex concept: the opening and closing brackets and matching character classes. Using the brackets simply means matching any one of the characters found inside the brackets. We've seen that the pipe character has special meaning, so [t|T] means to match either the character "t" or "T". So [t|T]est is just saying to match any string that starts with either "t" or "T", followed by "est".

It's also possible to specify a particular range of characters to match on. For example, if you want to match any letter in the alphabet, you would use [a-z]. This will match if any one of the letters of the alphabet is found anywhere in the string or line. Try the following (screen output not shown):

```
[curtis@mail ~]$ egrep -o '[a-z]' test.txt
```

or add uppercase letters to the list of possible matching characters:

```
[curtis@mail ~]$ egrep -o '[a-zA-Z]' test.txt
```

or search for any one digit:

```
[curtis@mail ~]$ egrep -o '[0-9]' test.txt
```

Later, we will see how we can use these concepts to specify the repetition of a pattern to simplify your regular expressions. Table 13-4 lists these and other useful regular expression character classes. To match the literal period (dot) character, remember to escape the dot to take away its special meaning (\.).

**Table 13-4.** *Regular Expression Character Classes*

| Regex Metacharacter(s) | Function |
| --- | --- |
| [....] | Match any one of the characters between the brackets. |
| [^....] | Match any one character not between the brackets. |
| . | Match any one character, except the newline. Equivalent to [^\n]. |
| \w | Match any one word character. Equivalent to [a-zA-Z0-9_]. |
| \W | Match any character not a word character. Equivalent to [^a-zA-Z0-9_]. |
| \s | Match any one whitespace character. Equivalent to [ \t\n\r\f\v]. |
| \S | Match any one character that is not a whitespace character. Equivalent to [^ \t\n\r\f\v]. |
| \d | Match any one digit. Equivalent to [0-9]. |
| \D | Match any one character that is not a digit. Equivalent to [^0-9]. |

Now add the following line to test.txt:

```
fooTestbar
```

and rerun the previous example:

```
[curtis@mail ~]$ egrep -c '[t|T]est' test.txt
```

```
3
```

This may or may not surprise you. Up to now I've been sloppy and saying that we've been matching the *words* "test" and "Test". However, this is not entirely accurate. We have been matching the *strings* "test" and "Test". The examples up to this point have been matching literally for any occurrence of the strings inside the line. To tighten up the regex a bit and only match on what we understand as a word, you would use a special regular expression anchor.

To match the strings "test" and "Test" anchored around word boundaries (essentially whitespace), use the special character \b around the pattern:

```
[curtis@mail ~]$ egrep -c '\b[t|T]est\b' test.txt
```

```
2
```

Aha! That's more like it. What if we wanted to match the strings inside other words, but not the strings as words themselves? Well, use the special character \B instead:

```
[curtis@mail ~]$ egrep '\B[t|T]est\B' test.txt
```

```
fooTestbar
```

Eureka!

It is also possible to anchor the pattern to a specific location in a line. That is to say, if you want to match an occurrence of the string "Test" at the beginning of a line, then use the ^ character to anchor the pattern to the beginning of a line:

```
[curtis@mail ~]$ egrep '^Test' test.txt
```

```
Test string this is.
```

or anchor a search pattern to the end of the line with the $ character:

```
[curtis@mail ~]$ egrep 'com$' test.txt
```

```
smith.999@example.com
```

Table 13-5 describes these anchor regular expressions.

**Table 13-5.** *Regular Expression Anchoring Patterns*

| Regex Metacharacter(s) | Function |
| --- | --- |
| ^ | Match the preceding character, or grouping, at the beginning of the string or line. |
| $ | Match the preceding character, or grouping, at the end of the string or line. |
| \b | Match a word boundary. |
| \B | Match anything not a word boundary. |

The final major concept I want to introduce is repetition of characters or groupings. The first way to specify the repetition of a pattern match comes in the form {n,m}, where n and m are integers, and m is optional. This can be a way to limit a pattern match to a specific number of matches, or to specify an unlimited number of matches. For example, to search for a string that is exactly four characters long, try the following, replacing 4 for n:

```
[curtis@mail ~]$ egrep -o '[a-z]{4}' test.txt
```

```
test
stri
smit
exam
stri
this
estb
```

or show off what we've learned so far, and limit this to any word exactly four characters long:

```
[curtis@mail ~]$ egrep -o '\b[a-z]{4}\b' test.txt
```

```
test
this
```

and include uppercase letters with the previous example:

```
[curtis@mail ~]$ egrep -o '\b[a-zA-Z]{4}\b' test.txt
```

```
This
test
Test
this
```

or modify the previous example to include any words, with uppercase or lowercase letters, that are four to six characters long, specifying a range by replacing 4 for n and 6 for m:

```
[curtis@mail ~]$ egrep -o '\b[a-zA-Z]{4,6}\b' test.txt
```

```
This
test
string
smith
Test
string
this
```

Finally, include any words, with uppercase or lowercase letters, that are four or more characters long:

```
[curtis@mail ~]$ egrep -o '\b[a-zA-Z]{4,}\b' test.txt
```

```
This
test
string
smith
example
Test
string
this
fooTestbar
```

I think you get the picture. Table 13-6 explains how to use the braces to define repetition or ranges, and includes a few other shorthand notations to make your regular expressions simpler.

**Table 13-6.** *Regular Expression Repetition Patterns*

| Regex Metacharacter(s) | Function |
| --- | --- |
| $\{n,m\}$ | Match the preceding character or grouping at least n times but no more than m times. |
| $\{n,\}$ | Match the preceding character or grouping n or more times. |
| $\{n\}$ | Match the preceding character or grouping exactly n times. |
| ? | Match the preceding character or grouping zero or one time. |
| + | Match the preceding character or grouping one or more times. |
| * | Match the preceding character or grouping zero or more times. |

So, do you remember the original regex I posed at the beginning of this section? Let me refresh your memory:

```
^[_a-z0-9-]+(\.[_a-z0-9-]+)*@[a-z0-9-]+(\.[a-z0-9-]+)*$
```

You should now have all the information you need to decipher this deceptively complex regular expression. *Hint 1*: the @ character is not a regular expression metacharacter. *Hint 2*: to use this regex on the command line with egrep, you would need to quote the pattern like so:

```
egrep '^[_a-z0-9-]+(\.[_a-z0-9-]+)*@[a-z0-9-]+(\.[a-z0-9-]+)*$' test.txt
```

Take some time to think about it if you wish. To put it simply: this regex matches or validates a properly formed e-mail address! This first chunk, ^[_a-z0-9-]+, matches any string of letters, numbers, or a hyphen or underscore at the beginning of the line. The second chunk, (\.[_a-z0-9-]+)*, matches any number of the same plus a period. Next, the literal @ character is followed by the same two chunks, except underscores are not allowed in domains. It's easier to decipher when you break the regex into chunks as indicated by the parentheses.

You'll find out why learning regular expressions is important as you develop procmail recipes, especially advanced ones. When doing so, think about ways to filter by more than just a literal word or phrase. Chances are you will be able to cut down on the number of recipes if you combine like filters into one recipe. Next, we'll take a look at how procmail simplifies filtering of common patterns for you through procmail macros.

## Special procmail Condition Macros

There are four special procmail expressions, or macros, that have special meaning and are replaced with a much larger and complex regular expression by procmail automatically. These can be used to simplify your conditions.

The expression ^TO_ is not a normal regular expression but rather a macro. Whenever procmail sees this macro, it expands the macro with the following regular expression (taken from the procmailrc(5) man page; note the regex is split across two lines, but it should be one single string):

```
(^((Original-)?(Resent-)?(To|Cc|Bcc)|(X-Envelope ➡
|Apparently(-Resent)?)-To):(.*[^-a-zA-Z0-9_.]))?)
```

This is meant to catch most of the possible destination message headers, not just the To or CC headers. When using the ^TO_ macro, do not add any spaces between the macro and the pattern to match on. For example, perhaps you forward the e-mail alias sales@example.com to your normal e-mail account but want to filter mail sent to that address separately from your other e-mail. To do so, you would use the ^TO_ macro in a procmail recipe like so:

```
^TO_sales@example.com
```

The macros ^FROM_DAEMON and ^FROM_MAILER are a bit different. Whenever procmail sees the ^FROM_DAEMON macro, it expands the macro with the following regular expression (taken from the procmailrc(5) man page; note the regex is split across multiple lines but it should be one single line):

```
(^(Mailing-List:|Precedence:.*(junk|bulk|list)|To: Multiple ➡
recipients of |(((Resent-)?(From|Sender)|X-Envelope-From):|>?From ➡
)([^>]*[^(.%@a-z0-9)])?(Post(ma?(st(e?r)?|n)|office)|(send)?Mail(er)? ➡
|daemon|m(mdf|ajordomo)|n?uucp|LIST(SERV|proc)|NETSERV|o(wner|ps) ➡
|r(e(quest|sponse)|oot)|b(ounce|bs\.smtp)|echo|mirror|s(erv(ices?|er) ➡
|mtp(error)?|ystem)|A(dmin(istrator)?|MMGR|utoanswer))(([^).!:a- ➡
z0-9][-_a-z0-9]*)?[%@>\t ][^<)]*(\(.*\).*)?)?)?$([^>]|$)))
```

And when procmail sees the `^FROM_MAILER` macro, it expands the macro with the following regular expression (taken from the `procmailrc(5)` man page; note the regex is split across multiple lines but it should be one single line):

```
(^(((Resent-)?(From|Sender)|X-Envelope-From):|>?From ➥
)([^>]*[^(.%@a-z0-9])?(Post(ma(st(er)?|n)|office)|(send)?Mail(er)? ➥
|daemon|mmdf|n?uucp|ops|r(esponse|oot)|(bbs\.)?smtp(error)?|s(erv(ices? ➥
|er)|ystem)|A(dmin(istrator)?|MMGR))(([^).!:a-z0-9][-_a-z0-9]*)?[%@>\t ➥
][^<)]*(\(.*\).*)?)?)?$([^>]|$))
```

Phew! Now those are some incredible regular expressions.

The `^FROM_MAILER` macro is a simpler subset of the `^FROM_DAEMON` macro, and they are meant to catch e-mail automatically generated and sent from a daemon, like a mailing list or SMTP server. For example, nondelivery reports (NDRs) are messages sent by a mail server itself, not a person, and usually have characteristics that identify it as such through headers or common subjects. You can filter such messages using a simple procmail recipe that uses `^FROM_MAILER` as its condition. Similarly, a mailing list manager like Mailman, which will be introduced in Chapter 19, will send various automatic bounce messages and other autogenerated e-mail messages like password reminders to the mailing list administrators and members. These can be filtered using the `^FROM_DAEMON` macro in a procmail recipe. Remember, if you choose to use both, any recipes using the `^FROM_MAILER` macro should occur before any recipes using the `^FROM_DAEMON` macro.

Basically, any well-behaving mailing list or e-mail server will try to identify administrative messages that are automatically generated by the system itself as such so you can easily filter these messages. This can be a handy procmail recipe to add at the end of your personal rcfile to catch autogenerated messages and filter them to a different e-mail folder so they do not clutter your Inbox.

## Special Advanced procmail Conditions

As I noted earlier, procmail conditions generally consist of a search pattern that is passed literally into procmail's internal egrep engine. The pattern can be as simple as a word or phrase to search for, or you can use your new regular expression skills to create complex patterns that match specific criteria. In addition, if more than one condition exists, all conditions must be met before the action is executed.

It is possible to modify conditions so they act differently. For example, you can negate a condition, effectively telling procmail to not match a message with a particular pattern. You can also use custom variables to hold values or patterns that can be reused. But to do so, you must tell procmail to expand that variable first before passing the literal test string to its internal egrep.

To create a special condition, the condition must start with the appropriate operator immediately preceding the condition search pattern. The regular expression follows the special character in the condition. You can add multiple operators where appropriate. Table 13-7 lists the special characters that mark the start of a special condition.

**Table 13-7.** *Special procmail Condition Characters*

| Character | Description |
|---|---|
| ! | Indicates that the condition should be negated, or inverted, allowing you to match on something other than the condition's pattern. |
| $ | Indicates that the remainder of the condition should be evaluated using sh(1) shell rules, substituting local variables with their assigned values, after which the literal pattern is passed to the internal egrep. |
| ? | Indicates that the exit status code of the program specified in the condition is used to decide whether or not a condition matches. |
| < n | Tests the total length of the message; if the total length of the message is less than the value n (in bytes), then the condition is true. |
| > n | Tests the total length of the message; if the total length of the message is greater than the value n (in bytes), then the condition is true. |
| variableName ?? | Indicates that the rest of the condition is compared to the value of the local variable variableName. This allows you to capture one part of a message, assign it to variableName, and compare or match that one part with another recipe condition. Special variables include: B, H, and HB, which have the same meanings as the recipe flags and override what part of the message is searched. |
| \ | To match any of the above literally as the first character or characters of a condition, they must be escaped with the backslash character. |

Table 13-7 contains advanced operations, and I only scratch the surface here. Later in this chapter, when I supply some sample recipes, I'll use some of these special conditions and explain them in more depth where appropriate.

## procmail Scoring

In its most basic form, procmail scoring can be a way to keep track of how many conditions in a recipe are matched. If a condition matches, then the score is incremented, and if the overall score is greater than 0, then procmail will execute the action (we discuss actions in the next section).

Normally, all conditions of a multicondition recipe must be matched for the action to be executed, but using scoring you can essentially make any number of conditions of a multicondition recipe sufficient to perform the recipe action.

By default, scoring starts at 0. Adding 1^0 immediately preceding the * that starts a condition will increase the score of the recipe by 1. If a recipe had two conditions, both starting with 1^0, then if either, or both, were matched, the score would be greater than 0 (either 1 or 2, depending on which conditions were fulfilled), and the action would be performed.

If you wanted to start the scoring at -1, effectively requiring more positive matches to tip the score over 0, you would start the first condition of the recipe with 8 -1^0, and assign each of the following conditions with 1^0. If you wanted to weight one condition more than another, then simply assign it a score of 2 with 2^0 or 3 with 3^0, and so forth, at the beginning of the condition.

Later in this chapter, I will provide an advanced recipe that will make use of scoring and the special condition operators discussed earlier. Learning these advanced features is easiest with examples.

But finally in this section, let's take a look at procmail recipe actions, the final component to a procmail recipe.

## procmail Recipe Actions

Aside from the very beginning :0, the only other necessary component to a procmail recipe is the action line. The action line is always the final line of the recipe. There are basically four general actions you can take:

- You can forward the message to another e-mail account.

- You can pipe the message to another program or script on the e-mail system.

- You can start a nesting block.

- You can deliver, or write, the message, or part of the message, to a mailbox file. This is probably the most basic and common use for procmail.

Table 13-8 lists each action, and the character, if any, that indicates the start of the action. Let's take a look at each of these in turn.

**Table 13-8.** *procmail Actions*

| Character | Description |
| --- | --- |
| *None* | Deliver the message to the specified mailbox file. |
| ! | Forward the message to the listed e-mail recipients. |
| \| | Pipe the message, or part of the message, to another program or script on the e-mail system. |
| { | Start a recipe nesting block. End and close the block with a final } character. |

If the action line starts with a ! character, often referred to as the *bang* character, then the action is to forward the message to the list of e-mail recipients. You should make sure that the e-mail addresses are valid and well formed. Also remember that this would be considered a delivering recipe, so unless you specified the c flag, a copy of the message would not be retained after the message is forwarded.

Next, if the action line starts with a | character, then the action is to pipe the message, or part of the message, to another program or script on the e-mail system. Uses of this type of action are nearly limitless; examples can be found later in this chapter.

If the action line starts with a { character, then the action isn't really an action. Rather, it's a beginning of a nesting block. A nesting block is a way to nest, or embed, additional recipes inside the parent recipe. To see the main advantage of this, you'll have to check out the example I explain later in this chapter. Usually, the same outcome as nesting recipes can be achieved with multiple individual recipes with the right flags. The end of the nesting block is signified by a closing } character.

Finally, if an action starts with anything else, it is assumed to be a mailbox filename to deliver the message to. If an absolute path is not given, then procmail assumes the filename is relative to the value of the MAILDIR variable. If the action is a directory, procmail will deliver each message to individual files in the directory. Each file is given a unique filename based on the Message-ID header.

Learning about regular expressions has been a lot of work, but it's well worth it, both for writing powerful procmail recipes but also to help you as a Linux system administrator in general. The power of server-side e-mail filtering through procmail should be obvious. Many of the concepts introduced here, such as regular expressions, will come in handy in other aspects of system administration. Now that I've introduced the basics of filtering, procmail configuration, and procmail recipes and search patterns, let's take a look at forwarding your mail to procmail to be filtered and delivered. Then I'll round this chapter off with some useful, real-world examples that apply this knowledge.

# Forwarding and Filtering Your E-mail

Now that we've gone over some of the filtering and procmail basics, and you've seen some pretty gnarly regular expressions and procmail recipes, let's look at how to actually send your e-mail through procmail for processing. There are two main ways to send mail through a filtering application like procmail. The first is by adding a mailer to sendmail.mc, and the second is through an individual .forward file.

Obviously, the first approach requires you to make a change to your sendmail configuration and allows you to send certain e-mail messages directly through procmail instead of delivering to the system default location. The second enables users to opt in themselves, thus giving users more control over their e-mail.

The most common use of procmail is calling it from a user's .forward file. A .forward is just what it sounds like: the mechanism to forward e-mail to another e-mail address or local script or application. For example, adding any other e-mail address to a file named .forward in your home directory will forward all e-mail to that address. If you want to forward e-mail to a remote address, add the following to a .forward file in your home directory, replacing forward@example.com with your forwarding address:

```
forward@example.com
```

If you want to forward your e-mail to a remote address and keep a local copy of your e-mail on the system, modify your .forward as shown here, replacing your local login and forwarding address:

```
\curtis, forward@example.com
```

Omitting the backslash would result in a mail loop, infinitely forwarding the same message to forward@example.com.

But we're interested in forwarding e-mail to procmail, not another e-mail account. To do so, we want to pipe the message to procmail by adding the following to .forward:

```
"|exec /usr/bin/procmail"
```

Make sure your .forward file is not group-writable by issuing the command chmod 644 .forward, and then try to send a test message, either from the command line or your mail client. If you try doing this but find that your test message is never delivered, then take a look at /var/log/maillog. Chances are you will find something like the following toward the end of maillog:

```
Nov 17 22:45:15 mail smrsh: uid 500: attempt to use "procmail" (stat failed)
Nov 17 22:45:15 mail sendmail[31852]: jAI3jEn3031851: to="|exec /usr/bin/procmail", ➥
ctladdr=<curtis@mail.ods.org> (500/500), delay=00:00:00, xdelay=00:00:00, ➥
mailer=prog, pri=30546, dsn=5.0.0, stat=Service unavailable
Nov 17 22:45:15 mail sendmail[31852]: jAI3jEn3031851: jAI3jFn3031852: DSN: ➥
Service unavailable
```

Hmm, so it looks like the delivery of the message failed. Notice smrsh in the first line? That is the sendmail restricted shell, designed to run external applications run from a .forward file in a safe and secure environment. It also restricts what applications can be called from a .forward. This keeps mischievous users from plotting some diabolical scheme to take over your server—or at least hampers them a bit by restricting their mail forwarding ability.

But you probably want to allow the use of procmail, so how do we rectify this situation? Well, it's very simple. Go ahead and check out the directory /etc/smrsh/. At this point, it should be empty. To permit specific commands to be allowed from within a .forward, simply populate this directory with a *symbolic*, or *soft*, link. A *symlink*, as they are typically called, is simply a pointer to a real or nonexistent file or directory. The former is very useful, while the latter, called a dangling link, isn't necessarily useful at all. So, to allow procmail, type the following at the command line:

```
[curtis@mail ~]$ cd /etc/smrsh/
[curtis@mail smrsh]$ sudo ln -s /usr/bin/procmail procmail
```

and check your handiwork:

```
[curtis@mail smrsh]$ ls -l
```

```
total 0
lrwxrwxrwx 1 root root 17 Nov 17 23:09 procmail -> /usr/bin/procmail
```

Now try sending your test message again. Voilà—instant delivery! If you create a working .procmailrc and add the simple test recipe suggested in the next section, you should also find that not only is the message delivered but it is also filtered into the e-mail folder Testing. Congratulations—you are on your way to more organized mail delivery. Let's take a look at some examples to get you started writing your own procmail recipes.

# A Cookbook of Sample procmail Recipes

In this section, I'll provide some sample procmail recipes. Many of these I use myself, but this does not mean you should simply copy them verbatim and put them in your .procmailrc. Please take the time to understand what they are doing, and adapt them to your specific needs. I'm providing them to help you develop your recipe-creation skills through example. You should find much of the foundational material introduced earlier in this chapter reflected in these examples. Let's start off easy and work our way into more complex recipes.

## A Simple Test Recipe

This is a good recipe that can be used to test procmail and make sure you are filtering your mail through procmail properly. You might use this as the first recipe in your .procmailrc, but comment it out after you've successfully tested procmail.

```
:0:
* ^Subject:.*test
Testing
```

As you can see from the first line of the recipe, no flags are used, so only message headers will be searched. In addition, procmail will use the default local lockfile for this recipe.

There is one condition, and it is a regular expression that looks for the string "Subject" at the beginning of the line (^Subject), followed by the colon character (:), followed by zero or more of any character at all (.*), followed by the string "test" (test). Because the regex is not anchored to the end but only the beginning of the line, anything at all, or nothing, can precede the string "test". Also remember that procmail conditions are not case sensitive, so any capitalization of the strings "Subject" and "test" will match.

If a message matches the condition, then the message will be delivered to the mailbox file $MAILDIR/Testing, as indicated by the final line of the recipe. Subsequently, we know that procmail will use $MAILDIR/Testing.lock as the local lockfile.

## Filtering E-mail from Your Mother

Because we know Mom is so dear to us, we want to make sure any messages from her are filtered to a special e-mail folder:

```
:0:
* ^From:.*mom@example.com
MailFromMom
```

As you can see from the first line of the recipe, no flags are used, so only message headers will be searched. In addition, procmail will use the default local lockfile for this recipe.

There is one condition, and it is a regular expression that looks for the string "From" at the beginning of the line (^From), followed by the colon character (:), followed by zero or more of any characters (.*), followed by the e-mail address mom@example.com. Because the regex is not anchored to the end but only the beginning of the line, anything at all, or nothing, can precede your mother's e-mail address. Also remember that procmail conditions are not case sensitive, so any capitalization of the strings "From" and your mother's e-mail address will match. Adding the .* between the ^From: and the e-mail address catches anything, like a name, that might come between the two.

If a message matches the condition, then the message will be delivered to the mailbox file $MAILDIR/MailFromMom, as indicated by the final line of the recipe. Subsequently, we know that procmail will use $MAILDIR/MailFromMom.lock as the local lockfile.

## Filtering E-mail from a Mailing List

Perhaps you are subscribed to an e-mail mailing list, the Central Ohio Linux Users Group (COLUG), for example. Keeping messages from various mailing lists separated makes following discussion threads much easier, and allows you to focus on more important mail in your Inbox.

We know that the e-mail address used to send to the COLUG mailing list is colug@colug.net, so perhaps that's a good search pattern to start with.

```
:0:
* ^TO_colug@colug.net
ColugMailingList
```

As you can see from the first line of the recipe, no flags are used, so only message headers will be searched. In addition, procmail will use the default local lockfile for this recipe.

There is one condition, and it is a procmail macro combined with a simple pattern that looks for the e-mail address colug@colug.net in the various delivery headers (using the ^TO_ macro discussed earlier in the chapter). We're smart enough to know that the mailing list address won't always be found on the normal To header, so instead of writing multiple recipes to match on the different places it could be, we'll let procmail do that for us with the ^TO_ macro. Also remember that procmail conditions are not case sensitive, so any capitalization of the COLUG e-mail address will also match.

If a message matches the condition, then the message will be delivered to the mailbox file $MAILDIR/ColugMailingList, as indicated by the final line of the recipe. Subsequently, we know that procmail will use $MAILDIR/ColugMailingList.lock as the local lockfile.

However, filtering mail from a mailing list can be tricky. Sometimes, the mailing list address itself cannot be found in any of the delivery headers. The reason for this can be that the mailing list software itself stripped the address per its configuration, or the original sender added the list address to the BCC line in their e-mail client. A better way to filter e-mail mailing lists is through a unique identifier. For example, Mailman, the mailing list software of choice introduced later in Chapter 19, and other properly configured and well-behaving mailing list servers will add a series of List- headers, per RFC 2369 (www.ietf.org/rfc/rfc2369.txt). It might be particularly useful to filter by the List-Id header, which (theoretically) should be unique to every mailing list and is added to every message handled by the mailing list server regardless of how the message is addressed or delivered:

```
:0:
* ^List-Id: Central OH Linux User Group <colug.colug.net>
ColugMailingList
```

The lesson to be learned from this exercise is to look for unique identifiers when filtering specific classes of e-mail. Mailing lists make it particularly easy for you in most cases. If in doubt, check the e-mail message headers with your mail client and look for the specific List-Id, or other unique identifier, for the types of e-mail you'd like to filter.

## Filtering E-mail with Undesirable Content

Nothing can take the place of a good antispam application, but there might be that one obviously offensive or annoying word or phrase you never want to see in any of your e-mail folders. Accepting the responsibility of deleting mail programmatically, you might decide to not even filter the message to an e-mail mailbox file at all. In addition, you might also want to search the entire e-mail message, including the header and body. Let's use the phrase from a popular e-mail scam as the simple search pattern in this next recipe:

```
:0HB
* Request for urgent business relationship\.
/dev/null
```

As you can see from the first line of the recipe, we use the H flag to explicitly search the e-mail header and the B flag to also search the e-mail body. In addition, procmail will not use a local lockfile, as indicated by omitting the second colon at the start of the recipe. I explain this in a bit when we look at the recipe's action.

There is one condition, and it is a simple regular expression that looks for the string "Request for urgent business relationship." anywhere in the e-mail message, regardless of its position on a line. Don't forget to escape the period so procmail matches the period itself. Also remember that procmail conditions are not case sensitive, so any capitalization of the search string will match.

If a message matches the condition, then the message will be delivered to the file /dev/null, as indicated by the final line of the recipe. In most UNIX and Linux operating systems, /dev/null is special. Officially called the *null device*, you might also hear others refer to /dev/null as the *bit bucket* or *black hole*. Anything written to /dev/null is simply discarded, essentially deleted and forever forgotten. This is why you do not need a lockfile; writing to /dev/null simultaneously has the same outcome as writing to /dev/null one at a time: nothing.

---

**Caution** Be sure a regular expression is thoroughly tested before adding it to a recipe that directs messages to /dev/null. One small typo and you could silently drop all of your mail.

---

## Filtering Unreadable E-mail

What, exactly, constitutes unreadable e-mail can be a hotly debated conversation. However, choosing certain unreadable character sets potentially used in an e-mail message is a good start. For instance, for English-speaking readers, e-mail composed and sent in an Asian character set will be completely unreadable; their e-mail reader will not recognize or translate the characters properly, regardless of whether or not the message was meant to be spam. The following are the very first few lines in my .procmailrc:

```
UNREADABLE='[^?"]*big5|iso-2022-jp|ISO-2022-KR|euc-kr|gb2312|ks_c_5601-1987'

:0:
* 1^0 $ ^Subject:.*=\?($UNREADABLE)
* 1^0 $ ^Content-Type:.*charset="?($UNREADABLE)
Unreadable-mail

:0:
* ^Content-Type:.*multipart
* B ?? $ ^Content-Type:.*^?.*charset="?($UNREADABLE)
Unreadable-mail
```

These are very complex recipes that use several advanced features of procmail I introduced earlier in the chapter. As you can see from the first line of each of the recipes, no flags are used, so only message headers will be searched initially. In addition, procmail will use the default local lockfile for these recipes. As such, keep in mind that the two recipes are mutually exclusive; if a message matches the first, it will not be run against the second, and vice versa.

The first recipe uses scoring to indicate that matching either condition is sufficient to execution of the action. If either conditions match, the recipe score will be incremented by 1, as indicated by 1^0 preceding each condition pattern.

The $ character indicates that the condition should be evaluated before being passed off to the internal egrep. In both conditions, this means that the variable UNREADABLE will be expanded to the regular expression previously assigned to it on the first line of the example. This means we don't have to explicitly reproduce the long regex every time we need it, and procmail will expand it for us. The rest of the condition pattern is a standard regex looking for the list of unreadable character sets in the Subject and Content-Type headers.

If a message matches either of the conditions of the first recipe, then the message will be delivered to the mailbox file $MAILDIR/Unreadable-mail, as indicated by the final line of the recipe. Subsequently, we know that procmail will use $MAILDIR/Unreadable.lock as the local lockfile.

The second recipe contains two conditions, but scoring is not used, so both conditions must match, or the action will not be executed. The first condition is a simple regular expression, looking for any Content-Type headers containing the string "multipart". The second condition is a special condition, overriding the recipe flags and comparing the pattern to the message body only, as indicated by the use of B ??. Similar to the conditions on the first recipe, this condition also uses the shell expansion option to expand the variable UNREADABLE first, as indicated by the $ character preceding the search pattern.

If a message matches both of the conditions of the second recipe, then the message will be delivered to the mailbox file $MAILDIR/Unreadable-mail, as indicated by the final line of the recipe. Subsequently, we know that procmail will use $MAILDIR/Unreadable.lock as the local lockfile.

## Forwarding Copies of E-mail Messages

In some cases, you might want to forward a copy of an e-mail to one or more e-mail recipients. Doing so is easy with the following (examples have been adapted from the procmailex(5) man page):

```
:0 c
* ^From.*jason@example.com
* ^Subject:.*review this
! jon@example.com

:0
* ^From.*jason@example.com
* ^Subject:.*review this
MailToReview
```

As you can see from the first line of the first recipe, the c flag is used, so only message headers will be searched and a carbon copy of the message is created and further processed against the second recipe. Doing so simply ensures you retain a copy of the message you are forwarding; otherwise, without the c flag the recipe would forward the message and stop. In addition, procmail will not use a local lockfile for the first recipe but will use the default local lockfile for the second recipe.

In both recipes, there are two conditions. Because we are making a copy of the message in the first recipe to be filed away locally, each recipe is identical aside from the action.

The first condition of each recipe is a regular expression that looks for the string "From" at the beginning of the line (^From), followed by the colon character (:), followed by zero or more of any characters (.*), followed by the e-mail address jason@example.com. The second condition of each recipe is a regular expression that looks for the string "Subject" at the beginning of the line (^Subject), followed by the colon character (:), followed by zero or more of any character at all (.*), followed by the phrase "review this" (test).

Because neither regular expression is anchored to the end but only the beginning of the line, anything at all, or nothing, can precede the search strings. Also remember that procmail conditions are not case sensitive, so any capitalization of the search strings will match.

If a message matches both conditions of the first recipe, then the message will be delivered to the e-mail account jon@example.com, as indicated by the final line of the first recipe. No lockfile is necessary to forward e-mail.

If a message matches both conditions of the second recipe, then the message will be delivered to the mailbox file $MAILDIR/MailToReview. Subsequently, we know that procmail will use $MAILDIR/MailToReview.lock as the local lockfile.

This example can be condensed into a shorter set of recipes, using a different combination of recipe flags:

```
:0 c
* ^From.*jason@example
* ^Subject:.*review this
! jon@example.com


:0 A
MailToReview
```

The first recipe of the previous two examples is identical; it creates a carbon copy of the message and forwards the original to Jon. However, the difference is in the second recipe. Using the A flag and chaining the two recipes together, thus making the first recipe a prerequisite to the second, reduces the number of redundant conditions. The second recipe will execute only if the conditions of the first recipe were matched.

Here's a third way to write these recipes using nested recipes:

```
:0
* ^From.*jason@example.com
* ^Subject:.*review this
{
  :0 c
  ! jon@example.com

  :0
  MailToReview
}
```

This is one parent recipe whose action is a nesting block that contains two more recipes. The parent recipe, which has no action other than to nest other recipes, needs no special flags or a local lockfile. Its two conditions, both of which must be met before executing the action, are meant to match on the e-mails we are interested in filtering to begin with. If a message matches, then the action is to process the message with the nested recipes, which are nearly identical to the previous two examples. First, a carbon copy of the message is created and the message is forwarded to Jon. Then the message is delivered to the mailbox file MailToReview. This demonstrates three different ways of achieving the same results, each using different procmail features we've seen throughout this chapter.

## Filtering Duplicate E-mail

This next recipe also has had a place in my .procmailrc for as long as I've used procmail. To give credit where due, this recipe is also taken direct from the procmailex(5) man page:

```
:0 Whc: msgid.lock
| formail -D 8192 msgid.cache
```

```
:0 a:
Duplicate-mail
```

Again, this example introduces the use of a different procmail feature, namely the use of additional flags and an action that pipes to a command.

First, you might notice that three flags are used in the first recipe: the W flag to make procmail wait for the execution of the action, suppressing any errors if the action is unsuccessful; the h flag to feed only the header of the message to the pipe; and the c flag to create a carbon copy of the message, turning what normally would have been a nondelivering recipe into a delivering recipe. In addition, procmail will use the local lockfile msgid.lock for the first recipe. Because we use the W flag and a specific local lockfile, other instances of procmail will not interfere with each other.

Because the first recipe has no condition, the action will always be executed. In this case, the action is the execution of another program, namely the formail command. formail is a mail formatter. In its simplest usage, any text piped through formail will be forced into proper mbox format. formail can also extract and manipulate header information found in a message in mbox format.

In this case, we are using formail to detect duplicate messages through the -D argument. This argument also requires a maximum length, in bytes, and a filename. It will use these to maintain a message ID cache file of the maximum length, compare the Message-ID header of the message piped through it to the message ID cache, and exit with a successful status code if the message is a duplicate.

The second recipe uses the a flag, which chains the two recipes and makes the successful execution of the first a prerequisite to the second recipe. It, too, has no conditions, so if the prerequisites have been fulfilled, the action will always be executed. The second recipe is a delivering recipe, writing mail that has been detected by the previous recipe as a duplicate message to the mailbox file $MAILDIR/Duplicate-mail, as indicated by the final line of the second recipe. Subsequently, we know that procmail will use $MAILDIR/Duplicate-mail.lock as the local lockfile.

This is such a deceptively simple-looking example, but it is a bit more complex than it appears at first blush. With the right, or, rather, the wrong combination of recipe flags, it would not work as expected and possibly drop or delete mail. This example is a conservative one that makes copies and filters duplicates instead of arbitrarily deleting any duplicate messages. This can be simplified into one recipe if you do not wish to receive the duplicates (also taken directly from the procmailex(5) man page):

```
:0 Wh: msgid.lock
| formail -D 8192 msgid.cache
```

Here, if formail detects the message as a duplicate, it will return a successful exit status code, thus satisfying the procmail condition. No carbon copy of the message is made, so the message is effectively dropped. If, for some reason, the action did not complete successfully due to error or because the message was not a duplicate, procmail would consider the message unfiltered and continue processing the message if there are any remaining filters in the rcfile.

This concludes the sampling of procmail recipes. These examples were meant to showcase most of the main features available to you through procmail. The bulk of your filters will probably be short and simple, but I challenge you to look for ways to streamline your filters or incorporate some of the examples listed here in your own environment. Do not forget to test a search pattern with egrep on some sample text before committing it to a recipe. Also remember that turning on verbose logging in procmail will tell you exactly what a recipe did—or did not—do, and therefore help you troubleshooting misfiring recipes. Next, let's take a look at how you can forward your mail through procmail to be filtered in the first place.

# Further procmail Resources

procmail is an extremely well-documented software package. Documentation can be found locally on your Fedora Core system in /usr/share/doc/procmail-[version]/, where [version] is replaced by the base version string of the RPM package installed. For example, at the time of the writing of this book, the RPM package installed was procmail-3.22-16, so documentation can be found in /usr/share/doc/procmail-3.22-16/; to check the version of procmail, run the following command:

```
[curtis@mail ~]$ rpm -qv procmail
```

---

```
procmail-3.22-16
```

---

In addition to the local documentation, or the documentation found with the source distribution, the three procmail man pages are exceptionally useful. For general procmail usage and information, see the procmail(1) man page. For information regarding procmail runtime configuration files and general recipe information, see the procmailrc(5) man page. Finally, for excellent procmail recipe examples with commentary, from which I've already referenced a great deal, check out the procmailex(5) man page. For community support, the procmail mailing lists are also an excellent resource. You can find list archives and subscription information at www.procmail.org/era/lists.html.

## Summary

There are two basic ways to filter e-mail: either on the client or on the server. It can get unwieldy if you have to manage more than a handful of filters in multiple e-mail clients on multiple computers, so server-side filtering is very convenient. procmail has been the e-mail filtering application of choice for years. It's a solid application with its flexibility rooted in regular expressions, a formulaic way of describing patterns. Filtering options are nearly limitless with procmail recipes, and in this chapter I supplied several examples designed to get you started. If you decide to forward your mail through procmail to filter your mail, be sure to configure `smrsh`, the sendmail restricted shell; otherwise messages will bounce.

In the coming chapters, we will build on these basic filtering fundamentals and find out how to put them to good use combating e-mail spam and viruses.

■ ■ ■

# CHAPTER 14

# Using MailScanner for Content Filtering

**A**t this point, you have a completely functional e-mail solution that some might think has all of the bare necessities: You have a working and customized MTA; you can offer remote mail access through POP3, IMAP, or the Web; and you can even handle basic message filtering and sorting. However, as I'm sure you have experienced with other e-mail accounts, you and your users can quickly become inundated with junk in your Inboxes, even if you sort the legitimate e-mail into different mail folders.

Unfortunately, the ubiquitous nature of e-mail means that a significant amount of malicious and unsolicited bulk e-mail is sent daily. Much of the junk e-mail is worse than a nuisance. We know that e-mail viruses can cause real damage in some cases, but what do you do about users that send large e-mail attachments or executable programs that can cause trouble on their recipients' computers? The latter examples might not be e-mail viruses per se; they could come from a clueless user with good intentions. Although you may have the absolute basic components necessary for a working e-mail solution, it's arguable that the basic components aren't enough in today's environments. Your abilities to scan messages and block or reject messages with questionable content are absolutely necessary. In this chapter, I introduce MailScanner, a free, open source product that allows you to do just that.

## Introducing MailScanner

MailScanner (www.mailscanner.info) is a complete e-mail security application designed to protect users from viruses, worms, unsolicited bulk e-mail, and any other harmful attachments or content. Whereas procmail excels at sorting e-mail based on matching patterns in the message header or body, MailScanner can do this and much more. For example, if you want to sort e-mail based only on certain criteria, procmail is much more efficient, but anything more complex, like scanning e-mail for any of the thousands of e-mail viruses out there, should be handled by MailScanner. This is not to say that procmail has no place in your environment; procmail can still filter your personal mail. MailScanner is meant as a gateway through which all mail is filtered to stop or tag harmful or potentially useless e-mail.

MailScanner can function as a complete antivirus and antispam solution, or it can act as a gatekeeper of sorts, sending the e-mail to another antivirus and antispam application for further analysis. In fact, MailScanner gives you the ability to send your e-mail through more than one antivirus application, if you are overly cautious enough to desire to do so. The point is that even though MailScanner alone is a complete content filtering solution, I am introducing MailScanner in the context of its role within a more complete antivirus and antispam solution. Using MailScanner is possible without changing your sendmail configuration directly. However, the mail delivery flow will change slightly.

## MailScanner and the Flow of Your E-mail

At this point, sendmail accepts mail from the outside world and delivers mail to the users' mailbox directly, effectively acting as both the MTA and the MDA, or forwarding mail through procmail to be filtered and delivered based on rules, in which case procmail acts as the MDA. With MailScanner, the flow of mail once it reaches your mail server is a bit more complex. The sendmail program still acts as the MTA, but it first routes the mail to an incoming queue instead of directly to your users' mailboxes or to procmail for additional filtering. MailScanner regularly takes the mail from the sendmail delivery queue, moves it to its own temporary mail queue, scans the message according to its configuration (which I cover later in the chapter), and finally acts on the message, again according to its configuration. If a message is to be delivered, MailScanner moves the mail to an outgoing queue, where a second sendmail process scans and delivers the message to either your users' mailbox or to procmail for additional filtering. This new flow of e-mail on your e-mail system is shown in detail in Figure 14-1.

The way MailScanner acts on the message depends on a number of criteria. For instance, if a message is passed on to the antivirus software and found to be infected, MailScanner can immediately delete the e-mail without delivering it to the recipient. Or before deleting the e-mail, the message can be quarantined in a special message queue for future review, in case the message was incorrectly identified as an infected message. If MailScanner determines it's OK to deliver the e-mail message to the recipient based on its configuration criteria, it delivers the message to an outgoing queue, from which sendmail scans and delivers messages normally. From there, delivery happens as it has previously, and messages can be forwarded through procmail for additional filtering and sorting.

Essentially, MailScanner splits the normal delivery process into three steps. First sendmail, the MTA, delivers the message to an incoming queue, which is used as input by MailScanner. Next, MailScanner delivers clean messages to an outgoing queue. Finally, sendmail completes the process by delivering directly to the recipient's mailbox or passes the message to procmail for sorting and final delivery.

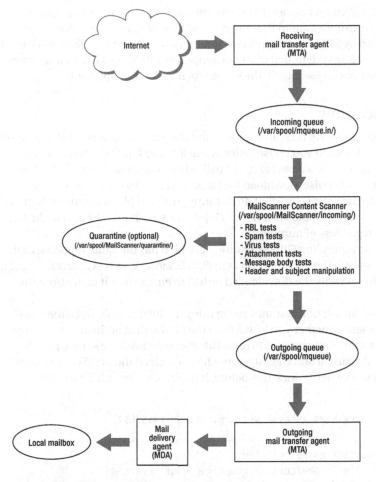

**Figure 14-1.** *MailScanner changes the flow of your e-mail by creating an intermediate step, during which messages are scanned for malicious content.*

# Installing MailScanner

Installing MailScanner will not directly affect your sendmail installation. The fact your send-mail configuration is not altered is a huge advantage of choosing to install MailScanner. If you need to temporarily suspend MailScanner and any related antivirus, antispam, or content filtering altogether, you can do so by shutting down MailScanner and restarting sendmail. Although MailScanner changes the flow of e-mail delivery, it does not do so through changes to your customized sendmail.mc. Instead, it starts sendmail with a few minor runtime configu-ration options that change only its delivery behavior. All of your other customizations remain intact.

The steps to install MailScanner are a bit different than some of the other applications we've seen so far. If you are using a system that supports RPM packaging, like Fedora Core, everything will be installed by RPM, and the process is automated by one installation script. If you are using a Linux operating system that does not support the RPM package management system, the installation process is essentially the same, albeit a bit more involved.

## Obtaining MailScanner

Visit the MailScanner website (www.mailscanner.info) and choose the latest stable installation tarball that matches your system. If you chose Fedora Core for your Linux distribution, download the latest MailScanner-x.xx.x-x.rpm.tar.gz tarball, where x.xx.x-x is replaced by the latest stable version string. Otherwise, download the latest MailScanner-install.x.xx.x-x.tar.gz tarball for Linux operating systems that do not support the RPM packaging system. At the time of this writing, the latest stable version is 4.47.4-1, but you should download the latest stable version available, regardless of numbering.

Also download the corresponding GPG signature file, which has the same filename as the installation tarball but ends with the file extension .sig (MailScanner-x.xx.x-x.rpm.tar.gz.sig, for example). We'll use this to verify the downloaded tarball to ensure that it came from the MailScanner developers.

The following example installation assumes you're using the RPM tarball; since the installation process is exactly the same whether you install from the RPM tarball or the regular source tarball, you can follow the same basic process to install MailScanner from the source tarball.

After you download the tarball and GPG signature file, download the MailScanner developer's GPG public key. If you've never done this before, it might look something like the following code:

```
[curtis@mail ~]$ gpg --recv-keys --keyserver pgp.mit.edu 1415B654
```

```
gpg: directory `/home/curtis/.gnupg' created
gpg: new configuration file `/home/curtis/.gnupg/gpg.conf' created
gpg: WARNING: options in `/home/curtis/.gnupg/gpg.conf' are not yet active during ➥
this run
gpg: keyring `/home/curtis/.gnupg/secring.gpg' created
gpg: keyring `/home/curtis/.gnupg/pubring.gpg' created
gpg: requesting key 1415B654 from hkp server pgp.mit.edu
gpg: /home/curtis/.gnupg/trustdb.gpg: trustdb created
gpg: key 1415B654: public key "Julian Field <Jules@Jules.fm>" imported
gpg: no ultimately trusted keys found
gpg: Total number processed: 1
gpg:               imported: 1
```

Otherwise, the same command might yield the following output:

[curtis@mail ~]$ **gpg --recv-keys --keyserver pgp.mit.edu 1415B654**

```
gpg: requesting key 1415B654 from hkp server pgp.mit.edu
gpg: key 1415B654: public key "Julian Field <Jules@Jules.fm>" imported
gpg: no ultimately trusted keys found
gpg: Total number processed: 1
gpg:           imported: 1
```

The first code snippet occurs if you've never used gpg, the GPG command, before. The gpg command illustrated previously is requesting the public key with the key ID of 1415B654 from the Massachusetts Institute of Technology (MIT) public key server pgp.mit.edu. Your personal key ring is created from scratch, and the public key you've requested is successfully imported into your key ring. The second code snippet occurs if you have used gpg before and a public key ring exists. In that case, the requested public key is imported into your key ring. Now use gpg to verify that the tarball you downloaded was signed by the MailScanner developer, replacing each filename in the following command line with those of the files you downloaded:

[curtis@mail ~]$ **gpg --verify MailScanner-4.47.4-1.rpm.tar.gz.sig** ➡
**MailScanner-4.47.4-1.rpm.tar.gz**

```
gpg: Signature made Sat 05 Nov 2005 11:04:03 AM EST using DSA key ID 1415B654
gpg: Good signature from "Julian Field <Jules@Jules.fm>"
gpg:        aka "Julian Field <jkf@soton.ac.uk>"
gpg:        aka "Julian Field <jules@zepler.org>"
gpg:        aka "Julian Field <jkf@ecs.soton.ac.uk>"
gpg:        aka "Julian Field <julianfield@acm.org>"
gpg:        aka "Julian Field <Julian.Field@fsl.com>"
gpg:        aka "Julian Field <julian@webcentre.net>"
gpg:        aka "Julian Field <Buyer@ecs.soton.ac.uk>"
gpg:        aka "Julian Field <Jules@JulianField.net>"
gpg:        aka "Julian Field <sysjkf@ecs.soton.ac.uk>"
gpg:        aka "Julian Field <J.K.Field@ecs.soton.ac.uk>"
gpg:        aka "Julian Field <postmaster@ecs.soton.ac.uk>"
gpg:        aka "Julian Field <mailscanner@ecs.soton.ac.uk>"
gpg: WARNING: This key is not certified with a trusted signature!
gpg:    There is no indication that the signature belongs to the owner.
Primary key fingerprint: EE81 D763 3DB0 0BFD E1DC 7222 11F6 5947 1415 B654
```

**■Note** This is just a quick introduction to one use of GPG and GPG signatures. For more information about the GPG and public key cryptography in general, visit www.gnupg.org.

The GPG fingerprint on the tarball matches the signature and appears to have been signed by the MailScanner developer, so you can be relatively certain that the files you downloaded are legitimate.

## Running the MailScanner Install Script

Installing MailScanner is as simple as unpacking the tarball, entering the MailScanner installation directory, and running the command install.sh. The command install.sh is a shell script that performs a series of tests to ensure that your environment is ready to build and install MailScanner RPMs. It is rather verbose and does a good job at letting you know what it is doing. If you've followed the Fedora Core 4 installation guidelines outlined in Chapter 2, this process should go especially smoothly.

First, unpack the installation tarball, and move it into the installation directory that is created:

```
[curtis@mail ~]$ tar zxvf MailScanner-4.47.4-1.rpm.tar.gz ; cd MailScanner-4.47.4-1
```

The installation tarball contains everything necessary for a complete MailScanner installation. The core of MailScanner itself is written in the Perl programming language. Perl can be extended with modules, which include some packaged with Perl and others created independently of the main Perl development process. Perl modules are reusable code packaged in such a way that it can be integrated into Perl programs. MailScanner takes advantage of several Perl modules that provide specific utilities, and these are bundled in the MailScanner installation tarball.

Run the installation script provided by the MailScanner developers inside the MailScanner installation directory:

```
[curtis@mail MailScanner-4.47.4-1]$ sudo ./install.sh
```

Now sit back and watch as the MailScanner install script runs through each of the several prerequisite Perl modules and applications. If the module isn't found on your e-mail system, the install script attempts to build and install it for you. The script is self-explanatory and is verbose in telling you what it's doing; just keep an eye on it. As the script says, do not worry too much about errors; they probably just indicate that a Perl module is already installed on the system. The only two important Perl modules required for the normal operation of MailScanner are perl-HTML-Parser and perl-MIME-tool, and we'll make sure they are installed properly after the script is complete.

Once the installation script completes, check to make sure the following RPM packages were installed successfully (your specific versions may vary if you installed a newer MailScanner release):

```
[curtis@mail i386]$ rpm -qv perl-HTML-Parser
```

```
perl-HTML-Parser-3.45-1
```

```
[curtis@mail ~]$ rpm -qv perl-MIME-tools
```

```
perl-MIME-tools-5.417-1
```

```
[curtis@mail ~]$ rpm -qv tnef
```

```
tnef-1.2.3.1-1
```

```
[curtis@mail ~]$ rpm -qv mailscanner
```

```
mailscanner-4.47.4-1
```

If any of these RPM packages are not installed, you must recheck the output from the MailScanner installation script to see why; these four packages are required for basic MailScanner operation. On Fedora Core 4, the perl-HTML-Parser RPM should be already installed as part of the default installation outlined in Chapter 2. If it isn't, the installation script should have rebuilt and installed from the local copy in the MailScanner installation tarball. The other three are installed by the MailScanner installation script and are not part of the default Fedora Core 4 installation.

If you are installing MailScanner from the source tarball distribution, you can check to make sure the required components were installed using a couple of quick commands. First, to check for the successful installation of the HTML::Parser Perl module, try the following command line in your e-mail system:

```
[curtis@mail ~]$ perl -e "use HTML::Parser;"
```

which runs a Perl command using the Perl interpreter. If there is no output or errors, then the module has been installed properly. If the module was not installed, you might see an error like the following one after running the previous command:

```
[curtis@mail ~]$ perl -e "use HTML::Parser;"
```

```
Can't locate HTML/Parser.pm in @INC (@INC contains: ➥
/usr/lib/perl5/site_perl/5.8.6/i386-linux-thread-multi ➥
/usr/lib/perl5/site_perl/5.8.5/i386-linux-thread-multi ➥
/usr/lib/perl5/site_perl/5.8.4/i386-linux-thread-multi ➥
/usr/lib/perl5/site_perl/5.8.3/i386-linux-thread-multi ➥
/usr/lib/perl5/site_perl/5.8.6 ➥
/usr/lib/perl5/site_perl/5.8.5 ➥
/usr/lib/perl5/site_perl/5.8.4 ➥
/usr/lib/perl5/site_perl/5.8.3 /usr/lib/perl5/site_perl ➥
```

```
/usr/lib/perl5/vendor_perl/5.8.6/i386-linux-thread-multi ➡
/usr/lib/perl5/vendor_perl/5.8.5/i386-linux-thread-multi ➡
/usr/lib/perl5/vendor_perl/5.8.4/i386-linux-thread-multi ➡
/usr/lib/perl5/vendor_perl/5.8.3/i386-linux-thread-multi ➡
/usr/lib/perl5/vendor_perl/5.8.6 ➡
/usr/lib/perl5/vendor_perl/5.8.5 ➡
/usr/lib/perl5/vendor_perl/5.8.4 ➡
/usr/lib/perl5/vendor_perl/5.8.3 ➡
/usr/lib/perl5/vendor_perl /usr/lib/perl5/5.8.6/i386-linux-thread-multi ➡
/usr/lib/perl5/5.8.6 .) at -e line 1.
BEGIN failed--compilation aborted at -e line 1.
```

Try testing the `MIME::Tools` Perl module next:

```
[curtis@mail ~]$ perl -e "use MIME::Tools;"
```

Again, if this commands exits without any output or errors, the module has been installed.

The TNEF and MailScanner binaries should have been installed in a system binary directory, like /usr/bin/ or /usr/sbin/. If you get no results when running either of the following commands, then the application is not installed properly:

```
[curtis@mail ~]$ locate tnef | grep bin/tnef
```

```
/usr/bin/tnef
```

```
[curtis@mail ~]$ locate MailScanner | grep bin/MailScanner
```

```
/usr/sbin/MailScanner
```

If any of these Perl modules of programs are not installed, you must recheck the output from the MailScanner installation script to see why; these four packages are required for basic MailScanner operation.

Now that MailScanner is installed, you're ready for the arduous task of configuring MailScanner and customizing its numerous configuration options. But before we move on to configuration matters specific to MailScanner's behavior, let's talk about some best practices for content filtering in general.

# Successful Content Filtering

My experience as a system administrator in general, and as an e-mail administrator in particular, teaches me that one of the most necessary features of any mail system is content filtering. However, experience also illustrates that this is the one of most difficult things to get right. Who's to say what's right, anyway? You might be saying, "My boss, silly." Well, maybe, but depending on the industry you're in, your users are also probably your bosses, at least indirectly.

Global content filtering is a balancing act. On one hand, you have to filter for content basically just to maintain an acceptable level of service; allowing too much bogus e-mail, whether it's offensive, unsolicited, or malicious, will fill up valuable disk space prematurely, and possibly result in a denial of service (DoS) from high volume and high server load or upset your general users, because they have to wade through too much extraneous material to get to their legitimate mail.

On the other hand, there's the saying, "One man's trash is another man's treasure." The same concept applies to e-mail. For example, many English-speaking users may consider e-mail written in an Asian character set to be spam. But my place of business employs numerous Asian faculty and staff members and students, meaning Asian character sets aren't at all uncommon. If we arbitrarily decided to block all e-mails written in Asian character sets, a significant percentage of our users would be unhappy (justifiably so!). You have to be careful what you filter, especially if you decide not to deliver certain classes of e-mail altogether.

In general, most e-mail content filtering applications, including MailScanner, allow you to do one of four things with an e-mail that matches a specific filter:

- Deliver the message normally, regardless of the filter match

- Reject the message, or bounce it back to the sender

- Quarantine the message in a temporary holding queue for further review by e-mail administrators

- Notify the sender or recipient(s) that a message matched a filter

With regards to MailScanner specifically, these options are not mutually exclusive. For instance, if you choose to reject, or bounce back, a message, it might also be a good idea to notify the recipient(s) that the message was rejected.

However, as I said earlier, false positives are a huge problem, especially when dealing with spam and phishing scams. If the e-mail system rejects a legitimate message, and that message is critical to a particularly import user, you probably want that message in a quarantine for easy retrieval.

---

**Caution** Best practices, and years of personal experience, illustrate that you would be highly ill-advised to simply discard any e-mail message without sending a rejection notification or quarantining the message for later retrieval. It's impossible to guarantee that you will never have false positives, and silently dropping e-mail with no backup is not a good idea.

---

The proliferation of e-mail viruses and phishing scams adds to the headache of dealing with the proper filtering of content. The headache isn't only in the sheer numbers of messages, although they can be staggering when there is a new virus outbreak, but in the fact that most messages infected with a virus payload are forged with valid e-mail addresses. An MTA uses the sender e-mail address found in the MAIL FROM: portion of a message's SMTP envelope to send a *nondelivery report (NDR)*. An NDR is the bounce message an SMTP server sends when an e-mail has invalid or undeliverable recipients. Because the addresses in an SMTP envelope are self-reported by the SMTP client, the addresses can really be anything at all, despite specific guidelines set forth in the RFCs. This can lead to a several problems.

First, if the originating e-mail address contains a valid email domain, an NDR will be sent to the originating email address. The remote MTA will accept the message, but if the recipient is not a valid user at that domain, the remote MTA will send an NDR, resulting in a double bounce. This second NDR will come back to you, the e-mail administrator, resulting in useless information, because the original message that caused the double bounce contained an invalid email address. Second, if the whole originating address is completely bogus, the NDR can't be sent at all. Both of these cases tie up CPU cycles, wasting time as the CPU tries to send e-mail that can't be delivered and taking computing power away from legitimate e-mail traffic.

Also, the originator address could be valid but forged to contain the address of someone other than the true sender. This problem, in my opinion, is the biggest in general. One infected computer, if left infected and connected to the Internet even for an hour, could send hundreds or thousands of infected e-mails, forging any e-mail address, yours for example—in which case you get stuck with all of the NDRs, infection notifications, and so forth, based on messages you never sent to recipients you may or may not know. We've all seen this before, and it has become quite a nuisance.

What started as a well-intentioned way of communicating infection, rejection, or undeliverable conditions to legitimate senders has become part of the problem of too much illegitimate e-mail. It is now considered proper administrative etiquette, and a courtesy to others, not to send notifications to either the originator or recipients when a message is caught by a common antivirus or antispam filter.

When we start configuring antivirus options, you'll see that most antivirus applications give you the option to clean an infected message and deliver it to the recipients. However, there has been a significant shift from e-mail viruses that surreptitiously attach their payload to legitimate e-mail messages to e-mail worms that create their own illegitimate messages and attach their payload for the express purpose of propagating themselves. So these days, it's simply a waste of time to clean infected messages, because typically the clean messages are garbage or unwanted. Besides that, current Internet etiquette, even if it's informally spoken, dictates that those who don't keep their computers clean of malicious content don't deserve to participate in the Internet e-mail community and should be blocked until they take responsibility for cleaning their computers.

Although MailScanner has some antivirus capabilities built in, I also introduce ClamAV, a free and open source antivirus application, in Chapter 15. I also further discuss the difficulties and best practices specifically regarding fighting e-mail viruses and worms in Chapter 15.

Having said all that about virus- or worm-infected e-mail messages, e-mail spam is a much more difficult problem. Typically, best practices dictate that spam must be tagged at least, but whether to deliver spam or not is a big decision. Phishing attacks and commercial e-mail evolve explicitly to beat antispam filters. Unlike most well-known e-mail viruses and worms that have specific signatures from which they can be detected, spam is much more difficult to accurately identify. Don't worry; I get into spam filtering in much more detail in Chapter 16. In addition, Chapters 17 and 18 are dedicated to introducing, installing, and configuring SpamAssassin, the antispam software of choice for this book. With three chapters dedicated to spam, one specifically dedicated to viruses and worms and two others to content and general e-mail filtering, you can expect to get serious exposure to combating these issues.

I hope the preceding pages convey that content filtering is a necessary evil. Mostly, how you decide to configure MailScanner, ClamAV, and SpamAssassin ought to be based on my and others' prior experiences, but you also need to balance those lessons with the specific, special needs of the user you're serving. Always quarantine whenever possible, just in case a filter goes bad or triggers a false positive. Over time, I'm sure you'll have to tweak policies and filters, but I hope this discussion presents a solid base from which to start. In subsequent chapters, minor changes to MailScanner will be necessary, but in the next section of this chapter, I cover the bulk of MailScanner configuration and customization.

# Configuring and Customizing MailScanner

Let's jump into the configuration and customization of MailScanner. Although MailScanner might actually work out of the box, I do not recommend running MailScanner before at least reading through the defaults. You've got to be aware, at least, of what MailScanner does. Otherwise, you're going to be constantly surprised when messages aren't delivered and will have to check the logs and quarantine in the hopes of finding useful information to determine why the message wasn't delivered. Although the default MailScanner is sane, you should not assume every choice the developers made in the default configuration matches your company's policies or specific needs.

If sendmail is the gate to your e-mail domain, MailScanner is the gatekeeper. Once a message is received and queued by sendmail, MailScanner starts the process of scanning every bit of the message for matches on a series of defined rules, alternatively handing off the message to another antivirus or antispam application for further scanning.

For every message that matches a rule, there is an associated action. I list the general types of actions possible in the previous section; please keep that discussion fresh in your mind when making your decisions.

MailScanner's entire configuration is found in the directory /etc/MailScanner/, regardless of whether you install from the RPM or source tarball, unless specifically configured otherwise at the time of installation. That directory looks like the one in the following example after a default installation of MailScanner version 4.47.4-1:

```
[curtis@mail ~]$ cd /etc/MailScanner/
[curtis@mail MailScanner]$ ls -l
```

```
total 184
-rw-r--r--  1 root root  6701 Nov  5 09:23 filename.rules.conf
-rw-r--r--  1 root root   787 Nov  5 09:23 filetype.rules.conf
-rw-r--r--  1 root root 87161 Nov  5 09:23 MailScanner.conf
drwxr-xr-x  2 root root  4096 Dec  8 18:58 mcp
-rw-r--r--  1 root root 13889 Dec 10 04:02 phishing.safe.sites.conf
drwxr-xr-x 17 root root  4096 Dec  4 14:16 reports
drwxr-xr-x  2 root root  4096 Dec  8 18:58 rules
-rw-r--r--  1 root root 10312 Nov  5 09:23 spam.assassin.prefs.conf
-rw-r--r--  1 root root  2969 Nov  5 09:23 spam.lists.conf
-rw-r--r--  1 root root  2538 Nov  5 09:23 virus.scanners.conf
```

As you can see, there are also three subdirectories: `mcp`, `reports`, and `rules`; we'll take a look at those later, so disregard them for now. The file naming scheme is straightforward: any file ending with a `.conf` file extension is a configuration file, and any file ending with a `.rules` file extension defines a series of rules.

The main MailScanner configuration file is `/etc/MailScanner/MailScanner.conf`, and this is where we begin. As you work through `MailScanner.conf`, you will see how the rest of the configuration and rules files are used and referenced. When you open `MailScanner.conf` for the first time, you'll find that there are over 250 configuration directives! Combined with all the blank lines and comments (i.e., any line beginning with a # character), `MailScanner.conf` may seem like an awfully lengthy configuration file. Don't worry, though. It is extremely well organized into a couple dozen main sections and self-documented through excellent comments. Later, if you ever get stuck with a particular configuration option, don't forget to consult the `MailScanner.conf(5)` man page.

## Defining MailScanner Configuration Variables

The first configurable options in `MailScanner.conf` are a set of variables. A MailScanner configuration variable is surrounded by a percent symbol, `%sampleVariable%`, for example. The first variable you will find in `MailScanner.conf` is `%etc-dir%`:

```
# Configuration directory containing this file
%etc-dir% = /etc/MailScanner
```

This variable is set at installation time and should be left as the default value. The next variable, `%report-dir%`

```
%report-dir% = /etc/MailScanner/reports/en
```

points to the directory containing scanner reports in the language of your choice. MailScanner supports some 15 languages, but let's assume English reports and notifications will be sent.

The variable `%rules-dir%`

```
%rules-dir% = /etc/MailScanner/rules
```

points to the directory containing MailScanner rules used later in the MailScanner configuration. Later in this chapter, I discuss what rules are within a MailScanner configuration context and how they can be used.

The variable `%mcp-dir%`

```
%mcp-dir% = /etc/MailScanner/mcp
```

points to the directory used for Message Content Protection, an advanced feature of MailScanner, which we won't cover in this book. Leaving it set to its default does not affect anything. All of these variables are also set at installation time and probably do not need to be changed, but it's good to know they are there and what they define.

### Specifying Your Organization's Name

The first variable you must change is `%org-name%`, so search for the following line in |MailScanner.conf:

```
%org-name% = yoursite
```

This variable is used in the X-MailScanner headers that are added to messages scanned by MailScanner. Instead of adding a generic header, MailScanner customizes the header it adds with what you define in %org-name% to make it easier to identify the headers added by your server. Adding such unique headers is useful for debugging and tracking mail delivery through your e-mail system. It also adds a bit of reassurance that messages were scanned by MailScanner in the first place.

There is a warning in MailScanner.conf not to use a period or underscore in this variable, because some other scanners incorrectly complain about finding these characters in a mail header. Therefore, for compatibility, set this variable to a word or two combined without a period, underscore, or space to briefly identify your organization, for example:

```
%org-name% = ExampleEnterprise
```

### Specifying Your Organization's Long Name

The next variable you must change is %org-long-name%. Search for the following line in MailScanner.conf:

```
%org-long-name% = Your Organization Name Here
```

This variable is just as it implies—a long description for your organization. It is used in the signature of the scanner report message bodies and can contain nearly anything at all. Although it's technically possible to make this span multiple lines by using \n, which indicates a new line, I don't recommend doing so for brevity sake. Go ahead and change this variable to more verbosely identify your organization.

### Specifying Your Organization's Website

The final configuration variable that needs to be changed is %web-site%. Change the following line:

```
%web-site% = www.your-organization.com
```

by adding the website address for your organization. This variable, like %org-long-name%, is also used in the signature of the scanner report message bodies.

## Setting MailScanner's System Settings

The next group of configuration options pertains to how the MailScanner processes themselves start and run. These options don't affect which messages are filtered, how they are filtered, or what happens when a message matches a filter. However, these options do tweak performance, for example, how often to scan the sendmail incoming queue, what user and group to run as, and so forth.

### Setting the Maximum Number of MailScanner Child Processes

The first option to change is the maximum number of child processes MailScanner starts. Because MailScanner is written in Perl, starting up a new MailScanner process has some overhead, as Perl is an interpreted language and not compiled code. To help compensate for the overhead, when you start the first, or parent, MailScanner process, it will start any number of extra child MailScanner processes. The idea is to find a balance between having enough extra processes to handle your e-mail load and not starting so many that you bring your server to a crawl when starting MailScanner for the first time. The general recommendation is to start with five child processes per CPU. Search for the line:

```
Max Children = 5
```

and change the value to whatever matches your specific system configuration. If you have a dual-CPU system, try 10 to begin with. As you begin testing your system, and after running in production for some time, you may find that you need to increase this value, especially if you experience higher e-mail traffic or too much delay in delivery. However, be careful not to increase this number too much, as you might hit hardware computing limitations in your system.

## Specifying a User and Group

The next two options

```
Run as User =
```

and

```
Run as Group =
```

do not pertain to our circumstances as mail is delivered by sendmail as the root user, the same system user that runs MailScanner. Combining MailScanner with some MTAs may require different user and group privileges. Leave both of these options blank.

## Specifying the Incoming Queue Scan Interval

Next, you can change how often the incoming mail queue, which sendmail delivers to, is scanned by MailScanner for processing new messages. This value is in seconds, and the default is set to 6 seconds. This is another option that is highly dependent on your specific circumstances. Increasing this value can reduce server load at the expense of slightly delaying the delivery of mail. Search for the following line:

```
Queue Scan Interval = 6
```

and change this to whatever you feel might be appropriate. If you're unsure, leave it at 6. Change it if you feel you can take the performance hit in order to deliver mail a few seconds faster. Messages delivered to the queue will be scanned by MailScanner in batches. If the queue is scanned too infrequently, you also run the risk of thrashing the system by starting too many MailScanner processes at the same time.

## Setting the Queue Directories

The next four system configuration settings define where the incoming, outgoing, temporary work, and quarantine mail queues are located. First, the incoming queue directory is where sendmail is configured to send all e-mail that it initially receives from the Internet to be scanned. MailScanner checks this directory to search for new messages to scan. The default is fine, and the option should remain configured as follows:

```
Incoming Queue Dir = /var/spool/mqueue.in
```

Next, the outgoing mail queue for MailScanner, which sends clean or disinfected messages destined for final delivery by sendmail, is set as follows:

```
Outgoing Queue Dir = /var/spool/mqueue
```

This queue is intentionally the delivery queue to which sendmail typically delivers when MailScanner is not running, so there should be no surprises in this setting.

MailScanner needs a working directory to split incoming messages to be scanned individually. This directory is only used while each individual part of an e-mail message, including any attachments or MIME parts that it might be composed of, is scanned. When MailScanner completes the scan of each part of a message, the original message is sent intact to the outgoing queue directory for delivery if it is clean. The default is adequate, unless you prefer to move it:

```
Incoming Work Dir = /var/spool/MailScanner/incoming
```

Lastly, if you decide later in the configuration process to quarantine infected messages before discarding them, you must set the quarantine directory:

```
Quarantine Dir = /var/spool/MailScanner/quarantine
```

Make sure the partition that the /var/ directory is in has plenty of disk space, especially if you decide to keep quarantined messages for some time.

### Setting the MailScanner MTA Options

The final two options that should be pointed out and ought to be checked to make sure they are set properly are the MTA and Sendmail options. Since MailScanner can support a number of MTAs other than sendmail, and each MTA has its own quirks and differences in the way it operates, MailScanner must know which MTA it is working with. This setting defaults to sendmail, but double-check to make sure this is the case, since sendmail is the MTA of choice for this book:

```
MTA = sendmail
```

In addition, you need to tell MailScanner where to find the sendmail binary executable, so it can send out notifications and so forth:

```
Sendmail = /usr/sbin/sendmail
```

That's it for the system settings that should be checked or changed. In most cases, the defaults suffice, but be aware that they can be changed, especially to improve efficiency and performance.

## Setting MailScanner Directory Options

The next two sections in MailScanner.conf are for tweaking the MailScanner incoming work, quarantine, and archive directories. If, in the previous system settings section, you changed the Run as User and Run as Group options, then you probably need to change the Incoming Work User and Incoming Work Group options to match. Otherwise, leave them blank, as they are by default. Also, you might have to change the permissions on the incoming work direc-tory with the option Incoming Work Permissions, but you need to be careful not to open this directory up to other users on the system. The default is set to mode 0600, which indicates user read and write permission only. In our case, MailScanner runs as the root user, and the resulting temporary work directory is only readable and writable by root. This prevents system users from reading others' e-mail messages as they enter the incoming work directory.

The same options exist for the quarantine directory. Quarantine User, Quarantine Group, and Quarantine Permissions should all be left as the default values (empty and mode 0600).

## Configuring How MailScanner Processes Incoming Mail

The next configurable options customize how MailScanner actually processes incoming mail. Some thresholds can be set in case a message is too large or contains too many problems. If these thresholds did not exist, it would be possible for someone, either intentionally or unin-tentionally, to cause a DoS on your mail system. For example, it's unreasonable to expect to send an e-mail message with a 10-GB file attachment (this is extreme; most sites today limit mail attachments to 10MB). If MailScanner is forced to scan just one of these messages and its attachments, much less 10, 20, or a 100 at once, your system will be effectively taken out of service, denying your customers legitimate use of the system.

The same applies for a message with dozens of embedded messages, which is possible if, when a message bounces numerous times, an e-mail server wraps an NDR around an NDR after an NDR and so on. Such examples seem extreme, but they are illegitimate uses of e-mail nonetheless, and less-extreme cases are common.

### Specifying Scanning Thresholds

The first four settings that can be adjusted to combat these problems follow:

```
Max Unscanned Bytes Per Scan = 100000000
Max Unsafe Bytes Per Scan = 50000000
Max Unscanned Messages Per Scan = 30
Max Unsafe Messages Per Scan = 3
```

These set various maximum thresholds. The first setting indicates that if roughly 100MB of a message cannot be scanned for whatever reason (whether it is an unknown attachment type, malformed message text, or otherwise), MailScanner considers it a bad or infected mes-sage and acts accordingly. The second setting indicates that if roughly the first 50MB of a message are found to be bad or infected, MailScanner stops scanning the message and acts accordingly. The last two settings are analogous to the first two, but they pertain to messages as a whole instead of partial messages.

### Conditionally Scanning Messages

The next option worth considering is

```
Scan Messages = yes
```

This option is enabled by default, and you might wonder why it exists. Of course you want to scan messages; that's why you're installing and configuring MailScanner! The real reason this option exists is so that you can optionally set this to point to a ruleset. If you do that, you can arbitrarily decide specific domains for which you do or don't scan. This is a good time introduce rulesets.

## Creating Rulesets for Conditional Scanning

*Rulesets* can be used in many MailScanner configuration options throughout MailScanner.conf. Typically contained in /etc/MailScanner/rules, or whatever you've set %rules-dir% to, rulesets are a way of customizing a configuration option according to one or more rules, conditionally applying the option to a subset of messages. A rule follows one of the following two formats:

*Direction MatchPattern Value(s)*

or

*Direction1 MatchPattern* and *Direction2 MatchPattern Value(s)*

The first is a simple rule with one condition, while the second allows you to define a maximum of two conditions, linked with the literal keyword and. Table 14-1 lists the possible values that can be substituted for Direction, Direction1, or Direction2.

**Table 14-1.** *Possible MailScanner Ruleset Directions*

| Direction | Description |
| --- | --- |
| From: | The rule will match if the message sender matches the match pattern. |
| To: | The rule will match if the message recipient matches the match pattern. |
| FromOrTo: | The rule will match if the message sender or recipient matches the match pattern. |
| FromAndTo: | The rule will match if the message sender and recipient match the match pattern. |
| Virus: | The rule will match if an attached virus report included an address that matches the match pattern. |

MatchPattern is a pattern that is used to decide which messages match the rule. Table 14-2 lists possible syntax for this field.

**Table 14-2.** *Example MailScanner Ruleset Match Patterns*

| Pattern | Description |
| --- | --- |
| user@example.com | Match a specific e-mail address |
| *@example.com | Match any e-mail addresses within a specific e-mail domain |
| user@* | Match a specific user with any e-mail domain |
| /regexPattern/ | Match using a standard regular expression |
| 192.168. | Match any SMTP client with an IP addresses that falls within the range 192.168.1.0 through 164.106.255.255 |
| /^192\.168\.1\.[1(25[0-5]\|2[0-4][0-9]\|[01]?[0-9][0-9]?)/ | Match any SMTP client with an IP address that matches the regular expression |

Value(s) is whatever the value would have been for the particular option had you not defined a ruleset in the first place, so possible values are impossible to list, as they're highly dependent on the specific configuration option you're conditionally setting.

To get back to our original task, set Scan Messages to a ruleset to conditionally scan some domains and not others by changing the following line:

```
Scan Messages = yes
```

to

```
Scan Messages = %rules-dir%/scan.messages.rules
```

Next create the file scan.messages.rules in the directory previously defined by the %rules-dir% variable, /etc/MailScanner/rules/ by default. Assuming you want to scan mail coming from, and leaving as, any e-mail domain except a few, the last line in scan.messages.rules must be as follows:

```
FromOrTo: default yes
```

Let's say, for example, you don't want to scan any e-mail sent from one of your e-mail domains. Add something like the following line, replacing subdomain.example.com with the domain of your organization:

```
From: subdomain.example.com no
```

## Specifying Message and Attachment Size Limits

Although you ought to read the rest of this section of MailScanner.conf to familiarize yourself with what's possible to do, the only other options I'm going to call your attention to are the following ones:

```
Maximum Message Size = 0
Maximum Attachment Size = -1
Minimum Attachment Size = -1
```

Setting Maximum Message Size to 0 disables filtering of messages based solely on message size, but I recommend setting this to a reasonable maximum value, something like the following:

```
Maximum Message Size = 100000000
```

which specifies a limit for how large a message can be without being blocked by MailScanner, roughly 100MB in this example.

Setting Maximum Attachment Size and Minimum Attachment Size to anything less than 0 disables attachment size checks altogether. I recommend setting a maximum attachment size to a reasonable value, for example:

```
Maximum Attachment Size = 20000000
```

which specifies that the limit for how large messages attachments can be is roughly 20MB.

Of course, you could create a ruleset that specifies these limits for some users, while disabling all these checks for others. MailScanner allows you the flexibility to be creative and to cater to special needs of a subset of your users, if such a need arises.

## Configuring MailScanner for Virus Scanning and Vulnerability Testing

The next section of MailScanner.conf is used to configure whether MailScanner performs virus scanning, whether to send the message to an external virus scanner, and how to handle infected messages and attachments. For now, keep the Virus Scanners option set as follows:

```
Virus Scanners = none
```

In Chapter 15, when we install and configure ClamAV, we will change this option. However, for testing purposes, we are leaving the default set until then.

Check the rest of this section to make sure the configuration matches your company's policies, but be sure to keep our best practice discussion from earlier in this chapter in mind. For instance, even though delivering clean messages that had contained infected attachments might show your boss that the new e-mail filtering system is working, receiving all of those annoying empty or useless messages will probably outweigh the benefits of showing off. These days, best practice and real-world experience also dictate that attempting to disinfect an infected file attachment is futile. Most files themselves are the viruses, so they are either unable to be disinfected or aren't worth delivering if they have been disinfected.

You can skip the sections labeled specifically for a particular antivirus application, but in Chapter 15, after we've installed the antivirus software ClamAV, we will go back and look at the section for ClamAV.

## Configuring MailScanner to Scan for Dangerous Content

The next section of MailScanner.conf is a fantastic set of options that offer true content filtering above and beyond the standard antivirus and antispam scanning. Although extremely important, antivirus scanners don't catch phishing scams, HTML e-mail messages with dangerous scripts designed to trick the user, or other potentially harmful content that looks like text or regular hyperlinks. However, MailScanner has been built to try to detect and mitigate some of these threats.

I highly encourage you leave this feature enabled by keeping the following option set to its default:

```
Dangerous Content Scanning = yes
```

You should read through this section, take note of the possible options and their default values, and customize according to your specific needs; everything is well documented and should be self-explanatory.

## Blocking Specific E-mail Attachments

MailScanner can arbitrarily block certain e-mail attachments with a specific filename, extension, or file type. For instance, it's not uncommon for e-mail viruses and worms to try to mask their true intent by setting their file extension to something more familiar and seemingly harmless. An example would be the file extension .ico, commonly used to indicate an icon. Most people don't equate an icon with an executable file, much less one with malicious content. However, various exploits exist that, if left unpatched on the user's computer, allow a seemingly harmless file be executed in an unexpected and devastating manner.

Blocking e-mail attachments by file extensions alone is a difficult balance between convenience and necessity. For example, the users I support would revolt if we decided to block the JPEG image format's .jpg file extension, even though there have been ways in the past to use a JPEG image to attack a vulnerable computer.

The list of file names and extensions is found in the file defined in MailScanner.conf with the following MailScanner configuration option:

```
%etc-dir%/filename.rules.conf
```

and the list of file types is found in the file defined in MailScanner.conf with the following MailScanner configuration options:

```
%etc-dir%/filetype.rules.conf
```

You can allow, deny, or deny and delete specific filenames, extensions, or file types. The syntax for these rulesets uses the following general form:

```
action  regex  [Text to log]  [Text to report to user]
```

Each of these fields is separated by one tab, not by spaces. An action can be one of the three keywords listed in Table 14-3. The regex is the regular expression used to look for the filename, file extension, or file type to allow or deny. The last two fields apply to only a deny rule, and each should simply contain a hyphen (-) in an allow rule. Otherwise, the third field is the short text that is used in the MailScanner logs to indicate a file was denied. The fourth and final field is the longer, more descriptive text that is used in notifications that are optionally sent to the user that a message contained a file that was denied.

Table 14-3. *File and File Type Ruleset Actions*

| Action Keyword | Description |
| --- | --- |
| allow | Explicitly allow any file or file type matching the regular expression |
| deny | Explicitly deny any file or file type matching the regular expression |
| deny+delete | Explicitly deny and immediately delete the offending file or file type |

For example, to deny any filename ending with the file extension .ico, you add the following in filename.rules.conf:

```
deny  \.ico$  Windows icon file security vulnerability ➥
  Possible buffer overflow in Windows
```

The example is on two lines here but should be one single line in the ruleset file itself.

Check these files, and make sure they aren't set to anything you or your organization might disapprove of, or add to the rules to increase the security of your organization's mail environment.

## Configuring Reports and Quarantine Options

The next section in `MailScanner.conf` deals with how infected messages are quarantined and with customizing reports and notifications. For example, I highly recommend previously that you quarantine message that are infected and subsequently blocked or rejected. Per the default configuration, make sure the following is set accordingly:

```
Quarantine Infections = yes
```

If you choose not to deliver infected message after they have been disinfected or stripped of their dangerous payload, you might want to change the following option from its default:

```
Quarantine Whole Message = no
```

to:

```
Quarantine Whole Message = yes
```

This makes it easier to retrieve entire messages, not just the attachments, in the case of a false positive. However, be aware that this may dramatically increase the size of your quarantine directory over time and consume more disk space faster than you originally intended.

The rest of the options in this section of `MailScanner.conf` allow you to choose the language in which reports are sent and point to the actual messages themselves in reports. If later you decide to configure MailScanner to actually send reports and notifications, you may want to modify the report files to customize their specific messages to your organization's needs, but I will not cover that here; doing so is a simple matter of finding the reports in the directory `/etc/MailScanner/reports/en/` and modifying the files to your liking.

## Configuring MailScanner Message Headers

MailScanner can add various additional informational message headers to each message it scans. I highly recommend configuring MailScanner to add informational headers for a couple of reasons. First, it gives the recipients something to filter with, should they choose to do so. Second, it is a quick and easy way for anyone to know whether a message has been scanned by your organization's instance of MailScanner. The more information available in the message headers, the easier it is to debug message delivery history.

Check this section out, starting with the following configuration option:

```
Mail Header = X-%org-name%-MailScanner
```

In particular, take a look at the following two options:

```
Add Envelope From Header = yes
Add Envelope To Header = no
```

Normally, these two pieces of information, the envelope sender and recipient addresses, are not explicitly recorded anywhere in the message or message header. The envelope sender and recipient addresses are reported in the SMTP `MAIL FROM` and `MAIL TO` commands. However, as we know, what's actually reported in the From and To headers of a message does not have to match the envelope sender and recipient addresses. If you need a refresher on the message envelope, see the discussion on STMP in Chapter 4.

Recording the envelope sender address can be extremely useful for further spam processing, especially if you start receiving large amounts of messages with the same bogus envelope sender address, in which case you could start filtering messages based on that bogus address. I recommend leaving this option enabled, which is the MailScanner default.

However, adding the envelope recipient address to a message header might not be desirable. The most common reason is for potential privacy concerns. The envelope recipient address, not the message To header, is used to determine who the message recipient(s) are. Normally, these two are identical, but they are not if you use the blind carbon copy (BCC) header in the message. When you enter one or more addresses on the BCC line of a message, the client uses those addresses to deliver the message, but the addresses do not appear anywhere else in the message headers or body itself. If you configure MailScanner to record the envelope recipient in a header, the recipient of a message in which others were blind carbon copied knows others were copied, when otherwise they would have been none the wiser. Depending on your organization's policies, divulging this information may or may not be appropriate, and I recommend not doing so and leaving this option disabled by default.

You probably want to customize the text that's put into the various information headers MailScanner can add to messages that have been scanned. The following configuration options all contain text you might want to modify:

```
Clean Header Value     = Found to be clean
Infected Header Value  = Found to be infected
Disinfected Header Value = Disinfected
Information Header Value = Please contact the ISP for more information
Unscanned Header Value = Not scanned: please contact your Internet E-Mail ➡
Service Provider for details
```

Finally, I would suggest changing the following configuration option:

```
Sign Clean Messages = yes
```

Enabling this option configures MailScanner to add a text or HTML signature to every scanned message. This text, although it alerts the recipient that their mail was scanned by MailScanner, is obtrusive and annoying in my opinion. Again, message headers are the best place to put information like this, unless you already have a policy of appending advertisements to your users' e-mail message bodies. Disable the configuration option by modifying it as follows:

```
Sign Clean Messages = no
```

## Configuring MailScanner Notifications

This section of `MailScanner.conf`, beginning with the configuration option

```
Notify Senders = yes
```

might be the most controversial of the bunch. It is where you configure whether or not MailScanner sends e-mail notifications when a message has been accepted for delivery, scanned for content, and subsequently blocked because of a match on a rule or configuration threshold. The MailScanner default behavior is to send such notifications, which in a perfect world, seems like the most polite, correct think to do. However, as much as I hate to say so, sending such notifications can actually contribute to the problem more than it helps. As I've said several times so far, this is especially true when so many of the viruses, spam, and phishing scams are forged, causing possibly hundreds of notifications to the wrong person.

To disable notifications altogether, simply disable the Notify Senders configuration option:

```
Notify Senders = no
```

and other notification options will be ignored.

After reading the previous section about best practices and taking into consideration the experiences from myself and others, you should read through this section of MailScanner.conf, check the defaults, and decide what's most in line with your organization's policies and best practices. Don't forget that most of these options can be used in a ruleset, so notification can be sent conditionally on certain criteria. MailScanner.conf itself has very good inline documentation, so you shouldn't have too much problem working through this section.

## Configuring Changes Made to Message Subjects and Bodies

The next two sections in MailScanner.conf control MailScanner's ability to modify the subject or the body of a message. The thought is, for example, to add something to the subject or body to inform the recipient of the status of the message, like tagging the message as spam. However, I strongly discourage modifying the content of a message body, including its subject. Message headers are the appropriate place to add informational and operational status messages.

Any tagging or modification of a message should occur only in the message header. Tagging messages with special informational message headers is unobtrusive to the users who don't care and useful for personal filtering for those users who do.

By default, some of the subject modification is turned off, but you should double-check for yourself. Specifically, to turn off subject modifications, disable the Scanned Modify Subject configuration option as follows:

```
Scanned Modify Subject = no
```

## Configuring MailScanner Notification to Administrators

MailScanner, starting with the following MailScanner.conf configuration option:

```
Send Notices = yes
```

allows for the possibility to send a notification to the e-mail system administrators every time a message is blocked. These notifications are similar to those that can be sent to the assumed message sender. The decision to leave these notifications on is up to you. However, be aware that if even if you only maintain e-mail services for a couple hundred users, you might become inundated with these notifications. Think about whether you really need to know when a message has been blocked, and keep in mind that all of this information is available to you in the system's mail logs. Checking the system and mail logs periodically is probably more efficient than wading through hundreds to thousands of blocked notifications.

I prefer not to receive these notifications, partly because of the extra load they incur on the system, but mostly because of information overload. I do, however, keep an eye on mail logs through some custom scripts and, mostly, through a great application called LogWatch. LogWatch is available as part of the base Fedora Core installation. To determine whether

LogWatch is installed on your Fedora Core system, run the following command to check if the `logwatch` RPM package is already installed:

```
[curtis@mail ~] rpm -qv logwatch
```

```
logwatch-7.2.1-1.fc4
```

This command shows the version of the RPM package, if it is installed. Of course, your version may vary. If you get the message "package logwatch is not installed", go ahead and install the `logwatch` RPM and its dependencies with yum (screen output truncated for brevity):

```
[curtis@mail ~]$ sudo yum install logwatch
```

This command searches for and installs, if found, the latest version of the LogWatch application available from the yum RPM package repositories you have configured on your system. Once installed, LogWatch runs as a daily system cron job; it checks the system and `maillog` files for unusual entries and e-mails the root user with an outline of what is found.

## Configuring MailScanner Spam Detection Options

MailScanner has the ability to perform a few spam detection operations itself and, optionally, pass messages off to SpamAssassin, an antispam application (see Chapters 17 and 18). I'm skipping over these few sections in `MailScanner.conf`, starting with configuration option:

```
Spam Checks = yes
```

I discuss a few of the options in much more detail in subsequent chapters, starting in Chapter 16, where I introduce additional antispam techniques and applications.

## Configuring MailScanner Logging

Now we've come to possibly the most important section in `MailScanner.conf`—at least from the e-mail system administrator's point of view! Logging is one of the most important things any application can do, if only for its audit trail. When a user or, worse, your boss calls to complain that he didn't receive a particular e-mail message or attachment, your logs should be the first place you check to get to the bottom of the problem. Many applications, including MailScanner, use something called syslog, the Linux system logging daemon.

syslog runs in the background all the time, accepting logs from other system applications and writing them to a file. Among the most powerful features of syslog are the notions of facilities and severities. Using different combinations of the facilities and severities, syslog can be configured to send different classes of log messages to different log files. On most contemporary Linux operating systems, including Fedora Core, log messages are found in the directory `/var/log/`. Mail logs are typically found in the file `/var/log/maillog`.

MailScanner is configured to send its log messages to the syslog facility `mail` with the following configuration option, found in `MailScanner.conf`:

```
Syslog Facility = mail
```

Read through this section of `MailScanner.conf` and adjust the settings according to your preferences. You might think that, with all the emphasis I'm putting on logs, you should turn on all the logging that MailScanner provides. However, the balance between too much, too little, and just enough logging is delicate. In addition, logging a lot of information might also slightly slow down MailScanner or the system itself, so try turning on a bit more logging while testing your system, but turn the verbosity and amount of information down a few notches when you're ready to release the system to your users.

## MailScanner Configuration Summary

The options left in `MailScanner.conf` that I have not covered in this chapter are either advanced options beyond the scope of this book or not worth explicitly mentioning at all. However, as a system administrator, you ought to be intimately in tune with how your system operates. I recommend checking through anything not covered in this chapter and reading the inline comments in `MailScanner.conf`, if only to be aware of the extra possibilities of MailScanner.

The possibilities of MailScanner are great, and the number of combinations of system and MailScanner configurations are too numerous to fully capture in this book. At minimum, what I've covered here will get your e-mail system running in tip-top shape, but you may find that your specific needs dictate tweaking these options. Perhaps what I've found to be unnecessary or appropriate for my environment isn't so for yours, so always be aware that your system may be a work-in-progress!

## Manually Starting and Stopping MailScanner

Starting MailScanner actually involves three things: first, the incoming sendmail daemon that accepts incoming mail on TCP port 25 and delivers to the incoming queue is started; next is the outgoing sendmail daemon that delivers mail from the outgoing queue to the final destination, be it the local system default mailbox, procmail, or a recipient on the Internet somewhere; and finally, the MailScanner parent process itself and any child processes (as defined by the Max Children configuration option in `MailScanner.conf`) are started.

One convenient init script will handle all this for you, but before we can start MailScanner and the incoming and outgoing sendmail daemons, we must shut down and disable the old sendmail init script we've been using up to now. To do so, first shut down the running sendmail with the original init script. On a Fedora Core system, this can be done with the `service` command:

```
[curtis@mail ~]$ sudo service sendmail stop
```

```
Shutting down sendmail:            [ OK ]
Shutting down sm-client:           [ OK ]
```

After sendmail has been shut down, you can run the MailScanner init script installed by the MailScanner installation script earlier. This script should operate like any other init script we've seen so far. On a Fedora Core system, you can start MailScanner with the service command:

```
[curtis@mail ~]$ sudo service MailScanner start
```

```
Starting MailScanner daemons:
    incoming sendmail:              [ OK ]
    outgoing sendmail:              [ OK ]
    MailScanner:                 [ OK ]
```

To see what happened, you can check /var/log/maillog. You should see three sendmail daemons start: the incoming sendmail, the client queuing daemon, and the outgoing send-mail daemon:

```
Jun 6 20:52:04 mail sendmail[9541]: alias database /etc/aliases rebuilt by curtis
Jun 6 20:52:04 mail sendmail[9541]: /etc/aliases: 107 aliases, ➥
longest 54 bytes, 2689 bytes total
Jun 6 20:52:04 mail sendmail[9549]: starting daemon (8.13.6): SMTP
Jun 6 20:52:04 mail sm-msp-queue[9553]: starting daemon (8.13.6): queueing@00:15:00
Jun 6 20:52:04 mail sendmail[9557]: starting daemon (8.13.6): queueing@00:15:00
```

You should also see several MailScanner processes start, depending on what the Max Children configuration option is set to (5 in the example given previously in this chapter):

```
Jun 6 20:52:05 mail MailScanner[9575]: MailScanner E-Mail Virus Scanner ➥
version 4.49.7 starting...
Jun 6 20:52:05 mail MailScanner[9575]: Read 721 hostnames from the ➥
phishing whitelist
Jun 6 20:52:05 mail MailScanner[9575]: Using locktype = flock
Jun 6 20:52:16 mail MailScanner[9579]: MailScanner E-Mail Virus Scanner ➥
version 4.49.7 starting...
Jun 6 20:52:16 mail MailScanner[9579]: Read 721 hostnames from the ➥
phishing whitelist
Jun 6 20:52:16 mail MailScanner[9579]: Using locktype = flock
Jun 6 20:52:27 mail MailScanner[9580]: MailScanner E-Mail Virus Scanner ➥
version 4.49.7 starting...
Jun 6 20:52:27 mail MailScanner[9580]: Read 721 hostnames from the ➥
phishing whitelist
Jun 6 20:52:27 mail MailScanner[9580]: Using locktype = flock
Jun 6 20:52:38 mail MailScanner[9582]: MailScanner E-Mail Virus Scanner ➥
version 4.49.7 starting...
Jun 6 20:52:38 mail MailScanner[9582]: Read 721 hostnames from the ➥
phishing whitelist
Jun 6 20:52:38 mail MailScanner[9582]: Using locktype = flock
Jun 6 20:52:49 mail MailScanner[9584]: MailScanner E-Mail Virus Scanner ➥
version 4.49.7 starting...
Jun 6 20:52:49 mail MailScanner[9584]: Read 721 hostnames from the ➥
phishing whitelist
Jun 6 20:52:49 mail MailScanner[9584]: Using locktype = flock
```

If there any errors or typos in your MailScanner.conf file, MailScanner complains when trying to start, for example:

```
Jun 6 21:00:58 mail MailScanner[9709]: Syntax error in line 1162, value "foo" ➥
for warnsenders is not one of allowed values "yes","no"
```

If you go back and examine line 1162 of MailScanner.conf, you find that Notify Senders is set to an invalid setting:

```
Notify Senders = foo
```

Fixing the error and restarting MailScanner resolves the issue.

If you wish to shut down MailScanner manually, you can use the service command to do so:

```
[curtis@mail ~]$ sudo service MailScanner stop
```

```
Shutting down MailScanner daemons:
    MailScanner:                [ OK ]
    incoming sendmail:          [ OK ]
    outgoing sendmail:          [ OK ]
```

Using this command results in the following message in /var/log/maillog for every MailScanner process shutdown:

```
Jun 6 21:04:51 mail MailScanner[9840]: MailScanner child caught a SIGHUP
```

Otherwise, you can configure MailScanner to automatically start up and shut down when appropriate, which I will show you next.

## Starting MailScanner Automatically

On a Fedora Core system, you can use the command chkconfig to configure an application to automatically start up and shut down in the appropriate runlevels:

```
[curtis@mail ~]$ sudo chkconfig --level 345 MailScanner on
```

Check your handiwork, and compare the following output to the output when you checked previously:

```
[curtis@mail ~]$ sudo chkconfig --list MailScanner
```

```
MailScanner     0:off  1:off  2:off  3:on  4:on  5:on  6:off
```

Next, don't forget to remove the sendmail init script from all system runlevels to prevent sendmail from automatically starting the old way; from now on, the MailScanner init script starts sendmail. You can remove the sendmail init script with the chkconfig command on a Fedora Core system:

```
[curtis@mail ~]$ sudo chkconfig --del sendmail
```

Check your handiwork with the chkconfig command:

```
[curtis@mail ~]$ sudo chkconfig --list sendmail
```

```
service sendmail supports chkconfig, but is not referenced in any runlevel ➥
(run 'chkconfig --add sendmail')
```

For a more complete introduction to Linux runlevels and Fedora Core init scripts, refer to Chapter 3.

Now that MailScanner is configured, customized to your organization's needs, and started properly, let's make sure your mail still delivers successfully.

## Testing MailScanner

Testing MailScanner is as simple as sending a test message to your e-mail account on your e-mail system. Compose a new e-mail to yourself with the subject "Testing MailScanner," and send it to your mail system. Within a few seconds, the message should be delivered. If you followed along in Chapter 13, and you've left your e-mail forwarding through procmail, then your test message might have been delivered to your Testing e-mail folder instead of your Inbox, if you still have the test recipe in your .procmailrc file.

A successful delivery can be verified through /var/log/maillog:

```
Jun 7 00:35:43 mail sendmail[11654]: k574ZhHZ011654: ➥
from=<curtis@example.com>, size=557, class=0, nrcpts=1, ➥
msgid=<45457.192.168.69.106.1149654943.squirrel@webmail.example.com>, ➥
proto=ESMTP, daemon=MTA, relay=localhost.localdomain [127.0.0.1]
Jun 7 00:35:44 mail MailScanner[10119]: New Batch: Scanning 1 messages, 1052 bytes
Jun 7 00:35:44 mail MailScanner[10119]: Virus and Content Scanning: Starting
Jun 7 00:35:44 mail MailScanner[10119]: Uninfected: Delivered 1 messages
Jun 7 00:35:44 mail sendmail[11661]: k574ZhHZ011654: ➥
to="|exec /usr/bin/procmail", ctladdr=<curtis@example.com> ➥
(500/500), delay=00:00:01, xdelay=00:00:00, ➥
mailer=prog, pri=120557, dsn=2.0.0, stat=Sent
```

From these logs, a message appears to have been successfully accepted and delivered from SquirrelMail to the incoming sendmail daemon. MailScanner has started its scheduled queue run, scanning for and detecting one new message in the incoming queue. MailScanner has started its scanning process and found the message to be uninfected by any malicious content and delivered the message to the outgoing queue. Finally, the outgoing sendmail daemon picked up the message and successfully delivered the message, forwarding it through procmail, as configured by the .forward file left over from the previous chapter's examples.

If we check the procmail log, we can see what procmail did:

```
procmail: Match on "^Subject:.*test"
procmail: Locking "Testing.lock"
procmail: Assigning "LASTFOLDER=Testing"
procmail: Opening "Testing"
procmail: Acquiring kernel-lock
procmail: Unlocking "Testing.lock"
From curtis@example.com Wed Jun 7 00:35:44 2006
 Subject: Testing MailScanner
 Folder: Testing                                    1035
```

As you know from our discussion of procmail in Chapter 13, this indicates a successful match on a procmail recipe, resulting in the message being successfully delivered to the Testing e-mail folder.

If you take a closer look at the message headers of the test message you sent, you can also see signs of MailScanner successfully scanning your message. Both Mozilla Thunderbird and SquirrelMail have the ability to view full e-mail headers, so let's do so.

To view the message headers of an e-mail in Thunderbird, highlight the e-mail in the folder index, and click View ➤ Headers ➤ All. Figure 14-2 shows you a sample of what an email with its message headers displayed looks like.

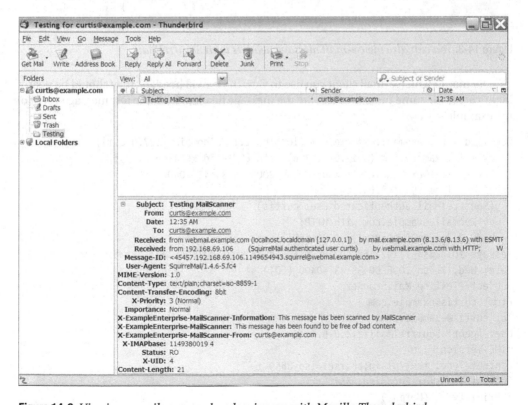

**Figure 14-2.** *Viewing e-mail message headers is easy with Mozilla Thunderbird.*

To view the message headers of an e-mail in SquirrelMail, view the message as normal, and click on the link "View full headers" under Options. Figure 14-3 shows you a sample of what a SquirrelMail message with visible message headers looks like.

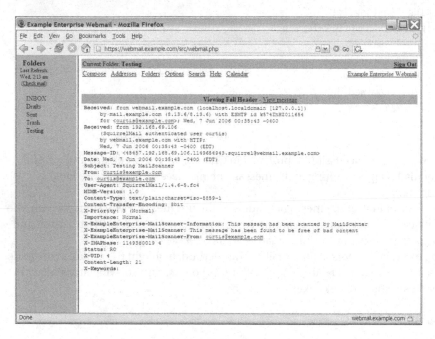

**Figure 14-3.** *You can also view e-mail message headers with SquirrelMail.*

No matter which e-mail client you use to view the e-mail headers, they should be nearly identical for the same message. Here are the message headers from the test message I sent on my example system:

```
Received: from webmail.example.com (localhost.localdomain [127.0.0.1])
   by mail.example.com (8.13.6/8.13.6) with ESMTP id k574ZhHZ011654
   for <curtis@example.com>; Wed, 7 Jun 2006 00:35:43 -0400
Received: from 192.168.69.106
   (SquirrelMail authenticated user curtis)
   by webmail.example.com with HTTP;
   Wed, 7 Jun 2006 00:35:43 -0400 (EDT)
Message-ID: <45457.192.168.69.106.1149654943.squirrel@webmail.example.com>
Date: Wed, 7 Jun 2006 00:35:43 -0400 (EDT)
Subject: Testing MailScanner
From: curtis@example.com
To: curtis@example.com
User-Agent: SquirrelMail/1.4.6-5.fc4
MIME-Version: 1.0
Content-Type: text/plain;charset=iso-8859-1
Content-Transfer-Encoding: 8bit
X-Priority: 3 (Normal)
Importance: Normal
```

```
X-ExampleEnterprise-MailScanner-Information: This message ➡
has been scanned by MailScanner
X-ExampleEnterprise-MailScanner: This message has been ➡
found to be free of bad content
X-ExampleEnterprise-MailScanner-From: curtis@example.com
X-IMAPbase: 1149380019 4
Status: RO
X-UID: 4
Content-Length: 21
X-Keywords:
```

Yours might look a touch different based on which e-mail client you used to send the message, but the key headers to point out, which should be there, are those that were added by MailScanner:

```
X-ExampleEnterprise-MailScanner-Information: This message ➡
has been scanned by MailScanner
X-ExampleEnterprise-MailScanner: This message has been ➡
found to be free of bad content
X-ExampleEnterprise-MailScanner-From: curtis@example.com
```

After taking the time to configure MailScanner, these should be a welcome sight. Congratulations, you've successfully installed and configured MailScanner!

# Further MailScanner Resources

As you work through the MailScanner configuration files, I think you'll find they are some of the best-documented files around. Just like the other open source packages highlighted in this book, MailScanner has a large, knowledgeable community backing and supporting it.

Don't forget to visit the MailScanner website at www.mailscanner.info for links to additional documentation and mailing lists. For additional user-contributed documentation, how-to articles, tips, and tricks, be sure to check out the MailScanner wiki at http://wiki.mailscanner.info.

# Summary

I realize this chapter may feel dense and that it contains a lot of material, but I feel it's very important to understand just how MailScanner operates and how it can be customized according to your needs. Introducing a layer like MailScanner is necessary to provide a high-quality service to your users, but it also takes up, by several notches, the level of complexity in configuration and e-mail delivery. Configuring MailScanner should not be taken lightly, and you should make sure its configuration is in line with your organization's policies and expectations. Otherwise, you might get caught unprepared in the future if proper measures are not taken to protect your email system and your users.

Subsequent chapters of this book depend and build on the information in this chapter. Before continuing, be sure you work through this chapter and are confident that you have at least a good start on customizing MailScanner. The next chapter introduces ClamAV, an outstanding antivirus application that works with MailScanner to add yet another layer of protection for your users.

# PART 6

###

# Fighting E-mail Viruses and Worms

■ ■ ■

# CHAPTER 15

# Using ClamAV to Block E-mail Viruses and Worms

**N**o e-mail system is complete without an antivirus mechanism of some sort. In Chapter 14, we saw how MailScanner can block file attachments based on filename, file extension, or file type, but it's necessary to take this one step further. E-mail virus authors constantly push the envelope, using sophisticated techniques to try to fool virus scanners and e-mail recipients alike. The worst part about modern viruses and worms is probably the fact that some don't even require a user to run the attachment to become infected. With certain recent image processing vulnerabilities, for example, simply *viewing* an e-mail with an infected file attachment was enough to infect a user's computer. Stopping these threats at the server level is imperative, both for the sake of your users and the integrity of your mail domain.

In this chapter, I will introduce ClamAV, an open source antivirus package. Just as complete, and every bit reliable, as any commercial antivirus software, ClamAV benefits from extensive community collaboration, both for code and virus database development. As we will see, more than just an antivirus scanner, ClamAV is truly the best of breed in the antivirus category. This is evident through findings by Electric Mail, one of the first e-mail service providers since 1994 (www.linuxpipeline.com/166400446).

## Introducing ClamAV

ClamAV (www.clamav.net) is an open source antivirus package for UNIX and Linux. ClamAV is more than just a virus scanner; it's a complete toolkit, including a command-line scanner; a fast, multithreaded daemon; and a virus-scanning C library for integration into other applications written in the C language.

ClamAV also boasts support for numerous compression and archive file formats, which are listed in Table 15-1. Support for these compression and archival file formats ensures that viruses can't hide inside a seemingly benign file attachment, an old trick used by virus writers for some time now.

**Table 15-1.** *Compression and Archive File Formats Supported by ClamAV*

| File Format | File Extension | Description |
|---|---|---|
| Bzip2 | .bz2 | Free and open source compression file format |
| Gzip | .gz | Free and open source compression file format |
| MS cabinet files | .cab | Microsoft Windows compressed archive file format |
| MS CHM | .chm | Microsoft compressed HTML help file format |
| MS OLE2 format | .shs_ | Microsoft Windows Object Linking and Embedding file |
| MS SZDD | .??__ | Microsoft Windows compressed installation file format |
| RAR 2.0 | .rar | Popular compressed archive file format |
| Tar | .tar | Free and open source archive file format |
| Compressed tar | .tar.gz, .tgz, .tar.bz2 | Tar archive compressed with Bzip2 or Gzip |
| Zip | .zip | Popular compressed archive file format |

There are several components to ClamAV; as I mentioned earlier, ClamAV is a complete *toolkit*, not just simply an antivirus scanner. But what does that mean, exactly? Well, let me show how each of the ClamAV components might come together in a stand-alone environment. Then I will illustrate how the ClamAV components fit into the bigger picture of our complete e-mail system design, integrating with MailScanner, which this book is all about.

## The ClamAV Big Picture

There are primarily four components that make up the complete ClamAV antivirus toolkit:

- *The ClamAV antivirus scanners*: clamscan and clamdscan

- *The ClamAV antivirus daemon*: clamd

- *The ClamAV antivirus database files, tools, and updater*: daily.cvd and main.cvd, sigtool, and freshclam, respectively

- *The ClamAV C antivirus library*: libclamav

The ClamAV antivirus scanner, clamscan, is the more basic of these components. The command clamscan is a command-line, on-demand file and directory antivirus scanner. The most basic use of clamscan is to feed it a list of files or directories and let it scan each for any known viruses interactively. Although ClamAV can be run interactively and on-demand, ClamAV can also run as a daemon, waiting for connections, forking a process to scan the file, and reporting back. Starting a command-line ClamAV scanner requires the scanner to read the database of over 40,000 viruses and worms, which can take considerable time and system resources, especially when you're receiving and scanning tens of thousands of e-mail messages a day. Running clamd, the ClamAV daemon, is one way to load the entire virus database into memory where it can be accessed quickly, potentially reducing the subsequent scanning times.

When clamd is run, scanning is initiated with clamdscan instead of clamscan. The command clamdscan acts as a client agent; it sends a file to clamd, waits for clamd to perform the actual scan of the file, and then receives a report back from clamd that indicates whether or not the file is infected. Example usage of, and results from, the ClamAV antivirus scanners can be found later in this chapter when we test ClamAV for the first time.

clamscan and clamd have to compare each file they scan with something to determine whether the file is infected; after all, there is no one intrinsic property or characteristic that makes a virus a virus. This is where the ClamAV antivirus databases come into play.

All viruses, even new variants of old viruses, have a unique quality about them, called their *signature*. An antivirus database contains a list of virus signatures, where each signature describes specific defining characteristics of known viruses. ClamAV has two antivirus databases: main.cvd and daily.cvd. The daily.cvd database gets updated, as its name implies, one or more times a day, as needed when new virus signatures are found. The main.cvd database is updated much less often, usually with new releases of the antivirus engine code itself. The default location of the ClamAV virus databases is typically /var/lib/clamav/.

You can view, create, and remove virus signatures from a database by using the ClamAV command sigtool. Example usage of sigtool will be smattered throughout the rest of this chapter. However, advanced usage, including creating and submitting a virus signature, is outside the scope of this book; check the section "Further ClamAV Resources" near the end of this chapter to get information on these advanced topics.

An obvious key aspect to the successful detection of viruses is to keep the ClamAV virus databases updated with new virus signatures. This is achieved with freshclam. The freshclam script connects to a mirror server, checks for a newer database, and downloads it if one exists; it's that simple. Later in this chapter I will show you how to make sure your ClamAV virus databases are always up to date.

I'm going to reiterate a popular mantra: there is more than one way to do the same job. Although running ClamAV configured to run clamd and interface with clamdscan for efficiency might be the preferred setup in a stand-alone ClamAV environment, let's look at a slightly different design we can use when integrating ClamAV into the complete e-mail system design we've been working on thus far.

## The MailScanner and ClamAV Bigger Picture

MailScanner will act as the gatekeeper for your e-mail. It will control what messages are scanned and how they are scanned, and then pass them on to be scanned by other applications like ClamAV. The ClamAV toolkit does one thing very well: detect viruses. ClamAV will not disinfect files, and it cannot do anything but tell you a file is infected. MailScanner takes care of this situation by handing off the file to scan, waiting for a response from ClamAV. Then MailScanner will act accordingly on the message based on the ClamAV scan results.

MailScanner can interface with ClamAV in two ways. The first is by using clamscan itself, which would prove to be too inefficient for even the average e-mail system. The other, preferred alternative is to use the ClamAV Perl module Mail::ClamAV.

## Introducing Mail::ClamAV

MailScanner is written in the Perl programming language. As alluded to earlier in Chapter 14, Perl can be extended with modules, some of which are packaged with Perl, and others that are developed independently of the main Perl development process. Perl modules are often referred to, or named for, how they are instantiated in a Perl program.

Mail::ClamAV is a simple, efficient Perl interface to the ClamAV C API library. Instead of having MailScanner fork clamscan, a separate binary application, and parse its output, you can use the native Perl interface Mail::ClamAV provides. By using the Mail::ClamAV module, MailScanner can load the ClamAV virus databases into memory when it starts each of its child processes, effectively achieving the functionality of running clamd and clamdscan without the overhead of maintaining an additional daemon process on your e-mail system.

So, let's take a look at the quick and simple ClamAV installation process. I think you'll see that getting ClamAV up and running is simple. Once we've tested ClamAV, we will install the Mail::ClamAV Perl module and configure MailScanner accordingly to the ClamAV into MailScanner.

# Installing ClamAV

ClamAV is available as a Fedora Core RPM package, or you can download and install from the source distribution found on www.clamav.net. The ClamAV RPM is not included in our default Fedora Core installation as outlined in Chapter 2; instead, it is an optional package available from the Fedora Extras project, which we discuss shortly. This and remaining chapters assume you are using the Fedora Extras RPM package, but the general topics we discuss here, as well as the specific configuration in this and subsequent chapters, should still apply to any instance of ClamAV installed from source. From which of the two, either the RPM package or the source distribution, you choose to install and maintain ClamAV is a matter of personal preference, but as always I prefer the RPM package for easy maintenance whenever possible.

## The ClamAV RPM Package

To determine whether ClamAV is installed on your Fedora Core system, use the following command to query the RPM database:

```
[curtis@mail ~]$ rpm -qv clamav
```

However, you will probably find that command will not produce the output you'd expect, which indicates the package clamav is indeed not installed. If you lack the ClamAV RPM package, you can install it with yum, but it won't come from the standard Fedora Core RPM repository. Instead, it's available through the Fedora Extras project.

### A Word about the Fedora Extras Project

The Fedora Extras project, found at http://fedoraproject.org/wiki/Extras, is an effort, led by a volunteer community, to provide a repository of packages that enhance and complement official Fedora Core packages. Packages found in the Fedora Extras repository are not part of the normal, official Fedora Core development process. However, they are built to be fully compatible with official Fedora Core packages.

Fedora Extras package repositories are built to be paired with specific releases of Fedora Core. For instance, there are separate repositories for Fedora Extras that pair specifically with Fedora Core 3 and Fedora Core 4. Packages developed and maintained for one specific Fedora Core release generally should not be installed on a mismatched Fedora Core release.

Fedora Core 4 comes with a Fedora Extras yum repository configured in /etc/yum.repos.d/. You should see the file fedora-extras.repo, which contains something like the following:

```
[extras]
name=Fedora Extras $releasever - $basearch
#baseurl=http://download.fedora.redhat.com/pub/fedora/linux/extras/ ➥
$releasever/$basearch/
mirrorlist=http://fedora.redhat.com/download/mirrors/ ➥
fedora-extras-$releasever
enabled=1
gpgkey=file:///etc/pki/rpm-gpg/RPM-GPG-KEY-fedora-extras
gpgcheck=1
```

If this repository is enabled, as the option enabled=1 indicates in this example, then yum will search in this repository, in addition to the other Fedora Core repositories, for RPM packages. If you are building your e-mail system with a Fedora Core release older than Fedora Core 4, or you'd prefer to download Fedora Extras RPM packages from a specific yum repository rather than allowing yum to choose from a list of mirrors, you will need to remove the comment from the baseurl option and comment the mirrorlist option like so:

```
[extras]
name=Fedora Extras $releasever - $basearch
baseurl=http://download.fedora.redhat.com/pub/fedora/linux/extras/ ➥
$releasever/$basearch/
#mirrorlist=http://fedora.redhat.com/download/mirrors/ ➥
fedora-extras-$releasever
enabled=1
gpgkey=file:///etc/pki/rpm-gpg/RPM-GPG-KEY-fedora-extras
gpgcheck=1
```

Now you're ready to install packages from the Fedora Extras yum repository. For additional discussion regarding yum, its configuration, and its repositories, refer back to Chapter 3. Installing ClamAV is no more difficult than installing any other RPM that we've encountered thus far in this book.

## Installing the ClamAV RPM

ClamAV is split into a couple of different packages, reflecting its different components. For instance, the command-line virus scanners and program documentation are installed by the clamav RPM package, whereas the clamav-update RPM package includes everything necessary to keep ClamAV updated. We will need to install the following RPM packages:

- clamav: Primary virus scanners and documentation

- clamav-update: Update scripts

- clamav-lib: ClamAV C library

- clamav-devel: Development headers and files

- clamav-data: Initial ClamAV database setup

To install the ClamAV RPM packages we need, simply use yum, specifying each package as arguments, provided the Fedora Extras repository is configured and enabled, as discussed earlier:

```
[curtis@mail ~]$ sudo yum install clamav clamav-update clamav-lib ➥
clamav-devel clamav-data
```

When you run this command, yum will calculate any RPM dependencies that need to be resolved, and may find additional packages to install. For example, on my default installation of Fedora Core 4 as outlined in Chapter 2, yum installed the following RPM packages in addition to the ClamAV RPM packages: `fedora-usermgtmt`, `fedora-usermgmt-setup`, and `fedora-usermgmt-shadow-utils`. So go ahead and accept the dependencies yum resolves, and complete the download and installation process. When finished with the process, yum should report success.

If this is your first time installing a package from the Fedora Extras repository, yum will automatically import the Fedora Packages GPG key for verifying the integrity of the Fedora Extras packages.

We will not need the following ClamAV RPM packages that are also available in the Fedora Extras yum repository:

- `clamav-exim`: ClamAV package specifically for the Exim MTA

- `clamav-milter`: The ClamAV sendmail milter interface

- `clamav-server`: `clamd` and supporting files for running the ClamAV daemon

These last three RPM packages do not apply to our implementation and are simply not needed. If you find any of these are installed, it's best to uninstall them with yum:

```
[curtis@mail ~]$ sudo yum remove clamav-exim clamav-devel ➥
clamav-milter clamav-server
```

---

**Note** Although ClamAV comes with a daemon, we will not be using it in our overall e-mail server system design. MailScanner provides its own mechanism for efficient antivirus scanning with ClamAV. I will discuss this further later in this chapter when we integrate ClamAV with MailScanner. If you install ClamAV by source, the daemon will get installed, but we'll just ignore it for our purposes; it won't be configured or turned on, so it won't waste system resources.

---

## The ClamAV Source Distribution

To install from source, download the latest source distribution (version 0.88 at the time of this writing). You can't easily use wget in this case, as ClamAV is hosted by SourceForge. When downloading files from a project hosted by SourceForge, visitors are redirected to select a local mirror to alleviate network congestion. Visit the ClamAV web site at `www.clamav.net` and click through the download links for the latest stable release. Eventually you will be led to ClamAV's SourceForge site and given the chance to download the ClamAV source distribution from a mirror close to you.

---

■**Note** SourceForge (`www.sourceforge.net`) is an open source software development and collaboration web site. Over 100,000 open source software projects use SourceForge as their web hosting provider and primary means of management.

---

Next, unpack, build, compile, and install the source distribution (the screen output is not shown for brevity):

```
[curtis@mail ~]$ tar xzvf clamav-0.88.tar.gz
[curtis@mail clamav-0.88]$ cd clamav-0.88
[curtis@mail clamav-0.88]$ ./configure
[curtis@mail clamav-0.88]$ make
[curtis@mail clamav-0.88]$ sudo make install
```

After this simple process, everything will be installed, including clamd, the ClamAV daemon that we won't be using. Again, you can simply ignore the bits we won't be using; they won't be configured or started, so there's nothing taking up precious system resources.

Whatever your choice of installation method might be, you're not quite ready to configure ClamAV. Before continuing we must install the Mail::ClamAV Perl module we will use to integrate ClamAV with MailScanner. This process is the same regardless of how you decided to install ClamAV itself.

## The Mail::ClamAV Source Distribution

The Mail::ClamAV Perl module does not come bundled or packaged with either the ClamAV RPM packages or source distribution, or the MailScanner installation distribution. Instead, the latest Mail::ClamAV module can be found at the Comprehensive Perl Archive Network (CPAN), at www.cpan.org. CPAN is one of, if not the primary, definitive sources of Perl documentation and software on the Internet. The best way to find Perl modules is through the CPAN search site at http://search.cpan.org.

### Installing Inline::C and Parse::RecDescent Perl Modules

Before downloading and installing Mail::ClamAV, we must ensure two prerequisite Perl modules are installed. The first is Inline::C, and the second is Parse::RecDescent, which is required by Inline::C. To test whether the Inline::C Perl module is installed, try the following from the command line of your e-mail system:

```
[curtis@mail ~]$ perl -e "use Inline::C;"
```

If this command exits successfully with no screen output, then you can skip the Inline::C and Parse::RecDescent installation and finish the Mail::ClamAV installation. Otherwise, test to see if you need Parse::RecDescent. To do so, try the following from the command line of your e-mail system:

```
[curtis@mail ~]$ perl -e "use Parse::RecDescent;"
```

Again, if this command exits successfully with no screen output, you can continue with the installation of Mail::ClamAV.

Otherwise, before installing the Inline::C Perl module, you must install Parse::RecDescent. Search for, and download, the latest Parse::RecDescent source tarball from CPAN:

```
[curtis@mail ~]$ wget http://search.cpan.org/CPAN/authors/id/D/DC/ ➥
DCONWAY/Parse-RecDescent-1.94.tar.gz
```

and unpack, build, compile, and install the Parse::RecDescent Perl module (the screen output is not shown for brevity):

```
[curtis@mail ~]$ tar zxvf Parse-RecDescent-1.94.tar.gz
[curtis@mail ~]$ cd Parse-RecDescent-1.94
```

Note the next step is a bit different. You actually use Perl to configure the source to prepare it to be built and compiled. The general concept is similar to that of using a configure script to do the same thing with most other software packages we've installed earlier in this book:

```
[curtis@mail Parse-RecDescent-1.94]$ perl Makefile.PL
```

```
Checking if your kit is complete...
Looks good
Writing Makefile for Parse::RecDescent
```

Then compile the Parse::RecDescent source as you normally would:

```
[curtis@mail Parse-RecDescent-1.94]$ make
```

```
cp lib/Parse/RecDescent.pm blib/lib/Parse/RecDescent.pm
cp lib/Parse/RecDescent.pod blib/lib/Parse/RecDescent.pod
Manifying blib/man3/Parse::RecDescent.3pm
```

Before installing Parse::RecDescent, run make test to test whether the build and compile was successful (the screen output is not shown here):

```
[curtis@mail Parse-RecDescent-1.94]$ make test
```

If all tests are successful, or any failures are noted as acceptable and subsequently ignored, finish by installing Parse::RecDescent:

```
[curtis@mail Parse-RecDescent-1.94]$ sudo make install
```

```
Installing /usr/lib/perl5/site_perl/5.8.6/Parse/RecDescent.pm
Installing /usr/lib/perl5/site_perl/5.8.6/Parse/RecDescent.pod
Installing /usr/share/man/man3/Parse::RecDescent.3pm
Writing /usr/lib/perl5/site_perl/5.8.6/i386-linux-thread-multi/ ➥
auto/Parse/RecDescent/.packlist
Appending installation info to /usr/lib/perl5/5.8.6/ ➥
i386-linux-thread-multi/perllocal.pod
```

Of course, you can check your handiwork with the Perl one-liner:

```
[curtis@mail Parse-RecDescent-1.94]$ perl -e "use Parse::RecDescent;"
```

Repeat the same steps if you need to install the Inline::C Perl module (the screen output is not shown for brevity):

```
[curtis@mail ~]$ wget http://search.cpan.org/CPAN/authors/id/I/IN/ ➥
INGY/Inline-0.44.tar.gz
[curtis@mail ~]$ tar zxvf Inline-0.44.tar.gz
[curtis@mail ~]$ cd Inline-0.44
[curtis@mail Inline-0.44]$ perl Makefile.PL
[curtis@mail Inline-0.44]$ make
[curtis@mail Inline-0.44]$ make test
[curtis@mail Inline-0.44]$ sudo make install
```

Check one more time to make sure Inline::C is available to the Perl interpreter:

```
[curtis@mail Inline-0.44]$ perl -e "use Inline::C;"
```

---

```
It is invalid to use 'Inline::C' directly. Please consult the Inline
documentation for more information.

 at -e line 1
BEGIN failed--compilation aborted at -e line 1.
```

---

Oops, not quite the output you were hoping for or expecting; it looks like there's still a problem with the Inline::C Perl module, Actually, that's not true—it's just that this particular Perl module is not meant to be used directly in the manner I've instructed you with the short Perl command. However, the fact that you got this error indicates the module was successfully installed and is available for use, so you can finish with the installation of Mail::ClamAV.

## Installing Mail::ClamAV

First, search for the Mail::ClamAV and download the latest version of the module as a source tarball:

```
[curtis@mail ~]$ wget http://search.cpan.org/CPAN/authors/id/S/SA/ ➥
SABECK/Mail-ClamAV-0.17.tar.gz
```

Next, unpack, build, compile, and install the Mail::ClamAV Perl module (the screen output is not shown for brevity):

```
[curtis@mail ~]$ tar zxvf Mail-ClamAV-0.17.tar.gz
[curtis@mail ~]$ cd Mail-ClamAV-0.17
[curtis@mail Mail-ClamAV-0.17]$ perl Makefile.PL
[curtis@mail Mail-ClamAV-0.17]$ make
[curtis@mail Mail-ClamAV-0.17]$ make test
[curtis@mail Mail-ClamAV-0.17]$ sudo make install
```

Check to make sure you were successful by giving the `Mail::ClamAV` Perl module a quick test; run the following from the command line of your e-mail system:

```
[curtis@mail Mail-ClamAV-0.17]$ perl -e "use Mail::ClamAV;"
```

If this command exits successfully with no screen output, then you have successfully installed the `Mail::ClamAV` Perl module. Congratulations, you're now ready to configure ClamAV for integration into your MailScanner installation!

# Configuring ClamAV

Configuring ClamAV is going to be even easier than installing it. Since we are not using ClamAV and `clamd` in a stand-alone implementation, most of the configuration of ClamAV is left to MailScanner. If you installed the `clamav-server` RPM package, or installed ClamAV from source distribution, you'll probably find the file `/etc/clamd.conf`.

This file is for configuring and customizing the behavior of `clamd` when installed in a stand-alone implementation. Since we will not be using the ClamAV daemon `clamd`, ignore `clamd.conf` for the purposes of this book. So, that leaves configuring MailScanner so it knows to pass e-mail and e-mail attachments to ClamAV and how to handle infected messages and files.

## Configuring E-mail Virus Scanning with MailScanner and ClamAV

You might recall that in Chapter 14 we configured MailScanner to perform virus scanning by setting the following option in `MailScanner.conf`:

```
# If you want to be able to switch scanning on/off for different users or
# different domains, set this to the filename of a ruleset.
# This can also be the filename of a ruleset.
Virus Scanning = yes
```

However, further down in `MailScanner.conf`, we did not specify any virus scanners since we had none installed at the time. Let's go ahead and configure MailScanner to use the `Mail::ClamAV` Perl module installed earlier in this chapter to scan e-mail for viruses. To do so, change the following configuration option in `MailScanner.conf` from

```
# This *cannot* be the filename of a ruleset.
Virus Scanners = none
```

to the following:

```
# This *cannot* be the filename of a ruleset.
Virus Scanners = clamavmodule
```

Note the comment before the configuration option; this cannot be a filename of a ruleset. However, it is possible to list more than one antivirus application, in a space-separated list, should you choose to implement more than one antivirus application. For a complete list of antivirus applications supported by MailScanner, see the extensive comments prior to this option in `MailScanner.conf`.

The final four MailScanner configuration options you should take a look at ClamAV scanning thresholds:

```
ClamAVmodule Maximum Recursion Level = 8
ClamAVmodule Maximum Files = 1000
ClamAVmodule Maximum File Size = 10000000 # (10 Mbytes)
ClamAVmodule Maximum Compression Ratio = 250
```

`ClamAVModule Maximum Recursion Level` sets the maximum number of times one file can be archived. It's a common practice by virus authors to hide the payload deep inside many recursive archives, expecting the antivirus not to un-archive more than the first level, thus missing the "hidden" payload. Of course, in practice, only viruses archive more than a few levels deep; anything else past this is assumed to be a virus.

`ClamAVModule Maximum Files` specifies the maximum number of files that will be passed to ClamAV in one batch. Scanning more than 1,000 will probably slow your system.

`ClamAVModule Maximum File Size` is the largest file that will be passed to ClamAV for scanning. This should be set in conjunction with the file attachment threshold you set in Chapter 14.

Set `ClamAVModule Maximum Compression Ratio` to something reasonable; otherwise it's possible for someone to launch a denial-of-service (DoS) attack on your e-mail system by sending many files with excessively high compression ratios, which take much longer to decompress. If the file is compressed way too much, then it's probably not legitimate.

That's it! There's nothing more to do; save the changes to `MailScanner.conf` and reload MailScanner for your changes to take effect:

```
[curtis@mail ~]$ sudo service MailScanner reload
```

```
Reloading MailScanner workers:
    MailScanner:                    [ OK ]
```

**Note** It's best not to restart MailScanner after making a minor configuration change. Instead, use the `reload` argument to the MailScanner init script, causing MailScanner processes to simply reread their configuration and thus not affecting or interrupting the sendmail processes at all.

Because MailScanner will load the ClamAV virus databases with the `Mail::ClamAV` Perl module each time MailScanner is started, there is no need to start or stop, manually or otherwise, ClamAV itself. If you did not install the `clamav-server` Fedora Extras RPM package, there is no ClamAV init script to worry about. Likewise, the source distribution does not install a ClamAV init script by default, either.

## Keeping the ClamAV Virus Databases Updated

The preferred mechanism for keeping the ClamAV virus databases updated is with the `freshclam` script and a cron job. How `freshclam` is run on a periodic basis depends on how you installed ClamAV to begin with.

## Configuring freshclam Installed from RPM

First, if you installed the `clamav-update` Fedora Extras RPM package, then the cron job has already been installed for you in `/etc/cron.d/clamav-update`. All you need to do is edit the file `/etc/sysconfig/freshclam`, which contains the following:

```
FRESHCLAM_DELAY=disabled-warn # REMOVE ME
```

Follow the comment and remove or comment the `FRESHCLAM_DELAY` option like so:

```
#FRESHCLAM_DELAY=disabled-warn # REMOVE ME
```

ClamAV will now be updated every three hours. Updating more than once an hour is not recommended as this causes undue stress to the ClamAV virus databases servers. To change the update frequency, first modify `/etc/cron.d/clamav-update` by modifying the cron entry. The default, shown here:

```
0 */3 * * * root /usr/share/clamav/freshclam-sleep
```

indicates the script `/usr/share/clamav/freshclam-sleep` ought to be run every three hours. True to traditional UNIX form, any line that starts with the # character in a crontab is a comment and will be ignored by cron. Any other line is a cron job definition and contains six fields: the minute, hour, day of month, month, day of week, and the full path to the command to execute. Table 15-2 lists the first five fields and allowed values.

**Table 15-2.** *Crontab Fields and Allowed Values*

| Field | Allowed Values |
| --- | --- |
| Minute | 0–59 |
| Hour | 0–23 |
| Day of month | 1–31 |
| Month | 1–12 |
| Day of week | 0–7 |

Consult the `crontab(5)` man page for further details on configuring a crontab.

If you modify the frequency in which the cron job is run, then you must also update the following configuration option in `/etc/sysconfig/freshclam` to match the update interval in minutes:

```
# FRESHCLAM_MOD=
```

For example, if you keep the cron job set to run every three hours, then `FRESHCLAM_MOD` would be set to 180:

```
FRESHCLAM_MOD=180
```

Finally, modify `/etc/freshclam.conf` and change the following lines:

```
# Comment or remove the line below.
Example
```

and follow the comment and remove or comment the line Example:

```
# Comment or remove the line below.
#Example
```

## Configuring freshclam Installed from Source

If you've installed ClamAV from the source distribution, then the basic steps are the same. First, create a file called /etc/cron.d/clamav-update with the following contents:

```
0 */3 * * * root /usr/local/bin/freshclam
```

Modify the interval if you wish and change the path to freshclam if you installed ClamAV in a nonstandard location. Consult the crontab(5) man page for further detail on configuring a crontab.

Finally, modify /etc/freshclam.conf and change the following lines:

```
# Comment or remove the line below.
Example
```

and follow the comment and remove or comment the line Example:

```
# Comment or remove the line below.
#Example
```

After you've configured freshclam, MailScanner may need to be modified a bit so it can monitor the ClamAV virus databases.

## Making MailScanner Aware of ClamAV Virus Database Updates

Next, in MailScanner.conf you may need to modify the following MailScanner configuration option:

```
Monitors for ClamAV Updates = /usr/local/share/clamav/*.cvd
```

This option must point to the location of your ClamAV virus databases. If you install ClamAV from the source distribution, then you can leave this option as it is. However, if you installed ClamAV from the Fedora Extras RPM package, then you will have to change this line to

```
Monitors for ClamAV Updates = /var/lib/clamav/*.cvd
```

This option will instruct MailScanner to periodically check to see if the ClamAV virus databases have been updated and to reload its configuration only when absolutely necessary. Now you can be sure that ClamAV virus databases will be updated in a timely manner, maintaining your e-mail system's ability to protect your users from malicious e-mail attachments. Next, I will show you how you can test ClamAV virus scanning and e-mail scanning with ClamAV and MailScanner.

# Testing Virus Scanning with ClamAV

Chances are you'll want to test your antivirus installation to see if it works. I'm going to go out on a limb and assume you don't have viruses just lying around, nor do you have the desire to risk infecting your computer. Well, do not despair! There are two safe ways to test ClamAV without putting your system at risk.

## Using clamscan to Search for Viruses

First, let's use clamscan, the command-line scanner, to make sure ClamAV has been installed properly. Doing so allows you to test ClamAV itself without MailScanner first. Then we can test actual e-mail–borne virus scanning with MailScanner and ClamAV later, once ClamAV has been proven to work properly. Make sure ClamAV can operate properly independently from any other application; otherwise you'll be troubleshooting too many components at once.

If you downloaded and unpacked the ClamAV source tarball, then let's use that for testing. Run clamscan on the unpacked tarball on your e-mail system with the following command:

```
[curtis@mail ~]$ sudo clamscan ~/clamav-0.88/*
```

On my test system, this produced the following output:

```
/home/curtis/clamav-0.88/test/README: OK
/home/curtis/clamav-0.88/test/clam.rar: ClamAV-Test-File FOUND
/home/curtis/clamav-0.88/test/clam.exe: ClamAV-Test-File FOUND
/home/curtis/clamav-0.88/test/clam-error.rar: OK
/home/curtis/clamav-0.88/test/clam.exe.bz2: ClamAV-Test-File FOUND
/home/curtis/clamav-0.88/test/clam.cab: ClamAV-Test-File FOUND
/home/curtis/clamav-0.88/test/clam.zip: ClamAV-Test-File FOUND
/home/curtis/clamav-0.88/TODO: Empty file
/home/curtis/clamav-0.88/UPGRADE: OK

----------- SCAN SUMMARY -----------
Known viruses: 42108
Engine version: 0.88
Scanned directories: 14
Scanned files: 207
Infected files: 5
Data scanned: 5.88 MB
Time: 3.141 sec (0 m 3 s)
```

Looks like ClamAV found some viruses! Don't worry, as their names indicate, they are simply harmless test viruses used just for these purposes and can be safely ignored. These files were created to test the various abilities of ClamAV to scan different file types. These file signatures are added to the ClamAV virus databases specifically for this purpose. Keeping these files around might be handy in the future if you ever suspect ClamAV or MailScanner is not working properly. Alternatively, similar files are also freely available on the Internet that provide similar test cases and are widely recognized by most antivirus applications.

## Using the EICAR Test Viruses to Test ClamAV

If you don't have the ClamAV source tarball readily available, another option is available. The European Institute for Computer Anti-Virus Research (EICAR) (www.eicar.org) has developed a standardized set of harmless test viruses. Most antivirus applications, including ClamAV, recognize these test viruses. You can download three test viruses from www.eicar.org/anti_virus_test_file.htm.

You can use wget to download each to your server, and try clamscan to see if ClamAV is working properly:

```
[curtis@mail ~]$ wget http://www.eicar.org/download/eicar.com
```

You can then initiate the scan like so:

```
[curtis@mail ~]$ clamscan eicar.com
```

On my test system, this produced the following output:

```
eicar.com: Eicar-Test-Signature FOUND

----------- SCAN SUMMARY -----------
Known viruses: 42108
Engine version: 0.88
Scanned directories: 0
Scanned files: 1
Infected files: 1
Data scanned: 0.00 MB
Time: 0.684 sec (0 m 0 s)
```

You can repeat as desired for each of the four EICAR test viruses. If ClamAV successfully detects all four EICAR test viruses, then you've got a successful ClamAV installation ready to stop e-mail–borne threats.

So, you've tested ClamAV independently from any other component of your e-mail system. Next, it would be prudent to test the MailScanner configuration changes you added after installing ClamAV. To do so, you can use the same EICAR test viruses.

## Testing E-mail Virus Scanning with MailScanner and ClamAV

Testing MailScanner for successful antivirus detection is as simple as sending an e-mail to yourself with one or more of the EICAR test viruses attached to the message. Doing so should at the very least result in MailScanner logging the incident in similar fashion to the following found in /var/log/maillog:

```
Jun 13 10:50:44 mail MailScanner[7068]: New Batch: Scanning 1 messages, 1429 bytes
Jun 13 10:50:44 mail MailScanner[7068]: Virus and Content Scanning: Starting
Jun 13 10:50:44 mail MailScanner[7068]: ClamAVModule::INFECTED:: ➡
Eicar-Test-Signature:: ./k5DEofvE011477/eicar.com
Jun 13 10:50:44 mail MailScanner[7068]: Virus Scanning: ClamAV Module ➡
found 1 infections
```

```
Jun 13 10:50:44 mail MailScanner[7068]: Infected message k5DEofvE011477 ➥
came from 127.0.0.1
Jun 13 10:50:44 mail MailScanner[7068]: Virus Scanning: Found 1 viruses
Jun 13 10:50:44 mail MailScanner[7068]: Filename Checks: ➥
Windows/DOS Executable (k5DEofvE011477 eicar.com)
Jun 13 10:50:44 mail MailScanner[7068]: Other Checks: Found 1 problems
```

As a matter of fact, in the case of the eicar.com test virus file, MailScanner recognizes the attachment as infected or unwanted content twice.

First, the ClamAVModule detected the file as matching a recognized virus signature and reported to MailScanner that the file was infected. Second, the filename checks configured in Chapter 14 recognized the file extension or file type as one that should be blocked or removed. This successfully proved that both virus detection with ClamAV and filename filtering is working through MailScanner; rest assured that your users will be safe from malicious e-mail attachments to the best of your ability.

## Further ClamAV Resources

As typical, the ClamAV documentation can be found locally on your Fedora Core system in /usr/share/doc/clamav-[version]/ where [version] is replaced by the base version string of the RPM package installed. For example, at the time of this writing, the RPM package installed was clamav-0.88-1.fc4, so documentation can be found in /usr/share/doc/clamav-0.88/; to check the version of ClamAV, run the following command:

```
[curtis@mail ~]$ rpm -qv clamav
```

```
clamav-0.88-1.fc4
```

Of particular interest is the file signatures.pdf, which details how the virus databases are created, how to create your own virus signature, and how to query and manipulate the virus databases. ClamAV succeeds in large part to its community support. If you feel that a new virus exists and has not been added to the ClamAV virus database, or is not yet detected by ClamAV, you can submit a sample for review by the virus database maintainer team through the form located at www.clamav.net/sendvirus.html.

In addition to the local documentation, or the documentation found with the source distribution, the most current information regarding ClamAV installation, configuration, and development status is also available from the ClamAV wiki found at http://wiki.clamav.net. For community support, the ClamAV mailing lists are also an excellent resource. You can find list archives and subscription information at www.clamav.net/ml.html.

## Summary

In this chapter, I introduced ClamAV, the free and open source UNIX antivirus toolkit. We saw how ClamAV is more than just a virus scanner. Comprised of various components, including command-line virus scanners, a virus-scanning daemon, and a C library, ClamAV can easily stand on its own, offering independent virus protection on a Linux system. However, I also showed how ClamAV can be integrated into our MailScanner implementation, using the `Mail::ClamAV` Perl module to interface with the ClamAV C API library.

Installation of ClamAV is very easy, and configuration is just as easy. With ClamAV integrated with MailScanner, our mail system is one step closer to a complete setup. In the next chapter, we start tackling the interminable job of fighting unsolicited bulk e-mail.

# PART 7

# Fighting Spam

# CHAPTER 16

■ ■ ■

# Introducing General Spam Countermeasures

It is apparent that spam has become an inevitable fact of life. In a way, the very openness and ubiquitousness of e-mail has become part of the problem; little prohibits any one person from sending huge amounts of bulk e-mail to millions of recipients. What's worse, the very e-mail system you're building could be used as a springboard for sending spam if you're not careful to properly configure it. Even when properly configuring your system, legitimate users might still attempt to take advantage of your system and services to send spam. My point is that spam can be a bigger headache for an e-mail administrator, as you have to both deal with receiving spam and take steps to ensure your system and users aren't contributing to the larger problem.

Most likely, your organization or customers will expect antispam services on your e-mail system. A successful antispam solution will take several components; there's no one killer application that can solve all of your spam problems. In this chapter I discuss various general tactics for fighting spam. Then, in Chapter 17, I introduce SpamAssassin, the real crux to any antispam solution.

## User Education: The First Line of Defense

Possibly the most important aspect to any antispam solution is the education of its users. The vast majority of information on the Internet is publicly accessible. If you are loose with your personal information, even your e-mail address, someone will find it. Harvesting valid e-mail addresses from various web resources is probably one of the best ways spammers have to get e-mail addresses. Teaching users to limit the amount of information they give out, and to whom they give it out, can help reduce the amount of spam your users receive.

Taking extra steps in limiting access to internal resources, and disallowing search engine crawlers from indexing internal, sensitive resources, is another way web administrators can help limit the amount of spam. Nearly all sites have a directory of e-mail addresses and contact information. Instead of making those directories textual e-mail addresses, generate dynamic images with the e-mail address in them; you can find resources and examples on the Internet. Of course, there's little you can do about e-mail addresses that are easily guessed.

> **■Note** Another tactic spammers incorporate is a sort of brute-force process, taking well-known dictionary words and proper names, and variations of each, and simply sending spam to them all. A spammer doesn't care that the majority will bounce; it is those that do not bounce that increase their chances. Typically, spam has an invalid envelope sender or From header, so bounce messages, or nondelivery reports (NDRs), never hit the spammers' real mailboxes.

Of course, the very fact that the amount of spam increases from year to year is apparently due to a significant amount of people buying into what unsolicited commercial e-mails are selling. Although it's easy to send millions of e-mail, it's not always cheap, especially at the staggering rate at which spammers send junk mail. However, it only takes a significantly small proportion of people to actually click through an embedded web link or buy a product to result in profitability for the spammer. Even if by accident, many affiliate click programs simply pay out when a web site is visited. When you talk about millions of clicks or purchases, it's not hard to imagine some are making money off these unsolicited attempts. In fact, the author of the sendmail program, Eric Allman himself, wrote an article about the economics of spam that is both humorous and insightful ("The Economics of Spam," `http://acmqueue.com/modules.php?name=Content&pa=showpage&pid=108`).

Educate your users that messages that look suspicious or obviously commercial in nature ought to be simply ignored and immediately deleted. Refraining from clicking through links found in spam, even if out of curiosity, can help reduce the profitability of engaging in spam.

## The Truth About Remove or Unsubscribe Links

Another sad but true matter of practical fact is that unsubscribe or remove links that appear at the end of spam can also be a part of the bigger problem. Oftentimes, a spam message will include a seemingly helpful notice of how the recipient can remove themselves from the list subscription should they feel they received the message in error. In fact, such notices are actually required of legitimate bulk e-mail messages by US law (more on that later in this chapter).

The most unscrupulous of e-mail spammers will add a notice to appear to be in accordance with the law, or to simply appear to be helpful. Somehow when you're given a way to opt out, unsolicited e-mail seems more legitimate. However, studies have shown that the bulk of those unsubscribe links are flat-out ignored. In fact, those very unsubscribe requests are often used as verification that an e-mail address is valid and active, alerting the spammer that there is somebody reading the mail. Such information can encourage an increased amount of spam if the spammers know there is a warm body behind that e-mail address, actively reading their mail.

Although rather unfortunate, it seems as if the best practical recommendation for users is to simply ignore the unsubscribe or remove links. It's best to give your customers the tools necessary to filter spam so that it is as unobtrusive and disturbing as possible. Unfortunately, this is a tough thing to do, and the proper use of such tools can also require proper user education for any solution to be successful.

Next, let's take a look at some of the methodologies that you might employ to help hinder or stop the proliferation of spam. There are several battlefronts from which to fight spam; let's look at measures you can take on your e-mail server itself first.

# Server-Side Antispam Measures

A complete antispam solution should include a method for server-side filtering and detection of e-mail spam. However, this isn't as easy as it might sound and may involve more than procmail-like filters. For instance, an e-mail administrator should be responsible for making sure their e-mail system is not illegitimately used as a springboard for spammers. There are also distributed efforts for stopping the proliferation of unsolicited bulk e-mail. Let's take a look at some of these server-side countermeasures you should consider implementing on your e-mail system.

## Eliminating Open Relays

There are several mechanisms you as an e-mail administrator might employ for fighting spam. You can take measures at the SMTP server level to inhibit or block the ability of certain classes, or types, of SMTP clients from sending e-mail through your server. These measures can be proactive, but they are not foolproof.

The first, and possibly most important, of the methods or mechanisms for stopping the proliferation of spam is the closing of open relays. An *open relay* is simply an MTA that will deliver e-mail for any sender. An open relay is essentially a free ride for spammers. If a spammer finds an open relay, they can send e-mail for free, taking up someone else's bandwidth and server computing cycles to do their dirty work.

What this really means is that your MTA should not attempt to deliver e-mail for a remote recipient unless that remote recipient is a local account or the sender is on your local network. When you allow anyone from a specific, local network, you are allowing relaying for that user. However, if anyone, including one of your users, outside your local trusted network attempts to send an e-mail to a remote recipient not hosted on your e-mail system, your MTA should refuse to deliver the message. This is a closed relay.

### WHITELISTS AND BLACKLISTS

A list in which you explicitly trust is called a *whitelist*. Conversely, a list in which you explicitly do not trust or automatically block is called a *blacklist*. You can probably see where the term *graylisting* comes from; this involves provisionally trusting clients individually using proactive, dynamic measures.

Typically, whitelists and blacklists are a retroactive measure. Only after repeated, unanswered, and unsolicited attempts at spamming your customers, you might decide to completely block a particular SMTP source by adding them to your blacklist. Or you might find that the same person trying to contact your VP of Sales is consistently getting hit by your antispam measures, so you add them to your system's whitelist, effectively allowing them to bypass your spam countermeasures.

A word of warning: use your whitelists and blacklists wisely, especially if basing them on e-mail addresses. We've seen how easy it is to forge an e-mail address. Also be careful about explicitly allowing or disallowing by IP address. If you block an IP address that is used by its owner as part of a dynamic DHCP range, you probably aren't blocking the same abuser after several days.

Whitelists and blacklists are all or nothing. Even basic content filtering has proven to be insufficient for the successful detection of most e-mail spam.

This approach has several disadvantages. For example, if you're a corporation with a network that covers only one building, your employees will not be able to send e-mail using your MTA from their home or a coffee shop—something that does not lend itself to mobile users in a fast-paced, always-connected environment. However, there are other alternatives, including using webmail (which we discussed in Chapter 12) and authenticating users before allowing them to send e-mail through your MTA (which I will discuss in more detail in Chapter 21).

Let's take a look at the sendmail configuration necessary for keeping your MTA from being an open relay.

## Configuring sendmail for Selective Relaying

In Chapter 6, we took a look at the sendmail configuration file /etc/mail/local-host-names. If you remember, this is where you put all of the e-mail domains you wish to receive e-mail for. In the context of open relays, this file lists all of the e-mail domains for which your MTA will always accept mail for local delivery, regardless of the sender or the sender's origin. If your e-mail domains were not entered in local-host-names, your MTA would not know it accepts mail for those domains locally.

I also briefly introduced the access database /etc/mail/access.db in Chapter 6. The access database is how you limit from whom and where you allow relaying. The flat-text file /etc/mail/access is used to generate the access.db file and should contain the list of rules, one per line, that define relaying access to your e-mail server.

For example, my local network is 192.168.69.1–192.168.69.255, so to allow relaying from that entire Class C IP subnet, I'd add the following to the access.db file:

```
192.168.69        RELAY
```

You'll also want to allow your e-mail system itself to relay, so make sure the following lines are also in the access.db file:

```
localhost.localdomain  RELAY
localhost              RELAY
127.0.0.1             RELAY
```

You can also explicitly reject mail from a particular Internet host or network. Adding a line like the following will reject mail from the IP address 192.168.69.100:

```
192.168.69.100    REJECT
```

Table 16-1 lists sample values for the key, or left-hand side (LHS), and Table 16-2 lists valid sample right-hand side (RHS) values. When combined into a rule in the access database, these values can be used to control relaying through your e-mail system.

**Table 16-1.** *Sample LHS Keys for the Access Database*

| LHS Key | Description |
| --- | --- |
| username@ | Match a specific username with any e-mail domain (the @ character is necessary). |
| username@example.com | Match a specific e-mail address. |
| example.com | Match a specific domain. |
| hostname.example.com | Match a specific hostname and domain. |
| 192.168.69 | Match a specific IP network (including the entire Class C subnet). |
| 192.168.69.100 | Match a specific IP address. |

**Table 16-2.** *Sample RHS Values for the Access Database*

| RHS Value | Description |
| --- | --- |
| RELAY | Allow an SMTP client matching the LHS relay through your e-mail system. |
| REJECT | Reject mail delivery from an SMTP client matching the LHS, with the standard SMTP reply code 5.7.1. |
| DISCARD | Accept mail delivery from an SMTP client matching the LHS, but silently drop the message after accepting it without notification to the sender or recipient. |
| ERROR:D.S.N: *Custom message* | Reject mail delivery from the SMTP client matching the LHS, with the custom SMTP reply code in the general form D.S.N as defined in RFC 1893 (www.ietf.org/rfc/rfc1893.txt) and custom error message. |

When you've finished making changes to /etc/mail/access, rebuild /etc/mail/access.db with the following commands:

```
[curtis@mail ~]$ cd /etc/mail/
[curtis@mail mail]$ sudo makemap hash access.db < access
```

Because we need to restart the sendmail daemons, use the restart, rather than the reload, argument to the MailScanner init script:

```
[curtis@mail mail]$ sudo service MailScanner restart
```

```
Shutting down MailScanner daemons:
    MailScanner:                [ OK ]
    incoming sendmail:          [ OK ]
    outgoing sendmail:          [ OK ]
Starting MailScanner daemons:
    incoming sendmail:          [ OK ]
    outgoing sendmail:          [ OK ]
    MailScanner:                [ OK ]
```

Pay special attention to what you relay, reject, and discard. Leaving your e-mail system configured as an open relay is a sure way to get your e-mail domain blocked by other administrators around the world. Also be careful of which networks or domains you reject mail delivery from, especially if the IP address is assigned to a dynamic DHCP pool. If you have one particular Internet host abusing your system, temporarily blocking it might be necessary, though.

## Introducing Real-Time Blackhole Lists

A *real-time blackhole list (RBL)* originally started out as a list of open relays. The idea is that a suspected open relay is submitted to an RBL database, an automated e-mail is sent using the suspect MTA to deliver the message, and if the message is received back, indicating the MTA is in fact an open relay, then the MTA is added to the RBL database. E-mail system administrators can use the RBL on their mail system and reject incoming mail originating from any system listed in the RBL.

I hesitate mentioning RBLs at all; the various RBLs have experienced a rather tumultuous history. Some have gained a reputation for listing too many legitimate, closed relays, or getting "de-listed" is difficult. Other RBLs require little by way of a verification process for determining whether or not a suspect MTA is really an open relay. And, because there are so many potential RBLs, if you get listed on one or more, even by mistake, it can be very difficult to get yourself removed or know for sure how many you are listed on. What's more, if e-mail systems cache RBLs and do not look them up in real time, then your MTA may continue to be blocked some time after you are removed.

However, this is not to say that RBLs cannot be used as just one more part of an overall antispam solution. Relying solely on RBLs, and blocking e-mail from hosts listed on one or more RBLs, is not a good idea and goes against best practices. RBLs should be used conservatively as a larger solution. So, in Chapter 18 we will see how SpamAssassin can use RBLs to increase the detection of spam. Table 16-3 lists some of the more respected RBLs that you might consider using in your SpamAssassin customization discussed in Chapter 18.

**Table 16-3.** *List of Real-Time Blackhole Lists*

| RBL Name | RBL Address | Web Site |
|---|---|---|
| Distributed Sender Blackhole List | list.dsbl.org | www.dsbl.org |
| SpamCop | bl.spamcop.net | www.spamcop.net/bl.shtml |
| Composite Blocking List | cbl.abuseat.org | http://cbl.abuseat.org/ |

You will have to decide whether to take the aggressive measures of using real-time blackhole lists. RBLs are created by people, and deciding who ought to be added to an RBL can be subjective. Too many RBLs are abused and are not managed well or regularly maintained. You should investigate any RBL you're considering and evaluate the risk.

## Introducing Graylisting

A relatively new method for combating spammers and other e-mail abusers is something called *graylisting*. Graylisting takes three pieces of information from all incoming e-mail messages: the message envelope sender (taken from the SMTP MAIL FROM command), the message envelope recipient (taken from the SMTP RCPT TO command), and the IP address of the SMTP client. The MTA uses this information to check against a local database on the e-mail system, determines the last time this combination connected to the MTA (if at all), and temporarily rejects the message if a predetermined amount of time hadn't elapsed since the last time the client connected.

The theory is if the sending MTA is a legitimate, properly configured MTA, it will retry message delivery again after a small delay when receiving the temporary rejection. Most spammers will simply connect and send e-mail to an MTA very quickly, and if messages are dropped or temporarily rejected, chances are they will not try to re-send at all. Spammers' tactics tend to be more brutish, relying on their sheer numbers to get through, and do not typically include following proper SMTP etiquette. Graylisting is usually not applied to outgoing mail sent from your local trusted network by your users.

Obviously, graylisting will result in delivery delays, but only for the first messages of their kind. Think of graylisting as a sort of throttle, forcing legitimate MTAs to retry delivery in an effort to weed out illegitimate MTAs. However, sometimes even legitimate MTAs do not always follow SMTP specifications properly; you might find that graylisting blocks those legitimate MTAs serving a large number of legitimate users. It's usually best to keep a list of such MTAs and treat them individually case by case.

Graylisting rejects mail, even temporarily, at the SMTP layer, without any human intervention. You should regularly test and update graylisting rules, and always keep an eye on mail logs to make sure the level of service your customers expect is not being compromised. Graylisting is also a new concept and is still not widely adopted yet.

The next few methodologies we will discuss are probably less aggressive, so they could be considered a little safer. However, they are effective tools nonetheless.

## Introducing Hash-Sharing Systems

In addition to support for traditional RBLs, SpamAssassin can also query one or more hash-sharing systems. A *hash-sharing system* is a collaborative and distributed catalog of spam messages. Suppose I am a contributing member of a hash-sharing system and my e-mail system receives a message that I classify as spam. I can send a checksum, or signature, unique to that spam message to the hash-sharing system's online database. Suppose you use the same hash-sharing system I contribute to and receive the same spam message after its checksum is submitted. Your e-mail system can check the hash-sharing system's online database to see if the message has been submitted previously by someone else, helping you decide whether or not the message is spam. You can also submit the same checksum to support my submission that the message is indeed spam. Hash-sharing systems can be very loosely compared to virus signatures and databases maintained by antivirus applications, although the checksums or signatures of spam e-mail messages ignore some aspects of a message and can be modified as spam evolves. SpamAssassin supports three hash-sharing systems: Vipul's Razor, Pyzor, and Distributed Checksum Clearinghouse (DCC). I'll briefly introduce each here, but I will not cover the installation and configuration of these hash-sharing system applications until Chapter 17.

Vipul's Razor (http://razor.sourceforge.net) is a Perl client written primarily by Vipul Ved Prakash that allows free UNIX client access to the commercial database owned and operated by Cloudmark (www.cloudmark.com).

Pyzor (http://pyzor.sourceforge.net) was originally written to be a replacement for the Razor client written in the Python programming language. However, Pyzor has evolved into its own hash-sharing system—both client front end and server and database back end—that is completely free and open source.

DCC (www.rhyolite.com/anti-spam/dcc/) is just one more hash-sharing system that has been widely successful and popular. One interesting aspect of DCC is that it uses UDP, rather than TCP, Internet traffic, so it typically requires little additional network bandwidth overhead. Any or all of these are excellent additional resources that can be used to increase your ability to detect and classify spam.

## Introducing Advanced Content Filtering

Everything I've discussed so far has occurred at the SMTP layer. If a message is rejected, even temporarily, the recipient is not notified as such. This means that mail from an ill-configured, but legitimate, mail domain could be sending mail to your VP of Sales, but if it's graylisted and never re-sent, your VP would be none the wiser. Of course, the rejections would be logged in the mail logs, but if your system handles as few as a thousand messages a day, a number not unreasonable even for a small to medium-sized company, you can't possibly be expected to catch every false positive.

But that same VP cannot be bothered with sorting through hundreds of unsolicited bulk e-mail in order to get at legitimate messages in his Inbox. So, you've got to do *something* but you need to make a compromise between too little and too much. Content-based filtering can be just such a compromise.

We've already talked about basic message filtering with procmail in Chapter 13 and content filtering in Chapter 14 when I introduced MailScanner. Here we're going to discuss content filtering specific to e-mail spam. Although MailScanner is a content filter itself by definition, it is a more general tool—one that can use additional applications to perform more specialized scanning. Just as we relegated antivirus responsibility to ClamAV, we will relegate the bulk of antispam detection to SpamAssassin.

## Introducing Bayesian Spam Filtering

The evolution of detecting and filtering e-mail spam from legitimate e-mail has taken a cue from the world of probability theory; specifically, Bayes's Theorem. According to the Stanford Encyclopedia of Philosophy (http://plato.stanford.edu/archives/win2003/entries/bayes-theorem/):

> *Bayes's Theorem is a simple mathematical formula used for calculating conditional probabilities.*

Bayesian spam filtering is a content filter, but different from traditional content filtering in that it is adaptive and learning. A Bayesian spam filter applies Bayes's Theorem by assigning the probability of whether an e-mail is spam, where the probability of legitimate e-mail is 0. Bayesian spam filters are trained to recognize spam e-mail from legitimate e-mail, typically on an individual user-by-user basis. Instead of looking for specific words, phrases, or patterns like a traditional spam content filter, a Bayesian spam filter will calculate the probability a message is spam based on analysis and comparisons made against characteristics of past mail received, both spam and legitimate. This means that over time, as more e-mail of both classes are scanned, a Bayesian spam filter continually has new data and conditions with which to adapt its ability to assign higher probabilities to spam.

Historically, traditional content spam filters do not take legitimate e-mail into account. Instead, potential characteristics of spam are stored and compared against incoming e-mail. However, over time, spammers will adapt and hide these characteristics from the filter, and effectively get past normal filters. We've seen these attempts in the spam in our mailboxes: add spaces in words, replace vowels with numbers, and so forth. These strategies do a good job of defeating traditional content filters, but humans recognize them immediately.

A good Bayesian spam filter will, over time, see that little to no legitimate e-mail contains words broken with spaces or numbers sprinkled within them. Messages that do contain such things will be given higher probabilities of being spam over time.

Bayesian spam filtering became widely accepted grossly thanks to Paul Graham's 2002 essay *A Plan for Spam* (`www.paulgraham.com/spam.html`). Since then a number of good antispam software packages have been developed with Bayesian filtering. SpamAssassin is one such Bayesian spam filter that is widely acclaimed. Chapter 17 dives into these concepts in much more detail, and you will learn how SpamAssassin uses the principles of Bayesian filtering to adapt and tune its ability to better detect spam from legitimate e-mail, possibly on an individual-user level.

# Client-Side Antispam Measures

In recent years, many contemporary client e-mail applications have been developed with their own built-in antispam mechanisms. Much of this development arose from the fact that few organizations have implemented a sitewide antispam solution. However, client spam detection and filtering can complement server-side detection and filtering. This should not be a reason to drop any plans for a server-side solution but, rather, should be used as one more component to the total solution. Think of client-side antispam measures as the last line of defense for your users, but these measures should not be relied on as the only line of defense.

The downside to using a client-side solution is that the functionality it provides is limited to that one client on a specific desktop computer or laptop. However, these features are standard on the two most popular e-mail clients today, and you may be asked to support users who wish to take advantage of them.

## Introducing Microsoft Outlook's Junk Mail Filtering

Microsoft Outlook has become almost as ubiquitous as e-mail itself, especially in the corporate world. Many businesses use the Microsoft Office suite of applications, of which Outlook is a standard component. Beginning with Outlook 2003, Microsoft has built in what they dub *junk mail filtering*. This feature is enabled automatically, but to check simply select Actions ➤ Junk E-Mail ➤ Junk E-Mail Options. As Figure 16-1 shows, Outlook has several levels of spam-detection filtering, allowing users to choose their level of protection. Once this feature is turned on, Outlook will attempt to detect spam and filter it to a user's Junk E-Mail folder while Outlook is open and receives mail.

**Figure 16-1.** *Microsoft Outlook 2003 allows users to select different levels of spam detection and filtering.*

Sometimes, Outlook will detect and filter a legitimate message as spam. To keep Outlook from doing so, right-click the message and from the context menu select Junk E-Mail ➤ Add Sender to Safe Senders List. This effectively adds the sender to Outlook's local sender whitelist. Conversely, you can tell Outlook to filter a message it missed by right-clicking the message and selecting Junk E-Mail ➤ Add Sender to Blocked Senders List. This effectively adds the sender to Outlook's local sender blacklist.

## Introducing Mozilla Thunderbird's Junk Mail Filtering

Mozilla Thunderbird also includes antispam measures. Indeed, Thunderbird's filter is a Bayesian spam filter. To enable Thunderbird junk mail filtering, select Tools ➤ Junk Mail Controls. As Figure 16-2 shows, Thunderbird has several options for configuring the behavior of junk mail detection and filtering capabilities. For instance, you can tell Thunderbird to trust mail that comes from anyone in your personal address book. If you implement SpamAssassin as detailed later in Chapters 17 and 18, I suggest selecting the option Trust Junk Mail Headers Set By and then choosing SpamAssassin from the accompanying drop-down list so it doesn't use those headers to taint its spam detection. Thunderbird can also automatically filter mail it detects as spam into an e-mail folder of your choice. Finally, to enable the Bayesian filter, called Adaptive Filtering in Thunderbird, click the Adaptive Filter tab and then select the option Enable Adaptive Junk Mail Detection.

When Thunderbird detects a message it thinks is spam, it will mark it as such with a warning and junk mail icon, as shown in Figure 16-3. If you have Adaptive Filtering enabled, you can click the This Is Not Junk button to make Thunderbird learn the message was detected incorrectly. Similarly, if spam slips through undetected, you can click the Junk button at the top of the Thunderbird toolbar. All in all, Thunderbird is fully equipped with tools to help you and your users detect and filter spam.

**Figure 16-2.** *Thunderbird offers additional antispam detection and filtering with its Junk Mail Controls.*

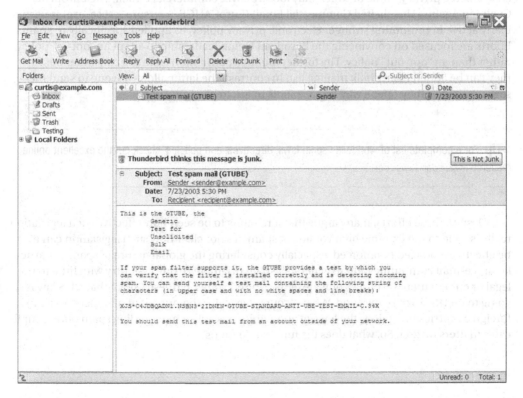

**Figure 16-3.** *When Thunderbird detects spam, it alerts you accordingly.*

# Attempting to Fight Spam with Legislation

Finally, one last class of methodology is a relative new one. Many governments and governmental agencies across the world have acknowledged there is a problem and have attempted to combat the problem through various legislation and policies. Although the overall impact of these measures isn't clear, it is an interesting angle from which to attack the problem, one few Internet pioneers years ago would have probably ever conceived to be necessary or possible.

One recently hyped example of such attempts was the Controlling the Assault of Non-Solicited Pornography and Marketing Act of 2003, which contains a list of requirements and criteria for legal commercial bulk mailers to follow, such as the following:

- Misleading or false e-mail header information should not be used.

- Messages should not contain misleading or deceptive subject lines.

- Each message must provide an opt-out request mechanism.

- Messages must be clearly marked as an advertisement and include a valid postal mailing address.

In addition to US federal law, numerous state legislative bodies have enacted some sort of law regarding commercial bulk e-mail.

Similarly, the European Union has also released several directives regarding online and e-commerce privacy, some of which may loosely cover commercial e-mail. The European Coalition Against Unsolicited Commercial Email (EuroCAUCE, www.euro.cauce.org) is particularly active in promoting stronger electronic privacy policy, as applied specifically to spam. Efforts are focused on convincing the European Union leadership to adopt an "opt-in" policy, rather than an "opt-out" policy. The former requires permission from the consumer before they can be added to any bulk mailing list. In contrast, the latter allows anyone to send messages as long as they offer a way for recipients to ask to be removed.

---

**Tip** For a complete list of worldwide spam laws, directives, and policies, check out the excellent online resource www.spamlaws.com.

---

Despite these efforts, many argue that it remains to be seen how effective such legislation really is. Due to the extreme high volume of spam, it's not clear how such legislation can even be effectively policed or enforced, especially considering the global nature of spam in particular and e-mail communication in general. If spam originates from a country with little to no legal or enforcement resources outside of the United States, it doesn't seem that a US law is going to do US citizens any good. What recourses exist for the pursuit of offenders based in foreign countries? Certainly, the level of anonymity possible when sending spam only complicates matters further. So, what does the future hold for us?

# Summary

In this chapter, we covered a lot of material. First, I advocated user education as one of the best ways to combat spam. As you learned, people need to start protecting their information more closely; your users need to know that signing up for any random request and clicking on suspect web links will only increase their chances of receiving more spam. Then, I surveyed a variety of approaches to fighting spam, both from the server side and client side.

One very important responsibility is to ensure your system isn't harboring spammers through an open relay, allowing anyone to send through your SMTP server to any e-mail address on the Internet. Relaying through your e-mail system should be selective, and the sendmail access.db database allows you to do just that. In addition, various RBLs maintained on the Web by the Internet community can be used to block spammers, but you've got to be careful with the legitimacy of those lists.

Of course, where spam is concerned, simple filtering isn't easy, either. Traditional content filters may not be sufficient in differentiating between unsolicited bulk e-mail and legitimate e-mail. By employing probability theory to the problem, a unique, adaptive method for detecting spam called Bayesian filtering has been developed.

Popular e-mail client applications like Microsoft Outlook 2003 and Mozilla Thunderbird also offer client-side e-mail spam detection and filtering that can be used by you and your users to combat spam. Perhaps sufficient by themselves, these client-side solutions can be used in conjunction with the server-side spam countermeasures you employ on your e-mail system.

Legislation is yet one more tool governments are trying to use to stop irresponsible mailers. However, while spam exists and flourishes despite legislation and education, e-mail administrators and users alike will have to continue adapting as best as possible. In Chapter 17, we continue our antispam discussion by introducing and installing SpamAssassin, the Bayesian spam filtering application.

■ ■ ■

# Introducing and Installing SpamAssassin

This is probably a highly anticipated chapter; I feel as if I've said so much about SpamAssassin already through the previous 16 chapters! Well, finally in this chapter I will formally introduce SpamAssassin, the free and open source Bayesian spam filter. We will work through the installation of SpamAssassin and explore how SpamAssassin fits into our larger overall system design. Just like MailScanner and ClamAV, SpamAssassin is one more important piece to a larger puzzle, specifically meant to help battle spam.

For the sake of the organization and flow of this book, I've decided to leave the configuration and customization of SpamAssassin, both for systemwide and individual use, as the focus of Chapter 18.

## Introducing SpamAssassin

SpamAssassin (http://spamassassin.apache.org/) is a free and open source project and a member of the Apache Software Foundation (www.apache.org), the same foundation of which the Apache HTTP server project is a member. SpamAssassin is an Internet electronic mail filter specifically designed to identify unsolicited commercial e-mail from legitimate e-mail.

Among the first open source spam filters, SpamAssassin was also one of the first to develop support for Bayesian spam filtering. However, Bayesian analysis is just one mechanism used by SpamAssassin. In general, the product's documentation categorizes its spam tests into the following general categories:

- *Basic message header and body text analysis*: SpamAssassin can detect spam through a number of content filters.

- *Bayesian spam filtering*: SpamAssassin can use probability principles developed from Bayes's Theorem to automatically learn the difference between spam and legitimate e-mail based on a number of criteria.

- *DNS-based blacklists*: SpamAssassin includes support to look up messages in a number of RBLs.

- *Other*: Optional general-purpose filtering databases developed by the community collaboratively.

The documentation also notes that SpamAssassin is designed to simply detect or classify spam, assigning a score to each message scanned that indicates how likely the message is spam. SpamAssassin does not delete or reroute messages it detects as spam. Determining what to do with a message that has been assigned a spam score is up to the e-mail administrator or the recipient through other means (e.g., with client-side filtering, procmail, or MailScanner). In our case, we will use MailScanner to handle the message accordingly after it has been scanned by SpamAssassin. Once a message has been scored, options for handling that message are virtually limitless. In Chapter 18, I will explore some of these options and best practices for configuring SpamAssassin and MailScanner, and describe how to handle messages found to be spam by SpamAssassin.

Like MailScanner, SpamAssassin is also developed and written in the Perl programming language. This ensures that SpamAssassin is built to be modular and extensible from the outset. SpamAssassin has evolved into a very robust, feature-rich application since its first official release in early 2001.

When SpamAssassin is installed, the spamassassin binary is installed, which is the primary means for scanning and tagging an e-mail message. Also included with SpamAssassin is the Mail::SpamAssassin Perl module, which is the core of the product itself. Mail::SpamAssassin can also be used to integrate spam detection into any other applications, similar to Mail::ClamAV Perl module, if so desired.

In addition, SpamAssassin supports a client/server design similar to ClamAV. It's possible to run spamd, the SpamAssassin daemon, and have it fork additional child processes as necessary. Then, spamc, the spamd client, can be used to send messages to spamd to be scanned and classified. This can help in some instances rather than having to execute a Perl interpreter each time a message is scanned. However, like our ClamAV installation, we will not use this particular SpamAssassin feature; instead, MailScanner will control SpamAssassin and the flow of mail to SpamAssassin using the Mail::SpamAssassin Perl module. This helps to ensure that there is a single point of failure, instead of having to rely on too many process daemons and determining where a message is dropped when passed from one daemon to another and back again.

# A Look at How SpamAssassin Works

SpamAssassin has a large number of tests it uses to classify spam. These tests are *heuristic*; in other words, the process involves trial and error and builds upon itself, iteration after iteration. Each subsequent test learns from the results of the preceding tests. Taken individually, any given test might not be very successful or accurate, but the results of each test taken as a whole can increase the chance of successfully classifying e-mail.

In fact, SpamAssassin boasts some very impressive statistics, given ideal circumstances. The following is taken directly from the SpamAssassin documentation (http://svn.apache.org/repos/asf/spamassassin/branches/3.1/README):

> *SpamAssassin typically differentiates successfully between spam and non-spam in between 95% and 100% of cases, depending on what kind of mail you get and your training of its Bayesian filter. Specifically, SpamAssassin has been shown to produce around 0.9% false negatives (spam that was missed) and around 0.1% false positives (ham incorrectly marked as spam).*

You can find more SpamAssassin statistics in the documentation online or distributed with SpamAssassin.

A series of tests are applied to each e-mail message. Some tests only apply the message header, while others examine the message body. When a message matches a test, a score is added to the message. This final total spam score is used to determine whether or not a message is spam. In Chapter 18, I will discuss using the spam score, understanding the recommended thresholds, and changing the score of individual tests.

The number of SpamAssassin tests total in the hundreds. Tests, or rules, are developed to look for patterns that might indicate a message is spam. Some rules are clear-cut instances of spam and assign higher scores to matching messages, while other rules use more fuzzy criteria and assign lower scores to matching messages. Rules range from tests for message bodies that contain 70 to 80 percent blank lines to tests for Subject headers that contain words or phrases in a custom blacklist.

---

**■Note** For a complete list of the tests SpamAssassin performs on an e-mail message, visit http://spamassassin.apache.org/tests.html.

---

Traditionally, spam tests are applied to e-mail messages individually, and the results are forgotten once the scanning process is complete. However, with Bayesian auto-learning enabled, previous results are remembered and used to influence the spam score of subsequent messages. In Chapter 18, you will see how to enable and make use of the SpamAssassin Bayesian auto-learn feature. Next, let's take a look at how to install SpamAssassin.

# Installing SpamAssassin

SpamAssassin is available as a Fedora Core RPM package, or you can download and install from the source distribution found at http://spamassassin.apache.org. The SpamAssassin RPM was included in our default Fedora Core installation as outlined in Chapter 2. This and subsequent chapters will assume you're using the Fedora Core RPM package, but the general topics discussed in this chapter and specific configuration in the next chapter should still apply to an instance of SpamAssassin installed from source (I will point out any differences where appropriate). As with anything else introduced earlier in this book, whether you choose to install and maintain SpamAssassin from the RPM or source distribution is a matter of personal preference.

## The SpamAssassin RPM Package

To determine whether SpamAssassin was installed on your Fedora Core system, you can use the following command to query the RPM package database:

```
[curtis@mail ~]$ rpm -qv spamassassin
```

```
spamassassin-3.0.4-2.fc4
```

This command displays the version of SpamAssassin and the revision number of the RPM package, if it is installed. Of course, your version may vary. Otherwise, if the package is missing, you will see an error message telling you that the SpamAssassin RPM package is not installed.

You can install SpamAssassin with the following yum command:

```
[curtis@mail ~]$ sudo yum install spamassassin
```

This command will search for, and install if found, the latest version of SpamAssassin available from the yum RPM package repositories you have configured on your e-mail system. In addition, any required prerequisite RPM packages will be downloaded and installed if they aren't already. In particular, you will need to have the perl-Digest-SHA1 and perl-HTML-Parser RPM packages installed on your e-mail system. These packages install the Digest::SHA1 and HTML::Parser Perl modules, respectively. Without them, SpamAssassin will not function properly.

If you decide RPM packages are not an option, then follow along in the next section to install SpamAssassin from the source distribution.

## The SpamAssassin Source Distribution

To install from source, download the latest stable source distribution from http://spamassassin. apache.org. You are given the opportunity to select a mirror site geographically close to you from which to download the SpamAssassin source distribution. At the time of this writing, version 3.1.3 was the latest stable release of SpamAssassin; however, it might be different by the time you read this.

Retrieving the latest source distribution is simple with the command wget; copy the URL to the source distribution from the download link on the SpamAssassin web site:

```
[curtis@mail ~]$ wget http://mirror.olnevhost.net/pub/apache/ ➥
spamassassin/source/Mail-SpamAssassin-3.1.3.tar.gz
```

First, start the installation process by unpacking the source tarball and configuring the build environment. Note that this process is a little different from the previous source installation processes earlier in this book. Here's some output from a build process on my example Fedora Core 4 system; not all screen output is shown for the sake of brevity:

```
[curtis@mail ~]$ tar xzvf Mail-SpamAssassin-3.1.3.tar.gz
[curtis@mail ~]$ cd Mail-SpamAssassin-3.1.3.tar.gz
[curtis@mail Mail-SpamAssassin-3.1.3]$ perl Makefile.PL
```

---

```
What email address or URL should be used in the suspected-spam report
text for users who want more information on your filter installation?
(In particular, ISPs should change this to a local Postmaster contact)
default text: [the administrator of that system]
```

---

When you start the build process, you will be prompted to enter a contact e-mail address or web site to direct people to should they receive notifications from your system. Most sites choose to use the postmaster address for this sort of thing; simply log into your e-mail system with another SSH session and add the following e-mail forward to /etc/aliases:

postmaster@example.com:      curtis@example.com

replacing example.com with your e-mail domain and curtis@example.com with the e-mail
addresses of the local e-mail administrators. Don't forget to run newaliases afterward:

[curtis@mail ~]$ **sudo newaliases**

Once you've finished adding the necessary aliases, go back to your other SSH session,
enter the e-mail address, and press Enter. The configure process will continue:

```
NOTE: settings for "make test" are now controlled using "t/config.dist".
See that file if you wish to customize what tests are run, and how.

checking module dependencies and their versions...
```

As you can see, the script performs checks to determine that other Perl module dependencies have been fulfilled. Some of these dependencies are optional, while some are not. Let
the script continue:

```
************************************************************************
NOTE: the optional Mail::SPF::Query module is not installed.

Used to check DNS Sender Policy Framework (SPF) records to fight email
address forgery and make it easier to identify spam.


************************************************************************
NOTE: the optional IP::Country module is not installed.

Used by the RelayCountry plugin (not enabled by default) to determine
the domain country codes of each relay in the path of an email.


************************************************************************
NOTE: the optional Razor2 (version 2.61) module is not installed.

Used to check message signatures against Vipul's Razor collaborative
filtering network. Razor has a large number of dependencies on CPAN
modules. Feel free to skip installing it, if this makes you nervous;
SpamAssassin will still work well without it.

More info on installing and using Razor can be found
at http://wiki.apache.org/spamassassin/InstallingRazor.


************************************************************************
NOTE: the optional Net::Ident module is not installed.
```

If you plan to use the --auth-ident option to spamd, you will need
to install this module.

****************************************************************************
NOTE: the optional IO::Socket::INET6 module is not installed.

This is required if the first nameserver listed in your IP
configuration or /etc/resolv.conf file is available only via
an IPv6 address.

****************************************************************************
NOTE: the optional IO::Socket::SSL module is not installed.

If you wish to use SSL encryption to communicate between spamc and
spamd (the --ssl option to spamd), you need to install this
module. (You will need the OpenSSL libraries and use the
ENABLE_SSL="yes" argument to Makefile.PL to build and run an SSL
compatible spamc.)

****************************************************************************
NOTE: the optional Archive::Tar module is not installed.

The "sa-update" script requires this module to access tar update
archive files.

****************************************************************************
NOTE: the optional IO::Zlib module is not installed.

The "sa-update" script requires this module to access compressed
update archive files.

optional module missing: Mail::SPF::Query
optional module missing: IP::Country
optional module missing: Razor2
optional module missing: Net::Ident
optional module missing: IO::Socket::INET6
optional module missing: IO::Socket::SSL
optional module missing: Archive::Tar
optional module missing: IO::Zlib

warning: some functionality may not be available,
please read the above report before continuing!

Every test that failed on my example Fedora Core 4 system involved optional modules that I will not use or reference in this book and thus can be safely ignored. However, you should make sure that none of the checks that fail on your system are required dependencies that need to be installed. In particular, two Perl modules that typically do not ship with the standard Perl distribution are required to build SpamAssassin: Digest::SHA1 and HTML::Parser. If you are alerted that either of these, or any other required modules, is missing, you will have to install them before proceeding. You can do so by downloading each module's source tarball from CPAN (http://search.cpan.org); make sure you download the latest version of each:

```
[curtis@mail ~]$ wget http://search.cpan.org/CPAN/ ➡
authors/id/G/GA/GAAS/Digest-SHA1-2.11.tar.gz
```

Unpack the source tarball:

```
[curtis@mail ~]$ tar xzvf Digest-SHA1-2.11.tar.gz
[curtis@mail ~]$ cd Digest-SHA1-2.11
```

Then build, compile, and install each module with the following commands for each:

```
[curtis@mail Digest-SHA1-2.11]$ perl Makefile.PL
[curtis@mail Digest-SHA1-2.11]$ make
[curtis@mail Digest-SHA1-2.11]$ make test
[curtis@mail Digest-SHA1-2.11]$ sudo make install
```

Once the required, or desired optional, Perl modules are successfully installed, rerun perl Makefile.PL. When success is reported:

```
Checking if your kit is complete...
Looks good
Writing Makefile for Mail::SpamAssassin
Makefile written by ExtUtils::MakeMaker 6.17
```

complete the compile process with the following two commands:

```
[curtis@mail Mail-SpamAssassin-3.1.3]$ make
[curtis@mail Mail-SpamAssassin-3.1.3]$ make test
```

If the previous two commands complete without any fatal errors, finish your source installation of SpamAssassin with the following:

```
[curtis@mail Mail-SpamAssassin-3.1.3]$ sudo make install
```

Although the source installation process is a bit different, it's not much more difficult than anything else we've installed from source thus far.

# Installing Optional Hash-Sharing System Software

Optional software you may decide to install includes Vipul's Razor, Pyzor, and DCC. In Chapter 16, I briefly introduced these hash-sharing systems. Here, I will show you how you can install them; it's up to you to decide which of the three systems you'd like to use. None are required, but they each increase your ability to successfully classify spam. If you install these optional packages now but later decide you'd rather not use them, you can leave them and disable their use in your SpamAssassin configuration. In Chapter 18, I will explain how each are used and show you how to configure each individually in more detail.

## Installing Vipul's Razor

Vipul's Razor client agent is available as an RPM package from the Fedora Extras yum repository. To install the RPM package, simply use yum to install:

```
[curtis@mail ~] sudo yum install perl-Razor-Agent
```

This command will search for (and install if found) the latest version of the Razor Perl client agent available from the Fedora Extras yum RPM package repository configured on your e-mail system.

If you prefer to install from source, then obtain the latest stable release of the razor-agents tarball only from http://razor.sourceforge.net (version 2.82 at the time of this writing). Once you've downloaded the tarball, unpacking it requires a slightly different command than you'd normally expect. Typically, the source tarballs we've seen thus far end with the .tar.gz or .tar.Z file extension, but the razor-agents tarball comes with a .tar.bz2 file extension by default. This indicates the tar archive was compressed with the Bzip2 compression utility rather than the Gzip compression utility. To unpack a Bzip2 compressed tar archive, use the j argument instead of the z argument to the tar command:

```
[curtis@mail ~]$ tar xjvf razor-agents-2.82.tar.bz2
```

From here, the process is the same as other Perl modules we've seen so far:

```
[curtis@mail ~]$ cd razor-agents-2.82
[curtis@mail razor-agents-2.82]$ perl Makefile.PL
[curtis@mail razor-agents-2.82]$ make
[curtis@mail razor-agents-2.82]$ make test
[curtis@mail razor-agents-2.82]$ make install
```

In Chapter 18, I will explain how to configure SpamAssassin to use Vipul's Razor.

## Installing Pyzor

The free and open source Pyzor client and server is also available as an RPM package from the Fedora Extras yum repository. To install the RPM package, simply use yum to install:

```
[curtis@mail ~] sudo yum install pyzor
```

This command will search for (and install if found) the latest version of the Pyzor client and server available from the Fedora Extras yum RPM package repository configured on your e-mail system. We will not use pyzord, the Pyzor daemon, so it can be safely ignored and left unconfigured.

If you prefer to install from source, then obtain the latest stable Pyzor release from http://pyzor.sourceforge.net (version 0.4.0 at the time of this writing). Once downloaded, the source tarball will need to be unpacked with the j argument to tar, as the default Pyzor tarball is also compressed with Bzip2:

```
[curtis@mail ~]$ tar xjvf pyzor-0.4.0.tar.bz2
```

The process of building, compiling, and installing Pyzor is different from the typical process we've seen. Pyzor is written in the Python programming language, and you use Python itself to build and install Pyzor, much in the same fashion as a Perl module installation:

```
[curtis@mail ~]$ cd pyzor-0.4.0
[curtis@mail pyzor-0.4.0]$ python setup.py build
[curtis@mail pyzor-0.4.0]$ python setup.py install
```

Voilà! That's all there is to it. Chapter 18 explains how to configure SpamAssassin to use the Pyzor client.

## Installing DCC

At the time of this writing, the DCC client is not available as an RPM package from either the base Fedora Core distribution or the Fedora Extras project. So, if you wish to use DCC with SpamAssassin, you will need to install it from the source distribution.

You can obtain the latest version of DCC (currently 1.3.38) from www.rhyolite.com/anti-spam/dcc/ with wget:

```
[curtis@mail ~] wget http://www.rhyolite.com/anti-spam/dcc/source/dcc.tar.Z
```

Next, unpack, build, compile, and install the source distribution (the screen output is not shown for the sake of brevity):

```
[curtis@mail ~]$ tar xzvf dcc.tar.Z
[curtis@mail ~]$ cd dcc-1.3.38/
[curtis@mail dcc-1.3.38]$ ./configure
[curtis@mail dcc-1.3.38]$ make
[curtis@mail dcc-1.3.38]$ sudo make install
```

That's it! In Chapter 18, you will learn how to configure SpamAssassin to use DCC. Whatever your choice of installation method, you're now ready to configure and customize SpamAssassin and plug it into your MailScanner installation, providing a complete antispam solution.

# Summary

In this chapter, I formally introduced SpamAssassin after much anticipation. SpamAssassin is one of the most anticipated topics in this book, and rightfully so. SpamAssassin is a fantastic application that will help you and your users cope with their e-mail spam woes. In this chapter, I also covered the simple SpamAssassin installation process.

In Chapter 18, we will look at configuring and customizing SpamAssassin for your organization's specific needs, completing the integration with MailScanner and the rest of your e-mail system. There will be some decisions to make, but we'll walk you through everything together. You will find that, like the installation process, configuring SpamAssassin isn't any more difficult than anything else we've seen thus far.

# CHAPTER 18

■■■

# Configuring SpamAssassin

**C**onfiguring SpamAssassin doesn't have to be any more difficult or complex than configuring Dovecot or ClamAV. However, we're doing things a little differently than the typical Spam-Assassin installation would, perhaps, dictate. SpamAssassin can be a fantastic resource in and of itself, and it is oftentimes called on a per-user basis by an individual procmail filter. But we're using SpamAssassin in a global, sitewide sense as one more component of a total anti-spam solution. Just as with ClamAV, MailScanner calls SpamAssassin to scan batches of e-mail messages to be tagged with a spam score.

In this chapter, I highlight what you need to decide to customize settings for your organization's specific environment. MailScanner comes bundled with a good SpamAssassin configuration that can be dropped in place to get you going quickly, but you should familiar-ize yourself with the configuration first. Over time, based on the success or failure of spam detection and user feedback, you might find you have to tweak your antispam settings and constantly adapt to an ever-changing environment.

In this chapter, we take a look at SpamAssassin configuration first. Then, we integrate SpamAssassin into the MailScanner configuration. Finally, we wrap up this chapter by dis-cussing how some of MailScanner's built-in antispam options can be used together with SpamAssassin to finalize your complete antispam solution.

## The SpamAssassin Big Picture

First, let's take a look at SpamAssassin configuration and customization in general and survey SpamAssassin options. SpamAssassin configuration files are in a Unix style similar to other configuration files we've seen in Dovecot, ClamAV, and MailScanner. A typical SpamAssassin installation loads its configuration from the following locations:

- `/usr/share/spamassassin/`: This is where all of the standard SpamAssassin rule definitions are found. In general, anything in this directory can be overwritten when you upgrade SpamAssassin, so you should not modify these files.

- `/etc/mail/spamassassin/`: You might remember seeing this directory in Chapter 5 when we were configuring sendmail. This is where site-specific, customized SpamAssassin configuration settings and rule definitions should be put, so they are not overwritten when you upgrade SpamAssassin.

- `~/.spamassassin/`: This directory is used as the state directory for each individual user. User preferences are also stored in this directory. In this book, I am outlining a sitewide installation and configuration, so individual users do not have this directory and configuration options in this directory are ignored if they exist.

A SpamAssassin configuration file typically ends with the file extension `.cf`. SpamAssassin configuration options can be grouped into three general classes:

- *User preferences*: These options are set to customize how SpamAssassin operates on e-mail messages, for example, setting the default total score necessary to tag a message as spam or modifying the individual score assigned to a message that matches a specific SpamAssassin rule or test. User preferences can be set in either a sitewide or a user preferences configuration file. Most configuration options fall within this class.

- *Rule definitions*: These options are set to create new rules, or SpamAssassin tests, which are used to detect spam in addition to the default SpamAssassin tests. Under most circumstances, these options are limited to system administrators or privileged users because of performance and security concerns.

- *Administrator settings*: These options are strictly limited to system administrators and are not available to individual users. These settings include the location of external applications necessary for spam tests and the ability to modify the default behavior SpamAssassin features.

As I've mentioned previously in this chapter, SpamAssassin can be configured to operate in two essentially different configuration environments: an individual, per-user configuration or a sitewide one.

## SpamAssassin Per-User Configuration

In a per-user SpamAssassin configuration, the e-mail system administrator creates custom global defaults that affect how SpamAssassin operates and that are common to all users running SpamAssassin on the e-mail system. Individual users are able to further customize SpamAssassin operation, filter their mail based on SpamAssassin results, and possibly opt in or opt out of having their mail scanned by SpamAssassin at all. Typically, this sort of environment dictates that SpamAssassin is called on a per-user basis to scan mail as it arrives on the SMTP server prior to final delivery through procmail, whether from a global procmail rcfile or individual procmail rcfile. Users may individually invoke SpamAssassin directly through the `spamassassin` binary. However, depending on the environment, the amount of e-mail traffic, and the number of users, the e-mail system administrator may choose to run the SpamAssassin `spamd` daemon and have users interface with SpamAssassin by invoking a message scan with `spamc`.

In this more-traditional SpamAssassin environment, users are also responsible for train-ing their own Bayesian filter, if they choose to do so. A certain amount of user education is necessary to make it clear that mail is scanned and tagged by SpamAssassin and to teach users what to do with messages classified as spam, how to tweak their user preferences if they wish to customize SpamAssassin, and how to retrain the Bayesian filter for better accuracy. Although this might sound ideal, in my experience, the majority of users don't want to fuss with spam and expect the spam filters put in place to just work with little or no intervention.

In addition to supporting such an environment, you must also manage the overhead of all of the different SpamAssassin components and the significant system performance hit your e-mail server could take if every single message is scanned by SpamAssassin. You might find the alternative sitewide SpamAssassin configuration environment easier to maintain and manage to provide an environment that can please the casual user and the power user.

## SpamAssassin Sitewide Configuration

An alternative SpamAssassin configuration is a more global, sitewide configuration—that is to say, all SpamAssassin configuration is maintained by you, the e-mail system administrator. In principle, this configuration can be achieved in essentially the same way as the per-user con-figuration environment; think of it as configuring SpamAssassin for one giant, all-encompassing user instead of many individual users.

One way of achieving this sitewide configuration is to continue to have procmail filter mail through SpamAssassin, either via the `spamassassin` binary or through `spamd` with `spamc`, but this approach has little benefit over the traditional per-user configuration environment.

Alternatively, I suggest taking advantage of the power and flexibility of MailScanner. By integrating SpamAssassin into MailScanner, we continue with the same gatekeeper architec-ture, letting MailScanner ultimately decide whether a message ought to be passed onto SpamAssassin or not. Integrating SpamAssassin into your MailScanner architecture also affords you the potential to use the same quarantine mechanisms for messages that have a very high spam score as those used to quarantine e-mail–borne viruses and worms, keeping the most dangerous e-mail content out of your users' mailboxes altogether.

One major difference between the sitewide approach and the per-user configuration envi-ronment is that any Bayesian learning and training occurs sitewide. That is not to say that Bayesian filtering still cannot work effectively. Indeed, you can offer a number of ways for users to pass along messages for retraining the sitewide Bayesian filter, contributing to the greater good of the whole e-mail environment. Later in this chapter, I will describe one such way.

One key consideration to keep in mind is how conservatively you might need to configure default SpamAssassin settings. For example, the most important decision might be the mini-mum SpamAssassin score necessary to tag a message as spam. By default, this value is 5.0 and is normally customizable by users' preferences. However, when considering a sitewide SpamAssassin configuration, a higher minimum score might be prudent. I point out other configuration options to keep an eye on for special consideration as this chapter continues, but I want to make the point now, so you're prepared. As with any other SpamAssassin set-tings, you may need to adjust thresholds beyond their default values to meet your organization's specific needs.

The benefits of a sitewide SpamAssassin configuration environment are numerous. First, you only have to worry about a single daemon process for all of your mail scanning. When MailScanner loads, it loads each component integrated into your e-mail architecture, including

SpamAssassin. Therefore, you should not run the SpamAssassin daemon spamd; MailScanner is written in Perl and can load SpamAssassin as a Perl module, much in the same way Mail-Scanner loads ClamAV. Second, MailScanner scans messages in batches rather than one at a time, making the process of scanning mail more efficient. Third, you can control what messages, or classes of messages, are actually scanned by SpamAssassin. For instance, maintaining your whitelists and blacklists with MailScanner is more efficient; it eliminates the need to scan particular messages with SpamAssassin, speeds up scanning times, and alleviates the strain on system resources.

In addition, MailScanner has some rudimentary antispam mechanisms built in. Although SpamAssassin is a very valuable and necessary component to your total antispam solution, it doesn't have to be the only component. MailScanner can perform a number of tests that might catch obvious spam without the overhead and delay of invoking SpamAssassin to do so.

## A Quick Look at the SpamAssassin Configuration Files

True to good programming practices, SpamAssassin is modular and very flexible. You've seen multiple ways of configuring and invoking SpamAssassin: through the spamassassin binary, using spamd and spamc, or as a Perl module. The layout and design of the SpamAssassin configuration files is also modular. Take a quick look at /usr/share/spamassassin/:

```
[curtis@mail ~]$ ls /usr/share/spamassassin/
```

```
10_misc.cf              20_phrases.cf           30_text_fr.cf
20_anti_ratware.cf      20_porn.cf              30_text_nl.cf
20_body_tests.cf        20_ratware.cf           30_text_pl.cf
20_compensate.cf        20_uri_tests.cf         50_scores.cf
20_dnsbl_tests.cf       23_bayes.cf             60_whitelist.cf
20_drugs.cf             25_body_tests_es.cf     languages
20_fake_helo_tests.cf   25_hashcash.cf          triplets.txt
20_head_tests.cf        25_spf.cf               user_prefs.template
20_html_tests.cf        25_uribl.cf
20_meta_tests.cf        30_text_de.cf
```

Each file ending with the file extension .cf is a SpamAssassin configuration file that is loaded when SpamAssassin is invoked. Each configuration file defines sets of rules, or spam tests, that are used to detect spam. Rule definitions are grouped into categories. Scores assigned to messages that match individual rules can be overridden in your customized configuration, or individual rules can be disabled altogether by assigning them a score of 0. The contents of this directory should not be modified; anything in /usr/share/spamassassin/ is overwritten when you upgrade SpamAssassin, deleting any changes you may have made.

Now take a look at /etc/mail/spamassassin/:

```
[curtis@mail ~]$ ls /etc/mail/spamassassin/
```

```
init.pre mailscanner.cf        spamassassin-helper.sh
local.cf spamassassin-default.rc spamassassin-spamc.rc
```

Each file ending with the file extension .cf is a configuration file defining custom sets of rules or custom configuration options—this is where your sitewide SpamAssassin custom configuration belongs. You are free to modify or add to the contents of this directory; changes to /etc/mail/spamassassin/ are not overwritten when you upgrade SpamAssassin.

Of particular note are init.pre and local.cf. The file init.pre is the only exception to the .cf file extension rule. This file is the first configuration file read and loaded when SpamAssassin is invoked. In the file init.pre, adding special SpamAssassin plugins or setting certain configuration defaults that other subsequent configuration options might depend on is appropriate.

The file local.cf is the traditional place to put custom SpamAssassin sitewide configuration options. In a per-user configuration environment, this configuration file is loaded before users' preferences, but values found in both local.cf and users' preferences are overwritten by the users' preferences.

The procmail rcfiles spamassassin-default.rc and spamassassin-spamc.rc and the spamassassin-helper.sh shell script are all useful if you decide to incorporate SpamAssassin into your environment using procmail, which is the most common method. For the purposes of this book, we are simply ignoring these files as we are not using procmail to invoke Spam-Assassin. If you follow the recommendations in this book, calling SpamAssassin from procmail is redundant and a waste of system resources. Therefore, let's jump right into configuring SpamAssassin with inclusion into MailScanner and a sitewide configuration environment in mind.

# Configuring E-mail Spam Detection with MailScanner and SpamAssassin

The last thing we come to in /etc/mail/spamassassin/ is mailscanner.cf. Take a closer look at mailscanner.cf:

```
[curtis@mail spamassassin]$ cd /etc/mail/spamassassin/
[curtis@mail spamassassin]$ ls -l mailscanner.cf
```

```
lrwxrwxrwx 1 root root 41 Jan 31 21:33 mailscanner.cf -> ➡
/etc/MailScanner/spam.assassin.prefs.conf
```

You can see mailscanner.cf is a symlink to the real file /etc/MailScanner/spam.assassin. prefs.conf. This symlink and file are installed as part of the default MailScanner installation detailed in Chapter 14. For the sake of simplicity, add all custom SpamAssassin configuration options for your SpamAssassin sitewide configuration environment to spam.assassin. prefs.conf, with the exception of any preconfiguration settings, which belong in init.pre.

■**Caution** This symlink *must* be in place, or your custom SpamAssassin settings will not be loaded when MailScanner invokes SpamAssassin, and SpamAssassin may not operate as expected. MailScanner itself does not load the SpamAssassin configuration; rather, it relies on SpamAssassin to read its own configuration when it is invoked for the first time.

## Modifying spam.assassin.prefs.conf

Before we make any changes, let's make a backup of the default file distributed with MailScanner:

```
[curtis@mail spamassassin]$ cd /etc/MailScanner/
[curtis@mail MailScanner]$ sudo cp spam.assassin.prefs.conf ➥
spam.assassin.prefs.conf.dist
[curtis@mail MailScanner]$ ls -l spam.assassin.prefs.conf*
```

```
-rw-r--r-- 1 root root 10327 Jan 1 08:52 spam.assassin.prefs.conf
-rw-r--r-- 1 root root 10327 Mar 15 12:50 spam.assassin.prefs.conf.dist
```

Now open spam.assassin.prefs.conf in your favorite text editor to take a look at what we need to modify. As you probably expect, a line starting with a number sign character (#) is a comment and is ignored by SpamAssassin when processing the configuration file. However, unlike Dovecot and MailScanner, SpamAssassin configuration options are not assigned with an equal sign character (=). Instead, configuration options are assigned in the following way:

```
<config_keyword> <value>
```

where config_keyword is the specific configuration option, and value is the desired value of the modified configuration option. I am only highlighting the important configuration options in spam.assassin.prefs.conf in this chapter. However, you should familiarize yourself with the entire file.

In addition, spam.assassin.prefs.conf does not contain all possible SpamAssassin configuration options. To get a full list of SpamAssassin configuration options for the version of Spam-Assassin installed on your e-mail system, with complete descriptions and examples, read the Mail::SpamAssassin::Conf Perl documentation using the following command on your e-mail system:

```
[curtis@mail ~]$ perldoc Mail::SpamAssassin::Conf
```

Simply think of perldoc as Perl's analogue to the man command and its man pages.

---

**Tip** You're sure to find configuration documentation on the SpamAssassin website, but it's important to read the documentation for the exact release you have installed; SpamAssassin is always changing and configuration options are added, changed, or removed from release to release.

---

### Specifying Whether DNS Is Available

The first configuration option you come across in spam.assassin.prefs.conf is dns_available:

```
dns_available yes
```

SpamAssassin must know whether DNS is available before it can attempt many of the network- and DNS-based spam tests. If DNS is down, these tests fail, so SpamAssassin skips them. Although you can configure SpamAssassin to perform a series of tests to guess whether DNS is available or not, doing so can waste precious seconds in delays.

I suggest leaving this option set to yes. If you cannot trust DNS to be available, you have other, larger issues with mail delivery in general. DNS lookup failures result in SpamAssassin time-out errors in your mail logs.

## Creating SpamAssassin Whitelists and Blacklists

Next, you can set whitelists and blacklists within SpamAssassin, but a better approach is to maintain your site whitelists and blacklists with MailScanner. This approach helps keep SpamAssassin from unnecessarily running on messages, reducing the total time needed to scan an e-mail message. I explain MailScanner whitelisting and blacklisting in more detail later in this chapter, when we finish configuring MailScanner antispam configuration options.

If, for some reason, you decide to maintain a whitelist or blacklist for SpamAssassin independent of MailScanner, you can add them to spam.assassin.prefs.conf. Whitelisting a full or partial e-mail address or e-mail domain sets a score of –100 to any matching messages, effectively classifying the message as "not spam;" blacklisting has exactly the opposite behavior, as expected.

You can define values using simple wildcard asterisk (*) or question mark (?) characters; other metacharacters and full regular expressions are not supported. You can also define more than one value per configuration option (separate values with a space), or you can define multiple, manual whitelists or blacklists with more than one occurrence of each configuration option.

For example, to whitelist any e-mail coming from curtis@example.com, add the following line to spam.assassin.prefs.conf:

```
whitelist_from curtis@example.com
```

If you'd like to whitelist the entire example.com e-mail domain, add the following line to spam.assassin.prefs.conf:

```
whitelist_from *@example.com
```

Table 18-1 lists the SpamAssassin whitelist configuration options, their descriptions, and the e-mail headers they apply to.

**Table 18-1.** *SpamAssassin Manual Whitelist Configuration Options*

| Keyword | Description | Applicable E-mail Headers |
| --- | --- | --- |
| whitelist_from email@domain.com | Whitelists a full or partial e-mail address or e-mail domain | Resent-From, Envelope-Sender, Resent-Sender, X-Envelope-From, or From |
| unwhitelist_from email@domain.com | Overrides the whitelist for a full or partial e-mail address or e-mail domain | Resent-From, Envelope-Sender, Resent-Sender, X-Envelope-From, or From |
| whitelist_from_rcvd email@domain.com domain.com | Whitelists a full or partial e-mail address or e-mail domain if the second value also matches the Received headers | Received plus Resent-From, Envelope-Sender, Resent-Sender, X-Envelope-From, or From |
| unwhitelist_from_rcvd email@domain.com domain.com | Overrides the whitelist for a full or partial e-mail address or e-mail domain if the second value also matches the Received header | Received plus Resent-From, Envelope-Sender, Resent-Sender, X-Envelope-From, or From |

Conversely, if you'd rather blacklist any e-mail coming from curtis@example.com, add the following line to spam.assassin.prefs.conf:

```
blacklist_from curtis@example.com
```

If you'd like to blacklist the entire example.com e-mail domain, add the following line to spam.assassin.prefs.conf:

```
blacklist_from *@example.com
```

Table 18-2 lists the SpamAssassin blacklist configuration options, their descriptions, and the e-mail headers they apply to.

**Table 18-2.** *SpamAssassin Manual Blacklist Configuration Options*

| Keyword | Description | Applicable E-mail Headers |
| --- | --- | --- |
| blacklist_from *email@domain.com* | Blacklists a full or partial e-mail address or e-mail domain | Resent-From, Envelope-Sender, Resent-Sender, X-Envelope-From, or From |
| unblacklist_from *email@domain.com* | Overrides the blacklist for a full or partial e-mail address or e-mail domain | Resent-From, Envelope-Sender, Resent-Sender, X-Envelope-From, or From |
| blacklist_from_rcvd *email@domain.com* *domain.com* | Blacklists a full or partial e-mail address or e-mail domain if the second value also matches the Received headers | Received plus Resent-From, Envelope-Sender, Resent-Sender, X-Envelope-From, or From |
| unblacklist_from_rcvd *email@domain.com* *domain.com* | Overrides the blacklist of a full or partial e-mail address or e-mail domain if the second value also matches the Received headers | Received plus Resent-From, Envelope-Sender, Resent-Sender, X-Envelope-From, or From |

## Configuring the Bayesian Filter Options

The next major set of configuration options to modify is the Bayesian filter options, starting with the use_bayes option:

```
# use_bayes 0
```

This option is commented out, because the Bayesian filtering engine is enabled by default. Although Bayesian filtering can potentially be more taxing on your e-mail system resources, I highly recommend using it; it is likely to increase SpamAssassin's ability to properly classify spam.

To explicitly enable Bayesian filtering, so it's clear at a quick glance that it is in fact running, modify the use_bayes option in spam.assassin.prefs.conf:

```
use_bayes 1
```

Alternatively, to explicitly disable SpamAssassin Bayesian filtering altogether, modify the use_bayes option in spam.assassin.prefs.conf thusly:

```
use_bayes 0
```

If you enable Bayesian filtering, SpamAssassin will maintain a Bayes filtering database. Normally, this database is maintained on a per-user basis for each user that runs SpamAssassin. Since we are not configuring a per-user environment, only one user will run SpamAssassin— the same system user that runs MailScanner. If you're following along with the installation and configuration of MailScanner as outlined in this book so far, the root user runs MailScanner and SpamAssassin.

Therefore, the default behavior of the Bayesian engine is to maintain the Bayesian database in the root user's SpamAssassin state directory in the root user's home directory, /root/.spamassassin/ by default. Typically, the / partition is not extremely large, so there is a danger of filling the / partition to capacity in allowing the Bayes database to grow too large. To avoid this, create a directory to hold the Bayes database on a disk partition with adequate disk space, like /etc/ or /var/, for instance:

```
[curtis@mail ~]$ sudo mkdir -p /var/spool/spamassassin/bayes/
```

Next modify the SpamAssassin default value of the configuration option bayes_path:

```
#bayes_path /etc/MailScanner/bayes/bayes
```

to match the directory in which you chose to create and store the SpamAssassin Bayesian database:

```
bayes_path /var/spool/spamassassin/bayes/bayes
```

---

**Note** Don't forget the final trailing bayes on the bayes_path option value. This is not a directory, but the prefix for all of the Bayes database filenames created in /var/spool/spamassassin/bayes/ by the SpamAssassin Bayesian filter engine.

---

If the configuration option bayes_auto_expire is enabled as follows:

```
bayes_auto_expire 0
```

SpamAssassin tries to automatically mark the old tokens as expired from the Bayes database when a certain threshold is exceeded. That threshold is set by the configuration option bayes_expiry_max_db_size, whose default value is 150,000 records. When this threshold is exceeded, SpamAssassin keeps 75 percent of the maximum value or 100,000 tokens, whichever is larger. The Mail::SpamAssassin::Conf documentation states that 150,000 tokens is approximately equivalent to an 8-MB file. If you'd like to increase this threshold, you need to add the following option to spam.assassin.prefs.conf:

```
bayes_expiry_max_db_size 300000
```

The expiration of tokens from the Bayes database can happen randomly, and if the automatic expiration process starts at an inopportune time, the Bayes filter engine could time out when performing an operation simultaneously. I recommend disabling the SpamAssassin Bayes database token automatic expiration, setting the maximum token number to a higher value, and allowing MailScanner and a simple script to run periodically when load is low to mark tokens as expired. To do so, add the following lines to spam.assassin.prefs.conf:

```
# Disable the SpamAssassin Bayes database token auto expiration.
# See "Rebuild Bayes Every" in MailScanner.conf
bayes_auto_expire 0
```

```
# Increase the maximum numbers of tokens in the Bayes database.
bayes_expiry_max_db_size 300000
```

Later in this chapter, when I explain the final MailScanner antispam configuration, you can find the rest of the information about setting up the MailScanner periodic Bayes database token expiration; further configuration is necessary in MailScanner.conf.

## Configuring SpamAssassin Bayes Auto Learning

SpamAssassin attempts to automatically train itself by feeding high-scoring spam and low-scoring nonspam back into itself. This feature is controlled with the bayes_auto_learn configuration option:

```
# bayes_auto_learn 0
```

This option is commented out, because the Bayesian auto-learn feature is enabled by default.

To explicitly enable the Bayesian auto-learn feature, so it's clear at a quick glance that it is in fact enabled, modify the bayes_auto_learn option in spam.assassin.prefs.conf:

```
bayes_auto_learn 1
```

To disable Bayesian auto-learning, modify the bayes_auto_learn option in spam.assassin.prefs.conf as follows:

```
bayes_auto_learn 0
```

If you decide to enable the Bayes auto-learn feature, you will need to set score thresholds that indicate to SpamAssassin which messages to feed back into itself to train the Bayes filter.

The configuration option bayes_auto_learn_threshold_nonspam is the minimum score threshold for messages to be fed back into SpamAssassin for auto-learning:

```
bayes_auto_learn_threshold_nonspam 0.1
```

The value 0.1 is relatively safe, but if you would prefer to be more conservative, try 0 or a lower number (negative numbers are OK). The lower the spam score, the less likely a message is to be classified as spam.

The configuration option bayes_auto_learn_threshold_spam is the maximum score threshold for messages to be fed back into SpamAssassin for auto-learning:

```
bayes_auto_learn_threshold_spam 14.0
```

The value 14.0 is higher than the default value (12.0); set this to what you feel is appropriate. Remember, the lowest value bayes_auto_learn_threshold_spam can be is 6.0, because a score of 3.0 from message header tests and a score of 3.0 from message body tests are the minimum points possible for the filter to auto-learn that a message is spam. The higher the spam score, the more likely a message is to be classified as spam.

One final configuration option with respect to Bayes auto-learning that *must* be modified to match your configuration is bayes_ignore_header. SpamAssassin must know which headers are added locally to ignore them so as not to taint the SpamAssassin scoring. You must use the value you assigned to the MailScanner configuration option %org-name% in MailScanner.conf to replace YOURDOMAIN-COM in the following four lines in spam.assassin.prefs.conf:

```
bayes_ignore_header X-YOURDOMAIN-COM-MailScanner
bayes_ignore_header X-YOURDOMAIN-COM-MailScanner-SpamCheck
bayes_ignore_header X-YOURDOMAIN-COM-MailScanner-SpamScore
bayes_ignore_header X-YOURDOMAIN-COM-MailScanner-Information
```

For example, if you set %org-name% = ExampleEnterprise in MailScanner.conf in Chapter 14, the previous four lines would be replaced with the following ones:

```
bayes_ignore_header X-ExampleEnterprise-MailScanner
bayes_ignore_header X-ExampleEnterprise-MailScanner-SpamCheck
bayes_ignore_header X-ExampleEnterprise-MailScanner-SpamScore
bayes_ignore_header X-ExampleEnterprise-MailScanner-Information
```

## Configuring SpamAssassin RBL and Hash-Sharing System Settings

Finally, the time has come to configure the SpamAssassin RBL and hash-sharing system settings. In the chapters leading up to this one, I've explained RBLs and how to install three hash-sharing system packages. If you decide to allow SpamAssassin to query various RBLs, and you installed Razor, Pyzor, or DCC, you can enable them in spam.assassin.prefs.conf.

SpamAssassin will run several RBL tests by default. If you wish to disable *all* RBL tests, use the skip_rbl_checks configuration option:

```
skip_rbl_checks    1
```

By default, Razor, Pyzor and DCC tests are enabled if the applications are properly installed. You can disable Razor tests with the use_razor2 configuration option:

```
use_razor2     0
```

You can disable Pyzor tests with the use_pyzor configuration option:

```
use_pyzor  0
```

You can disable DCC tests with the use_dcc configuration option:

```
use_dcc        0
```

If you installed Pyzor and DCC, you should set the pyzor_path and dcc_path options to point to the pyzor and dccproc binaries, respectively:

```
pyzor_path /usr/bin/pyzor
dcc_path /usr/local/bin/dccproc
```

If you installed Pyzor or DCC into nonstandard installation locations, set these previous two configuration options to the correct path on your e-mail system accordingly. Vipul's Razor client agent is a Perl module, so there is no binary to execute, thus it lacks an analogous option.

SpamAssassin waits for individual RBL tests to complete within specified time periods. To set these, use the following options:

```
rbl_timeout 20
razor_timeout 10
pyzor_timeout 10
```

Each value is the time, in seconds, to wait for each test to complete. Setting these values any higher can cause the entire SpamAssassin scan of a message to time-out without a spam score. The values shown here are the defaults.

## Configuring SpamAssassin Envelope from Header

SpamAssassin attempts to automatically figure out the envelope sender address from the message headers. To take the guess work out of this, you can explicitly configure SpamAssassin to look for the exact header with the envelope sender address. Set the envelope_sender_header option to match the value of the MailScanner Envelope From Header option:

```
envelope_sender_header X-ExampleEnterpriseMailScanner-From
```

SpamAssassin uses the envelope sender address for various header tests, including some of the whitelist and blacklist options discussed earlier in this chapter.

## Creating and Adding Your Own SpamAssassin Rules

The SpamAssassin development team does a terrific job of rigorously developing and testing spam rules. However, you might also find you want to create and add your own specific, custom rules to enhance the existing SpamAssassin rules and tests. A great resource for doing so is the SpamAssassin Rules Emporium, or SARE for short (www.rulesemporium.com).

There you can find resources for creating your own rules, or you can download community-contributed rules for inclusion into your installation. Of course, you should verify and thoroughly scrutinize any additional rules you choose to download and install before trusting your production e-mail environment to them.

You can also find an example of a custom rule in spam.assassin.prefs.conf:

```
header   FRIEND_GREETINGS   Subject =~ /you have an E-Card from/i
describe FRIEND_GREETINGS   Nasty E-card from FriendGreetings.com
score    FRIEND_GREETINGS   100.0
```

Although outdated, this rule is still useful for instructional purposes. The first line instructs SpamAssassin to perform a test, symbolically called FRIEND_GREETINGS, on headers for a specific string as defined by the regular expression. The second line simply defines a description for the FRIEND_GREETINGS test that can be used in a SpamAssassin report. The third and final line assigns a default score to the FRIEND_GREETINGS test, 100.0 in this case. A score of 100.0 indicates the message is 100 percent likely to be spam.

Custom rules, whether created by you or downloaded from the SARE, can also be installed in /etc/mail/spamassassin/, so they are automatically included when SpamAssassin is invoked. The default scores assigned to a rule are automatically inherited from the rule configuration file. You can also explicitly set or override the score of any SpamAssassin test in spam.assassin.prefs.conf.

> **Tip** A complete list of SpamAssassin tests distributed with SpamAssassin, and their corresponding assigned scores, can be found at `http://spamassassin.apache.org/tests.html`.

### Modifying SpamAssassin Rule Scores

As I have mentioned repeatedly, every SpamAssassin rule has a corresponding score that is added to the total score of a message when the rule is matched. Different rules are assigned different scores, and the SpamAssassin developers and contributors go to great lengths to test the rules and the attribution of scores.

If you feel its necessary, a rule's score can be modified in the following general way:

```
score SYMBOLIC_RULE_NAME n.nn
```

that is, the keyword `score`, followed by the symbolic name of the rule or test (e.g., `FAKE_HELO_MSN`) and the new score. Scores can be positive or negative integers (e.g., –2 or 10) or real numbers (e.g., –0.1 or 0.1).

Changing a rule's score might be particularly useful to completely disable a particular rule or test to keep it from ever running. To do so, simply assign a score of 0 to a rule. For example, to disable the `FAKE_HELO_MSN` test, add the following line to `spam.assassin.prefs.conf`:

```
score FAKE_HELO_MSN 0
```

That completes the bulk of the work in this chapter. Just a few more configuration options to change to get SpamAssassin fully integrated into MailScanner, and you'll be on your way to a complete antispam solution! Next let's jump into configuring SpamAssassin with inclusion into MailScanner and a sitewide configuration environment in mind.

## Modifying MailScanner.conf

Once the SpamAssassin-specific configuration is complete, you still need to finish a bit of MailScanner configuration that we skipped in Chapter 14. Although you have a working MailScanner installation and a customized SpamAssassin, you need to tie the two together.

I suggest creating a backup copy of `MailScanner.conf` before beginning:

```
[curtis@mail ~]$ cd /etc/MailScanner/
[curtis@mail MailScanner]$ sudo cp MailScanner.conf ➥
MailScanner.conf.nospamassassin
[curtis@mail MailScanner]$ ls -l MailScanner.conf*
```

```
-rw-r--r-- 1 root root 90636 Jan 1 08:52 MailScanner.conf
-rw-r--r-- 1 root root 90636 Mar 16 19:21 MailScanner.conf.nospamassassin
```

You can always go back to this copy of `MailScanner.conf` should you need to undo any changes and temporarily disable SpamAssassin scanning, if your SpamAssassin configuration isn't working properly.

Now open `MailScanner.conf` in your favorite text editor, and let's finish the MailScanner and SpamAssassin antispam configuration.

## Enabling MailScanner Spam Checks

Let's pick up our discussion of `MailScanner.conf` from the section that starts

```
#
# Spam Detection and Spam Lists (DNS blocklists)
# ----------------------------------------------
#
```

First look for the `Spam Checks` configuration option:

```
Spam Checks = yes
```

Setting this MailScanner configuration option to yes enables *all* antispam tests, including any built-in MailScanner and SpamAssassin tests. Setting this option to no disables all antispam tests. Presumably, you do not want to disable antispam countermeasures, so make sure this option remains set to the value yes.

## Configuring MailScanner RBL Settings

As I've stated before, MailScanner can perform a number of RBL checks itself. I recommend allowing SpamAssassin to use its RBL tests to add to the spam score of each message, but if you decide to do these checks with MailScanner instead, use the MailScanner `Spam List` configuration option:

```
Spam List = # ORDB-RBL SBL+XBL # You can un-comment this to enable them
```

As you can see, by default all MailScanner RBL checks are disabled. To add one or more RBL test to MailScanner, simply provide the specific test you'd like MailScanner to perform to the `Spam List` configuration option. The list of RBL tests available is configured by the `Spam List Definitions` option:

```
Spam List Definitions = %etc-dir%/spam.lists.conf
```

which points to the `/etc/MailScanner/spam.lists.conf` file, by default.

The `spam.lists.conf` file lists symbolic names for an RBL followed by the URL of the RBL itself. Use the symbolic name found there to add to the Spam List configuration option. For example, if you wanted to use SpamCop (`www.spamcop.net`) and Distributed Sender Blackhole List (`www.dsbl.org`), you would add the following line to `MailScanner.conf`:

```
Spam List = spamcop.net DSBL
```

To classify a message as spam using the MailScanner RBL tests, use the `Spam Lists To Be Spam` configuration option:

```
Spam Lists To Be Spam = 1
```

This option indicates how many MailScanner RBL tests a message must match to be classified as spam by MailScanner. Setting this to 1 tells MailScanner to automatically treat as spam any message that matches to a single RBL test. Depending on how aggressively you rely on any one RBL, set this value to one you feel comfortable with.

To set the time-out threshold on a particular RBL test, use the MailScanner Spam List Timeout configuration option:

```
Spam List Timeout = 10
```

If a test fails within the specified number of seconds, MailScanner ignores the test and continues processing the message.

## Creating MailScanner Spam Whitelists and Blacklists

You've seen how you can create SpamAssassin whitelists and blacklists in spam.assassin. prefs.conf. Those lists apply only to SpamAssassin. If a partial or full e-mail address or e-mail domain is in a SpamAssassin whitelist, MailScanner can still classify a message containing the same partial or full e-mail address or e-mail domain as spam through its other spam tests. If you truly want to whitelist or blacklist something, you should add it to a MailScanner whitelist or blacklist accordingly.

To create a MailScanner spam whitelist, use the MailScanner Is Definitely Not Spam configuration option in MailScanner.conf:

```
Is Definitely Not Spam = no
```

By default, this specifies that there is no MailScanner spam whitelist. Setting this to a rules file is best:

```
Is Definitely Not Spam = %rules-dir%/spam.whitelist.rules
```

Create /etc/MailScanner/rules/spam.whitelists.rules if it does not already exist, and add your MailScanner spam whitelist entries there. Make sure the very last entry in this file contains the following:

```
FromOrTo:    default    no
```

which is a catch-all default entry that says not to whitelist by default. To add a whitelist entry for messages that come from the e-mail address curtis@example.com, add the following line to spam.whitelist.rules:

```
From:    curtis@example.com    yes
```

You may consider whitelisting your entire local network, from which your users send outgoing mail, if you can trust your users not to spam others through your e-mail system. To do so, simply add your network subnets to spam.whitelist.rules:

```
From:    192.168.69.    yes
```

To create a MailScanner spam blacklist, use the MailScanner Is Definitely Spam configuration option in MailScanner.conf:

```
Is Definitely = no
```

By default, this specifies that there is no MailScanner spam blacklist. Setting this to a rules file is best:

```
Is Definitely Spam = %rules-dir%/spam.blacklist.rules
```

Create /etc/MailScanner/rules/spam.blacklist.rules if it does not already exist, and add your MailScanner spam blacklist entries there. Make sure the very last entry in this file contains the following:

```
FromOrTo:    default      no
```

which is a catch-all default entry that says not to blacklist by default. To add a blacklist entry for messages that come from the e-mail address curtis@example.com, add the following line to spam.blacklist.rules:

```
From:      curtis@example.com     yes
```

For a complete discussion on adding rulesets to a rules file, please refer to Chapter 14 and Table 14-1.

One additional MailScanner whitelist configuration option worth mentioning is Ignore Spam Whitelist If Recipients Exceed:

```
Ignore Spam Whitelist If Recipients Exceed = 20
```

A spammer might try to get past spam filters by adding a large number of e-mail recipients in hopes that any one of them will trigger a match to an address in a whitelist. To minimize the effectiveness of this tactic, MailScanner can ignore a whitelist entry if the number of recipients in an e-mail message exceeds this setting.

That's it for the main MailScanner spam settings. After just a few more SpamAssassin–specific MailScanner configuration in MailScanner.conf, we'll be ready to test the SpamAssassin and MailScanner antispam settings.

## Configuring MailScanner's SpamAssassin-Specific Settings

Next, configure MailScanner to use SpamAssassin for additional spam checks with the MailScanner Use SpamAssassin configuration option:

```
Use SpamAssassin = no
```

By default, MailScanner does not use SpamAssassin. To enable SpamAssassin checks through MailScanner, change the Use SpamAssassin option as follows:

```
Use SpamAssassin = yes
```

The SpamAssassin configuration option required_hits in spam.assassin.prefs.conf is the minimum score a message must exceed to be classified as spam. To override this threshold with MailScanner, override with the MailScanner Required SpamAssassin Score configuration option in MailScanner.conf:

```
Required SpamAssassin Score = 6
```

Because we've built a sitewide configuration, I suggest starting with a more-conservative minimum score first and changing this setting, if necessary, after some time:

```
Required SpamAssassin Score = 8
```

Likewise, the MailScanner High SpamAssassin Score configuration option

```
High SpamAssassin Score = 10
```

could be increased, too. This option sets the minimum score a message must exceed to be dealt with in a special manner, as dictated by the MailScanner High Scoring Spam Actions configuration option (see Chapter 14). The High Scoring Spam Actions option allows you the possibility of automatically quarantining messages with very high spam scores and hiding them from your users altogether. Be careful! You must check for false positives periodically, and if you set this value too low, important mail might not be delivered.

### Configuring MailScanner's SpamAssassin Bayes Token Expiration

Remember the Bayes database token expiration we discussed previously in this chapter? MailScanner can automatically clean up the Bayes data if you change the MailScanner Rebuild Bayes Every configuration option

```
Rebuild Bayes Every = 0
```

to every day (the value is the time in seconds)

```
Rebuild Bayes Every = 86400
```

Alternatively, leave this set to 0, and use a simple shell script to do it. Create a new file called something like /usr/local/sbin/rebuild_bayes_db.sh that contains the following script:

```
#!/bin/bash
# Rebuild the SpamAssassin Bayes database, cleaning out old tokens.
/usr/bin/sa-learn --sync --force-expire \
  -p /etc/MailScanner/spam.assassin.prefs.conf
```

Don't forget to make this script executable:

```
[curtis@mail MailScanner]$ sudo chmod 755 /usr/local/sbin/rebuild_bayes_db.sh
```

Next, add the script to the root user's crontab with the crontab command:

```
[curtis@mail MailScanner]$ sudo crontab -u root -e
```

The -u root argument tells the crontab command that you are editing the crontab for the root user, and the -e argument tells the crontab command that you want to edit the crontab. This command opens the default system text editor, typically vim, and you are editing what appears to be an empty file.

Enter the following line into the root user's crontab to run rebuild_bayes_db.sh every day at 3:00 a.m.:

```
0 3 * * *    /usr/local/sbin/rebuild_bayes_db.sh
```

Save your changes to the crontab, and exit the text editor. If there are no errors in the file, your crontab is automatically saved. For more detailed information about cron and crontab entries, refer to Chapter 15, or check out the crontab(5) man page.

## Configuring Vipul's Razor

If you decided to install Vipul's Razor in Chapter 17, and you've enabled it with the use_razor2 SpamAssassin configuration option in spam.assassin.prefs.conf, you need to set up Razor for use in a sitewide configuration.

To do so, you must first create a central Razor configuration directory; I suggest /etc/mail/spamassassin/razor/:

```
[curtis@mail ~]$ sudo mkdir /etc/mail/spamassassin/razor
```

Next, you must create your site's Razor identity, with which you authenticate your site to the Razor online database. The Razor servers keep track of your identity and anything submitted with the identity. The identity is created for you by the razor-admin command; you won't have to remember a username and password, the identity is automatically generated and stored in /etc/mail/spamassassin/razor/:

```
[curtis@mail ~]$ sudo razor-admin -home=/etc/mail/spamassassin/razor -register
```

Next, create a default Razor razor-agent.conf configuration file with the razor-admin command:

```
[curtis@mail ~]$ sudo razor-admin -home=/etc/mail/spamassassin/razor -create
```

Force a discovery of Razor servers, and add the servers to /etc/mail/spamassassin/razor/ with the razor-admin command:

```
[curtis@mail ~]$ sudo razor-admin -home=/etc/mail/spamassassin/razor -discover
```

Finally, configure SpamAssassin, so it can find the sitewide Razor configuration you just created by adding the SpamAssassin razor_config configuration option to spam.assassin.prefs.conf:

```
razor_config /etc/mail/spamassassin/razor/razor-agent.conf
```

Also configure the Razor sitewide configuration location in Razor's configuration itself by adding the following line to /etc/mail/spamassassin/razor/razor-agent.conf:

```
razorhome = /etc/mail/spamassassin/razor/
```

## Configuring Pyzor

If you decided to install Pyzor as described in Chapter 17, and you've enabled it with the use_pyzor SpamAssassin configuration option in spam.assassin.prefs.conf, you need to set up Pyzor for use in a sitewide configuration.

To do so, you must first create a central Pyzor configuration directory; I suggest /etc/mail/spamassassin/pyzor/:

```
[curtis@mail ~]$ sudo mkdir /etc/mail/spamassassin/pyzor
```

Next, use the pyzor command to discover the servers and download the list to the file /etc/mail/spamassassin/pyzor/servers:

```
[curtis@mail ~]$ sudo pyzor --homedir /etc/mail/spamassassin/pyzor discover
```

Finally, configure SpamAssassin so that it invokes `pyzor` with the proper sitewide configuration directory by adding the following line to `spam.assassin.prefs.conf`:

```
pyzor_options --homedir /etc/mail/spamassassin/pyzor
```

## Configuring DCC

If you decided to install DCC as discussed in Chapter 17, and you've enabled it with the `use_dcc` SpamAssassin configuration option in `spam.assassin.prefs.conf`, you do not need any additional configuration for the typical installation. The DCC installation process includes the creation of a sitewide installation location, `/var/dcc/` by default.

The critical MailScanner and SpamAssassin configurations are complete! Neither has to be as difficult or intimidating as you might think. Because MailScanner invokes SpamAssassin through the `Mail::SpamAssassin` Perl module, there is no SpamAssassin daemon to start. Once you've saved your changes to `spam.assassin.prefs.conf` and `MailScanner.conf`, don't forget to reload MailScanner:

```
[curtis@mail ~]$ sudo service MailScanner reload
```

That's it! Let's take a look at how to test your SpamAssassin and MailScanner configurations.

# Testing E-mail Spam Detection with SpamAssassin

Once you've completed your initial SpamAssassin configuration and made any changes to it, you can test SpamAssassin indirectly from MailScanner easily. You also want to make sure that Razor, Pyzor, and DCC can connect to their respective servers, if you installed and configured them. This section shows you how to check their connectivity and offer a few tips for troubleshooting connectivity problems. To start off, simply run the SpamAssassin executable `spamassassin` in debug mode using the sample spam message.

## Using the GTUBE to Test SpamAssassin

The Generic Test for Unsolicited Bulk E-mail (GTUBE) is similar in concept to the EICAR test viruses. The GTUBE can be used to safely test your SpamAssassin installation and configuration with a message recognized as definitely spam. The GTUBE can be found on your e-mail system if you installed SpamAssassin from the Fedora Core RPM package in `/usr/share/doc/spamassassin-[version]/sample-spam.txt`, or as a downloadable text file online at `http://spamassassin.apache.org/gtube`.

To test SpamAssassin for the first time, run the `spamassassin` command on your e-mail system, replacing the path to `sample-spam.txt` with the patch to your copy of the GTUBE:

```
[curtis@mail ~]$ sudo spamassassin -x -D -t ➥
< /usr/share/doc/spamassassin-3.0.6/sample-spam.txt
```

This command results in too many lines of output to reproduce here, but it should include output similar to the following:

```
Content-Transfer-Encoding: 7bit
X-Spam-Prev-Subject: Test spam mail (GTUBE)
X-Spam-Flag: YES
X-Spam-Checker-Version: SpamAssassin 3.0.6 (2005-12-07) on mail.example.com
X-Spam-Level: *************************************************
X-Spam-Status: Yes, score=1001.4 required=5.0 tests=DCC_CHECK,
    DNS_FROM_AHBL_RHSBL,GTUBE,NO_RECEIVED,NO_RELAYS autolearn=no
    version=3.0.6
X-Spam-Report:
    * -0.0 NO_RELAYS Informational: message was not relayed via SMTP
    * 1000 GTUBE BODY: Generic Test for Unsolicited Bulk Email
    * 1.4 DCC_CHECK Listed in DCC (http://rhyolite.com/anti-spam/dcc/)
    * 0.1 DNS_FROM_AHBL_RHSBL RBL: From: sender listed in dnsbl.ahbl.org
    * -0.0 NO_RECEIVED Informational: message has no Received headers


This is the GTUBE, the
    Generic
    Test for
    Unsolicited
    Bulk
    Email
```

If your spam filter supports it, the GTUBE provides a test by which you
can verify that the filter is installed correctly and is detecting incoming
spam. You can send yourself a test mail containing the following string of
characters (in upper case and with no white spaces and line breaks):

XJS*C4JDBQADN1.NSBN3*2IDNEN*GTUBE-STANDARD-ANTI-UBE-TEST-EMAIL*C.34X

You should send this test mail from an account outside of your network.

Spam detection software, running on the system "mail.example.com", has
identified this incoming email as possible spam. The original message
has been attached to this so you can view it (if it isn't spam) or label
similar future email. If you have any questions, see
the administrator of that system for details.

Content preview: This is the GTUBE, the Generic Test for Unsolicited
  Bulk Email If your spam filter supports it, the GTUBE provides a test
  by which you can verify that the filter is installed correctly and is
  detecting incoming spam. You can send yourself a test mail containing
  the following string of characters (in upper case and with no white
  spaces and line breaks): [...]

Content analysis details:  (1001.4 points, 5.0 required)

```
pts   rule name             description
----  -------------------   --------------------------------------------------
-0.0  NO_RELAYS             Informational: message was not relayed via SMTP
1000  GTUBE                 BODY: Generic Test for Unsolicited Bulk Email
 1.4  DCC_CHECK             Listed in DCC (http://rhyolite.com/anti-spam/dcc/)
 0.1  DNS_FROM_AHBL_RHSBL   RBL: From: sender listed in dnsbl.ahbl.org
-0.0  NO_RECEIVED           Informational: message has no Received headers
```

This summary output comes from the -t argument to the spamassassin command. It shows you the X-Spam message headers SpamAssassin would have added if the message was real and the results of all of the spam tests that matched the message. You can easily see here how a spam score is accumulated through several tests.

The rest of the output is verbose debugging information. When run in debug mode with the -D argument, SpamAssassin is very verbose and details each step it's taking. Scroll through the output and look for any glaring errors. You should also be able to spot blocks of output that indicate whether or not Razor, Pyzor, and DCC checks occurred successfully.

### Checking Vipul's Razor

The key output to search for to see if Vipul's Razor has been used by SpamAssassin starts with the following lines:

```
debug: Razor2 is available
debug: entering helper-app run mode
 Razor-Log: read_file: 16 items read from ➥
/etc/mail/spamassassin/razor/razor-agent.conf
 Razor-Log: Found razorhome: /etc/mail/spamassassin/razor/
```

If you find that Razor was not successfully loaded, check the errors. Also make sure the network traffic is not being blocked. The Razor agent sends requests to the servers on outbound TCP ports 2703 and 7, and incoming connections are typical TCP sessions, using a random TCP port greater than 1023. Razor does not use UDP or Internet Control Message Protocol (ICMP) except when SpamAssassin performs a typical DNS lookup on the Razor servers.

### Checking Pyzor

The key output to search for to see if Pyzor has been used by SpamAssassin starts with the following lines:

```
debug: Pyzor is available: /usr/bin/pyzor
debug: entering helper-app run mode
```

If you find that Pyzor was not successfully loaded, check the errors. Also make sure the network traffic is not being blocked. The Pyzor client uses UDP and TCP port 24441.

## Checking DCC

The key output to search for to see if DCC has been used by SpamAssassin starts with the following lines:

```
debug: DCC is available: /usr/local/bin/dccproc
debug: entering helper-app run mode
debug: setuid: helper proc 14217: ruid=0 euid=0
debug: DCC: got response: X-DCC-EATSERVER-Metrics: mail 1166; Body=many ➡
Fuz1=many Fuz2=many
debug: leaving helper-app run mode
```

If you find that DCC was not successfully loaded, check the errors. Also make sure the network traffic is not being blocked. DCC comes with a utility called cddc to test server connectivity (output is truncated for brevity):

```
[curtis@mail ~]$ cdcc info
```

```
# 06/29/06 05:10:45 EDT /var/dcc/map
# Re-resolve names after 06:53:09
# 1291.71 ms threshold, 1273.14 ms average  12 total, 10 working servers
IPv6 off

dcc1.dcc-servers.net,-   RTT+1000 ms anon
# 142.27.70.214,-                  CollegeOfNewCaledonia ID 1189
#   100% of 4 requests ok 1085.46+1000 ms RTT   2100 ms queue wait
# 194.109.153.82,-                      NIET ID 1080
#   100% of 3 requests ok 215.95+1000 ms RTT    64 ms queue wait
# 208.201.249.233,-               sonic.net ID 1117
#   100% of 3 requests ok 191.71+1000 ms RTT   105 ms queue wait

dcc2.dcc-servers.net,-   RTT+1000 ms anon
# 192.84.137.21,-                  INFN-TO ID 1233
#   100% of 3 requests ok 307.34+1000 ms RTT   100 ms queue wait
# 198.137.254.147,-              Misty ID 1170
#   100% of 4 requests ok 441.89+1000 ms RTT   558 ms queue wait
```

You should get a response from at least one server, but the more, the better. Your network firewall must accept incoming connections over UDP port 6277.

# Testing E-mail Spam Detection with MailScanner and SpamAssassin

Finally, the moment we've all been waiting for! It's time to test spam detection with MailScanner. Simply cut and paste the contents of the GTUBE into a new e-mail message and send it to yourself, or send a copy of the GTUBE to yourself from the command line of your e-mail system:

```
[curtis@mail ~]$ mail -s "GTUBE" curtis@example.com ➡
< /usr/share/doc/spamassassin-3.0.6/sample-spam.txt
```

If you watch /var/log/maillog, you should see lines like the following ones:

```
Jun 29 05:20:31 mail MailScanner[14400]: New Batch: Scanning 1 messages, 1682 bytes
Jun 29 05:20:34 mail MailScanner[14400]: Spam Checks: Found 1 spam messages
Jun 29 05:20:34 mail MailScanner[14400]: Virus and Content Scanning: Starting
Jun 29 05:20:34 mail MailScanner[14400]: Uninfected: Delivered 1 messages
```

MailScanner successfully detected and classified the sent message as spam! Open the message in your favorite e-mail client, and view full e-mail headers. The relevant headers of interest in this case include the following:

```
X-ExampleEnterprise-MailScanner-Information: This message has been scanned ➡
by MailScanner
X-ExampleEnterprise-MailScanner: This message has been found to be free of ➡
bad content
X-ExampleEnterprise-MailScanner-SpamCheck: spam, SpamAssassin (score=998.885, ➡
required 6, autolearn=not spam, ALL_TRUSTED -2.82, ➡
DNS_FROM_AHBL_RHSBL 0.07,GTUBE 1000.00, ➡
RAZOR2_CF_RANGE_51_100 1.49,RAZOR2_CHECK 0.15)
X-ExampleEnterprise-MailScanner-SpamScore: ➡
sssssssssssssssssssssssssssssssssssssssssssssssssssssssssssssssss
X-ExampleEnterprise-MailScanner-From: curtis@mail.example.com
```

Congratulations! Ample information appears to be given in the headers by MailScanner to indicate that the message is, indeed, spam. Now you and your users can use these results for filters to help you deal with the influx of spam.

# Further SpamAssassin Resources

SpamAssassin is an extremely well-documented software package. Documentation can be found locally on your Fedora Core system in /usr/share/doc/spamassassin-[version]/ where [version] is replaced by the base version string of the RPM package installed. For example, at the time of this writing, the RPM package installed is spamassassin-3.0.6-1.fc4, so documentation can be found in /usr/share/doc/spamassassin-3.0.6/. To check the version of SpamAssassin, run the following command:

```
[curtis@mail ~]$ rpm -qv spamassassin
```

```
spamassassin-3.0.6-1.fc4
```

In addition to the local documentation and the documentation found with the source distribution, the most current information regarding SpamAssassin installation, configuration, and development status is also available from the SpamAssassin wiki at http://wiki.apache.org/ spamassassin. For community support, the SpamAssassin mailing lists are also an excellent resource; you can find list archives and subscription information at `http://wiki.apache.org/spamassassin/MailingLists`.

## Summary

In this chapter, we completed the task of configuring and customizing SpamAssassin and MailScanner. Combined with the built-in tests MailScanner offers, SpamAssassin should provide a fine, reliable sitewide antispam mechanism to help your users deal with unsolicited bulk e-mail.

This chapter concludes the section of this book on e-mail–borne threats and countermeasures. It's unfortunate that we have to deal with these circumstances, but hopefully, you'll find the tools presented in this and the previous chapters useful for combating these threats.

Starting in Chapter 19, I will introduce the GNU mailing list manager called Mailman. With Mailman, mailing lists are a cinch, whether you use them for sending mass announcements or maintaining discussion lists. We're approaching the end of our endeavors toward a complete enterprise-quality mail system; I assure you, in the end, your hard work will pay off!

# PART 8

**■ ■ ■**

# Managing Mailing Lists

# CHAPTER 19

■ ■ ■

# Introducing and Installing Mailman

I'm sure you've received your fair share of electronic newsletters and corporate product announcements. Maybe you have even participated in online e-mail discussions. Each of these has something in common, aside from being e-mail—chances are a mailing list manager is involved in maintaining a list membership and sending the messages en masse to those subscribed to receive them.

Anyone can address an e-mail to multiple recipients. E-mail clients have offered the To, CC, and BCC lines since the early days of e-mail. Want to send one message to two people? That's easy. Want to send one message to 20 people? OK, that's easy, too. But what about 200 or 2,000 people? Even if you could add 2,000 addresses to the message, should you?

More than proper e-mail etiquette says you shouldn't address more than a handful of recipients per message. Addressing a single message to 2,000 recipients is more than just rude; it also taxes e-mail systems and can delay message delivery. And with the problem of spam, many mail servers won't allow messages with so many recipients to be sent in the first place. Besides, what if there's a need to send a different e-mail to those same 2,000 people once a week? Managing that many people with a simple address book can be unwieldy, especially if you have more than one set of 2,000 recipients.

In this chapter, I introduce the answer to these questions—Mailman. I also walk through the installation and initial configuration of Mailman. In Chapter 20, I continue the discussion on Mailman, focusing on what it means to be a Mailman site administrator and a Mailman mailing list administrator.

## Introducing the GNU Mailing List Manager

Mailman, the GNU mailing list manager (www.list.org), is the free, open source software of choice for countless e-mail domains for managing electronic newsletters and discussion mailing lists. Think of electronic newsletters and mailing lists as the same thing as their traditional postal equivalents; they are mechanisms for mass distribution of electronic communication. But electronic mailing lists have become much more than vehicles for one-way, announcement-style communication. Rather, mailing lists have become digital communities, fostering discussion and facilitating collaboration in much the same vein as usenet newsgroups.

The list of features to the credit of Mailman is extensive and includes the following:

- *Web integration*: Most of the mailing list and membership management features and tasks can be performed through an intuitive web interface.

- *Multilingual support*: E-mail notices and web pages can be localized; you can use over a dozen different languages.

- *Automatic bounce processing*: Mailman supports sophisticated mechanisms for managing messages that bounce back or are undeliverable. If specified criteria are met, list members can be automatically unsubscribed if too many messages bounce.

- *Easy mailing list management*: List and membership management can be delegated by the list administrator or owner to list moderators, allowing distributed mailing list management.

- *Digest subscriptions*: List members can optionally receive messages in a daily consolidated digest instead of individually.

- *Personal, custom list web pages*: Each mailing list has its own web page that can be customized.

- *Mailing list archives*: Messages sent to a mailing list can be saved in either publicly accessible or private, member-accessible archives with access through the web.

# Installing Mailman

Mailman is available as a Fedora Core RPM package, or you can download and install it from the source distribution found at www.list.org. The Mailman RPM is not included in our default Fedora Core installation (see Chapter 2). However, it's a cinch to install with yum. This chapter and subsequent chapters assume you're using the Fedora Core RPM package. The general topics and specific configuration in these chapters should still apply to an instance of Mailman installed from source code, and I will point out any differences where appropriate. Which of the two you choose for installing and maintaining Mailman is a matter of personal preference, but as always, I prefer to use the RPM package whenever possible for easy maintenance.

## The Mailman RPM Package

To determine whether Mailman is installed on your Fedora Core system, you can use the following command to query the RPM package database:

```
[curtis@mail ~]$ rpm -qv mailman
```

```
mailman-2.1.8-0.FC4.1
```

This command shows the version of Mailman and the revision of the RPM package, if it is installed. Of course, your version may vary. If the package is missing, the previous command indicates, with an error message, that the Mailman RPM package is not installed.

You can install Mailman with the following yum command:

```
[curtis@mail ~]$ sudo yum install mailman
```

This command searches for and installs, if found, the latest version of Mailman available from the yum RPM package repositories you have configured on your e-mail system. In addition, any required prerequisite RPM packages are also downloaded and installed if they aren't already.

If you decide RPM packages are not an option, follow the instructions in the next section to install Mailman from the source distribution.

## The Mailman Source Distribution

To install from source code, download the latest stable source distribution from www.list.org. At the time of this writing, this is version 2.1.8.

Throughout this book, I suggest using wget to download the latest stable source distribution, and Mailman is no different. Retrieving the latest source distribution is simple with the wget command; copy the URL to the source distribution from the download link on the Mailman website:

```
[curtis@mail ~]$ wget http://www.list.org/mailman.tar.gz
```

At this point, you might be anticipating the standard source code preparation, building, compiling, and installation steps that have become all too familiar so far—well, not just yet. A few tasks must be completed before we get to that process this time.

First, we must install a unique, unprivileged user and group for Mailman. This user and group own the Mailman files installed in subsequent steps. Proper user and group ownership and permissions are very important components to the basic security structure of a Mailman installation. The Mailman user and group must be created before you try to install Mailman.

To do so, use the groupadd and useradd commands. First, create the Mailman group:

```
[curtis@mail ~]$ sudo groupadd mailman
```

Second, create the Mailman user, assigning the mailman group you just created as the user's primary group:

```
[curtis@mail ~]$ sudo useradd -g mailman -c "GNU Mailing List Manager" ➥
-d /usr/local/mailman -M -s /sbin/nologin mailman
```

Adding the -d argument to useradd specifies the user's home directory, but we suppress the creation of the home directory (even if it already exists) with the -M argument; we will create this directory manually later in this chapter. Don't forget to restrict the Mailman user to a system account only, disallowing interactive logins, by assigning a fake shell like /sbin/nologin.

Next, create the Mailman installation directory. This directory can be located anywhere you like, but the default installation location is /usr/local/mailman/. Go ahead and create the directory, if it does not exist:

```
[curtis@mail ~]$ sudo mkdir /usr/local/mailman
```

Apply the proper group ownership and permissions on the Mailman installation directory you just created:

```
[curtis@mail ~]$ sudo chgrp mailman /usr/local/mailman/
[curtis@mail ~]$ sudo chmod a+rx,g+ws /usr/local/mailman/
```

Setting the group permission by adding the g+s argument to chmod sets the group to be sticky, which guarantees that all subsequent files or directories created in /usr/local/mailman/ are automatically owned by the Mailman group. Doing so ensures the proper group ownership and permissions necessary for Mailman to operate properly and securely.

When you're finished, your Mailman installation directory should look something like the following:

```
[curtis@mail ~]$ ls -la /usr/local/mailman/
```

```
total 12
drwxrwsr-x  2 root mailman 4096 Mar 18 16:52 .
drwxr-xr-x 12 root root    4096 Mar 18 16:52 ..
```

Remember, the directory indicated by the period (.) is the current working directory (/usr/local/mailman/ in the case of the previous example), and the directory indicated by two periods (..) is one directory higher in the file system tree than the current working directory (/usr/local/ in the case of the previous example).

Now its time to unpack, build, compile, and install the source distribution (the screen output is not shown here again for the sake of brevity):

```
[curtis@mail ~]$ tar xzvf mailman.tar.gz
[curtis@mail ~]$ cd mailman-2.1.8/
```

When you run the configure script, if you chose to install Mailman into a different installation directory from the default, do not forget to add the --prefix argument pointing to that directory. Adding --prefix=/usr/local/mailman is redundant, but OK; it explicitly configures the Mailman source to be installed in /usr/local/mailman/. Be sure not to run the configure script with sudo or as the root user. An example configure script follows:

```
[curtis@mail mailman-2.1.8]$ ./configure --prefix=/usr/local/mailman
```

Complete the installation by compiling and installing the Mailman source distribution:

```
[curtis@mail mailman-2.1.8]$ make
[curtis@mail mailman-2.1.8]$ sudo make install
```

The final step is to check the Mailman installation directory structure and permissions. The Mailman source distribution comes with a script that can do this for you. It must be run from the Mailman installation directory by the root user (screen output is not shown for the sake of brevity):

```
[curtis@mail mailman-2.1.8]$ cd /usr/local/mailman/
[curtis@mail mailman]$ sudo bin/check_perms
```

## THE IMPORTANCE OF RELIABLE DNS AND CACHING NAME SERVERS

It's important to note the importance of good, reliable, and redundant DNS servers. The ability to resolve human-readable domain names to IP addresses is crucial to the very essence of the Internet itself. In addition, when dealing with e-mail, SMTP servers, and mailing list servers, DNS is necessary for e-mail domain MX resolution. If a domain's MX record cannot be found, mail cannot be delivered to it.

Although DNS queries are thought to incur very little network bandwidth overhead, the sheer number of queries that an SMTP or mailing list server may generate could overload an already taxed DNS server. To help speed up DNS queries in general and reduce the overhead of querying a public DNS server, you may consider installing a caching name server on your e-mail system.

One such caching name server, called nscd, is installed on a Fedora Core 4 system by default. Enable the nscd init script with the chkconfig command:

```
[curtis@mail ~]$ sudo chkconfig --level 345 nscd on
```

Next, start nscd with the service command:

```
[curtis@mail ~]$ sudo service nscd start
```

You can change the behavior of nscd through its configuration file /etc/nscd.conf; consult the nscd.conf(5) man page for more information.

If the check_perms script reports any errors with a message like the following one

```
Problems found: 61
Re-run as mailman (or root) with -f flag to fix
```

go ahead and follow its suggestion to rerun check_perms with the -f argument to fix the problems:

```
[curtis@mail mailman]$ sudo bin/check_perms -f
```

until the check_perms reports that no more problems are found. Any warnings regarding private archive directory permissions are addressed later in this chapter and can be safely ignored for now.

Whatever your choice of installation method, you're now ready to configure Mailman.

# Configuring Mailman

Configuring Mailman to run on your system involves more than Mailman itself. We must also make some minor changes to the sendmail configuration and integrate the web-based components of Mailman with the Apache HTTP server (see Chapter 11). Some of the following configuration settings differ depending on whether you installed the Fedora Core Mailman RPM package or the Mailman source distribution; I note the differences where appropriate.

## Configuring Apache for use with Mailman

One of the more appealing aspects of using Mailman is its tight integration with a web server. Since we're already running a web server for webmail, it makes sense to leverage the web integration features of Mailman. If you have yet to bring a web server online, you should go back to Chapter 11 and follow instructions for the installation of the Apache HTTP server. In the remainder of this chapter, I assume you have already done so.

The reasons for integrating Mailman with a web server are numerous. First, mechanisms are built into recent releases of Mailman that allow administrators to add and remove mailing lists using a web interface. Second, mailing list administration and management can be done through the Mailman web interface. Finally, mailing list members and the general public may access and modify their membership to mailing lists hosted on your server, add and remove themselves from public mailing lists, and access public or private mailing list archives. In Chapter 20, I explain how all this can be done. Some tasks may only be performed from the Web, while other tasks have a Web and a command-line interface. In this chapter, I focus only on Mailman installation and configuration.

The first thing to do is configure your web server to execute the Mailman *Common Gateway Interface (CGI)* scripts. CGI is a standard way for data to be passed to and from a web page and a system application through server-side scripts. The locations of these scripts depend on whether you installed Mailman from the Fedora Core RPM package or the source distribution. If you installed Mailman from the RPM package, the CGI scripts can be found in /usr/lib/ mailman/cgi-bin/. If you install Mailman from the source distribution, the CGI scripts are found in /usr/local/mailman/cgi-bin/. Replace /usr/local/mailman/ with your particular installation directory if it's different.

If you installed Apache from the Fedora Core RPM package, you should add these configuration directives to the file /etc/httpd/conf.d/mailman.conf. If you installed the Fedora Core Mailman RPM package, much of this Apache configuration has been done for you, but you should continue working your way through this configuration to make sure nothing should be tailored for your installation. If you installed Apache from the source distribution, you can simply add the following configuration directives to httpd.conf itself, typically found in /usr/local/apache2/conf/.

Therefore, the first step is to add the following Apache configuration directive to link the URL /mailman/ to the Mailman CGI scripts:

```
ScriptAlias /mailman/ /usr/lib/mailman/cgi-bin/
```

The partial path /mailman/ is relative to what the ServerName directive is set to in httpd.conf, for example, http://mail.example.com/mailman/.

Next, set the security limitations and enable CGI for the Mailman CGI directory—this is the actual directory path found on your hard disk drive, not the URL:

```
<Directory /usr/lib/mailman/cgi-bin/>
  AllowOverride None
  Options ExecCGI
  Order allow,deny
  Allow from all
</Directory>
```

Mailman can archive mailing list messages using the archiving software called Pipermail. Originally written and developed on its own, Pipermail is now an integrated part of the Mailman source distribution. Mailing list archives can be either openly accessible to the general public or restricted to members of the mailing list. These archives are available through the Mailman web interface, historically accessed with the /pipermail/ URL path. Add the following Apache directive to add an alias for the URL path relative to your ServerName that points to the actual location of the public list archives, http://mail.example.com/pipermail/ for example:

```
Alias /pipermail/ /var/lib/mailman/archives/public/
```

Replace /var/lib/mailman/archives/public/ with /usr/local/mailman/archives/public/ if you installed Mailman from the source distribution.

The following directory options are necessary if you add the preceding /pipermail/ Alias:

```
<Directory /var/lib/mailman/archives/public>
  Options Indexes MultiViews FollowSymLinks
  AllowOverride None
  Order allow,deny
  Allow from all
</Directory>
```

The final Apache configuration is simply for the convenience of your users; it redirects requests for http://mail.example.com/mailman/ to the public mailing lists hosted on your site:

```
RedirectMatch ^/mailman[/]*$ http://mail.example.com/mailman/listinfo
```

Don't forget to restart Apache for your changes to take affect:

```
[curtis@mail ~]$ sudo service httpd restart
```

Figure 19-1 shows the default Mailman public mailing list information web page, which you should see if you point your web browser to http://mail.example.com/mailman/listinfo, replacing the domain in this example URL with your domain configured in the Apache ServerName configuration directive.

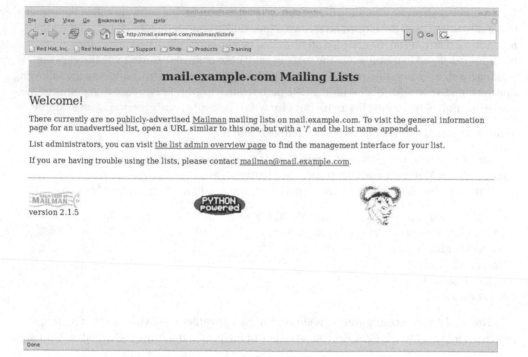

**Figure 19-1.** *The Mailman public mailing list information web page*

## Customizing Mailman Site Default Settings

Mailman sitewide configuration modifies how Mailman interacts with the system itself and sets default options for new mailing lists. Configuring Mailman is a bit different from anything else we've looked at so far. Because configuring Mailman is actually modifying Python scripts, configuration variables are set using Python syntax. Don't worry—it's not as intimidating as it sounds!

The primary Mailman sitewide configuration file is Defaults.py, found by default in /usr/lib/mailman/Mailman/Defaults.py, if you install Mailman by RPM, or /usr/local/ mailman/Mailman/Defaults.py, if you install Mailman from source code. This file is well documented, so always refer to it for options not discussed here. However, do *not* modify Defaults.py; any changes you make are guaranteed to be overwritten and lost when you upgrade Mailman. Instead, add any custom configuration options that override the default Mailman configuration to mm_cfg.py, which is found in the same directory as Defaults.py.

To get your Mailman installation up and running, surprising few Mailman configuration options need to be modified from the default settings in Defaults.py. The first modification is to configure the default e-mail domain that your mailing lists use with the Mailman DEFAULT_EMAIL_HOST configuration option. Assuming that it is the same as your primary e-mail domain already configured in sendmail, use the following command to set the domain:

```
DEFAULT_EMAIL_HOST = 'example.com'
```

Next, configure the default web site address, or URL, for your Mailman web interface with the DEFAULT_URL_HOST option; this URL should match the setting of the Apache ServerName directive:

```
DEFAULT_URL_HOST = 'mail.example.com'
```

The default URL through which users access the Mailman web interface must be defined with the DEFAULT_URL_PATTERN option. This URL should match the Apache ScriptAlias directive, which you set previously in this chapter:

```
DEFAULT_URL_PATTERN = 'http://%s/mailman/'
```

The special variable %s is replaced automatically by Mailman with the value of the DEFAULT_URL_HOST option.

Finally, tell Mailman through which e-mail SMTP server to send messages with the Mailman SMTPHOST configuration option:

```
SMTPHOST = 'mail.example.com'
```

That's all there is to it! This configuration customizes your Mailman installation to your site's specific environment. Next, a slight adjustment to your sendmail configuration is necessary, and then you're finished with the Mailman installation and configuration.

## Configuring sendmail for use with Mailman

Configuring sendmail to work with Mailman takes little effort, assuming sendmail has been configured properly and is passing e-mail already. However, you need to ensure that sendmail executes Mailman when called to do so. Specifically, smrsh, the sendmail restricted shell, must be configured to allow Mailman to process mailing list messages properly.

Configuring smrsh is quite easy. Simply create a symlink in /etc/smrsh/ to the Mailman wrapper script that handles the delivery of mailing list traffic. If you installed the Fedora Core Mailman RPM package, this should have been done for you, but double-check to make sure:

```
[curtis@mail ~]$ ls -l /etc/smrsh/mailman
```

```
lrwxrwxrwx 1 root mailman 29 Mar 20 23:25 /etc/smrsh/mailman -> ➡
/usr/lib/mailman/mail/mailman
```

If you find the symlink is missing, you can easily add the symlink:

```
[curtis@mail ~]$ sudo ln -s /usr/lib/mailman/mail/mailman /etc/smrsh/mailman
```

If you installed Mailman from source code, the symlink should point to the mailman wrapper inside the Mailman installation directory. Following the example earlier in this book, create the symlink to point to the mailman binary in /usr/local/mailman/mail/:

```
[curtis@mail ~]$ sudo ln -s /usr/local/mailman/mail/mailman /etc/smrsh/mailman
```

Replace /usr/local/mailman/ with the directory path in which you chose to install Mailman.

There's no need to restart sendmail or MailScanner after making this change. As I said, it's simple.

## Configuring the Mailman cron Jobs

Various Mailman features depend on several regularly scheduled cron jobs running at various times and frequencies. For example, automatic password reminders to list members are sent out monthly by a cron job.

Mailman comes with a crontab template already configured; all you have to do is add it to the Mailman user's crontab. If you installed Mailman from source code, add the Mailman cron jobs using the crontab command:

```
[curtis@mail ~]$ sudo crontab -u mailman /usr/local/mailman/cron/crontab.in
```

Replace /usr/local/mailman/ with your Mailman installation directory, if it's different. Check to ensure the crontab is installed successfully with the crontab command again:

```
[curtis@mail ~]$ sudo crontab -u mailman -l
```

```
# At 8AM every day, mail reminders to admins as to pending requests.
# They are less likely to ignore these reminders if they're mailed
# early in the morning, but of course, this is local time... ;)
0 8 * * * /usr/bin/python -S /usr/local/mailman/cron/checkdbs
#
# At 9AM, send notifications to disabled members that are due to be
# reminded to re-enable their accounts.
0 9 * * * /usr/bin/python -S /usr/local/mailman/cron/disabled
#
# Noon, mail digests for lists that do periodic as well as threshold delivery.
0 12 * * * /usr/bin/python -S /usr/local/mailman/cron/senddigests
#
# 5 AM on the first of each month, mail out password reminders.
0 5 1 * * /usr/bin/python -S /usr/local/mailman/cron/mailpasswds
#
# Every 5 mins, try to gate news to mail. You can comment this one out
# if you don't want to allow gating, or don't have any going on right now,
# or want to exclusively use a callback strategy instead of polling.
0,5,10,15,20,25,30,35,40,45,50,55 * * * * /usr/bin/python ➡
-S /usr/local/mailman/cron/gate_news
#
# At 3:27am every night, regenerate the gzip'd archive file. Only
# turn this on if the internal archiver is used and
# GZIP_ARCHIVE_TXT_FILES is false in mm_cfg.py
27 3 * * * /usr/bin/python -S /usr/local/mailman/cron/nightly_gzip
```

Compare this output to the content of /usr/local/mailman/cron/crontab.in; they should be identical.

If you installed the Mailman Fedora Core RPM package, this step is a bit different. When you start Mailman with the Fedora Core init script, the crontab template from /usr/lib/mailman/cron/crontab.in is copied to the system crontab, /etc/cron.d/mailman. You should not edit the file /etc/cron.d/mailman, as it will be overwritten the next time Mailman is restarted. If, for whatever reason, Mailman is shut off, the crontab will be removed from the system crontab.

## Starting and Stopping the Mailman Queue Runner

When a message is received by your e-mail system that is destined for a mailing list, the mailman wrapper delivers it accordingly to the Mailman queue for further processing and delivery to the mailing list's members. The Mailman process responsible for scanning the Mailman delivery queue and delivering those messages to their final recipients is called the Mailman qrunner. The qrunner process is controlled by the Mailman mailmanctl script. This script starts, stops, and checks the qrunner process and takes similar arguments to a traditional init script.

You can manually start the Mailman qrunner process with mailmanctl itself, or you can install the Mailman init script and have the Mailman qrunner process start and stop automatically when your e-mail system starts up and shuts down. The Fedora Core Mailman RPM installs a Mailman init script that will start, stop, and restart the Mailman qrunner and install the Mailman crontab.

To check if the Mailman init script is already installed properly by the Fedora Core RPM, use the chkconfig command:

```
[curtis@mail ~]$ sudo chkconfig --list mailman
```

```
mailman    0:off  1:off  2:off  3:off  4:off  5:off  6:off
```

In this example, the Mailman init script is installed but is not configured to automatically start or stop in any of the system runlevels. If the init script is not installed, the previous command would indicate that with an error or with no output at all.

The source distribution also comes with a similar init script that simply starts, stops, and restarts Mailman, but it needs to be installed manually. You can do so with the chkconfig command:

```
[curtis@mail ~]$ sudo chkconfig --add /usr/local/mailman/scripts/mailman
```

Finally, set Mailman to automatically start and stop when appropriate:

```
[curtis@mail ~]$ sudo chkconfig --level 345 mailman on
```

Double-check your handiwork once more with the chkconfig command:

```
[curtis@mail ~]$ sudo chkconfig --list mailman
```

```
mailman    0:off  1:off  2:off  3:on  4:on  5:on  6:off
```

Manually starting Mailman is simple with the service command:

```
[curtis@mail ~]$ sudo service mailman start
```

```
Starting mailman:                    [ OK ]
```

Manually stopping Mailman is equally easy:

```
[curtis@mail ~]$ sudo service mailman stop
```

```
Shutting down mailman:                    [ OK ]
```

That completes your Mailman installation, configuration, and integration with the Apache HTTP server and sendmail!

## Summary

Mailman can be an indispensable component to any organization serious about providing e-mail services to their users. Using the CC line in e-mail is fine when you have very few recipients, but when the number becomes unmanageable, mass distribution of Internet e-mail is best left to a quality mass mailer like Mailman.

Whether you use it to make announcements to your users or to offer public mailing lists for any number of reasons, Mailman makes managing mailing lists easy. In Chapter 20, I will conclude our discussion on mailing lists and the GNU Mailing List Manager by explaining what it means to be a Mailman site administrator and how to create, configure, and manage a mailing list.

■ ■ ■

# Mailman Site Administration and Mailing List Management

In Chapter 19, I covered the basics of mailing lists in general and explained how to install and configure Mailman, as well as how to configure your e-mail system to host mailing lists. This chapter builds on the previous one but focuses on what Mailman site administration and mailing list management entails. I will also touch on what average users ought to know if they are simply members of a public mailing list hosted on your e-mail system. We will see how to create new mailing lists, how to configure and manage mailing lists, and how to manage list membership.

## The Role of the Mailman Site Administrator

Now that you've completed Chapter 19 and have Mailman installed and configured, your responsibility does not stop there. Think of the Mailman site administrator as the root user of mailing lists. The Mailman site administrator is responsible for the creation and initial configuration of mailing lists. The administrator also has a set of command-line scripts available to help maintain the Mailman site installation and individual mailing lists. I generally categorize Mailman administrator commands into two primary classes: site administration and mailing list administration commands.

### A Survey of Mailman Administrator Commands

Throughout this chapter, there will be specific examples of how most of the commands I introduce here are used. All Mailman scripts support the command-line argument --help, which provides a complete synopsis of usage and command-line arguments.

You won't find the Mailman commands in your default command path, so you will find yourself constantly typing the full path to each command. I suggest adding the Mailman binary directory to your command path. If you installed the Fedora Core Mailman RPM package, then append /usr/lib/mailman/bin to your shell command PATH environment variable in ~/.bash_profile:

```
PATH=$PATH:$HOME/bin:/sbin:/usr/sbin:/usr/local/sbin:/usr/lib/mailman/bin
```

If you installed Mailman from source, then append /usr/local/mailman/bin, or whatever installation directory you chose at installation time, to your shell command PATH environment variable in ~/.bash_profile:

```
PATH=$PATH:$HOME/bin:/sbin:/usr/sbin:/usr/local/sbin:/usr/local/mailman/bin
```

You will have to either log out and log back in, or run the shell built-in command `source`, for your changes to take effect:

```
[curtis@mail ~]$ source .bash_profile
```

What I call *site administration* commands include commands to list, add, and remove mailing lists and manage mailing list administrators, owners, and the Mailman site password. Table 20-1 lists each command and provides a brief description of their purpose.

**Table 20-1.** *Command-Line Scripts Used for Mailman Site Administration*

| Command | Description |
| --- | --- |
| mmsitepass | Used to set the Mailman site password that can be used in place of any other password that Mailman prompts for. We will set this password later in this chapter. Choose wisely! |
| newlist | Used to create new mailing lists. |
| rmlist | Used to delete mailing lists, and optionally any associated list archives. |
| list_lists | Used to list mailing lists hosted on your e-mail system. |
| list_admins | Used to list the mailing list administrators, also called owners, of one or more mailing lists hosted on your e-mail system. |

What I call mailing *list administration* commands include commands to list, add, and remove mailing list members and manage mailing list passwords and configuration. Table 20-2 lists each command and provides a brief description of their purpose.

**Table 20-2.** *Command-Line Scripts Used for Mailman Mailing List Administration*

| Command | Description |
| --- | --- |
| config_list | Used to view, modify, or save a mailing list's configuration. |
| check_db | Used to verify the integrity of a mailing list's configuration database files. |
| change_pw | Used to change the list administrator password for one or more mailing lists; you can optionally e-mail the password to the list owner or owners. |
| add_members | Used to add, or subscribe, new list members en masse. |
| list_members | Used to list the members subscribed to a mailing list. |
| find_member | Used to find list members subscribed to one or more mailing lists. |
| remove_members | Used to remove, or unsubscribe, list members en masse. |
| sync_members | Used to synchronize a mailing list's membership to that in a flat-text file. If an address in the text file is not subscribed to the list, it will be added. If an address is subscribed to a list but not in the text file, it will be removed. |
| clone_member | Used to clone a list member's subscription from one address to a new address. All of the original subscription settings are inherited, and you have the option to remove the original address. This command is also useful for cloning list managers from one list to another. Future releases of Mailman will allow users to perform these tasks themselves. |

The majority of these commands, especially those that manipulate Mailman site or mailing list configuration, must be executed as root or as the mailman user itself. However, you can use sudo to do so, as explained next.

## Using sudo to Delegate Mailman Site Administration

We know using sudo will execute the command with the effective privileges as the root user, but you can also use sudo to execute commands as a different user. In addition, it's possible to limit what commands someone can execute with sudo. So, this is an extremely useful way of delegating Mailman site administration to another person without giving him the ability to use sudo with root privileges, and thus limiting him to only the Mailman commands.

Suppose you've created a user account called jon. Jon will be helping with Mailman site administration and will be given the privilege to run only the commands in the Mailman binary directory as the Mailman user. After you've created the account, you will need to make one small modification to sudoers, the sudo configuration file. Remember, use the visudo command; do not edit sudoers manually. Add the following line to sudoers:

```
jon     ALL=(mailman) /usr/lib/mailman/bin/
```

This will allow the user jon on any host to execute any commands in the directory /usr/lib/mailman/bin/ as the user mailman. If Jon tries to run a command that is not found in /usr/lib/mailman/lib/, it will not allow him to do so:

```
[jon@mail ~]$ sudo passwd root
```

```
Password:
Sorry, user jon is not allowed to execute '/usr/bin/passwd root'as root on mail.
```

Perhaps our friend Jon is inventive and tries to run a command as the mailman user:

```
[jon@mail ~]$ sudo -u mailman passwd mailman
```

```
Sorry, user jon is not allowed to execute '/usr/bin/passwd mailman' ➥
as mailman on mail.
```

Denied again. He knows he can run a Mailman command, so he tries that:

```
[jon@mail ~]$ sudo /usr/lib/mailman/bin/newlist
```

```
Sorry, user jon is not allowed to execute '/usr/lib/mailman/bin/newlist' ➥
as root on mail.
```

Oops, still denied. Because Jon was restricted to run commands only as the mailman user, he has to use the -u argument to the sudo command:

```
[jon@mail ~]$ sudo -u mailman /usr/lib/mailman/bin/newlist
```

```
Enter the name of the list:
```

Success! Locking down access to specific commands, instead of an entire directory, is left as an exercise to the reader; check the sudoers(5) man page for sample usage of Cmnd_Alias.

Now that you've been introduced to the Mailman commands, let's start using them. The very first thing you should do before creating any mailing lists is set the Mailman site password.

## Creating Your Mailman Sitewide Passwords

There are two Mailman sitewide passwords: the site password and the list creator password. Both are created using the same Mailman site administrator command, mmsitepass.

The site password is the master Mailman password. This password can be used anywhere Mailman asks requires a password. For obvious reasons, you need to choose this password wisely and protect it very carefully. To set the Mailman site password, use the mmsitepass command:

```
[curtis@mail ~]$ sudo mmsitepass
```

```
New site password:
Again to confirm password:
Password changed.
```

The sitewide list creator password is only good for creating new mailing lists. This optional password can be used to delegate new mailing list creation to others without giving access to any other Mailman administrative duties or elevated privileges. Of course, the e-mail system administrator, anyone delegated privileges with sudo, or anyone with the Mailman site password can also create mailing lists without the sitewide list creator password. To set the Mailman list creator password, use the mmsitepass command with the -c argument:

```
[curtis@mail ~]$ sudo mmsitepass -c
```

```
New list creator password:
Again to confirm password:
Password changed.
```

Next, you must create the Mailman site mailing list.

## The Mailman Site Mailing List

Every Mailman site needs a sitewide mailing list. This mailing list is for administrative use only by Mailman itself. For example, password reminders are sent out to list members using the Mailman site mailing list. It is required for Mailman to operate normally and must be set up, but it will not be used by your or anyone else as a regular mailing list.

Normally, the site mailing list is simply called Mailman. If you decide, for whatever reason, to change the name, modify the following configuration option to add the new name to mm_cfg.py:

```
MAILMAN_SITE_LIST = 'mmsitelist'
```

Replace mmsitelist with whatever you decide to name the Mailman site mailing list.

## Creating Your Mailman Site Mailing List

To create the Mailman site mailing list, use the Mailman newlist command:

```
[curtis@mail ~]$ sudo newlist mailman
```

---

Enter the email of the person running the list:

---

You can use any e-mail address here, but if multiple administrators will be helping with e-mail and Mailman administration, I suggest using the standard generic postmaster@example.com e-mail address, replacing example.com with your e-mail domain, of course, and making postmaster an e-mail alias for each administrator.

---

Initial mailman password:

---

Enter a password that you would like to assign as the Mailman sitewide mailing list admin password. If you ever need to modify the sitewide list configuration, you will need this password.

---

To finish creating your mailing list, you must edit your /etc/aliases (or equivalent) file by adding the following lines, and possibly running the 'newaliases' program:

```
## mailman mailing list
mailman:               "|/usr/lib/mailman/mail/mailman post mailman"
mailman-admin:         "|/usr/lib/mailman/mail/mailman admin mailman"
mailman-bounces:       "|/usr/lib/mailman/mail/mailman bounces mailman"
mailman-confirm:       "|/usr/lib/mailman/mail/mailman confirm mailman"
mailman-join:          "|/usr/lib/mailman/mail/mailman join mailman"
mailman-leave:         "|/usr/lib/mailman/mail/mailman leave mailman"
mailman-owner:         "|/usr/lib/mailman/mail/mailman owner mailman"
mailman-request:       "|/usr/lib/mailman/mail/mailman request mailman"
mailman-subscribe:     "|/usr/lib/mailman/mail/mailman subscribe mailman"
mailman-unsubscribe:   "|/usr/lib/mailman/mail/mailman unsubscribe mailman"
```

---

Stop here without pressing the Enter key. As the script prompts, you must create a series of entries into your system e-mail alias file for the mailing list to work properly. The newlist command conveniently gives you what you need to add, so simply open a new SSH connection to your e-mail system, open /etc/aliases in a text editor, and cut and paste the 11 lines to the end of the aliases file. Once you've made the changes, do not forget to run newaliases:

```
[curtis@mail ~]$ sudo newaliases
```

```
/etc/aliases: 87 aliases, longest 52 bytes, 1403 bytes total
```

These aliases are standard Mailman mailing list aliases that list members can use to interact with the list. Each alias simply redirects the e-mail message to the `mailman` command with the appropriate command arguments

Return to the SSH connection window that you ran `newlist` in and press Enter at the following prompt:

```
Hit enter to notify mailman owner...
```

Mailman will finish creating the mailing list and send an e-mail message to the owner of the mailing list just created, using the `mailman-owner` e-mail alias added to `/etc/aliases`, by default. You're now ready to configure your Mailman site mailing list.

### Configuring Your Mailman Site Mailing List

The Mailman installation, whether you installed the Fedora Core RPM or installed from source, comes with a configuration template suited specifically for the Mailman site mailing list. We will configure the list from the template with the command `config_list`; then later in this chapter when I describe mailing list management, I will describe how to configure a mailing list using the web interface.

The Mailman site mailing list configuration template is found in `/etc/mailman/sitelist.cfg` if you installed Mailman from the Fedora Core RPM package, or in `/usr/local/mailman/data/sitelist.cfg` if you installed Mailman from source code. To apply the configuration from the template, use the `config_list` command with the `-i` argument:

```
[curtis@mail ~]$ sudo config_list -i /etc/mailman/sitelist.cfg mailman
```

Now that you've taken care of some of the one-time administrative steps necessary for proper Mailman site administration, you're ready to create your first public mailing list.

# Creating Your First Public Mailing List

There are two ways to create a new mailing list. The first is with the Mailman command-line script `newlist`, and the second is with the web interface and list creator password. Let's take a look at both, beginning with the command-line script `newlist`.

## Creating Mailing Lists from the Command Line

When creating a new mailing list with the command `newlist`, you can run it interactively, allowing it to prompt you for each necessary piece of information. This is the same process we followed when creating the Mailman site mailing list. However, you can also create the list completely with command-line arguments to `newlist`. The synopsis of the `newlist` command usage from the output of `newlist --help` is shown here:

```
newlist [options] [listname [listadmin-addr [admin-password]]]
```

As you can see, any number of arguments is optional. So, you could specify the list name and nothing else and have newlist prompt you for the rest. Alternatively, you can create the list completely with one command, specifying the list name, list administrator (also referred to as the list owner), and list administrator password, in that order:

```
[curtis@mail ~]$ sudo newlist testlist curtis@example.com t3stp4ssw0rd
```

Again, when you create the list, newlist will print the lines that must be added to the aliases file:

```
## testlist mailing list
testlist:                "|/usr/lib/mailman/mail/mailman post testlist"
testlist-admin:          "|/usr/lib/mailman/mail/mailman admin testlist"
testlist-bounces:        "|/usr/lib/mailman/mail/mailman bounces testlist"
testlist-confirm:        "|/usr/lib/mailman/mail/mailman confirm testlist"
testlist-join:           "|/usr/lib/mailman/mail/mailman join testlist"
testlist-leave:          "|/usr/lib/mailman/mail/mailman leave testlist"
testlist-owner:          "|/usr/lib/mailman/mail/mailman owner testlist"
testlist-request:        "|/usr/lib/mailman/mail/mailman request testlist"
testlist-subscribe:      "|/usr/lib/mailman/mail/mailman subscribe testlist"
testlist-unsubscribe:    "|/usr/lib/mailman/mail/mailman unsubscribe testlist"
```

These aliases are standard Mailman mailing list aliases that list members can use to interact with the list. Each alias simply redirects the e-mail message to the mailman command with the appropriate command arguments. For example, the alias testlist is what list administrator, moderator, or members use to send a message to the mailing list itself (e.g., testlist@example.com). The alias testlist-owner is a convenient way to e-mail the mailing list owners (e.g., testlist-ownder@example.com).

Add these aliases by logging onto your e-mail system with another SSH session, cut and paste the aliases into /etc/aliases, and, of course, regenerate the aliases database with the newaliases command:

```
[curtis@mail ~]$ sudo newaliases
```

When you've added the aliases, pressing Enter will send an e-mail notification to the list administrator, using the testlist-owner e-mail alias added to /etc/aliases, by default.

I will use this test public mailing list as my example later in this chapter when discussing the role of the mailing list administrator and moderator. But first, let's take a look at creating a new mailing list from the web interface rather than the command line.

## Creating Mailing Lists from the Web Interface

If you'd rather enjoy the convenience of using your web browser to create mailing lists, or you want to delegate the ability of list creation to someone without a login account on your e-mail system, there is an alternative to using newlist at the command line: using the web interface. To begin, point your web browser at the following URL:

```
http://mail.example.com/mailman/create
```

Of course, replace this URL with the FQDN of your e-mail system, or whatever your HTTP server is configured to respond to with the Apache `ServerName` directive. Figure 20-1 shows how this web page looks when you first access it.

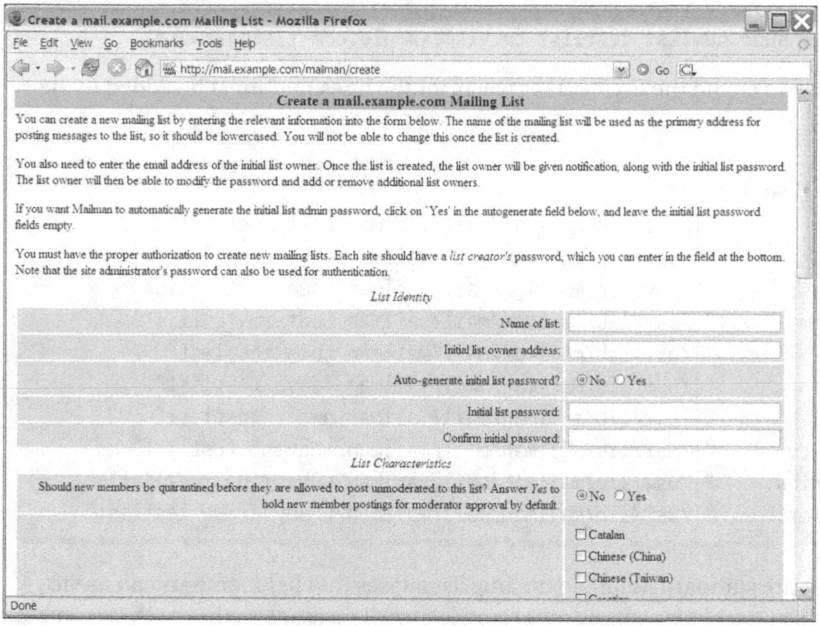

**Figure 20-1.** *It's possible to create a new Mailman mailing list through the web interface.*

You'll find that the mailing list creation web page prompts for the same information as the `newlist` command, with the addition of the list creator password. Go ahead and try creating a mailing list with this interface, making you the list administrator. You should receive the same e-mail notification that you received when you created a mailing list with the `newlist` command.

However, the list creation CGI script will also e-mail the root user, notifying the system administrator that someone has created a new mailing list from the Web. This provides an audit trail of what others are doing on your e-mail system; if you find the list creator password has been compromised, you'll know when it's used and have e-mail and web server logs recording the abuse. You will also receive the same aliases configuration that needs to be added to the `aliases` file manually before the list can be used. From there on, it's the same; add the aliases to `/etc/aliases` and run `newaliases`, and the list is ready to be used.

Now we're going to shift focus from Mailman site administration and mailing list creation and examine the Mailman mailing list administrator's role. Although you, the e-mail system administrator, can perform the duties of this role, individual mailing list administration responsibilities can also be delegated to anyone you trust.

# Mailman Mailing List Management

Mailman mailing list management can be split into roles or responsibilities: the list administrator, or owner, and the list moderator. Each of these can be a single person, or each role can be one or more individuals. Neither a list administrator nor a moderator requires an interactive account on your e-mail system. As long as they have a valid e-mail address, all list configuration and management can be done through the Mailman web interface.

First, let's take a look at the role of a mailing list administrator, focusing on list configuration and membership management. Then, we'll describe the typical duties of a list moderator, focusing on assisting with day-to-day management of a mailing list and list traffic.

## The Role of a Mailing List Administrator

The mailing list administrator is just that: the person, or persons, in charge of maintaining and running one or more mailing lists. This includes, but is not limited to, mailing list configuration, list membership management, and manual processing of moderated and bounce list traffic. The mailing list administrator is also often referred to as the list owner, which may describe the role much better; even though the Mailman or e-mail system site administrator can supersede anyone else in power over the lists, the list owner is the person delegated to be in charge of, and responsible for, the list.

As I've indicated earlier, the mailing list administrator does not need to have an interactive shell login account on the e-mail system itself. When the Mailman site administrator, or the list creator, creates a mailing list, the list owner is sent an e-mail notification listing the initial list password and explaining how to access the mailing list administrative web interface. From this list admin web interface, a list owner can perform all of her duties through her web browser. Let's take a look at this interface next.

## Configuring a Mailing List with the Mailman Web Interface

The mailing list administrative or configuration web page is the primary means for managing a mailing list. For a directory of sorts listing the links to the list admin page for all publicly advertised mailing lists, visit the following URL:

```
http://mail.example.com/mailman/admin
```

Replace this example with the FQDN of your web server and path to the Mailman virtual host, if configured differently. If you followed along with the examples in this chapter thus far, at the very least, you should see a link to your test mailing list, shown in Figure 20-2.

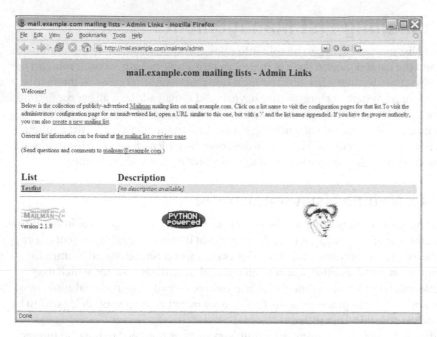

**Figure 20-2.** *An example of the directory of publicly advertised Mailman mailing list administrative links*

The basic URL for accessing any Mailman mailing list admin web page, publicly advertised or not, is of the following form:

```
http://mail.example.com/mailman/admin/[listname]
```

So, for example, to access the mailing list configuration web page for the mailing list `testlist` we created earlier, the list admin link would be

```
http::/mail.example.com/mailman/admin/testlist
```

If you visit the list admin web interface for the first time, you will be prompted to enter the list admin password, shown in Figure 20-3. This password is the one set by the Mailman site administrator or list creator when the mailing list was created and that was e-mailed to the list owner. Enter the list admin password and click the Let Me In button to enter the list admin web interface.

---

**Tip** You must enable HTTP cookies before visiting the list admin web page. In addition to maintaining your login session, cookies are necessary to effect any changes you make. Without cookies enabled in your web browser, the list admin web interface will not work properly.

---

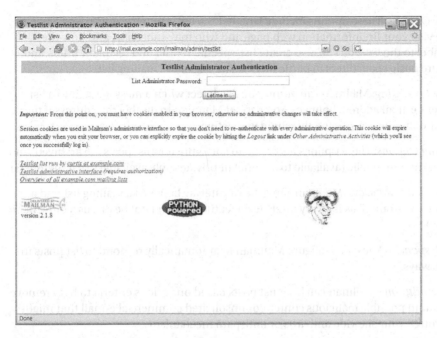

**Figure 20-3.** *You are required to authenticate with the list admin password before entering the list admin web interface.*

Once successfully authenticated, you are presented with a number of configuration categories and administrative activities. These include the following:

- *General Options*: These options let you configure and customize the mailing list description and basic list behavior, such as specifying how messages are delivered, indicating whether you want to send monthly password reminders to list members, and configuring list e-mail header settings.

- *Passwords*: You can change the list administrator and list moderator passwords.

- *Language Options*: Mailman supports numerous localized languages. You can change the default language or select supported languages.

- *Membership Management*: You can add, remove, search, and modify list members' subscriptions en masse.

- *Non-digest and Digest Options*: List members can subscribe to receive all individual messages as they are sent to the list (a nondigest membership), or subscribe to receive all message posts in one message periodically (a digest membership). These options allow you to set some basic defaults for each class of subscribers.

- *Privacy Options*: These options include whether the list is publicly advertised when people visit your list information web page and who may subscribe, and how they subscribe, to the list. You can also create list-specific sender and recipient filters and configure basic spam filters to battle illegitimate use of the mailing list.

- *Bounce Processing*: Mailman can automatically detect when a message sent to a list member's e-mail address bounces. You can set Mailman to disable the address if the number of bounces exceeds a threshold you define.

- *Archiving Options*: These options allow you to configure how list posts are archived, and whether they are public (available to anyone) or private (only available to list members).

- *Mail<->News Gateways*: Mailman can act as a gateway between a mailing list and a Usenet newsgroup. This is a very rarely used feature and will not be discussed further in this book.

- *Auto-Responder*: You can configure Mailman to automatically respond to list posts in various ways.

- *Content Filtering*: Mailman can filter list posts based on various criteria to help remove and contain possible malicious content or unsolicited commercial e-mail that might slip through your sitewide antivirus or antispam mechanisms.

- *Topics*: Mailman can filter messages based on regular expressions matched in the Subject and Keywords message headers for specific topics and categorize messages into topic buckets accordingly. List members can optionally register specific topic buckets, and only receive list messages that match their buckets, ignoring the rest.

Let's take a look at the configuration options of particular importance next. Listing or covering every single Mailman configuration option could consume an entire book, so I won't discuss them all here. There are features and options that I as a list owner don't modify or use. Luckily, many of the vast Mailman options do not require specific attention under most common circumstances. However, I will touch on a few key points, starting with some general options.

## Configuring General Options

The Mailman mailing list General Options category mostly includes customizations for personalizing a mailing list. This is also where you add or change the list administrators and moderators and customize some general delivery options. Figure 20-4 shows what this page looks like when you first log in.

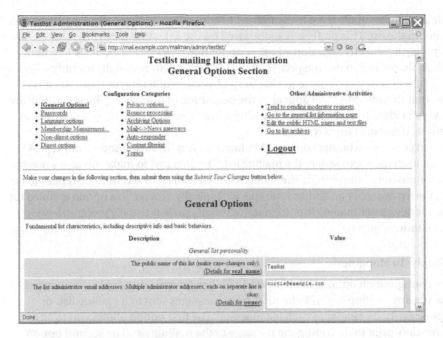

**Figure 20-4.** *The Mailman mailing list admin General Options web page*

## Customizing a Mailing List's Personality

The first configuration option is the public name of the mailing list. Modify this to make changes in capitalization *only*; changing the list name altogether will render the list unusable and undeliverable. I like to keep my list names all lowercase, but this is strictly subjective; you may prefer to modify the capitalization to make the list name easier to read.

Next, note the box for list administrators. The e-mail address you entered when you created the list should already be there. If you wish to allow more than one person to own a mailing list, simply add the additional e-mail addresses, one per line. You must have at least one list administrator defined. You can also modify the list of moderators. You can have multiple list moderators; again, add one per line in the appropriate box further down in the web page, scrolling if necessary. We will discuss the list moderator role later in this chapter. All list administrators share a single list admin password with which each administrator accesses the list admin web page. Likewise, all list moderators share a single list moderator password. I will show you how to change these passwords later in this chapter.

Further down the General Options web page, the next two boxes let you customize the list by adding a small phrase identifying the mailing list and a longer introductory description. The identifying phrase is simply a short but meaningful identifier that you see when you visit the list directory. Use the introductory description to more thoroughly explain the intent of the list, describe the intended audience of the mailing list, and so forth. This description will show up on a mailing list's individual list information web page, which we will see later in this chapter. Both descriptions simply personalize and identify the mailing list and are optional.

By default, a Mailman mailing list is configured to add a short prefix to the Subject header of messages sent to the list. This prefix is usually based on the list name itself, [testlist], for example. It is purely a subjective opinion whether or not this is necessary. Some list owners and list members do not like to use the prefixes, while others feel they visually identify a list post. Many mail clients mangle or move the list Subject prefix when replying, so you can't always assume that this identifier will appear at the beginning of the Subject header; there are other, better ways to identify and subsequently filter a Mailman mailing list. Remove or modify the list prefix as desired; I typically remove it.

Next, you can configure whether you want Mailman to strip the From, Sender, and Reply-To message headers from messages sent to the mailing list. The goal isn't to make messages posted to the list anonymous but to simply hide the sender's e-mail address and thus force replies to be sent to the list, the list owner, or an address you specify. Typically, you see this option enabled for announcement or newsletter mailing lists; interactive discussion lists usually prefer to leave the original sender's address intact.

### Configuring Reply-To Munging

The next three configuration options relate to *Reply-To header munging*. Reply-To munging involves removing any existing Reply-To headers from messages sent to a mailing list, or adding an explicit Reply-To header to each list message. The first option allows you to strip any Reply-To headers prior to delivering the message to the mailing list. The second option allows you to specify whether a reply to a message sent to the list ought to be directed to the original poster (resulting in no additional modification of a message's headers), to the list itself (adding an explicit Reply-To header, redirecting replies to the e-mail address of the mailing list), or to an explicit e-mail address set with the next option (adding an explicit Reply-To header, redirecting replies to an owner-specified e-mail address). The third option is where you enter the e-mail address to be added to the explicit Reply-To header. For most mailing lists, Reply-To munging is generally not recommended, and list posts usually ought to be directed to the original poster.

---

■**Caution** Many argue any Reply-To munging is not useful and can even be harmful and counterproductive (see, for example, "'Reply-To' Munging Considered Harmful," by Chip Rosenthal, at www.unicom.com/pw/reply-to-harmful.html). Others maintain that the practice can be helpful and friendly (see, for example, "Reply-To Munging Considered Useful," by Simon Hill, at www.metasystema.net/essays/reply-to.mhtml). I will not argue the point one way or the other here as it's been argued ad nauseam on the Internet. You should do what you feel is necessary for your specific needs.

---

### Configuring Notification Options

Mailman has the ability to send monthly subscription and password reminders to members of a mailing list. List passwords are used by members to modify their subscription settings, if they are administratively allowed to do so by list configuration. By default, this option is enabled.

Mailman can also send a welcome message to new list members when they first subscribe. This can be a useful way to alert new members of the rules and proper etiquette by adding your introductory text here. In addition, the welcome message includes a member's initial list password and the URL to the mailing list information web page. Similarly, you can configure Mailman to send messages to list members who unsubscribe from a list. You can add custom text to this message, if you wish. Even if either option is explicitly enabled or disabled for a mailing list by default, a list owner can override these options on a case-by-case basis when they (un)subscribe members as discussed later in the section "Managing Membership."

### Configuring Emergency Moderation of a Mailing List

By default, any member subscribed to a mailing list can also post to the mailing list. If a list member is moderated, then that means any message sent from the member is held temporarily for moderation until a list owner or list moderator explicitly approves the message for delivery to the list. Typically, announcement and newsletter mailing lists are moderated and only specific members are allowed to send messages to the list.

A mailing list can contain any number of moderated and unmoderated users. However, you can also temporarily moderate all users on the mailing list regardless of their specific subscription configuration by using the emergency moderation option. We'll cover configuring individual moderation later in this chapter.

### Configuring Message Size Limits

Mailing lists often set limits for the total size or length of messages. This is done for a variety of reasons—for example, to avoid list abuse. Setting the message size limit to 0 will incur no such limits. The default limit is 40KB, which is a nice starting point for most mailing lists.

### Configuring Mailing List-* Headers

Any well-behaving mailing list ought to include the List-* and List-Post messages headers as defined by RFC 2369 (www.ietf.org/rfc/rfc2369.txt). These headers easily identify messages as legitimate mailing list messages, and give e-mail administrators and list members a way to identify and track mailing list traffic. Both options are enabled by default, and I strongly encourage leaving them enabled no matter how the mailing list is used.

---

■**Tip** After making any changes on the General Options web page, do not forget to click the Submit Your Changes button at the bottom of the page. If you neglect to do so, your changes will be lost.

---

This concludes the high points of the mailing list General Options configuration page. Customizing many of these values is an important step that will give your list its individual personality. Next, let's take a look at how mailing list membership is managed.

## Managing Membership

The Mailman mailing list Membership Management category consists mostly of the Membership List, Mass Subscription, and Mass Removal (or unsubscription) pages. This is also where you modify list members' individual settings, including their moderation status. Figure 20-5 shows the Membership List web page when you first access it.

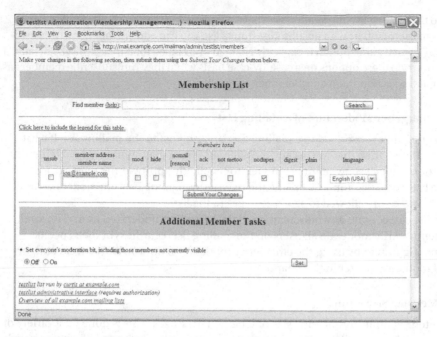

**Figure 20-5.** *The Mailman mailing list Membership List web page*

## Membership List

When you click the Membership Management link from the list admin web page, you are presented with the Membership List options page first. If the list of members is too large, they will be grouped together; simply click on a group to show its members. In addition, you can search for a specific list member by using the search feature.

This web page is where you modify the subscription status of individual members. You can unsubscribe a member by selecting the check box in the unsub column and clicking Submit Your Changes. Table 20-3 details the column headings found on the Membership List web page and their descriptions.

**Table 20-3.** *Mailman Membership List Column Heading Descriptions*

| Column Heading | Description |
| --- | --- |
| unsub | Select this box to unsubscribe the address from the mailing list. |
| mod | If this box is selected, this particular list member is flagged as moderated. Messages sent to the list by this address will be held for approval by the list owner or moderator. |
| hide | If this box is selected, this particular member's e-mail address is not shown in the list of subscribers. |
| nomail | Selecting this box will disable delivery to the e-mail address. If delivery was disabled for some other reason, it will be indicated by one of the following codes: U—the list member disabled delivery from their personal options page; A—delivery was manually disabled by the list owner; B—delivery was automatically disabled resulting from too many bounces; and ?—delivery was disabled for an unknown reason (sometimes due to an upgrade of Mailman from an older version). |

| Column Heading | Description |
|---|---|
| ack | Select this box if the list member should receive an automatic acknowledgment that a message he sends has been received by Mailman and will be processed and delivered to the list. |
| not metoo | Select this box if Mailman should not deliver copies of a list member's own messages to the list member herself. |
| nodupes | Select this box if Mailman should avoid delivery duplicate messages to this user. |
| digest | Select this box if the user should receive list traffic in digest mode instead of individual messages. |
| plain | If the user received list traffic in digest mode, digest messages should be sent in plain text rather than MIME. |
| language | Select from the drop-down list to change the user's preferred language. |

You can make as many batch changes as you want to multiple options on multiple accounts. In addition, you can change the moderation flag for all list members with one click. To activate the changes, do not forget to the click the Submit Your Changes button.

## Mass Subscriptions or Invitations

Click the Mass Subscription link under Membership Management when you want to add one or more e-mail addresses to a mailing list. Options include either automatically subscribing the addresses or inviting them to subscribe, sending a welcome message to new members, and sending a notification to the list owner containing the new subscriptions (overriding the list's default configuration of these settings).

Enter the addresses you want to subscribe or invite in the large box, one address per line. If you prefer, you can create a flat-text file on your workstation with one e-mail address per line, then click the Browse button and select your file to be uploaded and allow Mailman to use the file as the list of new addresses to add.

Note that you can add an additional message to the subscription or invitation message (if one is sent) beyond what may already be configured per the list's General Options settings. This allows further temporary customization of the welcome message. To activate the subscriptions or invitations, be sure to click the Submit Your Changes button.

## Mass Subscription Removal

Click the Mass Removal link under Membership Management when you want to remove one or more e-mail addresses from a mailing list. Options include sending a message to the addresses being removed, and sending a notification to the list owner containing the new "unsubscriptions" (overriding the list's default configuration of these settings).

Enter the addresses you wish to remove in the large box, one address per line. Again, if you prefer, you can create a flat-text file on your workstation with one e-mail address per line, then click the Browse button and select your file to be uploaded and allow Mailman to use the file as the list of new addresses to remove. To activate the subscriptions or invitations, be sure to click the Submit Your Changes button.

## Configuring Delivery Options

List members can receive mailing list messages in two different ways: in digest form or nondigest form. A list digest is simply one message containing all list traffic within a set period of time. If a list member would rather not receive every list message individually, he subscribes to the digest instead. A nondigest subscription is the exact opposite; list messages are delivered and received individually.

Users can select which delivery method they prefer when they subscribe to a list or through their personal options web page. As the list administrator or owner, you can change a list member's delivery method on the Membership List web page. Each form of delivery method has a set of customizable options, which we'll look at next.

### Nondigest Delivery Options

The first nondigest delivery option lets you specify whether list members can receive messages in nondigest form. Disabling this option limits members to digest message delivery only. Chances are you will want to leave this option enabled so that members can receive messages immediately.

If you'd like to add some text to the beginning of every message delivered from the list, you can do so here. Similarly, you can add text to the bottom of every list message. By default, no header is configured, but typical Mailman mailing lists are preconfigured with the following footer template:

```
%(real_name)s mailing list
%(real_name)s@%(host_name)s
%(web_page_url)slistinfo%(cgiext)s/%(_internal_name)s
```

Mailman will replace the Python strings starting with a % character with the list-specific information, resulting in the following text for the sample mailing list we created earlier in this chapter:

```
testlist mailing list
testlist@example.com
http://mail.example.com/mailman/listinfo/testlist
```

Simply remove the text from the box if you do not want to add a footer.

The last option is called Attachment Scrubbing, and it allows you to specify that any attachments will be removed from messages prior to delivery. An attachment is then archived on the e-mail system, and a URL link is added to the message telling members how to retrieve the original attachment. If you'd rather simply remove attachments from list messages altogether, then you will have to use content filters, discussed later in this chapter.

### Digest Delivery Options

The Digest Options web page contains the same option of enabling or disabling digest delivery for a mailing list. Disabling this feature will not allow list members to receive messages in digest form, forcing them to receive individual messages. In addition, you can add a header and footer to each digest message sent. You configure the footer in the same way as you do for the nondigest option.

You can also configure the default delivery method for newly subscribed list members. By default, this is set to regular, nondigest delivery. The format of the digest can be simply plain text or MIME encoded. Select the default format here; individual members can change this setting themselves or you can change this preference on a per-user basis on the Membership List web page. You can set the size threshold, in kilobytes, that the digest should reach before being sent, or you can configure the digest to be sent every day whether or not the threshold is met.

## Configuring Privacy Options

The Mailman mailing list privacy options are split into four categories: Subscription Rules, Sender Filters, Recipient Filters, and Spam Filters. Let's take a closer look at these options.

### Subscription Rules

When you click the Privacy Options link from the list admin web page, you are presented with the Subscription Rules category first. These options let you configure list policies, such as how the list and its membership are exposed to the public, and whether the list is publicly advertised. There are three subcategories of configuration options.

#### Subscription Privacy Options

The first option is whether to publicly advertise the mailing list. By default, lists are advertised. Advertising a list means that it will be listed in the mailing list directory discussed later in this chapter.

Next, you can define the conditions for member subscriptions. By default, every self-subscription request must be confirmed by the user. If a user subscribes to a public mailing list, a confirmation message is sent to the given e-mail address. The user must complete his subscription by clicking a unique URL e-mailed to him. This keeps someone from subscribing using an e-mail address that they do not own. You can alternatively require approval for all list subscriptions, thus making the list owner responsible for the e-mail address validation and subscription approval. Finally, you can combine the two and require user confirmation by e-mail (effectively validating the e-mail address) as well as administrator approval.

You can also require list owner or moderator approval for all unsubscribe requests. If this option is enabled, the list owner or moderator is notified of removal attempts and either the owner or moderator can subsequently approve the removal. Enabling this option is generally not recommended, especially for announcement and newsletter mailing lists.

#### List-Specific Membership Ban

If you have users from specific e-mail addresses consistently abusing their right to use a mailing list, you can add their addresses to a ban list. You can add multiple addresses, one per line. E-mail addresses in this list will not be allowed to subscribe to the mailing list.

#### List Membership Exposure Settings

You can limit who can view the mailing list members' e-mail addresses subscribed to a mailing list. By default, any list members can view the subscription list. However, for the sake of privacy, you may want to limit this ability to only the list admin or owner. Allowing anyone to view the subscription list can open you up to e-mail address harvesting. You can modify individual settings for specific addresses on the Membership List web page.

You can have Mailman obscure the e-mail addresses of list members so that they are not recognizable as e-mail addresses. This option is enabled by default, and should always remain so. This will make harvesting of addresses wherever they are seen much more difficult.

### Sender Filters

Clicking the Sender Filters link under Privacy Options allows you to define sender policies. These include the ability to define a default moderation policy, and actions to take when a message is held for moderation. There are two subcategories of configuration options.

### Member Filters

The first option is whether all new list members' moderation flag should be set. By default, this option is disabled, thus allowing all new list members to send to the list unless individually configured otherwise. Enabling this option will set this flag for all new subscriptions and hold messages for approval.

The second option specifies the action to take when a message is received from a list member who is flagged to be moderated. You can configure Mailman to hold the message and notify the list owner and moderator that a message requires their attention. The message can be rejected, with an optional personalized message entered in the box below. Or the message can be discarded, without any notification sent to the sender, list owner, or moderator. The default action is to hold the message for approval.

### Nonmember Filters

The rest of the options only apply to messages sent to the list from addresses not subscribed to the mailing list. There are four boxes where you can add explicit e-mail addresses of nonmembers that will be accepted, held for moderation, rejected, and simply discarded, respectively. These come in handy if you want to allow someone who isn't a subscriber to send a message to a mailing list.

You can also set the default action for messages sent to the list from nonmembers. By default, these messages are held for list owner or moderator approval, but you can also accept, reject, or discard these messages. In general, I do not recommend accepting these messages; spammers will only take advantage of this and pollute your mailing list. If you find that too many spammers attempt to send to the list, and the burden of moderation of these messages is too great, consider rejecting or even discarding messages from nonmembers, especially if the list is a controlled announcement or newsletter mailing list.

### Recipient Filters

Click the Recipient Filters link under Privacy Options to specify whether a message sent to the list will be accepted. If the first option is enabled, the mailing list address must be included somewhere in the e-mail headers (e.g., the To or CC headers). Many spam and virus messages do not include the real or valid destination address in the message itself. If you disable this option, you will open the mailing list to these sorts of illegitimate or ill-formed messages.

You can also limit the number of recipients that a message sent to the list may contain. Although you can limit and filter based on this same thing with MailScanner, you may decide to set this threshold lower for a particularly sensitive mailing list. The option is set to 10 recipients per message by default.

### Spam Filters

Click the Spam Filters link under Privacy Options when you want to define custom list-specific spam filters. Filters are simply regular expressions that are matched against message headers. Each filter can have multiple regular expressions and an associated action per filter. Actions include holding for moderator approval, rejecting the message with an error sent back to the sender, discarding the message with no notifications, or accepting the message for delivery. You can also defer a filter, which temporarily disables the regex filter until you reenable it by selecting a new action at a later time.

You can create multiple filters by adding the regex to the box, selecting an action, and activating your changes by clicking the Submit Your Changes button. Repeat for each filter you create for the list. Every rule is compared against message headers in turn until one matches, and the action is executed only if a filter matches. Otherwise, the message is delivered per list configuration.

## Configuring Archiving Options

Mailing list archives are a great resource, especially for interactive discussion lists. Any major mailing list with a community whose members help one another will always refer a "newbie" to the list archives to make sure their questions haven't already been answered.

Select the Arching Options link from the list admin web page to configure whether messages are archived. You can also configure archives to be accessible by the public or only by list members.

Finally, you can change when an archive volume is restarted: yearly, monthly, quarterly, weekly, or daily. An archive volume simply affects how messages are lumped together when viewed online and bundled together on the mailing list server. Monthly archive volumes are the default setting. Adjust this depending on the volume of the mailing list; if there is high volume, consider restarting archive volumes more often; if there is low volume, consider restarting archive volumes less often.

Public list archives are typically accessible online with the following general URL:

```
http://mail.example.com/pipermail/[listname]
```

So, for example, to access the public mailing list archives web page for the mailing list testlist we created earlier, the list archive link would be

```
http:://mail.example.com/pipermail/testlist
```

Private list archives are typically accessible online with the following general URL:

```
http://mail.example.com/mailman/private/[listname]
```

So, for example, to access the private mailing list archives web page for the mailing list testlist we created earlier, the list archive link would be

```
http:://mail.example.com/mailman/private/testlist
```

Figure 20-6 shows an example public list archive sorted by topic threads. As you can see, list archives can also be sorted by subject, author, or date. Mailman does not have a built-in archive search mechanism, so making your archive web-searchable is left as an exercise for the reader and well outside the scope of this book.

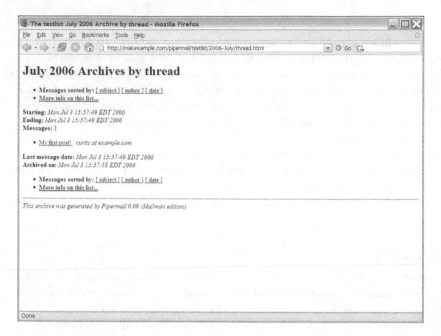

**Figure 20-6.** *Mailman mailing list public archive sorted by topic threads*

## Configuring Content Filtering

The final major category of Mailman mailing list configuration I'd like to discuss is content filtering. Here you can create additional filters that message bodies are matched against. This includes removal of certain message attachments or the ability to convert HTML messages to plain text.

Disabled by default, content filtering will activate any of the filters that are not blank. If a message sent to the list matches one of the filters, then the configured action is performed. Actions include Discard, Reject, Forward to List Owner, or Preserve. We've seen most of these actions, but Preserve is new. Preserve simply means to quarantine the original message and all attachments for later viewing by the site administrator and discard the message and all attachments without sending to the list.

If you do not want all filters or a particular filter to apply but want HTML conversion, leave all the boxes empty, enable Content Filtering, and enable HTML Message Body Conversion. Some of these settings and filters may be redundant and unnecessary if you also have MailScanner attachment blocking enabled, but you might want to tighten some of these filters for specific mailing lists to meet your needs.

This concludes our tour of mailing list configuration through the web interface. Much of list configuration is straightforward, but customizing privacy options or content filters can get a little complex. Take your time and be sure to check out the help available for every Mailman configuration option. Simply clicking on a link like Details for *real_name* will give you access to online help for that configuration option. Next, let's take a look at how to configure a mailing list from the command line using Mailman scripts.

# Configuring a Mailing List with the Mailman Command-Line Scripts

The Mailman site administrator, or anyone given command-line access to the Mailman scripts with sudo, can also configure a mailing list from the command line. The Mailman script config_list can be used to view or save a list configuration to the screen or a file, to configure a list using a properly formatted configuration file, or to check the configuration of a mailing list configuration for errors.

The general usage synopsis for the config_list command, available from config_list -help, is

```
config_list [options] listname
```

At least one option is necessary, either -i *filename* to configure a list or -o *filename* to view or save a list configuration. You must also specify a mailing list name, replacing it with *listname* in this example.

To view or save a list configuration to a file, for archival or revision control purposes perhaps, use the -o *filename* command-line argument to the config_list command:

```
[curtis@mail ~]$ sudo config_list -o testlist.cfg testlist
```

This command will save the mailing list configuration, with detailed comments, of the mailing list called testlist to the file testlist.cfg. Here's a small snippet of what this file looks like, generated from the list configuration of the test mailing list I've been using as an example throughout this chapter:

```
# -*- python -*-
# -*- coding: us-ascii -*-
## "testlist" mailing list configuration settings
## captured on Tue Jul  4 15:38:22 2006

## General options
#
# Fundamental list characteristics, including descriptive info and basic
# behaviors.

# The capitalization of this name can be changed to make it presentable
# in polite company as a proper noun, or to make an acronym part all
# upper case, etc.  However, the name will be advertised as the email
# address (e.g., in subscribe confirmation notices), so it should not be
# otherwise altered.  (Email addresses are not case sensitive, but they
# are sensitive to almost everything else :-)
real_name = 'testlist'

# There are two ownership roles associated with each mailing list.  The
# list administrators are the people who have ultimate control over all
# parameters of this mailing list.  They are able to change any list
# configuration variable available through these administration web
# pages.
#
```

```
# The list moderators have more limited permissions; they are not able
# to change any list configuration variable, but they are allowed to
# tend to pending administration requests, including approving or
# rejecting held subscription requests, and disposing of held postings.
# Of course, the list administrators can also tend to pending requests.
#
# In order to split the list ownership duties into administrators and
# moderators, you must set a separate moderator password, and also
# provide the e-mail addresses of the list moderators.  Note that the
# field you are changing here specifies the list administrators.
owner = ['curtis@example.com']
```

As you can see, a Mailman mailing list configuration file looks a lot like Defaults.py or mm_cfg.py, and follows the same order as each configuration category available through the list admin web page. Configuration option values are assigned the same way values are assigned in other Mailman configuration files, which are simply Python scripts, following the Python language syntax.

If you'd rather not save a list configuration to a file but would rather simply print to screen, replace the filename with a - character, which stands for standard out (the terminal display, normally):

```
[curtis@mail ~]$ sudo config_list -o - testlist
```

This will yield the same output but printed to your screen instead of saved to a file.

You can configure a list through the command line by using a valid configuration file and the -I *filename* argument to the config_list command:

```
[curtis@mail ~]$ sudo config_list -i testlist.cfg testlist
```

This command will configure the mailing list testlist using the configuration options found in the file testlist.cfg. This file can be the same one you just created but with changes. Do not worry about duplicate options; those options will be left the same.

If you'd rather check to make sure the configuration you want to apply to a mailing list is valid, then use the -c argument to the config_list command:

```
[curtis@mail ~]$ sudo config_list -c -i testlist.cfg testlist
```

```
attribute "reel_name" ignored
```

This will try to apply the configuration found in testlist.cfg without actually modifying the mailing list. As you can see here, I misspelled the Mailman configuration option real_name. Once you've fixed any errors, the previous command will exit with no screen output, and you're ready to rerun without the -c argument and apply the configuration and modify the mailing list.

The -i and -o arguments are mutually exclusive, which means they cannot be used together on the same command at the same time. Viewing a mailing list configuration from the command line is a great way to become more familiar with Mailman configuration options in a convenient way rather than clicking through the web interface. The same online help available in the web interface is printed in the config file, so every config file is self-documenting. You'll find that every check box, radio button, or text box you clicked or entered text into in the web interface will have a corresponding simple configuration option.

That's it for Mailman mailing list management and configuration, which concludes our discussion of the roles of the Mailman site administrator and mailing list administrator or owner. Although the next tasks we'll examine can also be performed by site or list administrators, I will frame my discussion within the context of a separate role.

## The Role of a Mailing List Moderator

The mailing list moderator's role is meant to be somewhat limited compared to the mailing list administrator. The role of the moderator is specifically limited to a particular set of mailing list administrative tasks to help delegate the responsibility of some of the day-to-day handling of administrative requests.

Moderated mailing lists, especially high-volume lists with a lot of traffic, can require extra work to maintain and keep up with approvals. Delegating one or more list moderators can help distribute the workload among multiple administrators without giving them full control or access to list administration and configuration.

You might be wondering what a moderated message might look like. My sample test mailing list, for which I am configured as the list administrator with the e-mail address curtis@example.com, is configured to only allow list members to post to the mailing list. A fellow administrator, Jon (jon@example.com), is configured to be a list moderator. When I try to send to the list with the address curtis@example.com, I receive an e-mail with the following response from Mailman running on my e-mail system:

```
Your mail to 'testlist' with the subject

    Mailman is a cool piece of software.

Is being held until the list moderator can review it for approval.

The reason it is being held:

    Post by non-member to a members-only list

Either the message will get posted to the list, or you will receive
notification of the moderator's decision.  If you would like to cancel
this posting, please visit the following URL:

    http://mail.example.com/mailman/confirm/testlist/➥
804cdfa499f356d858707e0705a2264249d5d710
```

As you can see, not even the list administrator is allowed to post to the mailing list, per configuration! If I follow the URL given at the end of the e-mail message, I can cancel my post request, but I really want my message to go through, so I will wait from the moderator's decision.

As list administrator and moderator, Jon and I each receive an e-mail with the following message:

As list administrator, your authorization is requested for the
following mailing list posting:

    List:    testlist@example.com
    From:    curtis@example.com
    Subject: Mailman is a cool piece of software.
    Reason:  Post by non-member to a members-only list

At your convenience, visit:

    http://mail.example.com/mailman/admindb/testlist

to approve or deny the request.

Following the URL given to the list administrative request web page, shown in Figure 20-7, the list owner or moderator can see all pending requests for the mailing list. Each request can be deferred, accepted, rejected, or discarded. Deferring the message will simply leave the request intact, but you can also select to preserve (i.e., quarantine) the message for further retrieval by the Mailman site administrator, or forward the message to another e-mail address. Accepting the message will result in the message being delivered to the mailing list; however, any subsequent posts from the same address will still be held for approval pending a change in the list configuration allowing posts. Rejecting the message will send a notification that the message has been rejected. Discarding the message will simply delete the message without any notification.

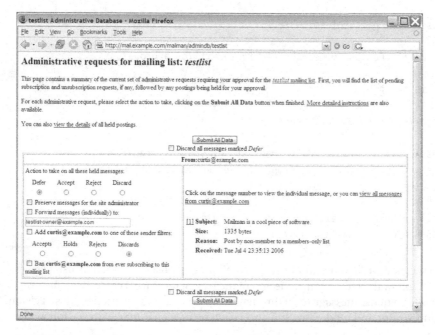

**Figure 20-7.** *A glimpse at the Mailman mailing list administrative requests web page*

In addition to the message approval request itself, you can optionally subscribe the address to the list, or decide to accept, hold, reject, or discard additional subsequent messages from the e-mail address. Each option would result in adding the e-mail address into the appropriate sender filter under the list configuration privacy options discussed earlier in this chapter.

---

■**Tip** Even list administrators or owners and moderators must also be added as a list member or to the privacy options sender filters for nonmembers to be permitted to post to a moderated mailing list.

---

That's basically all there is to the role of a list moderator. As with much of Mailman mailing list management, most tasks are fairly straightforward. There's one more quick topic left in this chapter: let's wrap up our Mailman discussion with a look at how users access your mailing lists.

## Viewing Public Mailing Lists from the Web

The Mailman mailing list information web page is a basic directory of publicly advertised mailing lists hosted on your e-mail system. This can be the first interface users will experience with your mailing list server. For a directory of sorts listing the links to the list for all publicly advertised mailing lists, visit the following URL:

`http://mail.example.com/mailman/listinfo`

Replace this with the FQDN of your web server and path to Mailman, if configured differently in Chapter 19. If you followed along with the examples in this chapter thus far, at the very least, you should see a link to your test mailing list, an example of which is shown in Figure 20-8.

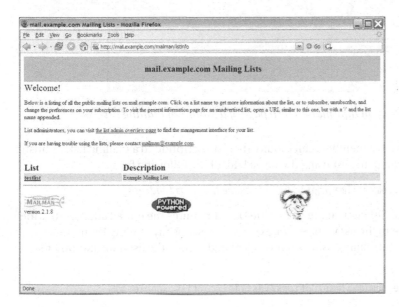

**Figure 20-8.** *An example of the directory of publicly advertised Mailman mailing lists hosted on your e-mail system*

The basic URL for accessing any Mailman mailing list information web page, publicly advertised or not, is of the following form:

```
http://mail.example.com/mailman/listinfo/[listname]
```

So, for example, to access the mailing list configuration web page for the mailing list `testlist` we created earlier, the list information link would be

```
http://mail.example.com/mailman/listinfo/testlist
```

This is where the list description you created earlier appears. Users can access the list archives, and they are offered the chance to subscribe to the list. In addition, users can view the list membership directory (if it's publicly accessible), or modify their subscription options. An example of a Mailman mailing list information web page is shown in Figure 20-9.

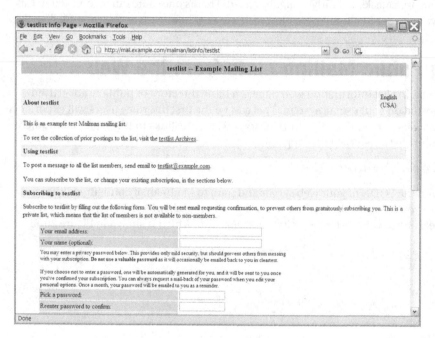

**Figure 20-9.** *An example of an information web page of a Mailman mailing list*

Finally, subscribed list members can modify their subscription to a mailing list, or unsubscribe themselves through the list using the basic URL of the following form:

```
http://mail.example.com/mailman/options/[listname]/[e-mailaddress]
```

This URL is a little different; at the end of the URL it requires the e-mail address that the user used to subscribe to the list with. So, for example, to access my mailing list member options web page for the mailing list `testlist` we created earlier, the list information link would be

```
http://mail.example.com/mailman/options/testlist/curtis@example.com
```

This is also where users can view their subscription to other mailing lists on the mailing list server. Think of this as a user's subscription control panel of sorts. The user will be prompted for his list subscription password, which can be retrieved from the same page if it has been lost. An example of a Mailman mailing options web page is shown in Figure 20-10.

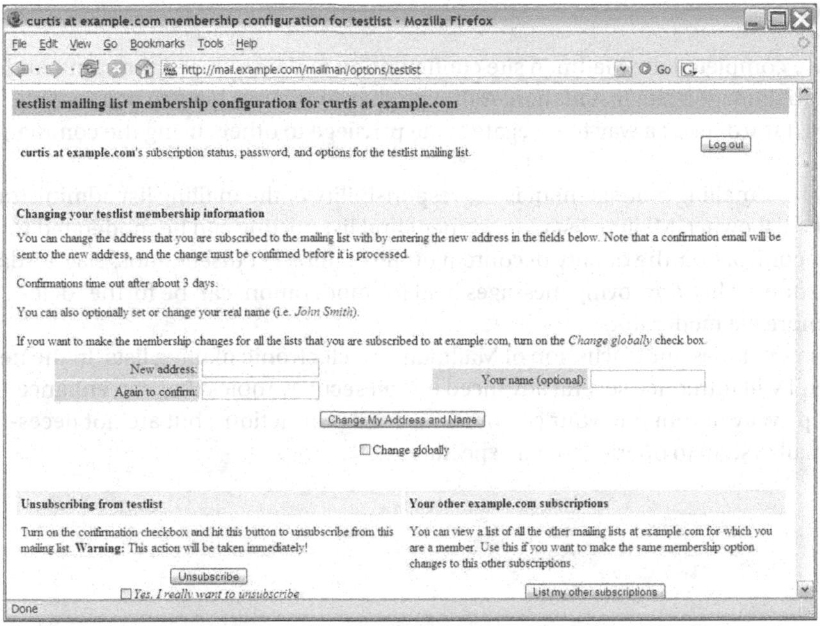

**Figure 20-10.** *An example of a user's Mailman mailing list subscription options web page*

And that completes our tour of Mailman, the GNU Mailing List Manager.

# Further Mailman Resources

Mailman is an extremely well-documented software package. Documentation can be found locally on your Fedora Core system in /usr/share/doc/mailman-*[version]*/, where *[version]* represents the base version string of the RPM package installed. For example, at the time of this writing, the RPM package installed was mailman-2.1.8-0.FC4.1, so documentation can be found in /usr/share/doc/mailman-2.1.8/; to check the version of Mailman, run the following command:

[curtis@mail ~]$ **rpm -qv mailman**

```
mailman-2.1.8-0.FC4.1
```

In addition to the local documentation, or the documentation found with the source distribution, the most current information regarding Mailman configuration is also available online and inline with each configuration option in the Mailman list admin web pages. Every option has a link next to it that will pull up detailed information about that option. For community support, the Mailman mailing lists are also an excellent resource. You can find list archives and subscription information at www.gnu.org/software/mailman/lists.html.

# Summary

In this chapter, we completed the Mailman site configuration and introduced the command-line scripts used to manage a site installation. Although the commands have to be run with special privileges, I introduced a way to delegate some privilege to others using the command sudo.

We also saw how mailing management is the responsibility of the mailing list administrator, also called the list owner. Mailing list management and list posting can be moderated to maintain greater control over the quality of content of the mailing list discussions. Day-to-day administrative requests, like approving messages held for moderation, can be further delegated to one or more list moderators.

This chapter concludes our discussion of Mailman and electronic mailing lists. In the next and final chapter, I will introduce several advanced e-mail security topics that can enhance the security and privacy of your and your customers' e-mail transactions, but are not necessary for your e-mail system to operate to full expectations.

# Advanced Topics

PART 9

Advanced Topics

# CHAPTER 21

■ ■ ■

# Advanced SMTP and E-mail Security

In this chapter, I introduce a couple of ideas for further increasing the security of your e-mail communications. In previous chapters of this book, most security concerns have been with the privacy of username and password pairs, specifically how to keep them private with protocol encryption, but what of privacy or security concerns with respect to e-mail transport and the content of e-mail message bodies? Just as a usernames and passwords are transmitted in clear text if they are not encrypted in a secure tunnel, e-mail message headers and bodies are sent in clear text, too.

Also, you truly have no idea what happens to an e-mail message as it travels along its path from one SMTP server to another on its way to its final destination. The potential for a message to be surreptitiously scanned and copied when it passes through an SMTP server is high. Sometimes e-mail users have little more than the integrity and reputation of their e-mail server administrators to ensure that messages are not needlessly scanned or archived for the wrong reasons. However, once a message leaves your SMTP server, you can't be sure what happens to your users' e-mail as it makes its way to its recipients.

In addition, you have to watch for users and miscreants who want to abuse their use of your SMTP server. We know that open relays are breeding grounds for spammers, but an increasing number of your users probably roam from location to location and continually need an outgoing SMTP server to send e-mail through. Limiting e-mail submission in a secure manner using user authentication is possible as an alternative to leaving your SMTP configured as an open relay, providing a value-added service to your users that satisfies both their mobile requirements and your security concerns.

In this chapter, I introduce a few mechanisms for addressing these issues. By no means are these mechanisms necessary for your enterprise-quality e-mail system to operate properly. In fact, some of these measures are so advanced that your administrative overhead and your users' educational requirements may be prohibitive, but you need to make that decision. First, I discuss advanced security measures that you, as the e-mail administrator, control from the SMTP server itself, securing communication between the client and server. Then I explain some advanced security concepts that are implemented on the client side, regardless of the security protocols or policies you implement on the SMTP server.

# Secure SMTP Relaying

If you've followed the recommendations of this book, your SMTP server relays e-mail to any recipient from users on your local network and only accepts messages destined for your local e-mail domain from all others. This setup has the unfortunate side affect of disallowing your users from sending mail from outside your local network through your SMTP server. This side affect is especially limiting for those who use an e-mail client application on a laptop and roam from your local network to their home network to hotel or coffee shop networks and so on. As soon as they leave your network, from which you allow e-mail relaying, they are not able to send e-mail to anyone outside of your e-mail domain without reconfiguring their e-mail client.

## Introducing Extended SMTP

SMTP has been found lacking, or limiting, in minor ways over the years. This fact shouldn't be completely surprising when you consider how long Internet electronic mail has been around and that it continues to change; the fact that the basic, underlying principles of SMTP are still untouched from the day they were adopted so many years ago is a testament to those originally responsible for developing the protocol.

However, SMTP has been enhanced and extended over the years to adapt to new demands. For example, SMTP itself didn't have any real concept of client authentication written into the original RFC. Instead of rewriting SMTP from scratch or developing a new, competing protocol, a standard framework for extending SMTP was created; it's typically referred to as *Extended SMTP*, or ESMTP for short. Guidelines were outlined for adding SMTP extensions without changing or conflicting with legacy SMTP clients and servers. ESMTP is generally optional, and an ESTMP server must be able to fall back and fully support SMTP if a client does not understand ESMTP.

---

■**Note** ESMTP is an IETF standard defined by RFC 1869 (www.ietf.org/rfc/rfc1869.txt).

---

An ESTMP session is initiated by the client with the EHLO command, rather than the standard SMTP HELO command. An ESMTP server responds with a success code (typically 200) and a multiline response listing the extensions it supports. Otherwise, a traditional SMTP server can respond with a failure error code (typically 500), and the client can either restart the session, falling back to standard SMTP, with an SMTP HELO command or stop the session with the QUIT command. ESMTP is used to provide a mechanism for authenticating SMTP clients; let's take a look at how this is possible.

## Introducing SMTP AUTH

Allowing complete, unauthenticated relaying is not an option, as we know from our discussion regarding spammer tactics (see Chapter 16). However, it is possible to relay selectively for those users who successfully electronically authenticate themselves. This selective relay is achieved through the *SMTP Service Extension for Authentication*, typically referred to as SMTP AUTH for short. Defined by the IETF standard RFC 2554 (www.ietf.org/rfc/rfc2554.txt), SMTP AUTH is based on the *Simple Authentication and Security Layer* (SASL) described in RFC 2222 (www.ietf.org/rfc/rfc2222.txt).

## Introducing SASL

SASL is an abstract framework with which authorization and authentication mechanisms can be achieved within network protocols like SMTP that do not inherently support such mechanisms. To provide client authentication, RFC 2554 defines a SASL profile with which an SMTP client and server can negotiate an authentication mechanism and perform an authentication exchange.

The SASL mechanism keywords are 1 to 20 characters long and must be registered with IANA (www.iana.org/assignments/sasl-mechanisms). The most common SASL mechanisms are listed in Table 21-1. In addition to server-side support for each mechanism, your e-mail client of choice must also support one or more of these authentication mechanisms.

**Table 21-1.** *Common SASL Mechanisms for Authorization and Authentication*

| Mechanism Keyword | Description |
| --- | --- |
| ANONYMOUS | Authorization is granted without authentication. |
| PLAIN | A simple password mechanism negotiated in clear text. The PLAIN SASL mechanism should not be used without further data security, like TLS. |
| EXTERNAL | Used with protocols like the Internet Security Protocol (IPsec) or TLS, in which authentication is implicit. |
| OTP | Authenticates using a one-time password mechanism. |
| CRAM-MD5 | A simple, challenge-response mechanism utilizing keyed hash message authentication code (HMAC) and the MD5 iterative cryptographic hash function. |
| DIGEST-MD5 | An HTTP digest–compatible, challenge-response mechanism that uses the MD5 iterative cryptographic hash functions. DIGEST-MD5 also offers a data-security layer to protect protocol communication. |
| GSSAPI | Short for Generic Security Services Application Programming Interface, a generic framework for client-server authentication necessary for use with Kerberos V authentication. GSSAPI also offers a data-security layer to protect protocol communication. |

## Introducing and Installing Cyrus SASL

You've probably guessed already that you need to install a SASL implementation. The most well-known open source SASL implementation was developed at Carnegie Mellon University and is called Cyrus SASL (http://asg.web.cmu.edu/sasl/).

### The Cyrus SASL RPM Packages

To determine whether the Cyrus SASL library is installed on your Fedora Core system, you can use the following command to query the RPM package database:

```
[curtis@mail ~]$ rpm -qv cyrus-sasl
```

```
cyrus-sasl-2.1.20-5
```

This command shows the version of the RPM package and the revision of the RPM package, if it is installed. Of course, your version may vary. If the package is missing, the previous command indicates, with an error message, that the Cyrus SASL RPM package is not installed.

You can install Cyrus SASL with the following yum command:

```
[curtis@mail ~]$ sudo yum install cyrus-sasl
```

This command searches for and installs, if found, the latest version of the Cyrus SASL library available from the yum RPM package repositories you have configured on your e-mail system. Any required prerequisite dependencies are also downloaded and installed if they aren't already.

In addition, the Fedora Core developers have packaged each SASL mechanism into their own RPM packages. For example, if you want to support the PLAIN SASL mechanism, install the cyrus-sasl-plain RPM package. To support the CRAM-MD5 or DIGEST-MD5 SASL mechanisms, install the cyrus-sasl-md5 RPM package. In fact, chances are good that these two packages are already installed. To check, use the following command:

```
[curtis@mail ~]$ rpm -qa | grep cyrus | sort
```

```
cyrus-sasl-2.1.20-5
cyrus-sasl-devel-2.1.20-5
cyrus-sasl-md5-2.1.20-5
cyrus-sasl-plain-2.1.20-5
```

To search for other available Cyrus SASL RPM packages, you can use the yum command:

```
[curtis@mail ~]$ yum search cyrus-sasl
```

This command shows you all known RPM packages with names containing the search string cyrus-sasl that are installed on your e-mail system or available for installation from the yum repositories configured on your e-mail system. If you require a specific SASL authentication mechanism, use yum to install it. Otherwise, you're ready to configure sendmail to support SMTP AUTH.

If you decide RPM packages are not an option, follow the instructions in the next section to install Cyrus SASL from the source distribution.

### The Cyrus SASL Source Distribution

To install from source code, download the latest stable source distribution from ftp://ftp.andrew.cmu.edu/pub/cyrus-mail/. At the time of this writing, the version is 2.1.21.

**Note** Installing Cyrus SASL 2.0 or a later version requires you to install and use sendmail version 8.13 or later; earlier versions of sendmail are not compatible with newer versions of Cyrus SASL.

Retrieve the latest stable release of Cyrus SASL by copying the full path to the source tarball and pasting it with wget in an SSH session on your e-mail system:

```
[curtis@mail ~]$ wget ftp://ftp.andrew.cmu.edu/pub/cyrus-mail/ ➥
cyrus-sasl-2.1.21.tar.gz
```

Next, unpack, build, compile, and install the source distribution (screen output is not shown for the sake of brevity):

```
[curtis@mail ~]$ tar xzvf cyrus-sasl-2.1.21.tar.gz
[curtis@mail ~]$ cd cyrus-sasl-2.1.21
[curtis@mail cyrus-sasl-2.1.21]$ ./configure
[curtis@mail cyrus-sasl-2.1.21]$ make
[curtis@mail cyrus-sasl-2.1.21]$ sudo make install
```

By default, Cyrus SASL is installed in /usr/local/lib/sasl2/. For the SASL library files to be accessible by other applications on your e-mail system, they must be included in a central directory. Typically, system libraries such as SASL can be found in /usr/lib/. Simply create a symlink pointing to the real location of the SASL library you just installed:

```
[curtis@mail ~]$ sudo ln -s /usr/local/lib/sasl2 /usr/lib/sasl2
```

or install Cyrus SASL directly into /usr/lib/ by providing the arguments --prefix=/usr/lib/sasl2/ to the configure script and rebuilding, compiling, and installing Cyrus SASL into the alternate installation location.

### Manually Starting and Stopping the SASL Authentication Server

One final component to the SASL installation is necessary. In order for sendmail to authenticate using SASL, the SASL authentication server saslauthd must be started. In addition, saslauthd must be started with a specific authentication mechanism, via the *Pluggable Authentication Modules* (PAM) or the system's shadow password file /etc/shadow. For a list of supported mechanisms, see the saslauthd(8) man page; see the pam(8) man page for more information about PAM.

If saslauthd is installed on a Fedora Core system from the RPM package, use the service command to start saslauthd with its init script for the first time:

```
[curtis@mail ~]$ sudo service saslauthd start
```

```
Starting saslauthd:                                    [  OK  ]
```

Look for the saslauthd processes running on your system with the following command:

```
[curtis@mail ~]$ ps auxw
```

You'll notice that saslauthd is running with the -a shadow command line argument:

```
root     15560  0.0  0.0   4456   436 ?        Ss   23:22   0:00 ➥
/usr/sbin/saslauthd -m /var/run/saslauthd -a shadow
```

This example output indicates that saslauthd is configured to use the standard system shadow password file /etc/shadow to authenticate local users. If you'd rather change the authentication method—to PAM, for instance—change the following MECH option in the file /etc/sysconfig/saslauthd:

MECH=shadow

to

MECH=pam

Run the following command to get a list of supported mechanisms:

[curtis@mail ~]$ **saslauthd -v**

and read the saslauthd(8) man page for a description of each available supported mechanism.

If you wish to shut down saslauthd manually, you can use the service command to do so:

[curtis@mail ~]$ **sudo service saslauthd stop**

```
Stopping saslauthd:                              [  OK  ]
```

Otherwise, you can configure saslauthd to automatically start up and shut down when appropriate, which I show you next.

### Starting the SASL Authentication Server Automatically

On a Fedora Core system using saslauthd installed from the RPM package, you can use the chkconfig command to configure an application to automatically start up and shut down. By default, the SASL authentication server is preconfigured not to start up at all. You can see this default configuration by passing the --list argument to chkconfig:

[curtis@mail ~]$ **sudo chkconfig --list saslauthd**

```
saslauthd       0:off   1:off   2:off   3:off   4:off   5:off   6:off
```

As you can see, saslauthd is disabled for all runlevels. To configure saslauthd to start up when your system comes online, use the chkconfig command again:

[curtis@mail ~]$ **sudo chkconfig --level 345 saslauthd on**

Check your handiwork by comparing the following output to the output when you checked previously:

[curtis@mail ~]$ **sudo chkconfig --list saslauthd**

```
saslauthd       0:off   1:off   2:off   3:on    4:on    5:on    6:off
```

For a more complete introduction to Linux runlevels and Fedora Core init scripts, refer to Chapter 3. Now that saslauthd is turned on and listening for SASL authentication requests, let's build and configure sendmail to support SMTP AUTH.

## Building sendmail to Support SMTP AUTH

sendmail must be compiled with particular options to link to the SASL library on your system to offer SMTP AUTH. If your copy of sendmail was compiled with SASL support, SASL should be listed somewhere in the output of the following command; it's indicated in bold in the following sample output:

```
[curtis@mail ~]$ sudo sendmail -d0.1 -bv root | grep SASL
```

```
NETUNIX NEWDB NIS PIPELINING SASLv2 SCANF SOCKETMAP STARTTLS
```

If SASL or SASLv2 is not listed in the output, your instance of sendmail was not compiled with SASL support and does not offer SMTP AUTH.

**Note** The sendmail version packaged as part of any standard default Fedora Core installation is compiled with SASL support out of the box.

If you compiled sendmail from source code, compiling sendmail with SASL support is easy. Before building sendmail, create the file devtools/Site/site.config.m4 inside the sendmail source distribution, and add the following two lines for Cyrus SASL version 1.x:

```
APPENDDEF(`conf_sendmail_ENVDEF', `-DSASL')
APPENDDEF(`conf_sendmail_LIBS', `-lsasl')
```

or for the preferred Cyrus SASL version 2.x, add the following lines:

```
APPENDDEF(`conf_sendmail_ENVDEF', `-DSASL=2')
APPENDDEF(`conf_sendmail_LIBS', `-lsasl2')
```

You should use Cyrus SASL version 2.0 or newer, as it's the latest, stable, and preferred release of the Cyrus implementation of SASL; development of the older versions of Cyrus SASL has halted.

Next, simply build sendmail as explained in Chapter 4. When you finish building sendmail, try the previous sendmail command again; SASL or SASLv2, depending on which you compiled with, should now be listed in the output. Once SASL is listed in the test sendmail output, you must configure sendmail to accept SMTP AUTH connections and indicate which SASL authentication mechanisms to support.

## Configuring sendmail to Support SMTP AUTH

We need to make a couple of additions or changes to your sendmail configuration, so I suggest creating a backup copy of /etc/mail/sendmail.mc before continuing. First, you must add the following line in /etc/mail/sendmail.mc, or verify that it exists:

```
define(`confAUTH_OPTIONS', `A')dnl
```

This line instructs sendmail to accept SMTP AUTH connections.

Next, add or uncomment the following two lines in /etc/mail/sendmail.mc:

```
TRUST_AUTH_MECH(`EXTERNAL DIGEST-MD5 CRAM-MD5 LOGIN PLAIN')dnl
define(`confAUTH_MECHANISMS', `EXTERNAL GSSAPI DIGEST-MD5 CRAM-MD5 ➥
LOGIN PLAIN')dnl
```

The TRUST_AUTH_MECH option lists the authentication methods that are trusted. Any user authenticating with a trusted authentication method is allowed to relay mail through your SMTP server. The AUTH_MECHANISMS option lists the authentication methods supported by your SMTP server. You should support the PLAIN mechanism, as this is the preferred mechanism used by Mozilla Thunderbird and Microsoft Outlook. Older e-mail clients may use the LOGIN mechanism.

---

**■Caution** Insecure SASL authentication mechanisms like PLAIN and LOGIN should *not* be used without an encrypted tunnel, if possible. In the next section, I introduce SMTP STARTTLS, a standard for protecting SMTP client-server communication, and explain how to limit these insecure methods to secure, encrypted communications.

---

After you've made you changes, you must recreate /etc/mail/sendmail.cf by running the following command:

```
[curtis@mail ~]$ sudo make -C /etc/mail
```

Finally, do not forget to restart sendmail with the MailScanner init script:

```
[curtis@mail ~]$ sudo service MailScanner restart
```

Let's test your changes to see if using SMTP AUTH is possible now.

## Testing SMTP AUTH

Connect to your sendmail instance using the following telnet command from the command line of your e-mail system, and issue the EHLO command (user input shown in bold):

```
[curtis@mail ~]$ telnet localhost 25
```

---

```
Trying 127.0.0.1...
Connected to localhost.localdomain (127.0.0.1).
Escape character is '^]'.
220 mail.example.com ESMTP Sendmail 8.13.6/8.13.4; Wed, 12 Apr 2006 23:02:51 -0400
```

```
EHLO localhost
250-mail.example.com Hello localhost.localdomain [127.0.0.1], pleased to meet you
250-ENHANCEDSTATUSCODES
250-PIPELINING
250-8BITMIME
250-SIZE
250-DSN
250-ETRN
250-AUTH DIGEST-MD5 CRAM-MD5
250-DELIVERBY
250 HELP
QUIT
221 2.0.0 mail.example.com closing connection
Connection closed by foreign host.
```

If sendmail is linked properly, with the SASL library successfully loaded, and is configured to support SMTP AUTH, the server responses to your ESMTP EHLO command should include the following:

```
250-AUTH
```

If not, check your mail logs for any errors related to loading SASL or for any security-related problems. For example, the following error message is commonly found in /var/log/maillog:

```
SASL error: listmech=0, num=0 or AUTH warning: no mechanisms
```

This error message indicates that, although sendmail is properly loaded and linked to SASL, no SASL authentication mechanisms could be found. On a Fedora Core system, this sort of error probably means you haven't installed any of the additional RPM packages like cyrus-sasl-plain. Review the previous section of this chapter, making sure you install the prerequisite components of SASL and at least one SASL authentication mechanism, and try testing SMTP AUTH again.

Once SMTP AUTH is properly configured and a session is negotiated, a security layer may be inserted to protect the authentication exchange and subsequent protocol operations. This security layer is achieved by securing SMTP AUTH with our old friend TLS, which we used in Chapters 10 and 11 to secure POP3, IMAP, and HTTP sessions.

## Securing SMTP AUTH with TLS

SMTP AUTH alone can pose significant security concerns. Just as POP3 and IMAP authentication occurs in plain text without securing the client/server communication with SSL or TLS, SMTP AUTH is just as vulnerable to packet sniffing techniques described in Chapter 10. This is especially true if you decide, for whatever reason, to support the SASL PLAIN authentication mechanism. Any passwords used to authenticate an SMTP client with the PLAIN mechanism are sent in clear text and are unencrypted.

Perhaps after learning about SMTP AUTH, you had hoped to use that as an antispam measure, forcing anyone to authenticate prior to allowing mail relaying. This policy is sound and highly useful, if it's supportable and enforceable within your particular organization. However, consider the security risks of potentially exposing your user's authentication credentials to the world, especially if you use the PLAIN SASL mechanism. The solution is to secure the communication with TLS, similar in concept to the way you secure POP3 and IMAP.

Securing SMTP sessions is commonly achieved through SMTP STARTTLS and is defined in RFC 2487 (www.ietf.org/rfc/rfc2487.txt). Like SMTP AUTH, SMTP STARTTLS is an SMTP service extension designed within the ESMTP framework. As such, SMTP over TLS requires an ESMTP-compatible client and server. As luck would have it, sendmail fits the bill perfectly! Let's take a look at sendmail's compatibility with SMTP STARTTLS next.

## Building sendmail to Support SMTP STARTTLS

sendmail must be compiled with particular options and linked with the proper libraries to support SMTP STARTTLS. The first requirement, OpenSSL, should already be satisfied, since we're using the OpenSSL implementation of SSL and TLS to secure other network protocols like POP3 and IMAP (see Chapter 10) and HTTP (see Chapter 11).

If your copy of sendmail is compiled with TLS support, STARTTLS should be listed somewhere in the output of the following command (indicated in bold in the sample output):

```
[curtis@mail ~]$ sudo sendmail -d0.1 -bv root | grep TLS
```

```
NETUNIX NEWDB NIS PIPELINING SASLv2 SCANF SOCKETMAP STARTTLS
```

If STARTTLS is not in the output, your instance of sendmail is not compiled with TLS support and does not offer SMTP STARTTLS.

**Note** The sendmail packaged as part of any standard default Fedora Core installation comes compiled with SMTP STARTTLS support out of the box.

If you compiled sendmail from source code, compiling sendmail with TLS support is easy. Before building sendmail, create the file devtools/Site/site.config.m4 inside the sendmail source distribution, and add the following four lines:

```
APPENDDEF(`confINCDIRS', `-I/usr/local/include')
APPENDDEF(`confLIBDIRS', `-L/usr/local/lib')
APPENDDEF(`conf_sendmail_ENVDEF', `-DSTARTTLS')
APPENDDEF(`conf_sendmail_LIBS', `-lssl -lcrypto')
```

Then simply build sendmail as explained in Chapter 4. When you finish building it, try the previous sendmail command again; STARTTLS should be listed in the output. Before you can restart sendmail and start serving secure SMTP sessions, you need to do a bit of configuration, too.

## Configuring sendmail to Support SMTP STARTTLS

First, like secure POP3 and IMAP, you need an SSL server certificate to identify and verify your SMTP server's identity to SMTP clients. If you need a refresher on requesting and obtaining an SSL certificate, please refer to Chapter 10. Remember, using a self-signed, snake-oil certificate is OK for testing purposes, but if you plan to roll this service out to your users, you should use a certificate signed by a well-known root CA.

Once you've generated the certificate key and CSR and received the signed certificate, you need to install the certificate and configure sendmail to point to your new certificate. On a Fedora Core system, search for the following four lines in /etc/mail/sendmail.mc:

```
dnl define(`confCACERT_PATH',`/etc/pki/tls/certs')
dnl define(`confCACERT',`/etc/pki/tls/certs/ca-bundle.crt')
dnl define(`confSERVER_CERT',`/etc/pki/tls/certs/sendmail.pem')
dnl define(`confSERVER_KEY',`/etc/pki/tls/certs/sendmail.pem')
```

Uncomment these lines by removing dnl from the beginning of each line, and change them to point to your certificate file. The directory /etc/pki/tls/ is a good place to store your sendmail server certificates, private key, and CA certificate or certificate bundle:

```
define(`confCACERT_PATH',`/etc/pki/tls/certs')
define(`confCACERT',`/etc/pki/tls/certs/ca-bundle.crt')
define(`confSERVER_CERT',`/etc/pki/tls/certs/sendmail.pem')
define(`confSERVER_KEY',`/etc/pki/tls/private/sendmail.key')
```

If you are running a different Linux distribution, or if you built sendmail from source, simply add these lines to sendmail.mc, modifying the paths and filenames to your sendmail SSL server certificate, private key, and CA root certificate or chain bundle accordingly.

In addition, as I caution in the previous section, you should limit insecure, plain-text authentication (i.e., PLAIN and LOGIN) to only SMTP sessions secured with SMTP STARTTLS. To do so, change the following line, added in the previous SMTP AUTH section, from

```
define(`confAUTH_OPTIONS', `A')dnl
```

to

```
dnl define(`confAUTH_OPTIONS', `A')dnl
```

and add the following line:

```
define(`confAUTH_OPTIONS', `A p')dnl
```

This configuration still allows relaying from authenticated SMTP sessions but limits the plain text authentication mechanisms to secure SMTP sessions.

Don't forget to rebuild sendmail.cf after you've made your changes. Now restart sendmail:

```
[curtis@mail ~]$ sudo service MailScanner restart
```

You're ready to test your new TLS configuration.

## Testing SMTP STARTTLS

Connect to your sendmail instance using the following `telnet` command from the command line of your e-mail system, and issue the `EHLO` command (user input shown in bold):

[curtis@mail ~]$ **telnet localhost 25**

```
Trying 127.0.0.1...
Connected to localhost.localdomain (127.0.0.1).
Escape character is '^]'.
220 mail.example.com ESMTP Sendmail 8.13.6/8.13.4; Wed, 12 Apr 2006 23:02:51 -0400
EHLO localhost
250-mail.example.com Hello localhost.localdomain [127.0.0.1], pleased to meet you
250-ENHANCEDSTATUSCODES
250-PIPELINING
250-8BITMIME
250-SIZE
250-DSN
250-ETRN
250-AUTH DIGEST-MD5 CRAM-MD5
250-STARTTLS
250-DELIVERBY
250 HELP
QUIT
221 2.0.0 mail.example.com closing connection
Connection closed by foreign host.
```

If sendmail is linked and configured properly and has successfully loaded the appropriate SSL certificates, the server responses to your ESMTP `EHLO` command should include the following:

250-STARTTLS

If not, check your mail logs for any errors related to loading `STARTTLS` or for any security-related problems. For example, the following common mistake might be indicated in your mail log:

```
STARTTLS=server: file /etc/pki/tls/certs/sendmail.pem unsafe: ➡
No such file or directory
```

This mistake is easy to fix; it indicates that you probably mistyped or forgot the filename of your SSL certificate. Resolve any issues as indicated in the logs and restart sendmail. Once your installation is free of errors, you are ready to start using `SMTP STARTTLS`.

---

**SMTP AUTH AND SMTP STARTTLS CAVEATS**

Please note that SMTP AUTH and SMTP STARTTLS are *not* useful for securing the contents of a message or ensuring the integrity of an e-mail message through its life from submission to delivery. These features should be used simply to restrict relaying through secure, authenticated means. Even though communication between an SMTP client and server is encrypted with SMTP STARTTLS, there is no way to guarantee secure, encrypted transmission through subsequent hops to the message's final destination.

In addition, once a message is submitted to an SMTP server, it's impossible to know what processes that message is subjected to, how many times it's scanned, and whether it's been copied on its way to its destination. Look at the scanning measures of the system we're developing in this book. Server-side security mechanisms are generally limited to restricting or controlling access to the SMTP server and those who send messages through it. You need to consider measures to ensure message security, message content integrity, and user privacy to be client-side mechanisms.

---

# Server-Side Sender Verification

A couple of recent initiatives are meant to change the way e-mail communication occurs. Although not explicitly meant to stop Spam, these efforts seek to reduce the effectiveness of phishing scams. As we've seen, anybody can register a domain, build an e-mail system, and send e-mail to their domain. Even worse, there's no way to know if a well-formed e-mail message with all the right headers and addressed with a particular domain was really sent from that domain. Three dominant technologies specifically designed to battle e-mail forgery are being independently developed and are competing for acceptance by the commercial companies and the Internet community: Sender Policy Framework, Sender ID, and DomainKeys.

## Introducing Sender Policy Framework

Originally called Sender Permitted From and described by Paul Vixie in his 2002 document "Repudiating MAIL FROM", the *Sender Policy Framework* (SPF) was developed because of the lack of sender authentication, verification, or accountability in SMTP as we know it. In his proposal, Vixie states:

> *Simply put, there is no cause for any confidence in the proposition "this e-mail came from where it says it came from."*

This lack of confidence is one of the inherent design flaws of our current e-mail system, which spammers and irresponsible mailers take advantage of in deceptive and dishonest practices.

Essentially, SPF requires two things. First, DNS is extended to provide a way for domain administrators to publicize which Internet hosts are allowed to represent their domains through e-mail. Second, recipient MTAs must request these DNS records and verify that the e-mail message was sent from one of the e-mail domains' representative Internet hosts. If not, the message is rejected.

In 2003, Meng Weng Wong, the founder of pobox.com, started a community-driven effort to develop SPF into a viable standard, combining Vixie's ideas and two other proposals into one single framework. In 2004, the IETF created the MARID working group to use SPF and another competing proposal to begin the creation of a true standards-track technology for future adoption.

## Introducing the IETF MARID Working Group and Sender ID

The IETF's MTA Authentication Records in DNS (MARID) working group used SPF and a competing proposal by Microsoft called Caller ID to develop *Sender ID*. However, the Sender ID protocol was almost doomed from the beginning. Few industry pundits felt the Sender ID proposal could stand up to the lofty goals set by the MARID working group. In addition, SPF supporters were not happy with the inclusion of portions of the Microsoft Caller ID proposal, as these portions were encumbered by pending US patents. The licensing conditions imposed by Microsoft were incompatible with the GNU General Public License, (GPL). Intellectual property and licensing concerns, incompatibilities, and feuding working group members prompted the IETF to disband the MARID working group later that year.

Microsoft still backs its original proposal, billing it as Sender ID and hosting the project at www.microsoft.com/mscorp/safety/technologies/senderid/default.mspx. Microsoft Sender ID does not support the sendmail program. The SPF community members have returned to their classic proposal and host their efforts at www.openspf.org. Various competing implementations of SPF for sendmail can be found at the SPF project web site, but none are clear winners or considered more than experimental. Each group continues to engender support for its preferred solution. Unfortunately, we now have two opposing technologies battling for industry acceptance instead of one being cooperatively developed through an international standards body like the IETF. However, another technology has promise and is quickly gaining industry acceptance and community support: DomainKeys Identified Mail.

# Introducing DomainKeys Identified Mail

The IETF *DomainKeys Identified Mail* (DKIM) working group (www.ietf.org/html.charters/dkim-charter.html) is an Internet standards-track effort to combine the original DomainKeys and Identified Internet Mail specifications. DomainKeys was originally developed by Mark Delany of Yahoo! (http://antispam.yahoo.com/domainkeys), with comments and a prototype implementation from Eric Allman, the author of the sendmail program. DomainKeys has been patented in the United States but is released under a dual proprietary commercial license and the GNU GPL 2.0. Identified Internet Mail was originally designed by Jim Fenton and Michael Thomas of Cisco Systems (www.identifiedmail.com).

The DKIM specification includes a DomainKey-Signature e-mail message header that includes an encrypted base64-encoded digital signature of the message contents, added by the sender's MTA. The receiving MTA uses the domain of the originating MTA to look up the e-mail domain's public key used to sign the message. The receiving MTA also recalculates the signature of the message and matches it to the unencrypted hash value contained within the DomainKey-Signature message header. If everything matches, the message is proven to have originated from the domain it claimed to come from. The receiving MTA can then deliver the message to the recipient or recipients.

Basically, the originating MTA and receiving MTA act on behalf of the sender and recipients to sign and verify a message's origin. This method makes it impossible for phishers to forge messages with e-mail domains from which they cannot send and allows e-mail administrators the ability to track phishing attempts that originate from their networks. This can also be used as one more test to add or subtract from the SpamAssassin message spam score.

Implementing DKIM does not mean that MTAs that do not support DKIM will reject your mail. The DKIM draft standard does not affect SMTP itself. Rather, if an MTA does not recognize the DKIM `DomainKey-Signature` message header, it simply ignores it and delivers the message normally.

The combined effort of these original authors and others in the IETF working group is backed by numerous commercial organizations, including AOL, Cisco, Sendmail, Inc., Verisign, and Yahoo!. More information about these efforts can be found at `www.dkim.org`. For an up-to-date list of organizations pledging support for DKIM, please visit `http://mipassoc.org/dkim/deploy/supporters.html`.In addition, an official project developing an implementation of DKIM for use with the sendmail program can be found at `http://sourceforge.net/projects/dkim-milter`.

This completes our discussion of advanced server-side security measures. I hope you consider these as you develop your e-mail system. Next, let's switch gears and focus on client-side security and privacy measures you and your users can take.

# E-mail Message Security and Privacy

It's generally accepted that you should never provide sensitive information through e-mail communication; phishing attempts only underscore the need for extreme caution when replying to messages. This should always be emphasized to your users whenever possible.

However, that is not to say that there aren't measures available for ensuring secure e-mail communication or identifying the origin and verifying the integrity of an e-mail message. Other than the potential server-side solutions to this problem, namely SPF, Sender ID, or DKIM, client-side solutions are also available today.

The rest of this chapter is dedicated to two client-based e-mail security concepts. The first is identification and verification through digital signatures and certificates, and the second is privacy through encryption of e-mail message bodies. There are two competing and incompatible solutions to providing e-mail authentication and privacy: S/MIME and OpenPGP.

## Introducing S/MIME

Originally developed by RSA Data Security, Inc., *Secure Multipurpose Internet Mail Extensions* (S/MIME), is one popular and generally prevailing method for providing e-mail message security and privacy. S/MIME fulfils three primary security functions: message integrity, nonrepudiation of the messenger sender, and message privacy through encryption.

Although not an official IETF Internet standard, S/MIME v2, which was developed by a private consortium of vendors, has become an industry standard in much the same way that SSL has over time. The S/MIME v2 message specification is described in RFC 2311 (`www.ietf.org/rfc/rfc2311.txt`) and handling certificates for use with S/MIME v2 is described in RFC 2312 (`www.ieft.org/rfc/rfc2312.txt`). These RFCs are informational only; they are not approved IEFT Internet standards and are not standards-track documents.

Though widely adopted by many e-mail application vendors today, S/MIME v2 has had two potential flaws or concerns. First, S/MIME v2 is based on the RSA key exchange, which until recently was encumbered by US patents held by RSA Data Security, Inc. Second, S/MIME v2 specifies the use of 40-bit cryptographic keys, which most consider too weak by today's cryptography standards.

To address these concerns, an IETF working group was created to develop the S/MIME v3 Internet standard. The IETF standards-track documents describing the S/MIME v3 message specification and certificate handling are RFC 3851 (www.ietf.org/rfc/rfc3851.txt) and RFC 3850 (www.ietf.org/rfc/rfc3850.txt), respectively. S/MIME v3 is being developed with stronger cryptographic requirements and with technology unencumbered by patents.

## Digitally Signing E-mail Messages with S/MIME

Using S/MIME to digitally sign an e-mail message is one way for e-mail recipients to trace and verify the message originator without a doubt. This digital signature can be equated to the use of fingerprints to track and verify the identity of one specific individual. Instead, we're attaching a digital SSL certificate to an e-mail message, providing a way for recipients to trace the identity of the sender similar to the use of SSL certificates when validating a web server during the process of initiating a secure HTTP session.

### Obtaining a Personal E-mail Certificate

Before you can digitally sign outgoing e-mail messages, you need a personal e-mail certificate. Several of the organizations that offer free personal e-mail certificates are listed in Table 21-2. Of course, you could create a self-signed e-mail certificate, just like you can for your web or e-mail servers. However, self-signed certificates are impossible for others to verify, since they are not signed by a well-known root certificate authority.

Another interesting point to note is that most personal e-mail certificate providers, free or otherwise, typically initially limit your certificate to contain only your e-mail address. Many certificate authorities allow you to add additional identifying information, including your full name, to your certificate only after collecting enough trust or assurance points through their specific web of trust program.

**Table 21-2.** *Organizations Offering Free Personal E-mail Certificates*

| Organization | Web Site URL |
| --- | --- |
| thawte | www.thawte.com/secure-email/personal-email-certificates/ |
| CAcert | www.cacert.org |
| Comodo InstantSSL | www.instantssl.com/ssl-certificate-products/free-email-certificate.html |
| ipsCA | http://certs.ipsca.com/Products/SMIME.asp |

Once you've obtained your personal e-mail certificate, its time to install it and make it available for use to digitally sign e-mail messages.

### Installing and Configuring Your Personal E-mail Certificate in Thunderbird

Installing your personal e-mail certificate is easy with Mozilla Thunderbird. Download and save the certificate to your computer, and start Thunderbird. Next create a master password, if you have not done so before. Setting a master password in Thunderbird allows Thunderbird to securely store sensitive information, like account passwords and your personal e-mail certificate, on your computer. The master password restricts access to this sensitive information; without it, sensitive data is potentially available to anyone who gains physical access to your computer.

To set the master password in Thunderbird version 1.5 on a Windows XP workstation, select Tools ➤ Options. Click the Privacy button from the list of categories at the top of the Options window, and select the Passwords tab. Figure 21-1 shows the Thunderbird Passwords configuration screen.

**Figure 21-1.** *Creating and using a master password keeps all of your sensitive information secure in Thunderbird.*

Enable the checkbox next to "Use a master password to encrypt stored passwords", and click the Set Master Password button. Thunderbird prompts you to enter your password twice.

Thunderbird next prompts you for your master password the first time you access any secure resource, like your personal e-mail certificate, during a session. You can also allow the Thunderbird password manager to save all of your passwords, like you can for IMAP authentication. At the beginning of a session, you are prompted for your master password, and Thunderbird automatically submits the appropriate saved password when necessary. Also, if Thunderbird needs your e-mail certificate to digitally sign, encrypt, or decrypt an e-mail message, you are prompted for your master password to unlock access to those sensitive resources.

Now let's import your personal e-mail certificate into the Thunderbird certificate store. In the Thunderbird Options window, click to select the Security tab under the Privacy category, and click the View Certificates button (shown in Figure 21-2). Next click the Import button to access the Certificate Manager.

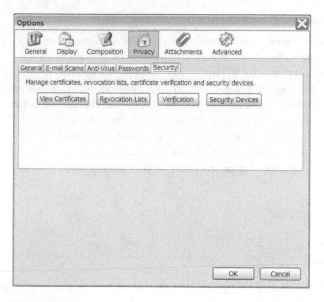

**Figure 21-2.** *Access the Thunderbird Certificate Manager from the Security tab under Thunderbird Privacy options.*

In the Certificate Manager, select the personal e-mail certificate you saved to your computer. You are prompted for your Thunderbird master password and the password used to protect the certificate file, if one is set. If your certificate is imported successfully, like the one shown in Figure 21-3, click the OK button twice to bring you back to the main Thunderbird message index screen.

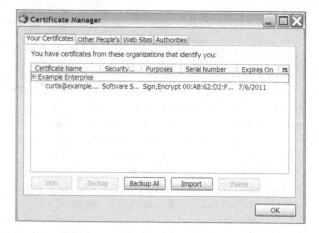

**Figure 21-3.** *The Thunderbird Certificate Manager stores all of your personal certifcates, other peoples' certifcates, and web site and certificate authorities' certificates for e-mail security and privacy.*

Now that your personal certificate is imported into the Thunderbird certificate store, you can configure your account settings to use your certificate to digitally sign outgoing messages.

### Configuring Thunderbird to Digitally Sign Your E-mail Using S/MIME

To configure your account settings to use your certificate to digitally sign outgoing messages in Thunderbird version 1.5 on a Windows XP workstation, click Tools ➤ Account Settings. Click to expand your e-mail account, if it's not already expanded, and click the Security item on the left. You should see a heading for Digital Signing. At this time, you can click the Select button and select the imported personal e-mail certificate you just installed. Thunderbird suggests using the same certificate to encrypt outgoing messages; go ahead and do so by clicking the OK button. Now the Digital Signing and Encryption boxes should both be configured with your imported certificate, as shown in Figure 21-4.

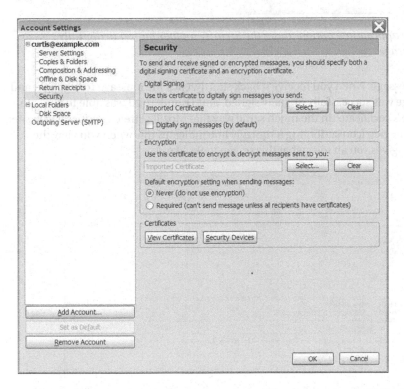

**Figure 21-4.** *Select your imported personal e-mail certificate for digitally signing and encrypting e-mail messages in the Security category in Thunderbird's Account Settings.*

Click the OK button to save your settings. From now on, when you compose new outgoing e-mail messages, Thunderbird digitally signs the message using your personal e-mail certificate.

Go ahead and try this; compose a new message to yourself. Clicking the arrow next to the Security button in the toolbar (the icon that looks like a padlock) reveals options to encrypt and digitally sign the message. The Digitally Sign This Message option should be checked; if it's not, select it to sign the message. When a message is digitally signed, a little pen icon is displayed in the right corner of the window's status bar. Figure 21-5 shows what this screen looks like.

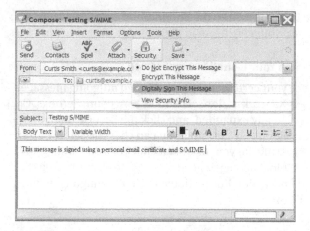

**Figure 21-5.** *Select the appropriate option under the Security toolbar button to digitally sign an outgoing e-mail message.*

Send the test message. When you receive it back shortly, click the message to highlight and read it. If the message was successfully digitally signed, and Thunderbird was able to verify the validity of the sender's certificate (in the much same way that Mozilla Firefox verifies a web site; see Chapter 10), a little pen icon scribbling a squiggly line indicates this when you view the message. Figure 21-6 gives you an idea what this screen looks like.

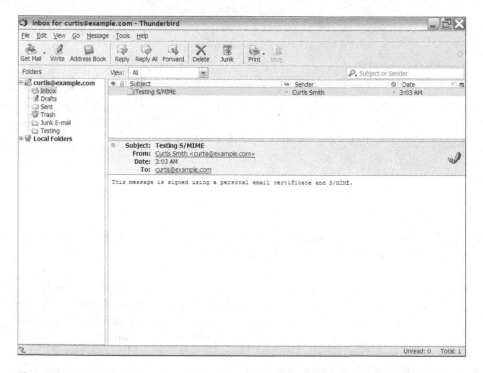

**Figure 21-6.** *Digitally signed e-mail messages are indicated as such with an icon showing a pen scribbling a squiggly line.*

Clicking on the scribbling pen icon shows you detailed information about the security of the message.

When recipients receive a message signed by your personal e-mail certificate with an S/MIME-compatible e-mail client, they can be sure the messages came from the sender they claim to have come from, providing instant verification of the source of the e-mail. Perhaps you want to take this one step further and encrypt the e-mail contents to allow a specific recipient or recipients to read only the contents of the message to ensure privacy from start to finish?

## Encrypting E-mail Message Bodies with S/MIME

Encrypting an e-mail message using the S/MIME standard requires one additional thing—the public key of the recipient you wish to send an encrypted message to. The recipient's public key is used as part of the encryption process to ensure that only the person who has the private key matching the public key you used can decrypt the message.

The easiest way to obtain someone's public key is by simply having them send you an unencrypted, digitally signed e-mail message. After all, if you remember our discussion about SSL certificates in Chapter 10, a digital certificate contains a public and private key, and the public key is attached to a digitally signed e-mail message. When you view a signed message, and the certificate is verified, Thunderbird automatically adds the sender's certificate, which is also his public key, to your personal certificate store. Certificates of other people can be found under the Other People's tab of the Certificate Manager, shown in Figure 21-7.

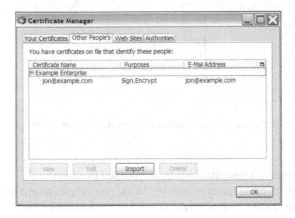

**Figure 21-7.** *Other people's certificates are stored in the Thunderbird Certificate Manager.*

Once you have a recipient's public key, and she has yours, you can send encrypted messages to that recipient and vice versa. Let's take a look at how this is done next. Before continuing, make sure you have read and followed the instructions in the previous section to set your master password and have installed your personal e-mail certificate.

For the purposes of illustration, send an encrypted e-mail message to yourself, which is easy, as you already have your own public key to encrypt the message. You also need to make sure that Thunderbird is configured to use your personal e-mail certificate for encrypting e-mail messages. To do so in Thunderbird version 1.5 on a Windows XP workstation, click Tools ➤ Account Settings. Click to expand your e-mail account, if it's not already expanded, and click the Security item on the left. Refer to Figure 21-4 to see this window.

Under the Encryption heading, you must select the same personal e-mail certificate for encrypting and decrypting e-mail messages as the one you use for digitally signing e-mail messages. This certificate may have been selected for you automatically when you selected your certificate for digitally signing e-mail. If not, go ahead and click the Select button to select the personal e-mail certificate that matches the e-mail address associated with this e-mail account. Click the OK button until you've returned to the main Thunderbird window.

Now, compose a new e-mail message, and address it to yourself. Before sending the message, though, click the arrow next to the Security button in the toolbar, the icon that looks like a padlock. In addition to the option to digitally sign the outgoing e-mail message, you can also select to encrypt the message. When a message is going to be encrypted, a little key icon is displayed on the bottom-right corner of the status bar of the window. Figure 21-8 shows an example of a message displaying the key icon.

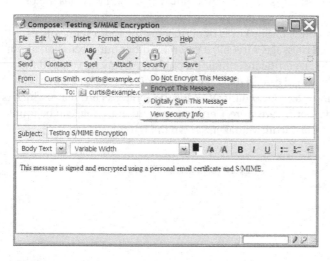

**Figure 21-8.** *Select the appropriate option under the Security toolbar button to encrypt an outgoing e-mail message.*

Now send the message. You should receive a new message from yourself in a few moments. When you receive the message, it's completely readable! "What gives?" you might be asking. If all went well, you should also notice two little icons to the right of the message headers. One is the little scribbling pen icon indicating that the message has been digitally signed, and the other is a golden key icon indicating that the message has also been encrypted by the sender (see Figure 21-9). Because this graphic indicates the message is encrypted and you can read the contents of the message, you have successfully encrypted and subsequently decrypted an e-mail message for the first time!

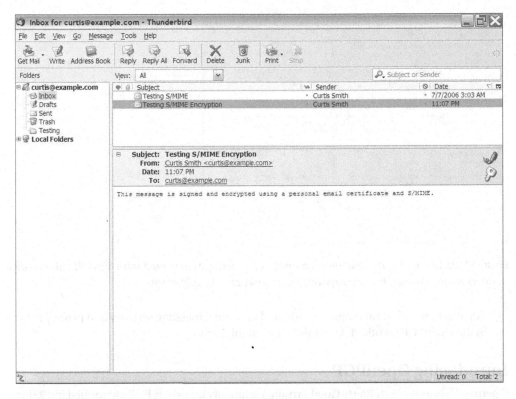

**Figure 21-9.** *Encrypted e-mail messages are indicated as such with a golden key icon.*

To prove the message really is encrypted, click to select the encrypted message, click the View menu, and click the Message Source menu item. After all of the standard e-mail message headers, you should come to a block of continuous and seemingly random characters, shown in part in Figure 21-10. This text block is the contents of the message body, safely encrypted using S/MIME and digital certificates.

**Caution** You may or may not be surprised to see that all message headers are intact, clearly containing all e-mail addresses and the complete delivery path of the message itself. Encrypting messages, with S/MIME or OpenPGP, does not necessarily entail complete anonymity. Masking identities and e-mail source is neither the topic nor the intent of this chapter.

**Figure 21-10.** *When viewing the message source of a message encrypted with S/MIME, all message headers remain intact, but the message body appears to be gibberish.*

An alternative, but incompatible, method for e-mail message security and privacy is the use of the OpenPGP standard. Let's take a look at this next.

## Introducing OpenPGP

OpenPGP has its roots in Pretty Good Privacy, commonly known as PGP. Developed in 1991 by Philip Zimmermann, PGP has since become prevalent in the security world. In fact, it's become the de facto standard for digitally signing software packages, as you've seen throughout this book. However, PGP was originally designed specifically to encrypt the contents of e-mail.

PGP has grown and evolved into OpenPGP through the contributions of Zimmermann and various commercial and open source software developers. OpenPGP is now an IETF standards-track specification governed by an IETF working group. The OpenPGP message format is described in RFC 2440 (www.ietf.org/rfc/rfc2440.txt) and the integration of OpenPGP and MIME is described in RFC 3156 (www.ietf.org/rfc/3156.txt).

In addition to the IETF working group dedicated to the standards-track specifications, the OpenPGP Alliance (www.openpgp.org) also exists to maintain interoperability and cooperation among the OpenPGP implementations. The OpenPGP Alliance provides a wealth of information regarding all things relating to OpenPGP.

OpenPGP is a specification, and it has several implementations. You should already be familiar with one implementation, namely GNU Privacy Guard (GPG) (www.gnupg.org). Throughout this book, we use GPG to verify the source of downloaded RPM packages and source tarballs. GPG can also be used to digitally sign e-mail messages or to encrypt the contents of e-mail bodies.

S/MIME and OpenPGP work nearly the same in principle, and both have a common goal of protecting e-mail security and privacy. However, the details and design of each are different and are not compatible. In particular, S/MIME uses standard digital certificates, while OpenPGP uses a different certificate format based on the original PGP specification. In addition, S/MIME is strictly limited to e-mail security, while an OpenPGP implementation like GPG can also be used to digitally sign and encrypt any file, e-mail or otherwise.

## Digitally Signing E-mail Messages with OpenPGP

Using the GPG implementation of OpenPGP to digitally sign an e-mail message is one more way for e-mail recipients to trace and verify without a doubt who the message originator was. This can be equated to the use of S/MIME and personal e-mail certificates to track and verify the identity of one specific individual. Instead, we're attaching a digital certificate based on the OpenPGP specification to an e-mail message, providing a way for recipients to trace the identity of the sender in similar fashion when using GPG to validate the source of a software package.

### Generating Your GPG Key

Before you can digitally sign outgoing e-mail messages, you need a GPG public/private key pair. To generate your key pair on a Linux system, use the gpg command:

```
[curtis@mail ~]$ gpg --gen-key
```

First, you are prompted to select the type and length of the new keys from the following list. For the average person, the defaults are perfectly acceptable and reflect current best practices and recommendations. Example user input throughout the following examples is in bold font:

```
Please select what kind of key you want:
   (1) DSA and Elgamal (default)
   (2) DSA (sign only)
   (5) RSA (sign only)  .
Your selection? 1
```

The *Digital Signature Algorithm (DSA)* and RSA are two different cryptographic algorithms for signing e-mail messages only. The original PGP specification made use of RSA, an older and previously patent-encumbered algorithm, and is only really supported by GPG for compatibility. DSA is newer and thought to be more cryptographically sound. ElGamal is a key-exchange mechanism and encryption algorithm that is used for encrypting e-mail message bodies and files. You must select option 1 if you want to digitally sign and encrypt e-mail messages. Next, you must specify the key pair sizes:

```
DSA keypair will have 1024 bits.
ELG-E keys may be between 1024 and 4096 bits long.
What keysize do you want? (2048) 2048
Requested keysize is 2048 bits
```

DSA key pairs cannot be larger than 1,024 bits and should not be smaller. The ElGamal keys can, however, be up to 4,096 bits long. Choosing a high key length will make the key stronger and less susceptible to brute-force attacks, but it also means greater overhead when encrypting and decrypting files or e-mails with your key. Choosing a key size of 2048 is acceptable for the average person.

Next, you are asked if and when you would like your key to expire:

```
Please specify how long the key should be valid.
      0 = key does not expire
   <n>  = key expires in n days
   <n>w = key expires in n weeks
   <n>m = key expires in n months
   <n>y = key expires in n years
Key is valid for? (0) 2y
Key expires at Sun 04 May 2008 12:35:01 PM EDT
Is this correct? (y/N) y
```

This choice can be debated for days and days. I think something middle of the road is perfectly acceptable for the average person. Two years is probably a good choice for most; I do not recommend creating a key without expiration. Remember, if a key expires, everyone who has your keys needs to receive your replacement key. If you limit who you share keys with, this is probably no problem at all.

Next, you need to provide your full name, e-mail address, and an optional comment. These, as noted in the program output shown next, are used to identify your key. Later, if you'd like to associate other identities, namely additional e-mail addresses, with your GPG key, they can be added; you don't need to generate additional GPG keys for each of your different e-mail addresses.

```
You need a user ID to identify your key; the software constructs the user ID
from the Real Name, Comment and Email Address in this form:
    "Heinrich Heine (Der Dichter) <heinrichh@duesseldorf.de>"

Real name: Curtis Smith
Email address: curtis@example.com
Comment:
You selected this USER-ID:
    "Curtis Smith <curtis@example.com>"
If you're satisfied with your key's user ID, then simply continue on; ➥
otherwise, change the part you don't like and continue.
Change (N)ame, (C)omment, (E)mail or (O)kay/(Q)uit? O
```

When you continue, you are prompted for a passphrase, which is one of the more important aspects to the security of your private key. This passphrase is used to keep your private key private. Using something more complicated than a standard 6- to 8-character password is best. For example, a password like l33t 5p3k with mixed capitals and punctuation is better. However, the phrase should not be easily guessable. GPG prompts you to enter your passphrase twice.

Now GPG needs to generate random bytes and collect entropy from the operating system, which is used by the cryptographic algorithms to create as random and secure a private key as possible. If your system is running idle, you might get the following error message:

```
Not enough random bytes available. Please do some other work to give
the OS a chance to collect more entropy! (Need 283 more bytes)
```

If you're generating your GPG on the same local computer you're working from, moving the mouse or typing a bunch of gibberish in a text document suffices. If you are generating your GPG key on a remote Linux system, what you do on your local workstation won't matter. Log in to the system with another SSH session, and run a command like the following one, so the OS can collect sufficient entropy:

```
[curtis@mail ~]$ while [ 1 ]; do find / -name \*; done
```

This command starts an infinite loop running a find on all files starting from the / directory. Once GPG has generated enough random bytes, you can stop this loop by typing Ctrl+C a couple of times to interrupt it. Keep running this as long as necessary. On computers with little activity or limited computing resources, it may take several minutes to generate enough entropy to create the key pair.

Finally, GPG reports when it's complete, noting your new key's fingerprint and the user ID associated with the key:

```
gpg: key 078208A4 marked as ultimately trusted
public and secret key created and signed.

gpg: checking the trustdb
gpg: 3 marginal(s) needed, 1 complete(s) needed, PGP trust model
gpg: depth: 0  valid:   1  signed:   0  trust: 0-, 0q, 0n, 0m, 0f, 1u
gpg: next trustdb check due at 2008-05-04
pub   1024D/078208A4 2006-05-05 [expires: 2008-05-04]
      Key fingerprint = D219 BB32 8A9E 40C0 4F22  4908 51E4 76EB 0782 08A4
uid                  Curtis Smith <curtis@example.com>
sub   2048g/E81313A4 2006-05-05 [expires: 2008-05-04]
```

Congratulations, you have a new GPG public/private key pair that can be used for signing and encrypting e-mail and files. However, to use your GPG keys to encrypt e-mail with Thunderbird, you need an extension to provide the required functionality.

### Introducing and Installing the Enigmail Extension for Thunderbird

You'll find that few e-mail applications natively support OpenPGP, and specifically GPG, for e-mail digital signing, though some do. For example, the Linux mail application Evolution actually now supports both OpenPGP and S/MIME as standard features. However, there is a freely available extension that adds OpenPGP support to the Mozilla Thunderbird e-mail application for all operating systems supported by Thunderbird.

This extension is called Enigmail (http://enigmail.mozdev.org/). Enigmail is a cross-platform extension for Mozilla Thunderbird. An extension is similar in concept to a browser plugin; it's a piece of software that adds features or enhancements to the base application. Enigmail only supports the GPG implementation of OpenPGP at this time, so you can reuse the same GPG keys you created on your Linux system or elsewhere.

You must download the extension from `http://enigmail.mozdev.org/` with your web browser; this is a file ending in `.xpi`. Note that you may have to right-click the download link and tell your browser to save the file to your local computer; simply clicking the link may not do it. Although Mozilla Firefox also supports extensions, this extension must be installed with Thunderbird only. Also note that you must download and install the specific version of the Enigmail extension for the exact operating system *and* version of Thunderbird you are using.

---

■**Note**  Note you must also have a working copy of GPG running on the computer where you wish to use the Enigmail extension for Thunderbird. GPG has been ported to Windows XP, Mac OS X, and Linux. Before continuing to download and install Enigmail, visit `www.gnupg.org` to find the version of GPG for your operating system of choice, and follow the provided instructions for installing GPG.

---

After you've installed GPG, downloaded the Enigmail extension file, and saved it to your workstation with your Internet web browser, start Thunderbird, and click Tools ➤ Extensions. Click the Install button at the bottom of this window, select the Enigmail extension downloaded and saved on your local computer previously, and click the OK button. After a few seconds, you can click the Install Now button to start the installation. Once complete, Thunderbird needs to be restarted for the new extension to be available.

When Thunderbird restarts, you should notice a new menu labeled OpenPGP; you're ready to start digitally signing e-mail with OpenPGP and GPG.

### Configuring Enigmail and Thunderbird to Digitally Sign Your E-mail

To enable the use of Enigmail in Thunderbird 1.5 on a Windows XP workstation, click Tools ➤ Account Settings. Select your e-mail account to expand it, if it isn't already expanded. You should see a new item called OpenPGP Security, shown in Figure 21-11. Select OpenPGP Security, and click "Enable OpenPGP support (Enigmail) for this identity". Click the OK button to save the settings and return to the Thunderbird main window.

You must add your GPG key pair to Enigmail or generate a new one. To do so, click OpenPGP ➤ Key Management. Enigmail may automatically detect your GPG keys if you're running Thunderbird on the Linux system from which you created your GPG keys previously. If not, you can import those keys, but most people simply want to generate a new key pair here by clicking on the Generate menu and selecting New Key Pair. This brings up a new screen, shown in Figure 21-12, which prompts for the same information the command-line gpg command does. Enter a passphrase, and select a key expiration, key size, and key type. Click the Generate Key button, and generate some activity on your workstation, for example, by surfing the web. You are notified when the key pair has been generated.

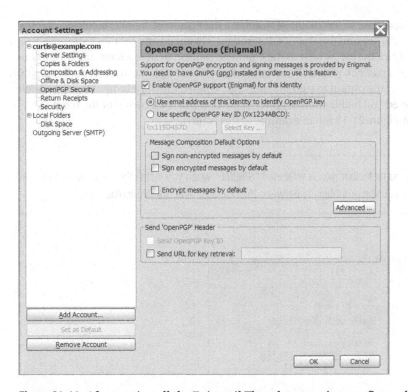

**Figure 21-11.** *After you install the Enigmail Thunder extension, configure the extension settings from the Account Settings window.*

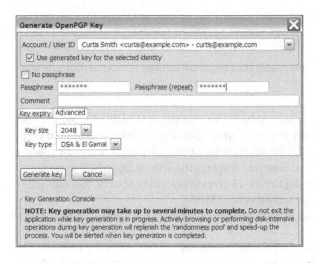

**Figure 21-12.** *If you do not import the GPG key generated from the command line, you can use the Enigmail GUI to create a new GPG key.*

Now, when you compose a new message, you have the option of digitally signing outgoing messages with your GPG key and the OpenPGP standard. Go ahead and try this. Compose a new message to yourself. Click the arrow next to the OpenPGP button in the toolbar (the button has an icon that looks like a padlock with PGP written on it) to reveal options to encrypt and digitally sign the message. Select the option to sign the message. When a message is digitally signed, a little pen icon is displayed and highlighted in green in the bottom-right corner of the window's status bar. Check out Figure 21-13 for an example of this screen.

---

**Note** The original Security toolbar icon is relabeled "S/MIME" when you install the Enigmail Thunderbird Extension to minimize confusion or ambiguity between the OpenPGP and S/MIME toolbar items.

---

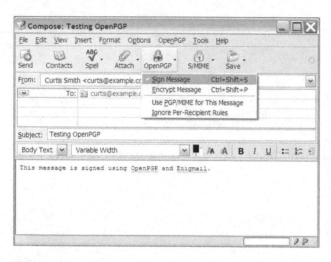

**Figure 21-13.** *Select the appropriate option under the OpenPGP toolbar button to digitally sign an outgoing e-mail message.*

Send the test message. When you receive it back shortly, click it to highlight and read the message. If the message was successfully digitally signed, and Thunderbird was able to verify the validity of the sender's GPG key, the little pen icon scribbling a squiggly line indicates this when you view the message. In addition, Enigmail displays the special OpenPGP message header indicating the signature details. Figure 21-14 gives you an idea of what this message looks like; it should similar to a message signed with S/MIME.

Clicking on the pen icon shows you additional detailed information about the security of the message.

When a recipient receives a message signed by your personal GPG DSA key with an OpenPGP-compatible e-mail client, he can be sure the message came from the sender it claims to have come from, providing instant verification of the validity of the source of the e-mail. Perhaps you want to take this one step further and encrypt the e-mail contents, allowing only a specific recipient or recipients to read the content of the message, ensuring privacy from start to finish? This, too, is possible with GNU Privacy Guard and Enigmail.

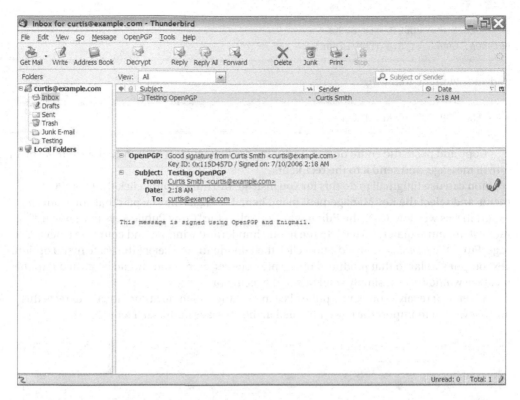

**Figure 21-14.** *OpenPGP digitally signed e-mail messages are indicated as such with an icon showing a pen scribbling a squiggly line and the OpenPGP message header.*

## Encrypting E-mail Message Bodies with OpenPGP

Encrypting an e-mail message using the OpenPGP specification requires one additional thing—the public GPG key of the recipient to whom you wish to send an encrypted message. The recipient's public key is used as part of the encryption process to ensure that only the person who has the private key matching the public key you used can decrypt the message. This principle is the same as encrypting message bodies with S/MIME and personal e-mail digital certificates, but the underlying technology is different.

The easiest way to obtain someone's public key is simply by having them send it to you in an e-mail message, which can be done safely in an unencrypted message, as your public key is just that—public. A public key, when exported to a file, is typically a binary file, which can get mangled when attached to an e-mail message. GPG can export a public key in an ASCII-armored format that is more conducive to sharing via e-mail or the web. To export your public key from the command line, simply run the following gpg command:

```
[curtis@mail ~]$ gpg --armor --export curtis@example.com
```

Don't forget to replace the example address with your email address. An example ASCI-armored public key begins with the following:

```
-----BEGIN PGP PUBLIC KEY BLOCK-----
Version: GnuPG v1.4.4 (GNU/Linux)
```

and ends with the following:

```
-----END PGP PUBLIC KEY BLOCK-----
```

Copy and paste the entire output, including the first and last lines, into the contents of an e-mail message, and send it to the recipient.

You can use Enigmail to do this for you instead. In Thunderbird, click the OpenPGP menu, and select the Key Management menu item. Highlight the key pair that you want to export in this window. Click the Edit menu, and select the "Copy Public Keys to Clipboard" menu item. Immediately go back to the main Thunderbird window, and compose a new message. From the message body edit box, click the Edit menu, and select the Paste menu option. Text output similar to that produced by the previous gpg command should be pasted into the message window. Next, simply send this to the recipient.

When you receive someone's public key in this way, Enigmail automatically detects this and allows you to import the key embedded in the message body; see Figure 21-15.

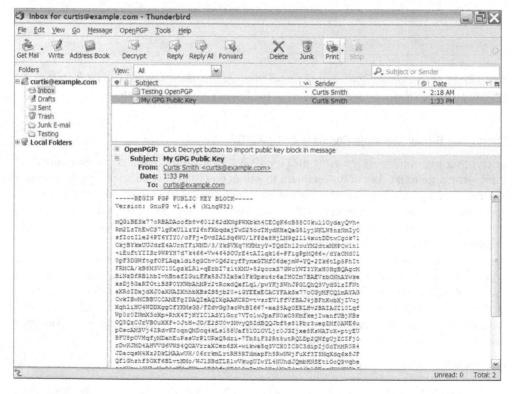

**Figure 21-15.** *When you receive someone's GPG public key embedded in an e-mail message, you can import the key straight from Thunderbird by clicking the Decrypt toolbar button.*

Click the Decrypt button in the Thunderbird toolbar, and click OK when prompted to import the public key.

Once you have a recipient's public key, and she has yours, you can send encrypted messages to that recipient and vice versa. Let's take a look at how this is done with Enigmail next. Before continuing, make sure you have read and followed the previous section to set up your GPG public/private key pair and have imported any recipients' public keys.

For the purposes of illustration, send an encrypted e-mail message to yourself, which is easy as you already have your own public key to encrypt the message. Compose a new e-mail message, and address it to yourself. Before sending the message, though, click the arrow next to the OpenGPG button in the toolbar (the button has an icon that looks like a padlock with PGP written on it). In addition to the option to digitally sign the outgoing e-mail message, you can also click to encrypt the message. When a message is going to be encrypted, a little key icon is displayed and highlighted in green in the bottom-right corner of the window's status bar. Check out Figure 21-16 for an example of this screen.

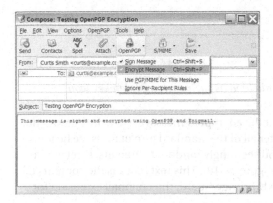

**Figure 21-16.** *Select the appropriate option under the OpenPGP toolbar button to encrypt an outgoing e-mail message.*

Now send the message. You should receive a new message from yourself in a few short moments. When you receive the message, you might notice that it's completely readable, much the same as S/MIME! If all went well, you should also notice the two familiar little icons to the right of the message headers indicating the message has been digitally signed and encrypted by the sender (see Figure 21-17). In addition, the OpenPGP header indicates whether the message was successfully decrypted and by whom the message body was encrypted.

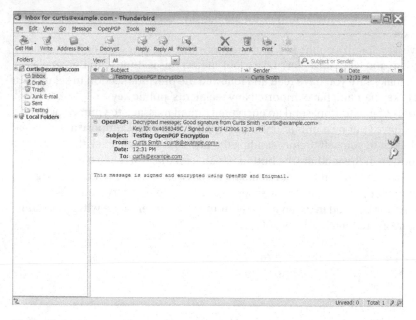

**Figure 21-17.** *Encrypted e-mail messages are indicated as such with a golden key icon.*

To prove the message is encrypted, select the encrypted message, click the View menu, and click the Message Source menu item. After all of the standard e-mail message headers, you should come to a block of continuous and seemingly random characters, similar to a message body encrypted with S/MIME (see Figure 21-18). This text block is the contents of the message body, safely encrypted using GNU Privacy Guard, the Enigmail extension for Thunderbird, and the OpenPGP standard.

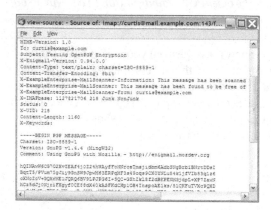

**Figure 21-18.** *When viewing the message source of an e-mail encrypted with OpenPGP, all message headers remain intact, but the message body appears to be gibberish.*

# Summary

This chapter explored a lot of advanced topics. Although optional, these topics are worth considering to improve the security of your e-mail system itself and the integrity and privacy of users' e-mail messages. First, I introduced the SMTP AUTH extension, which allows for the possibility of authenticating SMTP clients. It can be a useful way to provide your remote users, who travel frequently, a safe way to use one SMTP server for outgoing mail by authenticating with their usernames and passwords. Second, you saw how to secure SMTP session using TLS with the SMTP STARTTLS extension. If you choose to use SMTP AUTH, I highly recommend also employing SMTP STARTTLS to keep your users' e-mail passwords private.

However, these features do little for the security and privacy of individual e-mail messages themselves. I introduced two different ways you and your users can provide for message recipients to authenticate and validate the origin of specific messages. It's also possible to encrypt the body of an e-mail message, providing secure communication between two participating individuals. S/MIME probably has a wider and more general adoption by more e-mail clients, but if you're an applications developer or systems administrator, using OpenPGP and the GNU Privacy Guard implementation of the OpenPGP standard might be the more logical choice, and you can optionally use the Thunderbird extension Enigmail if your e-mail client does not support the OpenPGP standard.

In the appendix, you will find the sendmail.mc I use on my development system throughout this book. Use it as a reference for building your own sendmail configuration.

We've come to the end of the main topic of this book. What a ride it's been—complete with a couple of side trips into to the worlds of vi, regular expressions, and general system administration. This book has shown you a number of tools at your disposal to create a great e-mail system that meets the needs of your users. I've chosen the tools that I feel represent the best of breed in their classes. I am confident that you will find an e-mail system built with these tools capable of providing an inexpensive, dependable, stable, and easily maintained platform from which you can host your very own enterprise mail system. Good luck!

# PART 10

...

# Appendix

# APPENDIX

■ ■ ■

# sendmail.mc

The following code listing is the sendmail.mc file introduced in Chapter 5 and built on throughout this book. It contains all of the options discussed within this book and should work without modification with a sendmail installation on a modern Linux distribution.

This file is adapted, with slight modifications and customizations, from the sendmail.mc file that is shipped with the Fedora Core 4 sendmail RPM package. The file is self-documenting, meaning comments are spattered within the configuration file itself; the comments are the lines that start with dnl.

```
divert(-1)dnl
dnl #
dnl # This is the sendmail macro configuration file for m4.
dnl # If you make changes to /etc/mail/sendmail.mc, you need
dnl # to regenerate the /etc/mail/sendmail.cf file with
dnl #
dnl #     make -C /etc/mail
dnl #
include(`/usr/share/sendmail-cf/m4/cf.m4')dnl
VERSIONID(`Config last revised 2005-08-17 cjs')dnl
OSTYPE(`linux')dnl
dnl #
dnl # Set the default logging level.  Level 9 is the default;
dnl # set it to a higher number to debug your configuration.
dnl #
dnl define(`confLOG_LEVEL', `9')dnl
dnl #
dnl # Uncomment the following line to force the FQDN of your email
dnl # system.  Otherwise, sendmail will get this from a DNS lookup.
dnl #
dnl define(`confDOMAIN_NAME', `mail.example.com')dnl
dnl #
dnl # Uncomment and edit the following line if your outgoing mail
dnl # needs to be sent out through an external mail server:
dnl #
dnl define(`SMART_HOST',`smtp.your.provider')
dnl #
define(`confDEF_USER_ID',``8:12'')dnl
```

```
define(`confTO_CONNECT', `1m')dnl
define(`confTRY_NULL_MX_LIST',true)dnl
define(`confDONT_PROBE_INTERFACES',true)dnl
dnl #
dnl # Set the following line to the full path to procmail:
dnl #
define(`PROCMAIL_MAILER_PATH',`/usr/bin/procmail')dnl
define(`ALIAS_FILE', `/etc/aliases')dnl
define(`STATUS_FILE', `/var/log/mail/statistics')dnl
define(`UUCP_MAILER_MAX', `2000000')dnl
define(`confUSERDB_SPEC', `/etc/mail/userdb.db')dnl
define(`confPRIVACY_FLAGS', `authwarnings,novrfy,noexpn,restrictqrun')dnl
dnl #
dnl # The following allows relaying if the user authenticates
dnl # with SMTP AUTH.
dnl #
dnl # Caution! If users authenticate with a plain text authentication
dnl # mechanism like PLAIN or LOGIN, their passwords will be exposed.
dnl # I recommend leaving this option disabled and enabling the
dnl # following option.
dnl #
dnl define(`confAUTH_OPTIONS', `A')dnl
dnl #
dnl # The following allows relaying if the user authenticates with
dnl # SMTP AUTH, and also disallows plain text authentication
dnl # (i.e., PLAIN and LOGIN) on SMTP sessions not secured with SMTP
dnl # STARTTLS.
dnl #
define(`confAUTH_OPTIONS', `A p')dnl
dnl #
dnl # Define the supported SASL authentication mechansims next.
dnl #
dnl # PLAIN is the preferred plain text authentication method
dnl # and is used by Mozilla Thunderbird and Evolution, although
dnl # Outlook Express and other older MUAs do use LOGIN.
dnl #
dnl # Other mechanisms should be used if the connection is not
dnl # guaranteed secure with SMTP STARTTLS.
dnl #
dnl # Please remember that saslauthd needs to be running for
dnl # SMTP AUTH.
dnl #
TRUST_AUTH_MECH(`EXTERNAL DIGEST-MD5 CRAM-MD5 LOGIN PLAIN')dnl
define(`confAUTH_MECHANISMS', `EXTERNAL GSSAPI DIGEST-MD5 CRAM-MD5 LOGIN PLAIN')dnl
dnl #
dnl # Define the full path to the server certificates for
dnl # SMTP STARTTLS.
```

```
dnl #
define(`confCACERT_PATH',`/etc/pki/tls/certs')
define(`confCACERT',`/etc/pki/tls/certs/ca-bundle.crt')
define(`confSERVER_CERT',`/etc/pki/tls/certs/localhost.crt')
define(`confSERVER_KEY',`/etc/pki/tls/private/localhost.key')
dnl #
dnl define(`confTO_QUEUEWARN', `4h')dnl
dnl define(`confTO_QUEUERETURN', `5d')dnl
dnl define(`confQUEUE_LA', `12')dnl
dnl define(`confREFUSE_LA', `18')dnl
define(`confTO_IDENT', `0')dnl
dnl FEATURE(delay_checks)dnl
FEATURE(`no_default_msa',`dnl')dnl
dnl #
dnl # Use the sendmail secure shell (smrsh) for the safe execution of
dnl # external programs.
dnl #
FEATURE(`smrsh',`/usr/sbin/smrsh')dnl
FEATURE(`mailertable',`hash -o /etc/mail/mailertable.db')dnl
FEATURE(`virtusertable',`hash -o /etc/mail/virtusertable.db')dnl
FEATURE(redirect)dnl
FEATURE(always_add_domain)dnl
FEATURE(use_cw_file)dnl
FEATURE(use_ct_file)dnl
dnl #
dnl # The following limits the number of processes sendmail can
dnl # fork to accept incoming messages or process its message
dnl # queues to 12.  sendmail refuses to accept connections once
dnl # it has reached its quota of child processes.
dnl #
dnl define(`confMAX_DAEMON_CHILDREN', 12)dnl
dnl #
dnl # Limits the number of new connections per second. This
dnl # caps the overhead incurred because of forking new sendmail
dnl # processes. May be useful against DoS attacks or barrages of
dnl # spam. (As mentioned later, a per-IP address limit would be
dnl # useful but is not available as an option at the time of this
dnl # writing.)
dnl #
dnl define(`confCONNECTION_RATE_THROTTLE', 3)dnl
dnl #
dnl # The -t option retries delivery if, for example, the user
dnl # runs over his quota.
dnl #
FEATURE(local_procmail,`',`procmail -t -Y -a $h -d $u')dnl
FEATURE(`access_db',`hash -T<TMPF> -o /etc/mail/access.db')dnl
FEATURE(`blacklist_recipients')dnl
```

```
EXPOSED_USER(`root')dnl
dnl #
dnl # The following causes sendmail to only listen on the
dnl # IPv4 loopback address 127.0.0.1 and not on any other
dnl # network devices. Remove the loopback address restriction to
dnl # accept email from the internet or intranet.
dnl #
DAEMON_OPTIONS(`Port=smtp,Addr=127.0.0.1, Name=MTA')dnl
dnl #
DAEMON_OPTIONS(`Port=smtp,Addr=192.168.69.4, Name=MTA-Public')dnl
dnl #
dnl # I strongly recommend not accepting unresolvable domains if
dnl # you require rudimentary spam detection.
dnl #
FEATURE(`accept_unresolvable_domains')dnl
dnl #
dnl # Also accept email sent to "localhost.localdomain" as
dnl # local email.
dnl #
LOCAL_DOMAIN(`localhost.localdomain')dnl
dnl #
dnl # The following example makes mail from this host and
dnl # any additional specified domains appear to be sent from
dnl # example.com:
dnl #
MASQUERADE_AS(`example.com')dnl
dnl #
dnl # Masquerade not just the headers but the envelope as well
dnl #
FEATURE(masquerade_envelope)dnl
dnl #
dnl # Masquerade not just @mydomainalias.com, but @*.mydomainalias.com
dnl # as well
dnl #
FEATURE(masquerade_entire_domain)dnl
dnl #
MASQUERADE_DOMAIN(localhost)dnl
MASQUERADE_DOMAIN(localhost.localdomain)dnl
MASQUERADE_DOMAIN(example.com)dnl
dnl MASQUERADE_DOMAIN(mydomain.lan)dnl
dnl #
dnl # Define your mailers.  These must be last in this file.
dnl # The SMTP mailer is the only one used in this book.
dnl #
MAILER(smtp)dnl
```

# Index

# forums.apress.com

FOR PROFESSIONALS BY PROFESSIONALS™

JOIN THE APRESS FORUMS AND BE PART OF OUR COMMUNITY. You'll find discussions that cover topics of interest to IT professionals, programmers, and enthusiasts just like you. If you post a query to one of our forums, you can expect that some of the best minds in the business—especially Apress authors, who all write with *The Expert's Voice*™—will chime in to help you. Why not aim to become one of our most valuable participants (MVPs) and win cool stuff? Here's a sampling of what you'll find:

## DATABASES
**Data drives everything.**

Share information, exchange ideas, and discuss any database programming or administration issues.

## PROGRAMMING/BUSINESS
**Unfortunately, it is.**

Talk about the Apress line of books that cover software methodology, best practices, and how programmers interact with the "suits."

## INTERNET TECHNOLOGIES AND NETWORKING
**Try living without plumbing (and eventually IPv6).**

Talk about networking topics including protocols, design, administration, wireless, wired, storage, backup, certifications, trends, and new technologies.

## WEB DEVELOPMENT/DESIGN
**Ugly doesn't cut it anymore, and CGI is absurd.**

Help is in sight for your site. Find design solutions for your projects and get ideas for building an interactive Web site.

## JAVA
**We've come a long way from the old Oak tree.**

Hang out and discuss Java in whatever flavor you choose: J2SE, J2EE, J2ME, Jakarta, and so on.

## SECURITY
**Lots of bad guys out there—the good guys need help.**

Discuss computer and network security issues here. Just don't let anyone else know the answers!

## MAC OS X
**All about the Zen of OS X.**

OS X is both the present and the future for Mac apps. Make suggestions, offer up ideas, or boast about your new hardware.

## TECHNOLOGY IN ACTION
**Cool things. Fun things.**

It's after hours. It's time to play. Whether you're into LEGO® MINDSTORMS™ or turning an old PC into a DVR, this is where technology turns into fun.

## OPEN SOURCE
**Source code is good; understanding (open) source is better.**

Discuss open source technologies and related topics such as PHP, MySQL, Linux, Perl, Apache, Python, and more.

## WINDOWS
**No defenestration here.**

Ask questions about all aspects of Windows programming, get help on Microsoft technologies covered in Apress books, or provide feedback on any Apress Windows book.

**HOW TO PARTICIPATE:**
Go to the Apress Forums site at **http://forums.apress.com/**.
Click the New User link.

# FIND IT FAST
## with the Apress *SuperIndex*™

### Quickly Find Out What the Experts Know

Leading by innovation, Apress now offers you its *SuperIndex*™, a turbocharged companion to the fine index in this book. The Apress *SuperIndex*™ is a keyword and phrase-enabled search tool that lets you search through the entire Apress library. Powered by dtSearch™, it delivers results instantly.

Instead of paging through a book or a PDF, you can electronically access the topic of your choice from a vast array of Apress titles. The Apress *SuperIndex*™ is the perfect tool to find critical snippets of code or an obscure reference. The Apress *SuperIndex*™ enables all users to harness essential information and data from the best minds in technology.

No registration is required, and the Apress *SuperIndex*™ is free to use.

❶ Thorough and comprehensive searches of over 300 titles

❷ No registration required

❸ Instantaneous results

❹ A single destination to find what you need

❺ Engineered for speed and accuracy

❻ Will spare your time, application, and anxiety level

Search now: ***http://superindex.apress.com***

# You Need the Companion eBook

**Your purchase of this book entitles you to buy the companion PDF-version eBook for only $10. Take the weightless companion with you anywhere.**

We believe this Apress title will prove so indispensable that you'll want to carry it with you everywhere, which is why we are offering the companion eBook (in PDF format) for $10 to customers who purchase this book now. Convenient and fully searchable, the PDF version of any content-rich, page-heavy Apress book makes a valuable addition to your programming library. You can easily find and copy code—or perform examples by quickly toggling between instructions and the application. Even simultaneously tackling a donut, diet soda, and complex code becomes simplified with hands-free eBooks!

Once you purchase your book, getting the $10 companion eBook is simple:

❶ Visit **www.apress.com/promo/tendollars/**.

❷ Complete a basic registration form to receive a randomly generated question about this title.

❸ Answer the question correctly in 60 seconds, and you will receive a promotional code to redeem for the $10.00 eBook.

2560 Ninth Street • Suite 219 • Berkeley, CA 94710

**eBookshop**

THE EXPERT'S VOICE™

All Apress eBooks subject to copyright protection. No part may be reproduced or transmitted in any form or by any means, electronic or mechanical, including photocopying, recording, or by any information storage or retrieval system, without the prior written permission of the copyright owner and the publisher. The purchaser may print the work in full or in part for their own noncommercial use. The purchaser may place the eBook title on any of their personal computers for their own personal reading and reference.

**Offer valid through 3/25/07.**